Anni

This is your great-great grandyarnie
Cannon

An *Apostle's* Record

Abraham Hoagland Cannon, 30 March 1891

An Apostle's Record

THE JOURNALS OF ABRAHAM H. CANNON

EDITED BY

DENNIS B. HORNE

GNOLAUM BOOKS

CLEARFIELD, UTAH

Other books by Dennis B. Horne:

~ *Bruce R. McConkie: Highlights from His Life and Teachings* (2000)
Eborn Books

~ *Called of God, by Prophecy: Spiritual Experience, Doctrine, and Testimony
from Church Leaders Reveal How God Chooses His Servants* (2001)
Eborn Books

CONTENTS

THE ABRAHAM H. CANNON JOURNALS

MEMBER OF THE FIRST SEVEN PRESIDENTS OF THE SEVENTY (FIRST COUNCIL OF THE SEVENTY)

Call to the Seventy—Plural marriage—Illness—Polygamy raid—Robbed—Pres. George Q. Cannon's capture and injuries—AHC's trial—Prepares for incarceration—Admitted to Penitentiary—Conditions and occupations in "Pen"—Released—Pres. Cannon's business affairs—John Q. Cannon confession and excommunication—Illness and passing of Pres. Taylor—Life of Joseph Smith—John Q. rebaptized—Manti Temple dedication

THE APOSTOLIC YEARS (1889-1895)

Pres. Cannon released from prison—Pres. Woodruff's opinion of Pres. Cannon—Pres. Cannon's doctrine—Counsel to Saints—Baseball—Blasphemy—Sacrament—O. F. Whitney vision of Savior—Calling and sustaining of AHC to Apostleship—AHC's ordination and charge—Church financial policy discussion—Voting strategy—Gentile hypocrisy—Endowment oath court battle—Joseph Smith story—Amasa Lyman—Church loses naturalization-Endowment oath case—Retaliatory defense—Profanity—Blood atonement—Pres. Woodruff revelation—Hydraulic Canal Co. difficulties—Fast-day—Provo temple land—Publishing

INTRODUCTORY ESSAY

Elder Abraham Hoagland Cannon (1859-1896) is historically remarkable for one thing above all others—his marvelous journal. This becomes especially significant when it is remembered that he was a member of the Quorum of the Twelve Apostles of The Church of Jesus Christ of Latter-day Saints for seven years, and the son of President George Q. Cannon. It is this rare perspective—this fortunate position—that makes the journal so valuable. Elder Cannon faithfully recorded much of the deliberations, discussions, and decisions of his Brethren of the Twelve and the First Presidency during his years as one of their number.[1]

Abraham H. Cannon, commonly known as Abram in his time, was called as a member of the First Seven Presidents of the Seventy in 1882 at age 23 and then served as a member of the Quorum of the Twelve Apostles from 1889 until his death in 1896. His journals cover several historically critical events, and many quorum discussions, in a detail almost unequaled elsewhere—except perhaps in the official quorum minutes themselves. It is a rare opportunity to be able to read of these deliberations, for there are precious few other historical sources that grant such a chance.[2]

While the journals are not official Quorum of the Twelve minutes, Abraham's quotations and summaries offer the next closest thing. In the process, they become a prime example of how President Gordon B. Hinckley counseled we should view the history of the Church: "I do not fear truth. I welcome it. But I wish all of my facts to be in their proper context."[3] Elder Cannon's diary gives the most accurate and truthful context possible—a witnesses perspective—from which to view Church history and those who made it—as they made it. The journals are candid and do not whitewash what they record. Abraham wrote frankly and without guile, recording meetings and events as they transpired.

The value of such a primary source is appreciated by historians and scholars. In his officially approved work *A Comprehensive History of the Church of Jesus Christ of Latter-day Saints*, Elder B. H. Roberts wrote the following tribute regarding Wilford Woodruff's journal, which also applies in principle to Abraham Cannon's: "As historian President Woodruff rendered a most important service to the church. His *Journals* regularly and methodically and neatly kept...constitute an original documentary historical treasure which is priceless." Continuing he wrote: "The same is true as to the discourses and sayings of Brigham Young, and other leading elders of the church; while for minutes of important council meetings, decisions, judgments, policies, and many official actions of a private nature, without which the writer of history may not be able to get right viewpoints on many things—in all these respects these *Journals* of President Woodruff are invaluable."[4] (President Woodruff himself understood this, stating in Elder Cannon's presence that "the writing of Church History...is very much needed" [12 December 1895].)

Other scholars have recognized a similarly precious contribution from Abraham Cannon's journal, praising it as a "magnificent diary, almost equal in importance to his father's for the years it covers."[5] It joins a growing number of recently published original sources—including the diaries, journals, and papers of such men as Joseph Smith, Brigham Young, Heber C. Kimball, Wilford Woodruff, George Q. Cannon, William E. McClellan, William Clayton, Rudger Clawson, John Henry Smith, Marriner W. Merrill, and others—that now become so specially helpful in expanding and improving our understanding of Church history. Joseph Smith himself gave instructions that minutes of Quorum meetings should be carefully kept and published so that decisions and doctrine would not be lost to the Church.[6]

The journals are a high-grade gold mine for seven-plus years of LDS Church history and doctrine. Though they cover many items of interest, among the most significant is the material on plural marriage, including the 1890 Manifesto issued by President Wilford Woodruff. Here is found a first-hand historical view of the true inspiration—and overlooked complexity—of this pivotal period in Church history. For instance, the charge that "[Wilford] Woodruff's Manifesto of 1890 evolved from a tactic to preserve polygamy into a revelation," is discredited.[7] Also important is the announcement and discussion by Church leaders of the 1894 revelation on adoptions and sealings, received by President Woodruff: "The Lord has told me that it is right for children to be sealed to their parents, and they to their parents just as far back as we can possibly obtain the records."[8] This revelation clarified that children should be sealed to parents instead of Church leaders, as had been the case previously.

The following list summarizes some of the more interesting subjects, discussions, and events highlighting Abraham H. Cannon's journals:

1) *Doctrinal and policy discussion*: Doctrinal questions frequently came before the First Presidency and the Twelve for clarification. These deliberations become some of the finest gems found in the journals. From this seven year period we can construct what could be termed a brief doctrinal history, where we can follow the establishment of policy, the reliance on precedent from former Church presidents' decisions, and the sincere efforts of quorum members striving to teach only sound doctrine to the Church and themselves.

2) *Spiritual experiences of members of the First Presidency and Twelve*: When a group of faithful Apostles meet in sweet counsel to deliberate sacred matters, a natural consequence is the sharing of spiritual experiences. Abraham recounts many of these. He relates their accounts of dreams, visions, prophecies, healings, spirit world visitations, and other like manifestations. Many of these experiences have found their way into other published LDS sources, but some appear in print for the first time in this volume.

3) *LDS Church history*: Abraham met weekly with a few men who personally knew the Prophet Joseph Smith. These men would occasionally tell stories and experiences from their past, often providing insights, interpretations, and explanations of Church history not well known today. A common theme in President Lorenzo Snow's remarks to the quorum concerned the Kirtland era apostasy and the need to avoid a similar spirit amongst themselves.

One interesting subtext which comes through clearly is that whatever else may happen to the Church, whatever governmental persecution must be endured, whatever financial burden must be shouldered, whatever ill-health, apostasy from within, or anything else—the one thing which these men insisted upon was that Joseph Smith was a prophet of God, even with his human weaknesses. In the midst of it all, these men refused to waver on that point—be it public or private.

4) *Polygamy or plural marriage*: Abraham Cannon had three wives during the greater portion of his adult life, and most of his closest associates were also living in plural marriage. They spent considerable time and effort avoiding corrupt law enforcement officials who saw catching the Cannons as a boon to their careers. One of the most important aspects of the journals is the documentation of the complexity of the plural marriage issue (including the 1890 Manifesto) as lived and understood by the First Presidency and Twelve.

5) *The life of President George Q. Cannon* (1827-1901): As a son of President Cannon, Abraham became a confidante, perhaps the most trusted member of his very large family. This opened the door to privileged conversations with a highly prominent political leader and member of the First Presidency. Through the son we learn much about the father that is not available elsewhere. Of special note is the recognition which emerges of President Cannon as a powerful force in Council meetings—in doctrinal interpretation, policy formulation, and political strategy. After he spoke, matters were often decided.

6) *Late 19th century LDS publishing*: George Q. Cannon and Sons Company, owned by the Cannon family and managed on a daily basis by Abraham, published many Church-related works, including the *Juvenile Instructor*, the *Contributor*, the *Young Woman's Journal*, and various other items. Of particular interest are those entries dealing with the *History of the Prophet Joseph Smith*, a Cannon family collaboration, though with George Q. Cannon's name as author; and the four volume *History of Utah*, by Bishop (later Apostle) Orson F.

Whitney. George Q. Cannon and Sons was the forerunner of Deseret Book Company, and the journals contain information about that company which Deseret Book's own official history considered unknown and lost.

7) *The fall of Elder Moses Thatcher* (1842-1909): The Thatcher episode is one of the saddest in Utah period Church history. Moses Thatcher was a member of the Twelve whose stubborn political independence, morphine addiction, and careless attitude toward his calling cost him his Apostleship. His fall and the continued attempts of the Brethren to rescue him are often recounted at length.

8) *The adventures of Frank J. Cannon*: Frank Cannon was Abraham's older brother. Historically he is considered by many as being even more prominent than his Apostle brother. His name and adventures are occasionally mentioned in the journals. As a youth, he led a checkered life, sometimes bringing public shame to the Cannon family name. He later reformed and experienced some varied success in business and prominence in politics, becoming an early United States senator from Utah, but after his brother and father died he quarreled with Church leaders and became bitterly apostate for the rest of his life. He used his insider status first to help the Church, and then later to harm it. Most of the entries about Frank during Abraham's apostolic years are favorable.[9]

9) *Politics*: Partisan politics are a major theme running through the journals and unfortunately were a source of some occasional unpleasantness in quorum discussions. Beyond that, political themes such as statehood and plural marriage in the courts and law enforcement are prominently mentioned, as is women's suffrage. Also, the question in late 1895 of whether George Q. Cannon should run for the senate is discussed.

10) *Business affairs—including church, personal, and Cannon family*: Abraham was constantly and heavily involved in a multitude of business dealings. He invested heavily and then usually paid heavily

for those investments. The greatest trials of his life were probably financial, most noticeably in the panic of 1894 when the distress became acute. The journals also open a window upon Church finances, including its crushing burden of debt.

11) *The Salt Lake Temple dedication*: Abraham offers an Apostle's perspective on this momentous event (including the earlier laying of the capstone) and the spiritual outpouring experienced by the members who attended.

12) *The Mountain Meadows Massacre*: Abraham toured Mountain Meadows in 1895 and interviewed a local rancher who had witnessed a part of the massacre. His narration is appalling but constitutes a written (though second-hand) eyewitness account of the tragedy.

13) *Addresses given at general conference and in other gatherings*: Abraham wrote summaries of many general conference talks he heard as an Apostle. During these years, Church publications such as the *Latter-day Saints Millennial Star* and the *Deseret Weekly News* printed lengthy summaries, but not exact stenographic reports of these addresses. Elder Cannon's own summaries as found in his journal offer another perspective on the salient points of these discourses. Of special interest are the quotations and summaries of talks given by Church leaders at special priesthood meetings, funerals, stake and ward conferences, and other assemblies of Church leaders and members, many of which could be the only surviving account extant.

14) *Prisoner for polygamy*: Like many of his contemporaries, Elder Cannon was convicted of unlawful co-habitation and served for six months in the Utah State Penitentiary. While there, he became something of a leader of the other "co-habs" and also managed to upgrade his short-hand skills from 50 words per minute to 88. His descriptions of prison life for the Mormon men and their leaders are some of the most detailed available. I have chosen to include only some highlights of his prison experience, which has been treated in greater detail elsewhere.[10]

The First Presidency and the Quorum of the Twelve in the 1890s

At this point in Church history, most of the major players in the Restoration had passed away. Wilford Woodruff became President of the Church in 1889, and Lorenzo Snow was sustained as President of the Twelve Apostles. These were the quorum leaders Elder Cannon served with. His father, President George Q. Cannon, and Joseph F. Smith were known as strong and capable counselors, giving wise and inspired counsel to their President under very trying circumstances. A new generation of men had been called to the apostleship, several of them being sons of members of the First Presidency. John W. Taylor, Heber J. Grant, Abraham O. Woodruff (who was called soon after Abraham Cannon died), Brigham Young Jr., and Abraham himself (the junior member) all fit this category (John W. Young, though an apostle, served as a counselor to the Twelve). Franklin D. Richards, Francis M. Lyman, Moses Thatcher, Marriner W. Merrill, George Teasdale, John Henry Smith, and Anthon H. Lund rounded out the Quorum.

These were good men, chosen and called of God to the holy Apostleship, but cannot all be fairly compared to today's Apostolic leaders in the ministry. Most of their time was spent in business and financial pursuits. They had large plural families that they supported the best they could. As is seen from the journals, fully half of them struggled under the burdens of debt during very difficult economic times. The Church itself was often on the verge of financial disaster because of United States government persecution.[11] The weekly duties of some of these men were usually more business oriented than ecclesiastical. Elder Heber J. Grant ran several businesses. Elder John W. Taylor spent much of his time in land speculation. Elder Merrill was President of the Logan Temple. Elder Cannon ran a publishing establishment, and for a while a newspaper (the *Deseret News*), along with varying degrees of involvement in a multitude of other business enterprises, and hence could not spend much time in the work of the ministry. Aware of his consuming business distractions, Elder Cannon told his brethren of the Twelve that: "I would like to be in a position to labor more than I now do for the work of God and the salvation of souls" (2 April 1895). Others were engaged in politics to the neglect of more weighty matters.

While there were usually good reasons for these departures from the ministry, the Brethren realized that they were not the highest priorities. In Council meeting "Father and Joseph F. Smith addressed us in regard to our duties as the leaders of the people. The latter was very vehement in telling us that our duties required us to be out among the people, teaching them the ways of God, instead of spending our time at home with our business. He said in substance, to me, 'Here is Bro. Abram H. Cannon with the work of two or three men on his shoulders. I say to him in the name of Israel's God that it is his duty to get relieved as soon as possible, and get out among the people.' He also felt that the apostles should be relieved of work in the temples. The counselors to the President should also travel and not be shut up to do the work which clerks can be hired to do" (Oct. 4, 1894).

It is also true that a few of the Apostles of this time period eventually lost their positions. John W. Taylor would not obey the prevailing interpretation of the Manifesto and was eventually excommunicated. Moses Thatcher lost the spirit of his calling and was dropped from the Quorum. John W. Young followed business interests instead of the ministry, and was also removed from his position as a counselor to the Quorum of the Twelve.

Others of his quorum were of a kind that their loyalty and commitment remained unquestioned, no matter what the circumstances. Lorenzo Snow, president of the Twelve during Elder Cannon's entire tenure, demonstrated this on one occasion as the First Presidency and Twelve discussed a large and risky financial transaction. The Prophet and his Counselors were optimistic, but most of the Twelve were skeptical. Then "Pres. Snow remarked that the Presidency would have the support of the Quorum of the Twelve in whatever they decided to do, even though the course they took resulted in financial failure." Such was Elder Cannon's file leader.

This was the makeup of the presiding quorums when Elder Cannon entered, and these were the men with whom he sat and deliberated as the junior member. The Lord shepherded His Church through a time when the national sentiment was strongly against the Mormon people. These journals help us recognize just how trying a time it really was.

THE SELECTION PROCESS

The voluminous extent of Abraham H. Cannon's journals (19 volumes, or roughly 4,000 pages) made the consideration of publishing all of them impractical. With this limitation in mind, I made the decision to concentrate on Elder Cannon's Apostolic years, selecting the most historically and doctrinally interesting and relevant excerpts. This largely follows precedent set by other similar works and is the only practical way to bring the best of these documents before the interested reader. Along with the material from the Apostolic years, I have sought to include other entries which have some kind of special significance. Of course, when dealing with such a lengthy collection, mistakes can be made and material overlooked that should have been included. And there is also the consideration that my judgment of what to select for inclusion may well differ from someone else's. I placed special priority on Quorum council meetings; however, not all of these entries are included since sometimes nothing of interest transpired.[12] This brings up consideration of material which has been purposefully omitted.

There are three small categories of purposefully omitted material. The first consists of entries which I considered to be too sacred to publish. The second concerns the problems and transgressions of Church members which Elder Cannon recorded as they came before him personally in an ecclesiastical capacity or as they were brought to the presiding quorums for judgment. The third category involves a doctrinally controversial item.[13]

As for the first category, there are several entries which contain descriptions of or remarks about what Elder James E. Talmage referred to as the "highest blessings" of the temple.[14] These have been omitted because of their sacred character. No actual wording of any temple ordinances has been included. I believe Elder Cannon himself would insist upon this, for reasons known to those who have made the same sacred covenants he did. For those who wish further information, the journals themselves are available for consultation. An appropriate exception to this is the mention of participation in prayer circles which were held at most Quorum meetings and are often included (see 17 October 1889 and note).[15]

As for the second category, in my judgment these entries have little historical value. For example, after sitting through the trial of a disgraced mission president, Abraham wrote: "How terrible is the lesson which this event conveys! A man whose whole life has been spent in the service of God allowing himself to be overtaken in sin when his race is nearly run! It shows us that no man is safe till he is dead, and the very strongest are liable to fall when they least expect to yield. I hope to be able to profit by this sad scene."[16] Such a lesson is the only practical value that can be taken from a recitation of such events. An exception is the John Q. Cannon scandal, which is included here because it is a matter of official record in church history.

Some other items which have not been included here have to do with business and politics. There is copious discussion of passing political strategy and opposing party platforms. While this may be of interest to the political historian, it seemed overly cumbersome for my purposes, so I have included only the most important material that develops and continues the larger story. (See also *Annotation* below.)

A wide variety of business and financial matters were recorded in careful detail, but as with political matters, they tend to distract from the central purpose of this work. I have included these entries when the material seemed important, or had some historical significance. Historians seeking more of this kind of information should take the time to peruse the journals in their entirety.

CONTENT

Because of Elder Cannon's position as an apostle, his journals contain the discussions and deliberations of his associates in the highest councils of the Church—which is what makes them so important and valuable. In their private councils, these men spoke candidly, at times offering opinions, ideas, and speculation which they would not have shared with church members generally. After one such meeting, President Lorenzo Snow closed by reminding the Twelve that "it would not do to teach such things in public." To open another "Pres. Snow felt that we should keep in the utmost secrecy the proceedings and counsels of our meetings. 'I do not care what the brethren say so long as they close with the desire to do as our leaders direct.'" Today, official minutes of meetings of the First Presidency and Twelve are considered confidential and sacred. It is reasonable to suppose that portions of Elder Cannon's journal could be categorized similarly. It then becomes necessary to carefully consider the criteria for making an exception and publishing them. The following reasons would seem to be sufficient justification:

1) Copies of the journals have been fully available to the public in several archival repositories since 1967, and written permission to publish has been secured from the current owner of the originals, Brigham Young University.

2) Many scholars, historians, and researchers, as well as some sensationalists, have already thoroughly examined the journals contents and published their various findings. There are no "skeletons" uncovered here. See the bibliographic essay for further information on these works.

3) With the passage of time, considerations of confidentiality may change. For example, Church leaders have given formal permission for the complete papers of Joseph Smith to be published, including official minutes of meetings of the First Presidency and the Twelve. The question of how much time must pass before papers and journals such as these become appropriately justifiable for publication is highly subjective.

4) Church leaders have indicated that the death of a general authority writer or speaker may have significant bearing on whether their sacred experiences or discussions may be publicly shared. Such are "generally made known after they [are] gone."[17]

5) Following appropriate precedent can be a helpful guide. Sensitive items such as minutes[18], patriarchal blessings[19], spiritual experiences, and disagreements among Church leaders[20], have all been published before by church owned or approved presses, and have consequently been of interest and value to the scholarly community.

6) Finally, there is the question of whether this historical document is of sufficient intrinsic value to outweigh all other considerations. Even the Book of Mormon contains textual problems and graphic descriptions which today might cause someone who seeks to be sensitive to acceptable Church publishing parameters to pause before rushing to press—yet such difficulties quickly fade when compared with the true worth of the book. As previously stated, we do not fear truth.[21] It then follows that we do not fear true and unbiased church history—a history conscientiously recorded by one who deeply believed in his Church's truth and the divine calling and inspiration of its human leadership.

Having the foregoing rationale in mind, we must still exercise wisdom and care when reading and interpreting this primary but unofficial and nonbinding historical document.

FORMAT OF A TYPICAL JOURNAL ENTRY

Elder Cannon was very consistent in his journal writing, and though he missed some days, he usually gave a synopsis of what had happened during that time. It is unclear whether he meant for the public to read his journals at some future day. (He did write a note at the end of one of the mission journals that he would probably find enjoyment in reading it later in life, and at the end of his prison or

"Pen" journal he created a register which included the names, birthdates, prison terms, and autographs of his fellow "co-habs." This included such notables as Rudger Clawson and Lorenzo Snow.) He began keeping his journal at the start of his first mission, and ended the last in 1896, the year he died. The journals are handwritten from 1879 until 1891, and then are typewritten till his death.

The format for the beginning of an entry evolved over the years Elder Cannon wrote, but by the time he became an Apostle, the following description is normal. Each entry begins with a day, then a date, and usually a place, most commonly Salt Lake City. Next he almost always gave a brief weather report, such as "very nice day" or "very hot day" or "cloudy today but no storm." Then followed the bulk of the entry, which usually included Abraham going to the office and "posting the books." Then the rest of the entry, which was commonly one quarter page to several pages, with general conference and quorum meeting days often even longer.

EDITORIAL PROCEDURES

Editing Elder Abraham H. Cannon's journals has not been as complex as projects of this kind usually are. The reason is because Abraham was an excellent writer and editor. He proofread material for publication almost every working day of his adult life, and wrote many articles for publication in the *Juvenile Instructor*. For a late 19th century diarist and author, he possessed remarkable competency in spelling and writing. He often corrected his own infrequent mistakes, using proper editorial notation. He did this with both his handwritten and typewritten journals. The result is that they have needed very little clarifying editorial work.[22]

PUNCTUATION

Sentence structure: As stated, Elder Cannon's writing needed little work. I have made some few minor changes to clarify sentence meanings, usually consisting of modernizing punctuation or capitalization. These are exceedingly rare and do not alter the meaning of a sentence. With relatively few exceptions the journal entries remain unchanged.

Ellipsis: It should be understood that the material selected from Abraham's journal for this publication is almost never the actual beginning of the entry. I have not used beginning ellipses (...) except in the rare instances in which I start quoting an entry in the middle of a sentence. I have made extensive use of ellipses where I have skipped material in the middle or at the end of an entry.

Abbreviations: Elder Cannon typically abbreviated the name George as Geo., as in George F. Gibbs, (which name was almost always abbreviated). I have elected to expand this to the proper name. I also did this with Jos. for Joseph and Jno. for John. Also, Bp. has been changed to Bishop and Mss to Manuscript.

Initials: Initials are usually left as initials, except where it seemed wise to clarify the full name of a person to avoid identity confusion. This helped with J. F. Smith and J. H. Smith for Joseph F. Smith and John Henry Smith, and a few other similar uses. Abraham sometimes wrote of Pres. W., which meant President Woodruff, and which I have rendered Pres. Woodruff. I have almost always left Pres. in this abbreviated form to remain consistent with Elder Cannon's usage.

[*Bracketed words*]: Words in brackets are sparingly used to give the meaning of archaic or confusing words and also to fix some poorly worded sentences, such as when an obviously needed word has been unintentionally left out. In one case (see 24 Oct. 1894) they are used with a ? to provide my best guess for material which has been partially removed from the original text (see below).

Missing entries: A few brief portions of the journals are missing and presumed lost. When the journals were donated to Brigham Young University, some excerpts were cut from some pages; in other cases entire pages are missing. The assumption is that this was done by the Cannon family before donation. BYU Special Collections staff were unable to provide further information as to the missing pages.[23] Though Elder Cannon died in July 1896, and it is certain he continued keeping his journal until shortly before this, BYU Special Collections does not possess any journal after 31 December, 1895.

Quotations and quotation marks: This is an area in which Elder Cannon's journals are inconsistent, and this becomes frustrating because of the importance of accurate quotations from brethren in Quorum council meetings. While he made frequent use of quotation marks, he did not always insert one at the end of the quotation, which leaves us to guess where it ends. Since he often summarized what was said by others, but would also quote them without using marks, it often becomes impossible to discern which is which. With these difficulties in mind, I was very reluctant to insert a quotation mark unless I was positive it was in the correct place. However, it is evident that there are a number of quotations from the Brethren in council that are not marked as such.

Other changes: The word "Tithings" has been changed to "tithes", the name Anton to Anthon (as per LDS Church History Department procedure), and I have dropped the cent notation from monetary values, such as $25,000.00 to $25,000. I also italicized the titles of books, magazines and newspapers.

While I have striven for editorial accuracy in this work, its length and complexity proportionately increase the possibility of error. Hopefully these are few and will minimally affect the integrity of the text.

ANNOTATION

Annotation is an immensely subjective process. Some editors outdo themselves explaining everything, and others clarify very little. I have seen critiques of both extremes. For this particular project, I found myself in agreement with Jean B. White (editor of the John Henry Smith diaries) who wrote: "There is no end to the possibilities for annotation if an editor is determined to explain every unclear entry. I decided to keep annotation to a minimum."[24] I commented very little on the political and business entries, as ample information about these subjects is available elsewhere.[25] Basic information about the main characters mentioned in the journals is included in the biographical register and the biographical essay.

Provenance

I mostly worked with photocopies obtained from the Brigham Young University L. Tom Perry Special Collections archives—the owner of the journals. BYU Special Collections received them in 1967 as a gift from Rachel Cannon Heninger, a granddaughter (deceased) of Abraham H. Cannon through his first wife Sarah Ann Jenkins' son George J. Cannon.[26] They are located at Vault MSS 62. They are published here by permission of BYU Special Collections. Copies of the journals may be found in the Utah State Historical Society Library, the University of Utah J. Willard Marriott Library Special Collections, the Family and Church History Department archives of The Church of Jesus Christ of Latter-day Saints,[27] and some are in private hands.

Previous Treatments

A number of scholars have used the Abraham H. Cannon journals—some extensively—though none have compiled and published them as found in this volume. Since the journals are an indispensable source for inside information on Church leadership deliberations for the years 1889-95, they are relied upon heavily and consequently most studies of the period would be seriously weakened without the material gleaned from them (see the bibliographical essay for further information on these publications).

A historian named William C. Seifrit became interested in the journals as he searched for references to one Charles H. Wilcken, an early Latter-day Saint and Cannon family acquaintance, about whom he was preparing an article. He quickly recognized the tremendous value of the journals but also realized that few researchers had made use of them because of the lack of an index or guide to their extensive contents. He spent three years preparing a register or index of over 200 pages, along with a brief inventory or summary of each journal volume. The index is invaluable for finding names mentioned in the journals, but falls short as a subject aid. Nevertheless, this labor constituted one of the earliest attempts at thorough scholarly examination of the journals and serves as a needed time-saving resource for historians researching the journals for specific references to the many people Abraham knew and wrote about.[28]

In 1970 a document appeared entitled *Excerpts from the Journal of Abraham H. Cannon.* The compiler of this 28-page booklet selected only the most sensational items, mostly regarding plural marriage. There was no introduction, annotation, or explanation included. Elder Cannon's journals deserve better than such tabloid treatment.[29]

This publication, *An Apostle's Record: The Journals of Abraham H. Cannon* remedies the lapse in the historical record, making readily available a little-known document of tremendous worth and justifying the immense labor of its author. As Elder Francis M. Lyman of the Quorum of the Twelve and a close associate of Elder Cannon's told a Utah (Provo) stake conference audience two hours after he learned of Abraham's untimely death: "He has been a model in keeping a history of his life, and has done more in detail work than any other man of his age in the Church."[30]

---

[1] Davis Bitton, in his *Guide to Mormon Diaries and Autobiographies* (Provo, Utah: Brigham Young University Press, 1977), wrote: "Important diary due to author's unusual position as General Authority in Mormon Church, publisher and editor, and business investor in many Utah enterprises.... Detailed reports of 'council' meetings, especially valuable after 1889 for deliberations of the Twelve and the First Presidency. Valuable glimpses into decision-making process, differences of opinion, repeated efforts to achieve greater unity" (55).

[2] The most notable would be the journals of Rudger Clawson. See Stan Larson, ed., *A Ministry of Meetings: The Apostolic Diaries and Journals of Rudger Clawson* (Salt Lake City: Signature Books, 1993). These journals offer a similar scope and detail to the A. H. Cannon journals, but for different years.

[3] Gordon B. Hinckley, "The Continuing Pursuit of Truth," *Ensign*, April 1986, 2-4. Continuing, President Hinckley stated: "We recognize that our forebears were human. They doubtless made mistakes. Some of them acknowledged making mistakes. But the mistakes were minor when compared with the marvelous work which they accomplished."

[4] B. H. Roberts, *A Comprehensive History of the Church of Jesus Christ of Latter-day Saints*, 6 vols. (Salt Lake City: The Church of Jesus Christ of Latter-day Saints, 1930), 6:354-55. Elder Roberts' tribute concluded: "Other men may found hospitals or temples or schools for the church, or endow special divisions or chairs of learning in them; or they may make consecrations of lands and other property to

the church, but in point of important service, and in placing the church under permanent obligations, no one will surpass in excellence and permanence or largeness the service which Wilford Woodruff has given to the Church of Jesus Christ in the New Dispensation, by writing and preserving the beautiful and splendid *Journals* he kept through sixty-three eventful years—so far do the things of mind surpass material things" (ibid.). Elder Franklin D. Richards agreed with Elder Roberts, stating: "The journal of Pres. Woodruff has furnished the Church with much valuable information, which would otherwise have been lost" (A. H. Cannon journal, 6 April, 1895, cited hereafter as AHC journals).

[5] Davis Bitton, *George Q. Cannon: A Biography* (Salt Lake City: Deseret Book, 1999), 262. See also Paul H. Petersen in *BYU Studies,* vol. 32, no. 3 (Summer 1992), 116.

[6] At the time the first Quorum of the Twelve Apostles was chosen by the Three Witnesses in 1835, the Prophet Joseph Smith spoke to them about the necessity of keeping records and minutes of their meetings, and of the "deep sorrow" he felt at not having always done this in the past. He told them:

> It is a fact, if I now had in my possession, every decision which had been had upon important items of doctrine and duties since the commencement of this work, I would not part with them for any sum of money; but we have neglected to take minutes of such things, thinking, perhaps, that they would never benefit us afterwards; which, if we had them now, would decide almost every point of doctrine which might be agitated. But this has been neglected, and now we cannot bear record to the Church and to the World, of the great and glorious manifestations which have been made to us with that degree of power and authority we otherwise could, if we now had these things to publish abroad.

> Since the Twelve are now chosen, I wish to tell them a course which they may pursue, and be benefited thereafter, in a point of light of which they are not now aware. If they will, every time they assemble, appoint a person to preside over them during the meeting, and one or more to keep a record of their proceedings, and on the decision of every question or item, be it what it may, let such decision be written, and such decision will forever remain upon record, and appear an item of covenant or doctrine. An item thus decided may appear, at the time, of little or no worth, but should it be published, and one of you lay hands on it after, you will find it of infinite worth, not only to your brethren, but it will be a feast to your own souls.

> Here is another important item. If you assemble from time to time, and proceed to discuss important questions, and pass decisions upon the same, and fail to note them down, by and by you will be driven to straits from which you will not be able to extricate yourselves, because you may be in a situation not to bring your faith to bear with

sufficient perfection or power to obtain the desired information; or, perhaps, for neglecting to write these things when God had revealed them, not esteeming them of sufficient worth, the Spirit may withdraw and God may be angry; and there is, or was, a vast knowledge, of infinite importance, which is now lost. What was the cause of this? It came in consequence of slothfulness, or a neglect to appoint a man to occupy a few moments in writing all these decisions....

Now, if you will be careful to keep minutes of these things, as I have said, it will be one of the most important records ever seen; for all such decision will ever after remain as items of doctrine and covenants. (Joseph Smith Jr., *History of the Church of Jesus Christ of Latter-day Saints*, 7 vols. (Salt Lake City: The Church of Jesus Christ of Latter-day Saints, 1948), 2:198-99.

[7] For the charge see the back dust jacket flap of B. Carmon Hardy, *Solemn Covenant: The Mormon Polygamous Passage* (Urbana and Chicago: University of Illinois Press, 1992). For the refutation, see AHC journals, 29 September 1890: [Franklin D. Richards] "When Pres. Woodruff prepared his manifesto it was without the aid or suggestions of his counselors. He took a clerk and went to a room alone. There *under the spirit of inspiration* he dictated the declaration he desired to make, and there was only one slight change made therein when it was read to Counselors Cannon and Smith. Therefore I feel it is from the almighty." See also 6 October 1890 [Pres. Woodruff in general conference as recorded by Elder Cannon]: "His course had been taken *under direction of God*, and rather than do anything contrary to the will of God, he would allow himself to be taken out to his death." See also 2 April 1891: [Pres. Woodruff] "In the name of Jesus Christ I say that God has not forsaken the Presidency or Twelve. *He inspired me to issue the manifesto* and if he had not done so I should never have taken that course even though all ordinances for the living and the dead had ceased, and our temples had fallen into the hands of our enemies" (emphasis added). Lastly, see Appendix One: Plural Marriage Issues in the Abraham H. Cannon Journals.

[8] See AHC journals, 5 April 1894. Interestingly, President Woodruff also stated that "there is yet very much for us to learn concerning the temple ordinances, and God will make it known as we prove ourselves ready to receive it" (ibid.).

[9] See also the biographical essay.

[10] See William C. Siefrit, "The Prison Experience of Abraham H. Cannon," *Utah Historical Quarterly* 53, no. 3 (1985): 223-36. See also Abraham H. Cannon, "Mormons in Prison," in *Voices from the Past: Diaries, Journals, and Autobiographies* (Provo, Utah: Brigham Young University Press, 1980), 97-100.

[11] For example, in the late 1890s, Elder Rudger Clawson (who was called into the Quorum of the Twelve Apostles a couple of years after the passing of Elder Cannon) audited the Church's financial books at President Lorenzo Snow's request. His findings: "[that the Church] if not bankrupt, was surely on the verge of bankruptcy." (David S. Hoopes and Roy Hoopes, *The Making of a Mormon*

Apostle: The Story of Rudger Clawson [Lanham: Madison Books, 1990], 178). The fact that the Church for most of the 1890s verged on financial collapse—but never did—is most telling.

[12] As with any lengthy journal, Abraham's included much that could be categorized as mundane, trivial, and commonplace. Weather reports, meals, purchases, travel, theater and play plotlines, family interaction, and recitations of daily routine account for large portions of many journal entries. Those interested in this material can consult the originals.

[13] This material relates to the so-called "Adam-god theory." See 10 March 1889, 23 June 1889, and 26 May 1892 in the original journals.

[14] In his officially commissioned work, *The House of the Lord*, Elder James E. Talmage used these words to describe the ordinance work performed in the Holy of Holies of the Salt Lake Temple: "This room is reserved for the *higher ordinances* in the Priesthood relating to the exaltation of both living and dead." (James E. Talmage, *The House of the Lord: A Study of Holy Sanctuaries both Ancient and Modern,* 1st ed. [Salt Lake City: The Church of Jesus Christ of Latter-day Saints, 1912], 194; emphasis added.) Elder Abraham H. Cannon had personal knowledge of these ordinances.

[15] For a description of prayer circles held by the First Presidency and the Twelve, see N. Eldon Tanner, "The Administration of the Church," in *Ensign*, Nov. 1979, 47. See also Joseph Fielding Smith, comp., *Life of Joseph F. Smith* (Salt Lake City: Deseret Book, 1969), 226.

[16] See AHC journals, 20 January 1892.

[17] Boyd K. Packer, "Keeping Confidences," Church Employees Lecture Series, 18 January 1980, 4.

[18] For an explanation and overview of general meetings and minutes of the First Presidency and the Twelve, see N. Eldon Tanner, "The Administration of the Church," *Ensign*, Nov. 1979, 47-48.

For precedent for the use of Quorum of the Twelve minutes found in a general authority's journal see Sheri L. Dew, *Go Forward With Faith: The Biography of Gordon B. Hinckley* (Salt Lake City: Deseret Book, 1996), 241 n. 15 and 609 ("Excerpt from Minutes of Council of Twelve Meeting, GBH Journal, undated"); and 383 n. 5 and 618 ("Minutes of the Council of the Twelve, 23 July 1981, as recorded in GBH Journal, 23 July 1981"); and 291 n. 1 and 612 ("See Gordon B. Hinckley, Notes from Special Meeting, 12 May 1968") This biography of President Hinckley also makes copious use of material from the journals of other members of the Twelve.

For further explanation of how minutes are taken and used, see Lucile C. Tate, *Boyd K. Packer: A Watchman on the Tower* (Salt Lake City: Bookcraft, 1995), 243. A perusal of sources cited in this biography of President Packer shows that discussions and talks from these meetings were often used. The same is true for the biography of President Marion G. Romney. See F. Burton Howard, *Marion G.*

Romney: His Life and Faith (Salt Lake City: Bookcraft, 1988), 109, 125, 170-71, 184, 186, and 219. See also note 6 above.

For an example of published official minutes, see H. Donl Peterson, *The Story of the Book of Abraham: Mummies, Manuscripts and Mormonism* (Salt Lake City: Deseret Book, 1995), 217-20.

[19] A few examples from LDS literature that contain excerpts from or entire patriarchal blessings are Joseph Fielding Smith Jr. and John J. Stewart, *The Life of Joseph Fielding Smith* (Salt Lake City: Deseret Book, 1972), 194-95; Bryant S. Hinckley, *Sermons and Missionary Services of Melvin Joseph Ballard* (Salt Lake City: Deseret Book, 1949), 70; Bryant S. Hinckley, *The Faith of our Pioneer Fathers* (Salt Lake City: Deseret Book, 1956), 234-35; Sheri L. Dew, *Go Forward With Faith: The Biography of Gordon B. Hinckley* (Salt Lake City: Deseret Book, 1996), 21-22; and Alan K. Parrish, *John A. Widstoe: A Biography* (Salt Lake City: Deseret Book, 2003), 49.

[20] For a frank acknowledgment that Church leaders occasionally disagree amongst themselves, including the fact that such disagreements are part of their life experience and associations in the ministry, see Dallin H. Oaks, *The Lord's Way* (Salt Lake City: Deseret Book, 1991), 150 and 152 n. 11. From this source we learn that modern Church leaders are well aware that past and present general authorities have dealt with occasional disagreement within their quorums. Even so, they largely choose to ignore it and focus on the good and the positive, which accounts for the great majority of the work and discussion between them. While Elder Cannon recounted the disagreements he witnessed amongst his brethren of the Twelve, he also wrote of their reconciliations and the remarkable unity and brotherly love that these strong-minded, independent-thinking men had for each other.

[21] LDS scripture states: "And truth is knowledge of things as they are, and *as they were*, and as they are to come; and whatsoever is more or less than this is the spirit of that wicked one" (D&C 93:24-25; emphasis added).

[22] I have not sought to provide an as-close-as-possible typographical reproduction of his writing, as there is no justification for it.

[23] Davis Bitton explained: "A few gaps due to lapses by author. Also unexplained removal of pages or clipping out of portions of pages. Still, coverage is remarkably complete and frank" (*Guide to Mormon Diaries and Autobiographies*, 55). Another puzzled author wrote: "There were many such excisions in his record—whether made by Abraham or someone else is uncertain—and we can only guess at their contents." Further, "Abraham's extant journals end with the year 1895. He had been a faithful diarist for many years and it is likely that he continued to be so into 1896. But the location of his records for that year are unknown." (Hardy, *Solemn Covenant*, 215-16.) In September of 2002, I interviewed Harvard Heath, a former employee of BYU library's special collections, who related that about five years previously he himself had interviewed Jean Cannon Willis, another granddaughter of Elder Cannon (and also President Heber J. Grant) and a sister of Rachel Cannon

Heninger. Mr. Heath said that he asked her if she knew who had excised the material from the journal and she replied, "We did," meaning the family. From their conversation, he got the impression that the family had removed portions from the journals, perhaps years before their donation to BYU. When asked what the missing material contained, she explained that it was mostly personal and private items which family members felt were not the business of the public. Mr. Heath had no information regarding the missing 1896 journal.

[24] Jean Bickmore White, ed., *Church, State, and Politics: The Diaries of John Henry Smith* (Salt Lake City: Signature Books, 1990), xiii.

[25] See Edward Leo Lyman, *Political Deliverance: The Quest for Utah Statehood* (Urbana and Chicago: University of Illinois Press, 1986); Gustive O. Larson, *The "Americanization" of Utah for Statehood* (San Marino: The Huntington Library, 1971); and Davis Bitton, *George Q. Cannon: A Biography* (Salt Lake City: Deseret Book, 1999). These publications provide an excellent commentary if the readers turn to the notes and scan them for the plentiful references to the AHC journals, by date, and then read the appropriate text.

[26] The best date of donation I could obtain from BYU Special Collections was the very early 1970s, as they did not keep accurate records at that time. The 1967 date used here is from Lyman, *Political Deliverance*, 304.

[27] Access is restricted at this library.

[28] The register is located with the University of Utah Special Collections library copy.

[29] The publisher was Pioneer Press; the compiler was Ogden Kraut.

[30] Francis M. Lyman, "The Yoke of Christ," discourse delivered at the Utah Stake Conference, Provo, 19 July 1896. Cited in Brian H. Stuy, ed., *Collected Discourses: Delivered by President Wilford Woodruff, His Two Counselors, the Twelve Apostles, and Others*, vol. 5 (Burbank, CA: B.H.S. Publishing, 1992), 163.

ACKNOWLEDGMENTS

I have received helpful advice regarding this project from a number of knowledgeable people. Davis Bitton and Dean Jessee each read a late draft and gave me valuable critiques that I used to improve the finished product. Lee Donaldson, Jerry Baker, Joseph Muren, and Myron Horne, all with Church Educational System backgrounds, read the manuscript and made suggestions. None of the foregoing share any responsibility for this volume. Each reviewed with me their thoughts relative to the inherent difficulties involved in a project such as this, and the impossibilities—which I had already begun to realize—of satisfying all interested parties: general readers, scholars and historians, and Church leaders. While I cannot hope to achieve universal approval, hopefully a fair and justifiable middle ground has been found.

Appreciation is tendered the Brigham Young University L. Tom Perry Special Collections archives and Russ Taylor for making copies of the journals available and for furnishing information on their provenance. Thanks also to the BYU Copyrights and Permissions Office for granting publication rights. Staff members from the LDS Family and Church History Department archives made available material from the Brigham Young Jr. diary, which is normally under restricted access, and furnished a photograph of Abraham H. Cannon (both used by permission).

Thanks are due Dan Hogan, Jeanna Mason, David Stevens, and Kent Minson for their help and expertise in the various aspects of book production.

This book is not an official publication of The Church of Jesus Christ of Latter-day Saints and the content of the journal entries and other accompanying explanatory materials are the sole responsibility of the author and editor and do not necessarily represent the position of the Church.

Biographical Essay

Elder Abraham Hoagland Cannon lived his life in the shadow of his father, the prominent politician, businessman, and LDS Church First Presidency member George Q. Cannon. Abraham died fairly young and spent his entire Apostolic tenure as the junior member of the Quorum of the Twelve Apostles. For these and other reasons he is almost unknown in the Church today. Perhaps the single most important thing he did in his life—after his Apostolic ministry—was to keep a marvelously complete and detailed journal. It is this journal that brings him out of historical obscurity and grants us the precious record of an Apostle who witnessed Church history in the making.

Ancestry and Parents

Abraham, or Abram as he was commonly known, was the fifth child (fourth biological) of George Q. Cannon (1827-1901) and the third child of his first wife, Elizabeth Hoagland (1835-1882).

Elizabeth was the daughter of Abraham Hoagland, who helped settle Royal Oaks, Michigan, where she was born and where the family heard and accepted the gospel message of The Church of Jesus Christ of Latter-day Saints. Abraham Hoagland was a blacksmith by trade and a bishop by calling. He served as a bishop in Nauvoo, where the family moved when they joined the Church, and also at Winter Quarters, Iowa, and then later as the first bishop of the fourteenth Ward in Salt Lake City. It was on the pioneer trek westward that Elizabeth and young George first met and became friends. They traveled in the company of President John Taylor, from whom George had learned the printing trade in Nauvoo. George was called on a mission to the California gold fields and then to Hawaii, but on his return he and Elizabeth were married in December of 1854. Their honeymoon consisted of a perilous journey across Nevada to California where George had been called to publish a mission newspaper, *The Western Standard*. Their first baby died after only a few weeks, and money was scarce. While thus living at the poverty level, a "wealthy Hawaiian planter called on them and, sensing their dire straits, made them a gift of $3,000. George was not insensitive to his family's needs, but he was painfully aware of the precarious situation of the church he loved and, after serious deliberation, he sent the entire amount to the First Presidency. President Young later told the dedicated elder (in David H. Cannon's presence) that, coming when it did, that money had saved the Church from a dangerously critical financial crisis."

The Cannons were called home at the approach of Johnson's army, sent by U.S. President Buchanan to squelch the nonexistent Mormon rebellion against the federal government. Upon arriving in Utah, the Cannons were sent to Fillmore to publish the *Deseret News*. When the threat subsided, they were returning to Salt Lake City with the newspaper press, a pregnant Elizabeth, her second baby John Q., and George's second wife, Sarah Jenne. They were met by a messenger from President Young, requesting George to come to President Young's office at once, as he had been called on another mission. He left with Elizabeth and their new baby, John Q., and rode all night from Payson to Salt Lake. Upon arriving at the President's office, George heard President Young say to those assembled, "Didn't I tell you it would be so? I knew I had but to call; here he is!" George was then sent out as the Eastern States Mission President.

George Q. Cannon

Meanwhile, on 12 March 1859, Abraham Hoagland Cannon (named after Elizabeth's father) was born in Salt Lake City. His mother endured the trials of having a Church leader husband who was gone much of the time in the service of the Lord and of losing several children in their infancy. She herself died while her sons John Q. and Abram were serving missions.[1]

George was ordained an apostle and set apart as a member of the Quorum of the Twelve Apostles in 1860 on his return from his Eastern States mission. George Q. Cannon became perhaps the most well-known (at least to the world) Latter-day Saint of the last third of the nineteenth century. His life has been well chronicled in several publications, and his journals are being published by the Family and Church History Department of the LDS Church.[2] Therefore, only a few highlights will be mentioned here. In 1873 Elder Cannon was named a counselor (one of five) to President Brigham Young; in 1880 he became First Counselor to President John Taylor; then in 1889 he was sustained as First Counselor to President Wilford Woodruff; and finally in 1898 he was again called as First Counselor to Lorenzo Snow. He was elected multiple times by the people of Utah as a territorial delegate to congress, where he rubbed elbows with the powerful men of the country and fought for Mormon causes. This service in the nation's capital served to increase his political influence and personal prominence, until the time came that President Young warned him to be careful, for "he said that next to himself I was the most hated of any of the authorities…. They would seek my life with the greatest of anxiety after seeking his, and I ought to be careful of myself."[3]

As is seen from the Abraham H. Cannon journals, President Cannon had amassed a fortune, mostly through mining stock investments, but hard economic times had affected him along with others, until he struggled mightily under the burdens of debt and obligations to a very large plural family. This he endured quietly, though Abraham felt deeply for him.

President Cannon spent years hiding from law enforcement officials, though he was eventually caught and served several months in prison.[4] Upon his release, he continued his duties as counselor to President Woodruff, who told Abraham privately that "your Father has…the best mind of any man in the Kingdom, without exception." Abraham also reported that President Woodruff had "remarked to Charles Wilcken [a family friend] that Father is the humblest man in the Church." Such was the regard the President had for his First Counselor.

On another occasion, during a priesthood meeting, President Woodruff let it be known that President Cannon was "the largest tithe-payer in the Church, but Father in explaining this matter later said that he had tried for many years to pay something as a consecration, and as there was no other fund in which to get credit than that of tithing, he had obtained credit for a larger tithing than he really should pay. He wanted by this means, however, to prepare himself and his family for the adoption of the law of consecration when it is again restored. He had sometimes borrowed money in order to pay into the Church for a consecration."[5]

President Cannon's years in the First Presidency were not without trial and controversy. He suffered embarrassing financial setbacks and was forced to live on the "underground" because of the unrelenting pursuit of federal marshals determined to be the one who caught George Q. Cannon. At President John Taylor's request he invested considerable resources in the Bullion, Beck, and Champion mine, which paid well at first, but then became a loss and a source of unpleasantness between him and at least one member of the Twelve. His dealings with political lobbyists in Utah's eventually successful quest for statehood drained him emotionally and financially. He even deeded his valuable "big house" downtown Salt Lake City property to these men—in behalf of the Church—in order to allay their greed ("[6 April 1895, Abraham wrote] I…was also at the President's office for a short time talking with Father, who was transferring his 17th Ward property to Hiram B. Clawson [agent for the lobbyists]").

To some in the public press and even the Church, he was viewed as the "real" president of the Church, for age was beginning to affect President Woodruff. One member of the Twelve mentioned this perception in council meeting: "Every dog in the country seems to be barking at Pres. George Q. Cannon. He is a man of God, and the Spirit of the Lord is upon him, and I do not care if he is the power behind the throne, so long as he stands as he thus has done to protect the interests of the Church and people."

When his son Abraham died in 1896, it wrenched President Cannon's heart, as Abram had been reliable and trustworthy in everything asked of him by his father, and such was not the case with some of President Cannon's other sons. When Abraham's body was being prepared for burial, Elder Brigham Young Jr. wrote in his journal that "Bro. George Q. tried to remain in the room but [the] sight of Abraham's face quite unnerved him. He requested me to remain and that all went well."[6] This sudden, tragic death seemed to be the beginning of the end for President Cannon himself, whose health declined until after returning from the Church Hawaiian Jubilee celebration in December, he died a few months later on 12 April 1901 in Monterey, California.

Though an author, printer, publisher, businessman, politician, congressman, board member and director of several corporations and railroads, as well as president of the family businesses, the most important thing to George Q. Cannon was his Apostleship and his testimony: "I know that God lives. I know that Jesus lives, for I have seen him."[7] And when determining the doctrine of the Church on the personage of the Holy Ghost, President Cannon could disclose to his Brethren "that he had heard the voice of the third member of the Godhead, actually talking to him...."[8]

Abraham Hoagland Cannon

Abraham Cannon grew up in Salt Lake City, in what was referred to as the Cannon "Big House" a large four-apartment home which President Cannon built so his wives could be close together but still live separately.

Elder Matthias Cowley, apostle and boyhood friend, wrote the following regarding Abraham's early life: "As a boy he was given the best opportunity that the times afforded for an education and being of a studious nature, he availed himself of that privilege, finishing his studies in the Deseret University. For a time when his father was editor of the *Deseret News* he was employed in that office as errand boy. Later, he learned the carpenter's trade at the Church carpenter shop, and worked on the Temple Block. He also studied architecture under...Obed Taylor, and became an architect." As one of his eldest sons, President Cannon also asked Abraham to teach Sunday School classes for his other children.

MARRIAGE AND MISSION

On 16 October 1878, Abraham, age 19, married Sarah Ann Jenkins. Almost exactly one year later, on 15 October 1879, he married his Uncle Angus' daughter Wilhelmina (whom he called "Mina") Cannon, his first plural wife. Soon after this second marriage, "he was called on a mission to Europe. After laboring for some time in the Nottingham conference, [in] England, he was assigned to the Swiss and German Mission, where he mastered the German language and traveled as a missionary in both Switzerland and Germany. He wrote some of the hymns which the German saints now sing in their congregations."[9] Young Elder Cannon took advantage of his connections to the *Juvenile Instructor* office to share many of his mission experiences, which he published with the title "Jottings by a Young Missionary" but under the name "Streben." These stories are scattered throughout the periodical in the years 1880 to 1882. Later he also helped translate the Book of Mormon into German. As noted previously, it was while on his three-year mission that his mother passed away, a sore trial for her son. Abraham returned from Europe in June of 1882.

At this point, at the age of twenty-three, he went to work as "Business Manager" of the *Juvenile Instructor*, a Church organ published by George Q. Cannon & Sons, his father's publishing company. Abraham Cannon would spend the rest of his life closely associated with this establishment, helping it grow from a small printing office to a large publishing house, though it barely weathered the panic of 1894. He also managed an Ogden book store, at first owned by the Cannon family, but which he later bought and managed himself. Abram paid rent to his father on these properties and family members owned the company stock.

He had not been home from his mission long when on 8 October 1882 he was called into the First Council of Seventy, then known as the First Seven Presidents of the Seventy. Of this occasion he wrote: "I then accompanied Mina to meeting [general conference], and shortly after arriving there I was invited to the stand, where my name, together with that of Bro. T. B. Lewis, was mentioned by Pres.

Woodruff before the conference, and we were selected to fill the vacancies in the Quorum of the First Seven Presidents of Seventies. I was chosen in Bro. Joseph Young's place and Bro. Lewis for John Hancock, both deceased. I was never more surprised in my life, as I had received no intimation of this appointment." Then, the next day "I went to a meeting at the Council house. Pres. Woodruff there set me apart with an excellent blessing." T. B. Lewis was not set apart, as it was discovered that he had already been ordained a high priest.[10] On 9 October 1884, Elder Cannon was admitted to the Council of Fifty, a private theocratic-political council first organized by Joseph Smith in the early 1840s, but now briefly reconstituted by President John Taylor. This occasion was also the last time the council met.[11]

Life continued normally for Abraham, until September 5, 1885, when he "was taken down with a severe illness.... Dr. Seymour B. Young…pronounced my disease a case of Typhoid fever. It proved to be very severe as I lay for seven weeks in bed, during part of which time I was delirious." His wives, Sarah and Mina, nursed him day and night. Even with this care, he became so deathly sick that he had an experience which he later shared with his brethren of the Quorum of the Twelve Apostles in a council meeting: "I spoke of my experience when my spirit left the body during my illness with the typhoid fever." And on another occasion he added this extra detail: "I also told of…having seen my mother when I was dead during the typhoid fever.…"

PRISONER FOR POLYGAMY

On 17 February 1886, Elder Cannon was tried for "illegal co-habitation" one of the new anti-polygamy laws which had been passed by the U. S. government to stamp out Mormon polygamy: "I reached the Court Room at 11:20 a.m. whither Mina and the other witnesses in my case had already gone. After receiving assurances through F. S. Richards from [Prosecuting Attorney] Dickson that if I would cause them no trouble my sentence shouldn't be passed until March 17th, I went on the stand after pleading "not guilty" and testified in my own case. In answer to Dickson's question whether

Sarah and Wilhelmina were my wives, I replied, 'They are, thank God,' and I further admitted having lived with them during the dates mentioned in the indictment. A verdict of "guilty" was immediately rendered by the jury...."

When March seventeenth arrived, Abraham "bid the family 'Goodbye'":

> I then went to the Federal Court House where at 10 a.m. I was called up to be sentenced. Upon Judge Zane giving me permission to speak I explained my position and stated that I had only sought to obey the law of God in doing as I had done, and if for doing that I deserved punishment I was prepared for sentence. He then sentenced me to six months imprisonment, to pay a fine of $300 and costs and stand committed till the fine and costs are paid. I immediately went into the marshals office under guard, and there remained until about 4 p.m., except for a few minutes when I went to a restaurant under guard, waiting for the Penitentiary wagon.... About 5 p.m. after riding over a very rough road and wet, I arrived at the "Pen" in charge of Guard Jancy. I was ushered into the dining room where I sat while the guards and working trusties ate. I was offered food but did not care for any. The turnkey, Mr. Curtis, then came in and in a very gentlemanly way performed his duties. He took my name, age, height, weight, color of hair and eyes, occupation, crime for which sentenced, etc. He then took from me my knife, money and a newspaper, the other things in my pocket he permitted me to retain. I was then taken and measured for a suit of clothes (prison stripes). I was then put in the yard where I met a number of the brethren.

Abraham's prison term was difficult, but not intolerable. He served out his sentence with other Mormon men who had been incarcerated for the same offence, and found himself supported by an enjoyable brotherhood. Though exposed to some degree to the many undesirable elements of prison life, he was able to shield himself from the worst of it. While enduring the endless monotony of prison, Abraham improved his shorthand skills, wrote articles for the *Juvenile Instructor* and authored a book entitled *Questions and Answers on the Book of Mormon* (referred to in the journals as *Book of Mormon Catechism*) which he published upon his release.

Elder Cannon's prison term ended 18 August 1886. He wrote: "At 5 o'clock, I was permitted to leave the yard with the trusties, who at that time went to work. I found John Q. waiting for me with a buggy, and, as Mr. Curtis did not desire to search my valise, I jumped in and we were soon in town. I called to see Sara and the children at her mothers and then went to Aunt Sarah's, where I had breakfast, and met the rest of my folks." Abram had been able to do a substantial amount of regular business through letters and visitors while in the Pen, as well as writing articles and books, and discussing doctrine with other brethren. He quickly resumed his personal management of the family businesses, especially the *Juvenile Instructor*, and also became increasingly involved with his father's financial affairs.

In 1886, after his release, he courted Mary E. Croxall, (usually referred to as M.E.C. in his journal) and then married her on 11 January 1887, as his third wife.

As the years passed, Abraham became increasingly involved with business affairs, both his own, his father's, and the Church's. However, it is often difficult to discern from the journals exactly whose business affairs he is writing about.[12] He did experience something of prosperity and success in his efforts, enabling him to support three separate residences, employ various numbers of workmen, and invest in railroads, mines, stock (horses and cattle), stock (corporate), and travel widely on both personal and Church business, all while receiving no compensation from the Church.

BUSINESS AND THE APOSTLESHIP

Then in 1889, his father dropped a hint that something was up. He "said the authorities of the Church had decided to appoint me to a mission, and he hoped I would round up my shoulders and take it." Abraham soon learned the nature of this mission. On 6 October 1889, he went by appointment "to the Gardo House where myself and Bro. Anthon H. Lund…were summoned into the presence of the First Presidency and Twelve Apostles. Pres. Woodruff then stated that Bro. Marriner W. Merrill and ourselves had been selected to fill the vacancies in the Quorum of the Twelve." As the son of the First Counselor in the First Presidency, he became a target for the charge of nepotism in the new call. However, a day later as the father and son discussed the matter, Elder Cannon recorded that "our conversation…gave me very great joy to see how happy he was at my call to the Apostleship without any suggestion from him. He said that the three men of all Israel whom he would have chosen had been selected." President Woodruff went to great lengths at the time of the new Apostle's sustaining in general conference to explain to the congregation that the Quorum of the Twelve Apostles had made the selection, and the First Presidency and the Lord had only confirmed their choices.[13]

Abraham's life did not change much with the new calling. At this time all the General Authorities did not yet receive a regular "living allowance" from the Church; some received a salary, others did not.[14] Though there was intermittent discussion amongst themselves regarding the need to alter this situation, many Church authorities were expected to provide for themselves and their families, all while engaged as much as possible in the ministry. Therefore, Elder Cannon continued managing the *Juvenile Instructor* office, as well as contracting further business obligations for himself, and becoming much more involved in both Church business and his father's. On 1 October, 1892 for example, he took over management of the *Deseret News*[15] and the *Contributor*, another Church magazine. His brother John Q.—an associate in some of these ventures—listed some of Elder Cannon's business activities: "He was the moving spirit in the Salt Lake and Pacific Railways…. He was elected director, vice president and assistant manager of the Bullion-Beck mining company. He was a director and one of the organizers of the State Bank of Utah; director of the Utah Loan and Trust Company,

Ogden; director in Z.C.M.I.; vice-president of George Q. Cannon & Sons Company; director in the Co-operative Furniture Company; first vice-president of the Chamber of Commerce.... He had also been an active promoter of canal and irrigation company enterprises, and was a member of the Deseret Sunday School Union Board."[16]

Elder Cannon's publishing establishment issued a number of excellent church-related works, such as Orson F. Whitney's *History of Utah*; books by Edward W. Tullidge, James A. Little, George Q. Cannon, and James E. Talmage; and various official Church works, handbooks, and scriptures. He seems to have held Dr. Talmage (who was but three years younger and would later become an Apostle) in high esteem. With the approval of the First Presidency and an official Church "committee on criticism" (of which Elder Cannon was a member), Dr. Talmage had been preparing lessons and holding well-attended religion classes, lecturing on the subject of the articles of faith. On 1 April 1894, Elder Cannon wrote: "I attended Dr. Talmage's theological class in the Assembly Hall at 12:30, and after he had delivered his lecture on the Gathering, I adjourned the class...by authority and direction of the First Presidency. He [Dr. Talmage] spoke first about the adjournment, and I then explained that it was because of his numerous duties in other directions, and because it was only designed originally to continue the class till April, that it was decided to close. I expressed my appreciation of Bro. Talmage's labors, and a hearty vote of thanks was tendered him."[17] This series of lectures was eventually published in book form with the approval of the First Presidency as *The Articles of Faith* and has since become a classic in LDS doctrinal literature.

A combination of factors were responsible for the decline in Elder Cannon's financial fortunes. He overextended and over-obligated himself both economically and physically. Some of his business deals stalled or failed.[18] He became mired in debt, and it was a constant struggle to repay and refinance loans and also make payroll for both the *Deseret News* and the other publications he managed. The primary reason for his difficulties came from the economic downturn of the early 1890s, which turned into the panic of 1893-94, and which affected the rest of the country as well. During this year banks throughout the United States failed on a daily basis. Once, when word reached the *Deseret News* office that several banks had failed in Denver, Colorado, the report was purposely withheld from readers in order to prevent a run on local banks. Panic became an apt word to describe the times. The Church, many of its leaders, and the financial institutions in which they had invested suffered severely. Bankruptcy and lawsuits became commonplace, with Elder Cannon barely avoiding the former and sometimes finding himself in court to battle the latter. It was at this point that he wrote the following entry in his journal:

> I was in the offices a good part of the day, and had one of the most trying financial experiences of my life. A [*Deseret*] *News* office check was protested, [so] we had no means with which to pay the *News* employees, and Dooley asked me to get Father's endorsement to a guarantee for our $15,000 overdraft. Father had me at the President's office, where he complained at my failure to give him a report of the *News* and *Juvenile* offices condition. His complaint is well-founded, and I intend to try and avoid giving him cause to find fault in the future. An attorney came to see me about the *History* [*of Utah*] account due Streicher, one of the canvassers, who threatens suit unless his account is paid in full. Skelton of Provo, who owes the balance of over $400 on an unpaid note, came to tell us he can do nothing at present, and apologize for his past failures to keep his word with us. Altogether I have had a most trying day, and one which I hope the Lord will enable me to avoid in my future experience.

While his journal is replete with this type of entry for later 1893 and 1894, most are not included in this compilation. Abraham was hard pressed to meet all his duties and obligations. At the same time he served as a member of the Quorum of the Twelve Apostles, he ran his own businesses, helped the First Presidency and his father with theirs, and became further involved with the Bullion-Beck and Champion Mining Company (B.B. & C.), the affairs of which were constantly intruding upon both his father's life and his own.[19] Added to this were his three families, each needing attention and support. It was about this time that he wrote something about a friend which proved remarkably prophetic for him as well: "Henry A. Woolley died this morning.... He was a very excellent man, and I have been associated with him in several businesses in which we were both directors. He is a young man who seemed likely to have a long lease on life. He died the victim of overwork and worry, and too many are following in his footsteps."

Through all his many successes and struggles with both Church and business, one quality that Elder Cannon continually demonstrated was loyalty to his fellowservants in the ministry. He always lined up solidly behind them. He took their direction with obedience, deferred to them in council, and accepted their rebukes both publicly and privately with genuine humility.[20] Conceivably, one may cover up and lie to others, but rarely to a journal, as seen above and also in the following experience.

In mid-1895, Elder Cannon visited southern Utah, scouting railroad locations and touring Mountain Meadows (site of the Mountain Meadows Massacre). Here he received a visit from a disgruntled Church member. Elder Cannon wrote:

> Just after finishing breakfast Mr. Thomas Taylor, ex-Bishop of the 14th Ward in Salt Lake City called to see me and gave vent to considerable abuse of the Authorities of the Church in general and Father in particular. He said that my visit to the city and to the South was calculated to defeat his plans for the construction of a road to San Diego, he having already secured the co-operation of influential and moneyed men to carry through his project. He says that the Authorities of the Church have persistently interfered with his arrangements, and they have followed him with a determination to ruin him, which he cannot understand. He threatens that a

continuation of this persecution, as he calls it, could lead him to publish a statement giving what he said would be damaging testimony against Father and the other members of the Presidency. He will then appeal to the people to know if they will sustain such men in the positions they occupy. His whole conversation was that of a man partially insane. I invited him to publish any statement which he might have or could procure, and assured him that nothing he could tell would injure Father or the brethren, as their whole conduct through life was of a character that they need not be ashamed of it. I told him further that his talk this morning had deprived me of all respect and regard which I had entertained for him in the past.

In his turn, President Cannon fully realized what kind of son he had in Abraham, and a great love and respect had long since grown between them. "I was much touched by the devotion of Abraham in this matter," wrote the father in regards to his request to Abraham to look after the affairs of his brother John Q. "And I could scarcely refrain from weeping in thinking about the manner in which he has helped me on various occasions and done what he could for my sons, some of whom seem inclined to lay heavy burdens upon me, without any design on their part to do so, but through mismanagement. Abraham has always stood by me and done all in his power to assist me, and I felt to bless him for it."[21] John Q. had been called as a counselor in the Presiding Bishopric in 1884 at age 27 but had sinned and been excommunicated two years later. In 1888 he was rebaptized, but because his business dealings were sometimes less than proper he acquired a poor reputation and became a burden to his family. The other prominently mentioned brother in the journals, Frank J., had a weakness for vice and speculation. His charm and skill with a pen won him some popularity and position in politics, but also scandal and misfortune in his personal life and business. Between the two, Abraham found himself forced into the role of rescuer on many occasions.

About this time Abraham mentioned a few health complaints, such as exhaustion (presumably from overwork) and ear trouble. Since the whereabouts of his journal for the first six months of 1896 is unknown, we have less information regarding his health and other doings for this time period.

1896, THE MISSING HALF YEAR

We can trace some of his whereabouts from the records of his colleagues. Elder John Henry Smith's journal records Elder Cannon's attendance at regular Quorum meetings on 9 and 16 January; 6 February; 5, 12, 19, 26 and 31 March; 1, 2, 5, 6, 16, 23, and 29 April; 7 and 28 May; and 4 June.

President Woodruff's journal also records the following: 28 January, "We had some business with A. H. Cannon on our money matters." 10 February, "A. H. Cannon got letters from Brothers Langford, Smith, and Hugh J. Cannon." 5 April, "A. H. Cannon [spoke for] 20 minutes." 29 April, "Abram H. Cannon was the purchaser for a railroad company." 7 June, "I attended the conference through the day. Abram H. Cannon and H. J. Grant spoke in the forenoon." From these entries, we discover what should be expected—that Elder Cannon continued living his normal life, attending his meetings, and furthering his and the Church's business interests.

In June of 1896, Abraham became involved with a struggling Ogden bank, the Utah Loan and Trust Company. His actions in this matter have been described as a "desperate scheme that required him to go deeply into debt" (which, as noted, simply contributed to where he already was).[22] Historian Ronald W. Walker explained the situation:

> Mormon apostle Abraham H. Cannon offered to buy controlling interest in the bank in June 1896, [and] the [Franklin D.] Richards family breathed a grateful sigh and relinquished their controlling interest at sixty cents on the dollar of their original investment. The depressed

Nineties had not been any more kind to Elder Cannon than to the Richardses, and he hoped to recoup his fortune by promoting a Salt Lake City to Los Angeles railroad which, by using the UL&T as its financial agent, would revivify the ailing bank. The details of the transaction reflected common desperation of both the buyer and the seller. To secure money to pay off the Richardses, the UL&T loaned Cannon $40,000 from its scanty reserves, with the apostle offering as collateral his newly acquired UL&T stock, along with some previously owned shares. As both partners in the transaction must have known, unless Cannon could quickly come up with money to pay off his debt, the deal seriously jeopardized the bank's liquidity.

Six weeks later Abraham Cannon was dead…. Despite a $50,000 life insurance policy, his estate could not begin to pay off his many debts, most substantial of which was the UL&T note. Since its default promised eventual bankruptcy to the financial institution, the UL&T stock which supposedly secured the loan was itself worthless.

At least for the moment, Elder Cannon's posthumous insolvency was concealed from public view.[23]

Abraham had been struggling with debt and heavy obligations during the early 1890s and had only just begun to recover in late 1895 and presumably 1896. Therefore, given his already precarious financial condition, his move with the U.L.&T. is perplexing, doubly so since we do not have his 1896 journal, which would undoubtedly have explained his reasoning. Evidently he was counting a great deal on his railroad project and other investments to improve his personal economic condition and allow for the rescue of the bank. It was Elder Heber J. Grant who posthumously saved him: "After five months of fund-raising, Grant triumphantly paid off Abraham Cannon's note. Executors of his estate had scraped together $15,000, but the bulk of the money came from Grant's campaigning. 'I have labored earnestly in this matter,' Grant wrote… 'and one of the main reasons for doing so has been my desire to maintain Abraham's good name. I feel confident that had I passed away from life, and he been permitted to live, that he would have labored with equal zeal to try and preserve my honor and good name in the community.'"[24]

ABRAHAM'S FOURTH WIFE

Curiously, in 1906, as part of the Reed Smoot Senate hearings, a brief national controversy developed over the final few weeks of Abraham's life, relating to his marriage to a fourth plural wife. Because of the missing 1896 journal, there is little known about it, and those who have researched and written about the circumstances have relied on scanty circumstantial evidence and theorizing—not a hallmark of reliable history.

It seems clear that President Woodruff's interpretation of the Manifesto allowed for limited plural marriage outside the boundaries of the country, either in another country or on the ocean. While historians have quibbled over the technicalities of this, it matters little since Wilford Woodruff was the President of the Church and the man who held the keys of the sealing power, and could interpret and enforce the revelation he had received as he wished and as the Spirit led.

The story actually begins earlier, on 19 October 1894, when Abraham wrote that "I also had a talk with Father about the *Juvenile* business, which made him feel somewhat discouraged because of our heavy indebtedness…. Father also spoke to me about taking some good girl and raising up seed by her for my brother David [David had died earlier on his mission]. He mentioned the daughter of Theophilus Davis, who has said she will never marry at all unless I become her husband, but I told him I knew but little of her character. He told me to think the matter over, and speak to him later about it. Such a ceremony as this could be performed in Mexico, so Pres. Woodruff has said."

A few days later on 24 October 1894 Abraham again wrote: "After meeting I went to the President's office and talked with Father about taking a wife for David. I told him David had taken Annie [Cannon his?] cousin, through the veil in life, and suggested she might be a good person [to have?] sealed to him for eternity. The suggestion pleased Father very much, and [as Uncle?] Angus was there, He spoke to him about it in the presence of the Presidency. [He does?] not object providing Annie is willing. The Presidents Woodruff and Smith both said they were willing for such a ceremony to occur, if done in Mexico, and Pres. Woodruff promised the Lord's blessing to follow such an act. Father said Uncle Angus should sound [question] Annie on the matter, and I was willing to leave it in that way."

Then, on Saturday, 27 October, Abraham recorded: "I had a talk with Uncle Angus about his daughter Ann, and he gave me full and free permission to ask her to become the wife of my brother David, and seemed to wish that she would look favorably on the proposition, though he did not want to influence her in the least against her own will. He said he would give her counsel if she desired it." Over the next few months there are several other journal entries that mention Annie Cannon and show that Abraham may have been courting her, presumably with the knowledge of his other wives (see, for example, 11 December 1894).

It is here that conjecture comes into play, for nothing else is found in the journals to reveal if Abraham ever asked Annie to be his wife for time and his brother David's wife for eternity, and thereby fulfill the wishes of his father. Again, the assumption is that some of the missing portions of the journals contained that information, but we do not know. All we know is that "there is no formal record of her ever having married" anyone.[25] It seems there is but a remote possibility that she became a plural wife to Abraham, but the stage was now set for other developments.

The story then jumps ahead to late 1895, when Abraham began keeping company with Lillian Hamlin, the former fiancée of his brother David (see, for instance, 29 December 1895). Apparently this continued until June, when Abraham approached his wife Mina about his marriage to Lillian (also spelled Lilian) for time only and her sealing to David for eternity. Mina rebelled against the proposition, as she periodically had on other occasions when dealing with the realities of life in polygamy. On 12 June Abraham attended the birthday party of his daughter. Lillian Hamlin received her endowments in the Salt Lake Temple on the 17th. The next day, according to the journal of Wilford Woodruff, "J. F. Smith and A. H. Cannon went to California." Joseph F. Smith was accompanied by one of his wives, and Abraham was accompanied by Lillian. Various theories have been advanced by writers concerning what happened over the ensuing days until 2 July, when the party returned to Utah. The prevailing family tradition was that President Smith sealed Lillian to Abraham for time—and to David Cannon for eternity—while aboard ship off Catalina Island in the Pacific Ocean. This scenario is complicated by President Smith's denial that he performed the sealing aboard ship.[26] Another theory postulates that President Smith sealed them in the Salt Lake Temple on 17 June, the day before they left, and that the trip to California constituted a honeymoon.[27] Whatever the truth of the matter, we do know that they were sealed together by one holding the keys, for Lillian became pregnant on the trip, nine months later giving birth to a girl she named Marba (Abram spelled backwards), and her surname was Cannon.[28]

The reason this last quiet marriage became a national issue was that it constituted a post-Manifesto plural marriage, something the anti-Mormons and the Church's political opponents were gleefully eager to prove the Church had sanctioned. They put the Church on trial nationally, in the name of Apostle Reed Smoot, and used the forum of senatorial hearings to their fullest advantage. Therefore, Church leaders and their relatives and enemies were subpoenaed to testify regarding their knowledge of post-Manifesto polygamy, including Abraham's marriage to Lillian Hamlin. The hearings produced a constant flow of headlines for newspapers more interested in circulation than truth.[29]

The second Manifesto by President Joseph F. Smith in 1904 halted all sanctioned plural marriages, including those outside the boundaries of the United States.[30]

As an apostle, Elder Cannon sat with members of the Twelve and the First Presidency who presided and conducted during the general conferences, stake conferences, funerals, and other meetings of the

Church. The Brethren were given no notice of when they would speak or what subject they should talk about. These extemporaneous exercises commonly kept the speakers in a state of nervousness until their turn came, at which time they often confessed an urgent reliance on the inspiration of the moment. It was under such circumstances that Elder Cannon declared: "I have always a pleasure in bearing my testimony of the Prophet Joseph. I have never had the pleasure of the visitation of angels, although I have seen great workings of the spirit of God, and the workings of the spirit which I have seen tell me that this is the work of God."[31] And a few years later: "I am pleased to…bear my testimony this day that…the sick are healed by the power of God. I believe and know that the dead have been raised to life. I know that the gifts of tongues and interpretation of tongues are experienced by the people. I know that the gift of prophecy is heard frequently among the people, and sometimes from those from whose mouths prophecy is least expected. I know that in the conferences of the people there is the power of God manifested to a remarkable degree."[32] As is apparent from his sermons, the apostolic ministry had magnified Elder Cannon's ability to teach and testify well beyond that of the average 35-year-old in the Church.

LAST DAYS AND DEATH

Wilhelmina, or Mina, testified during the Smoot hearings that Elder Cannon had returned from California on July 2 with a pain in his head and feeling very sick. She said he told her that "he had never had a well day since he had married her [Lillian]." The pain was "in his head; in his brain." Abraham stayed in Mina's home as he died, with his new wife Lillian visiting from time to time. Mina related that "he told me he had married her and asked my forgiveness," and she added her own opinion that she thought the trip and the marriage is what killed him. She also said that it was the general understanding of friends and relatives at the time that President Joseph F. Smith had performed the sealing ceremony, but that she no longer believed this, because she had since read his public denial.[33]

A few of Elder Cannon's colleagues recorded in their own journals what they personally observed of the last days of Elder Abraham H. Cannon:[34]

President Wilford Woodruff (President of the Church)— 7 July 1896: "President Cannon spent most of the day signing bonds. I spent the day in the office. Abram H. Cannon is a very sick man. He had a successful operation performed in taking of his ear in taking out a polipus [sic], a fungus growth. He is very sick." [This was the first operation.]

President Wilford Woodruff— 8 July 1896: "I spent the day in the office. I received a letter from Sarah. I wrote one in return. Abram H. Cannon is very sick."

Elder Marriner W. Merrill (of the Quorum of the Twelve Apostles)— 8 July 1896: "Attended Quorum meeting at 10 a.m. in Salt Lake. At noon went in company with John W. Taylor to see Brother Abram Cannon at his home. Found him very ill indeed; he could not speak above a low whisper, and was very weak. He has three beautiful homes close together and all well furnished."

Elder Brigham Young Jr. (son of Brigham Young and member of the Quorum of the Twelve Apostles)— 10 July 1896: "Have visited Bro. Abraham H. Cannon who is very ill. Administered to him several times; he is very low."

Elder Brigham Young Jr.— 11 July 1896: "Visited Bro. Cannon who is very low but I feel he will live."

President Wilford Woodruff— 13 July 1896: "We had a very hard rain this morning. Abraham H. Cannon is but very little better."

President Wilford Woodruff— 14 July 1896: "In company with President G. Q. Cannon and J. F. Smith visited A. H. Cannon and found him almost at deaths door. J. F. Smith anointed him and I administered to him. He seemed better after being administered to."

Elder Brigham Young Jr.— 15 July 1896: "Met with special circle at Temple to pray for Bro. A. H. C. who lies at point of death. Visited and administered to him. Four doctors made a cut or bored into his head behind the ear which gave Bro. A. H. C. relief. Seemed to be pressure on the brain certainly there is a drainage enough now. His ear aperture was too much inflamed to carry away the puss etc. Bro. C lies insensible and he looks more like a dead man than a live one but each time I have prayed to the Lord the Lords spirit has relieved my feelings of all anxiety." [This was the second operation.]

Elder John Henry Smith— 15 July 1896: "Elder A. H. Cannon is very bad today. A consultation Doctor was called and an operation performed which gave some relief. H. J. Grant and I went and administered to him."

President Wilford Woodruff— 15 July 1896: "Abram H. Cannon is worse today. Nothing but the power of God can save him."

Elder Brigham Young Jr.— 16 July 1896: "Bro. Cannon is a trifle better."

Elder Brigham Young Jr.— 17 July 1896: "Called at Bro. A. H. C. He is better so all think and he looks it."

President Wilford Woodruff— 17 July 1896: "I learned that A. H. Cannon was still very low but things on the improvement a little."

Elder Brigham Young Jr.— 18 July 1896: "Arose early, breakfast early. Said to my wife "Bro. Cannon is passing a crisis." I was awakened in the night and found myself plunged in grief; every breath was a prayer for Bro. Abraham's life. This continued for more than [an] hour as I suppose, then I sank away to sleep without realizing more than a partial relief from these terrible feelings.

"Took train at 7:40 U. P. Just before getting on train learned that Bro. A. H. C. took a turn for the worse about 1 o'clock this morning."

President Wilford Woodruff— 18 July 1896: "I visited A. H. Cannon. He seemed to be dying."

Elder Marriner W. Merrill— July 19, 1896: "Apostle A. H. Cannon died at his home in Salt Lake City."

President Wilford Woodruff— 19 July 1896: "Abraham Hoagland Cannon died this morning fifteen minutes past 6 [5?] o'clock. He was a member of the quorum of the Twelve Apostles having been ordained an apostle on the 7th day of October 1889 by President Joseph F. Smith. Brother Cannon's death is a great loss not only to his family but to the Church. Especially to the Presidency of the Church as he was attending to a good deal of our business. Very few purer or better men ever lived on earth than Abram H. Cannon. On Saturday the 18th Emma and myself visited Bro. Cannon at his death bed. He seemed to be dying when we were there."

Elder Brigham Young Jr.— (Sunday), 19 July 1896: "Word was brought last evening that Bro. A. H. C. is sinking more but Presidents Geo[rge] Q. C[annon] and J[oseph] F. S[mith] seem to have any hope left. Received telegram at 9:30 a.m. that Bro. Abraham died at 5:15 this morning. It is hard to believe that he is taken from us. He was needed so badly. I dreamed sometime during the night that he and [I] had a very satisfactory conversation and he reconnected [reconciled] me to his death. I remember these words that he said to me. 'Now you see it was all for the best' referring to his death.

"Meeting at 10 a.m. Bro. Lyman spoke of Abraham as we all have known him.... Visited Cannon's. Assisted placing the body in cold air chamber. Very tired and nerves much tried. Bro. Geo[rge] Q. C[annon]. tried to remain in the room but sight of Abraham's face quite unnerved him. He requested me to remain and see that all went well."

Elder Brigham Young Jr.— 20 July 1896: "It is decided that the Twelve take charge of the funeral ceremonies. Bro. Cannon bears up wonderfully well. So does the family of Bro. Abraham.

"The whole people are in mourning. Was at Bro. Abraham's in evening."

Elder Brigham Young Jr.— 21 July 1896: "President Snow, Richards, John H[enry] S[mith], H[eber] J. G[rant], [and] myself met at His[torian's] off[ice]. H. J. G. chair, J. H. S. and I members of Comm[ittee] to attend to the business of Bro. A. H. C.'s funeral. Drove to Cemetery with President Cannon. Selected S. E. corner Abraham's lot for his grave."

Elder Brigham Young Jr.— 22 July 1896: "Raining, President Wilford Woodruff did come to the office. His health is not good. Comm[ittee] met in A. M. C. office and arranged program for conducting funeral ceremonies. Took President Cannon home. Had supper and visit with him and my Sis. Carle. Bro. C[annon] bears up remarkably well."

Elder Marriner W. Merrill— 25 July 1896: "I left Richmond for Salt Lake to attend Apostle A. H. Cannon's funeral tomorrow, Sunday, at 2 p.m."

Elder Brigham Young Jr.— 26 July 1896: "The twelve left office at 12 o'clock. At Bro. Abraham H. Cannon's place viewed the remains. Family were all in tears though little boisterous crying. President G. Q. C. was affected but controlled his feelings. President Snow and F[ranklin] D. R[ichards] walked in front. Brothers Lyman, Smith, Taylor, Merrill, Teasdale and [my]self carried the coffin. President Woodruff is here and feeble. It made my heart ache to see decay so plainly in him, Pres. Snow and F. D. Richards. God help the people when these veterans in His service pass away which looks to be in the near future. Procession went without hitch to Tabernacle. Twelve pall bearers. Abraham looked natural. Bro. F. D. R. prayed. Presidents Snow and Woodruff spoke to the point. 'Oh my Father' was sung by Bro. Easton. President Joseph F. Smith made few remarks to the point and very pointedly. God blessed the speakers. Song and prayer by self closed the ceremonies. I prayed: I said it seems to me that Bro. Abraham is approved of God and man from the cradle to the grave. Very long procession. Twelve bore the coffin to the grave, let it down and Bro. Lyman dedicated the ground. How my heart burned for the grief stricken father and family. God comfort them. Returned home nearly sick. Now we shall feel the loss of our dear Bro. Abraham."

Elder Young's mention of a dream (see 19 July entry) involving Abraham is worth further notice. It is apparent that Abraham gave him some kind of explanation that reconciled or contented Elder Young that he needed to die, despite certain wording in his patriarchal blessings and the enormous amount of work which lay ahead for him to do in mortality. President Woodruff also recorded a personal revelation regarding this recently deceased youngest member of the Twelve: "While in San Francisco on the night of Tuesday August 18, I was very much troubled in the forepart of the night with evil spirits that tried to afflict me. Finally a spirit visited me that seemed to have power over the evil spirits and they departed from me.... This same spirit said to me not to grieve because of the departure of Abram Hoagland Cannon for the Lord had called him to fill a very important mission in the spirit world. As a pure, holy Apostle from Zion in the Rocky Mountains, a labor which would not only prove a great blessing to his fathers household but to the Church and kingdom of God on the earth. The spirit of God rested upon me at the close of this manifestation in a powerful manner and bore testimony to me of the truth of the revelation to me concerning Abram H. Cannon."[35] At the October general conference of the church, President Woodruff elaborated on this manifestation:

We lost one of our Apostles a short time since. He was about the youngest man in the quorum of the Apostles. He was called suddenly away from us. There is a meaning to this. Many times things take place with us that we do not comprehend, unless it is given to us by revelation. But there is a meaning in the loss of that young Apostle. I had a manifestation of that while in San Francisco recently. One evening, as I fell asleep, I was very much troubled with evil spirits, that tried to afflict me; and while laboring to throw off these spirits and their influence, there was another spirit visited me that seemed to have power over the evil spirits, and they departed from me. Before he left me he told me not to grieve because of the departure of Abraham Hoagland Cannon; for the Lord had called him to fill another important mission in the spirit world, as a pure and holy Apostle from Zion, in the Rocky Mountains—a labor which would not only prove a great benefit to his father's household, but to the Church and kingdom of God upon the earth. I feel to name this because it is true.... While in the St. George Temple I had a son, who was in the north country, drowned. He was 21 years of age, and was a faithful young man. He had a warning of this. In a dream he was notified how he would die. We had testimony of that after his death. I asked the Lord why he was taken from me. The answer to me was. 'You are doing a great deal for the redemption of your dead; but the law of redemption requires some of your own seed in the spirit world to attend to work connected with this.' That was a new principle to me; but it satisfied me why he was taken away. I name this because there are a great many instances like it among the Latter-day Saints. This was the case with Brother Abraham Cannon. He was taken away to fulfill that mission.[36]

Echoing the thoughts and feelings of his devastated father, one of Abraham's younger brothers, upon hearing of his death, wrote: "Our family I'm very proud of but there are few Abrahams in it."[37] Some historians mark the passing of Abraham as the beginning of the decline in health and vitality of President George Q. Cannon as well.

With Abraham's death, and the passing of his father in 1901, the two most prominent spiritual leaders had departed from the ever-enlarging Cannon family. Abraham's brother Frank J. soon thereafter apostatized and for years wrote bitter editorials in the *Salt Lake Tribune* (as well as in a book), slandering President Joseph F. Smith, who by then was the President of the Church. President Smith, out of respect for Frank's father, ignored the non stop public verbal assault (although his son, Joseph Fielding Smith Jr., did not).[38] Both Frank and John Q. died in the early 1930s.

In 1945 the Cannon family, in attendance at a family member's funeral, listened with rapt attention as President George Albert Smith delivered them a message from their common ancestor, President George Q. Cannon:

> In his address President Smith referred to the sudden and unexpected death of Mrs. Neslen as an example of the wisdom of keeping one's life in order and of being constantly prepared for whatever unforeseen eventualities may be awaiting. President Smith had felt for some time that it would be necessary for him to have a meeting with the Cannon family but did not know it would be under such circumstances. About three months before the accident, in the quiet of his room at home, he had strongly felt the influence of George Q. Cannon. He did not see a face and did not hear a voice, but, "was nevertheless as convinced as though he had both seen him and heard him speak that George Q. Cannon earnestly wished him to know that he was concerned about his family."
>
> Some time during his remarks his speaking changed, and those who listened had a penetrating conviction that

they were hearing a servant of the Lord speaking beyond himself, speaking words that were quickened somehow with meaning beyond the usual. They could not say that it was so much his voice or his manner that had changed. They would not dare say that President Smith was aware of it—but they did say that there came upon those in the chapel a "feeling of conviction that they had heard a message of advice and counsel prompted by the love of those who have passed beyond for those who still live in mortal life".[39]

---

[1] The preceding quotations and information are taken from Beatrice Cannon Evans and Janath Russell Cannon, eds., *Cannon Family Historical Treasury* (n.p.: The George Cannon Family Association, 1967; hereafter cited as *Cannon Family Historical Treasury*). Other following quotations in this essay without a reference are from the AHC journals.

[2] See Davis Bitton, *George Q. Cannon: A Biography* (Salt Lake City: Deseret Book, 1999), hereafter cited as *George Q. Cannon: A Biography*; Lawrence R. Flake, *George Q. Cannon: The Missionary Years* (Salt Lake City: Bookcraft, 1998); and Michael N. Landon, ed., *The Journals of George Q. Cannon, vol. 1, To California in '49* [Salt Lake City: Deseret Book and the Historical Department of The Church of Jesus Christ of Latter-day Saints, 1999]. Other volumes in this series are expected). See also *Cannon Family Historical Treasury*.

[3] *Cannon Family Historical Treasury*, 100.

[4] The first time President Cannon was caught by the federal marshals, he was released on a $45,000 bond. At President John Taylor's request, he did not appear for trial and forfeited his bond. President Taylor had a "presentiment" that President Cannon's life was in danger, and therefore he asked his counselor to do something totally out of character and not appear for trial as promised (*Cannon Family Historical Treasury*, 108). Abraham provided this further explanation in his journal: "I told of Father's failing to appear for trial, when I was sentenced to prison for cohabitation, when he would have most likely been killed, had he been present" (7 February 1895).

[5] President Cannon wrote the following in his own journal: "I have been desirous to…restore to the Church all I had ever drawn from it for services, so my labors might be gratuitous. I have paid tolerably heavy tithing and I felt if I could square up these credits I should be grateful" (*Cannon Family Historical Treasury*, 104-05).

[6] Brigham Young Jr. Diary, 19 July 1896. LDS Church Archives. As extracted by Church Archives staff. Used by permission.

[7] *Cannon Family Historical Treasury*, 116.

---

[8] Quotation taken from the journal of James E. Talmage, 13 January 1899; cited in James P. Harris, ed., *The Essential James E. Talmage* (Salt Lake City: Signature Books, 1997), 55-56. To a group of young people in Canada, President Cannon testified "that the Lord Jesus lived, for I had seen Him and heard His voice, and I had heard the voice of the Spirit, speaking to me as one man speaketh to another." (Quotation taken from the Journal of George Q. Cannon; cited in *George Q. Cannon, A Biography*, 523 n. 35 and 415.

[9] Cited in Matthias F. Cowley, *Prophets and Patriarchs of the Church of Jesus Christ of Latter-day Saints* (Chattanooga, Tenn.: Ben E. Rich, 1902), 288. Large portions of this Cowley article are copied virtually word for word from Andrew Jenson, *Latter-day Saint Biographical Encyclopedia*, Vol. 1, (Salt Lake City: Andrew Jenson Historical Company, 1901), 167-68. An article about Elder Cowley immediately follows (168) the A. H. Cannon article in *LDS Biographical Encyclopedia*. Abraham was well acquainted with both authors.

[10] For an explanation of this error and its resolution, see B. H. Roberts, *A Comprehensive History of the Church of Jesus Christ of Latter-day Saints*, 6 vols. (Salt Lake City: The Church of Jesus Christ of Latter-day Saints: 1930), 6:105-06; hereafter cited as *Comprehensive History of the Church.*

[11] See D. Michael Quinn, "The Council of Fifty and Its Members, 1844 to 1945," *BYU Studies* 20, no. 2, 181, 190. See also *Encyclopedia of Mormonism* 1:326-27.

[12] "Difficult to draw lines between holdings of Cannon and Sons, enterprises…fostered by the Church, and author's personal investments" (Davis Bitton, *Guide to Mormon Diaries and Autobiographies* [Provo, Utah: Brigham Young University Press, 1977], 55; hereafter cited as *Guide to Mormon Diaries and Autobiographies*).

[13] In his book *Builders of the Kingdom*, Merlo J. Pusey insinuates that President Woodruff, and by extension President Cannon, was responsible for Abraham's call, and not the Council of the Twelve. Evidence from these journals indicates that this conclusion is incorrect. See Merlo J. Pusey, *Builders of the Kingdom: George A. Smith, John Henry Smith, George Albert Smith* (Provo, Utah: Brigham Young University Press, 1981), 156.

[14] See, for example, AHC journals, 6 April 1888. See also Thomas G. Alexander, *Mormonism in Transition: A History of the Latter-day Saints, 1890-1930* (Urbana and Chicago: University of Illinois Press, 1986), 100; David S. Hoopes and Roy Hoopes, *The Making of a Mormon Apostle: The Story of Rudger Clawson* (Lanham: Madison Books, 1990), 189-90; and Melvin Clarence Merrill, ed., *Utah Pioneer and Apostle Marriner Wood Merrill and His Family* (n. p.: Marriner Wood Merrill Heritage Committee, 1980), 199.

[15] See Andrew Jenson, *Church Chronology*, October 1, 1892 (Saturday).

[16] Cited in Matthias F. Cowley, *Prophets and Patriarchs of the Church of Jesus Christ of Latter-day Saints* (Chattanooga, Tenn.: Ben E. Rich, 1902), 288.

17 For another account of the closing of these classes, see John R. Talmage, *The Talmage Story: Life of James E. Talmage—Educator, Scientist, Apostle* (Salt Lake City: Bookcraft, 1972), 154-59; and James P. Harris, ed., *The Essential James E. Talmage* (Salt Lake City: Signature Books, 1997), 52-55.

18 For an example of a business deal that failed, see Andrew Jenson, *Autobiography of Andrew Jenson: Assistant Historian of the Church of Jesus Christ of Latter-day Saints* (Salt Lake City: Deseret News Press, 1938), 186.

19 For a brief treatment of the B.B.&C. mine, see Thomas G. Alexander, *Things in Heaven and Earth: The Life and Times of Wilford Woodruff, a Mormon Prophet* (Salt Lake City: Signature Books, 1993), 244-45, 284-85; and A. H. Cannon journals, 28 January 1891 and notes.

20 One area in which Elder Cannon demonstrated loyalty and some few of his Quorum associates did not was politics. During the pre-statehood years of the 1890s, political aspiration became a source of occasional strife and unpleasantness in the highest councils of the Church, particularly between the First Presidency (mostly Republican), and Moses Thatcher and B. H. Roberts (Democrats). This conflict led to the eventual (1896) issuance of the so-called "Political Manifesto" which mandated that high church officials, mostly General Authority level, had to receive permission from the First Presidency before running for political office—this in accord with the charge they received at their acceptance of the call to full-time Church service, that they agree to put their callings first in their lives. For the text of the Political Manifesto, see James R. Clark, ed., *Messages of the First Presidency*, 6 vols. (Salt Lake City: Bookcraft, 1965-1975), 3:272-77.

As for Elder Abraham H. Cannon's personal politics, I do not remember seeing any entry in which he explicitly states his affiliation with either of the national parties. He was a member of the People's (Mormon) party until Church leaders dissolved it so that members could align themselves with the national parties—this as a step toward statehood. It was amusing to note that Truman Madsen, author of a biography of B. H. Roberts, announced that Abraham Cannon was a Democrat, while Thomas G. Alexander, author of a biography of Wilford Woodruff, made him a Republican. See Truman G. Madsen, *Defender of the Faith: The B. H. Roberts Story* (Salt Lake City: Bookcraft, 1980), 204; and Thomas G. Alexander, *Things in Heaven and Earth: The Life and Times of Wilford Woodruff, a Mormon Prophet* (Salt Lake City: Signature Books, 1993), 276. In this editor's opinion, Elder Cannon's journals give the impression of a sympathy toward the Republican party (see 23 October 1892, for example). Both Madsen and Alexander used the A. H. Cannon journals in writing their respective biographies.

Regarding the issue of fallibility of Church leaders, Elder Cannon stated: "It is the judgment of men not illuminated by the Holy Ghost which commits mistakes. Men's thoughts are not as God's. The men who lead this Church in this dispensation do not make mistakes, although, viewed by individuals devoid of the Holy Spirit, some of their acts may assume that appearance. I testify that President

Woodruff, who stands at the head of the Church, is directed by the revelations of God. So with those associated with him. They may make mistakes in their personal concerns, but the affairs of the Church of Christ are moved forward by the power of inspiration of the Almighty. The Church will not diminish in power, but will increase in every gift and grace and in the power of salvation from this time forward." (Abraham H. Cannon, "The Benefits of Persecution," 2 March 1890. Cited in Brian H. Stuy, ed., *Collected Discourses: Delivered by President Wilford Woodruff, His Two Counselors, the Twelve Apostles, and Others*, vol. 2, [Burbank, CA: B.H.S. Publishing, 1988], 22; hereafter cited as *Collected Discourses*). While Elder Cannon saw firsthand the occasional mistakes made by the men he served with, he also possessed a larger view, accorded him by the calling and faith he possessed.

[21] *George Q. Cannon: A Biography*, 409-10.

[22] *George Q. Cannon: A Biography*, 407.

[23] Ronald W. Walker, "Heber J. Grant and the Utah Loan and Trust Company," *Journal of Mormon History* 8 (1980): 22-23.

[24] Ibid., 33. Elder Grant and Elder Cannon, as two of the youngest of the Twelve, mutually respected and admired one another. Elder Cannon felt that Heber was "a very remarkable man for one so young," and that he "has done a vast amount of good in his time." Years later, Heber J. Grant related this story involving Abraham:

> Some years ago I preached a sermon in this Tabernacle. At the close of the service, on my way home, between here and the Eagle Gate, six or seven men complimented me for "spanking in public" Brother Abraham H. Cannon who had spoken just before I did. Two or three days later some seven or eight men were in the President's office, and I was summoned before them and taken to task for "spanking" Brother Cannon. They were very angry. They were all Republicans, and all those who had complimented me were Democrats. Brother Abraham and I were there at this meeting, and I asked him if he knew that he was spanked. He said, no, he did not; and I remarked, "If I spanked you in public, I must have done it in my sleep. I quite frequently sleep when other people are talking; but, up to date, I have not learned to sleep while I am talking. I am not aware of saying one single, solitary word that reflected on what you said."…
>
> I requested that those two sermons be published in the *Deseret News*, one following the other; that neither Abraham nor I be permitted to read them before publication. When they were published I was to appear at the President's office and I would make any apology that was necessary for spanking Brother Abraham in public. Brother Cannon and I read them to ourselves and then read them aloud, and we could not find one single, solitary word, wherein I had found any fault with what he had said,

neither could the Presidency. So I did not have to apologize. (Conference Report, June 1919, 142-43)

[25] B. Carmon Hardy, *Solemn Covenant: The Mormon Polygamous Passage* (Urbana and Chicago: University of Illinois Press, 1992), 215-16; hereafter cited as *Solemn Covenant*.

[26] Ibid., 217-18. See also *Collected Discourses* 5:168.

[27] See D. Michael Quinn, "LDS Church Authority and New Plural Marriages, 1890-1904," *Dialogue: A Journal of Mormon Thought* 18, no. 1 (Spring 1985), 84; and *Solemn Covenant*, 220 for other theories and guesswork. See also Merlo J. Pusey, *Builders of the Kingdom: George A. Smith, John Henry Smith, George Albert Smith* (Provo, Utah: Brigham Young University Press, 1981), 188-90.

[28] *Solemn Covenant*, 222.

[29] After Reed Smoot, an Apostle, was elected to the U. S. Senate, his and the Church's political opponents tried to deny him his seat, even though he himself was not a polygamist. They used the senate Committee on Privileges and Elections to hold hearings with which they sought to harm the reputation of the Church before the nation. While their success is debatable, the bigotry was unquestionable, and the enormous hypocrisy of the spectacle was the real reason Senator Reed Smoot kept his elected position. As one perceptive senator put it: "I don't see why we can't get along just as well with a polygamist who doesn't polyg as we do with a lot of monogamists who don't monog" (Cited in *Solemn Covenant*, 283 n. 157. The quotation is attributed to Pennsylvania Senator Boies Penrose). Appropriate care should be taken when using the Smoot hearing transcripts as source material. In context, the hearings were run by anti-Mormons and the senate committee's questioners were anti-Mormons. Church witnesses were forced to appear and were then faced with questioning from their enemies, which was immediately reported nationally in a biased form. Under those circumstances it should be expected that they said as little as possible and were not fully cooperative when asked about matters that could be used to harm them or their sacred institutions. Joseph Fielding Smith, son of President Joseph F. Smith, described his father's experience at the hearings:

> This case was first considered by the committee, commencing January 16, 1904, and hearings continued before that committee until June, 1906. It was very evident from the start that it was not Reed Smoot who was on trial as much as it was the Church of Jesus Christ of Latter-day Saints. Many witnesses were called, including President Joseph F. Smith, President Francis M. Lyman and other leading brethren of the Church. President Smith said that when he came before the committee as the first witness in this trial, March 2, 1904, and looked about him he was not slow to discover that he was in the house of his enemies. As he looked into the faces of the members of the Senate committee, he felt, as well as saw, a

spirit of antagonism and bitterness expressed in the countenances of most, if not all, of those who were there to investigate him....

President Smith was called to the witness stand before the committee at 10 a. m., March 2, 1904, and continued before that body under a very severe and in large part improper examination until near the close of the third day of the investigation. (Joseph Fielding Smith, *Life of Joseph F. Smith* (Salt Lake City: Deseret Book, 1938), 331–33).

[30] See Appendix One: Plural Marriage Issues in the Abraham H. Cannon Journals.

[31] Abraham H. Cannon, "The Benefits of Persecution," 2 March 1890. Cited in *Collected Discourses* 2: 22.

[32] Abraham H. Cannon, "Faith Brings Blessings," 6 April 1894. Cited in *Collected Discourses* 4: 26.

[33] Senate Committee on Privileges and Elections, *Proceedings before the Committee on Privileges and Elections of the United States Senate in the Matter of the Protests against the Right of Hon. Reed Smoot, a Senator from the State of Utah to Hold His Seat*, 59th Cong., 1st sess., 1906, Doc. 486, 2:141-46. Commonly known as the Smoot hearings.

[34] Entries are from the journals of Wilford Woodruff, John Henry Smith, Marriner W. Merrill, and the Brigham Young Jr. Diary (LDS Church Archives, as extracted by Church Archives staff. Used by permission). One author has written the following account of Elder Cannon's death: "Sometime during their stay in California, perhaps while at Catalina harbor, Abraham got water in his ear while relaxing on the beach. This aggravated an earlier condition, causing him great distress, and soon led to serious complications. After returning to Salt Lake City, he suffered from intense head and ear pain that grew progressively worse. His condition deteriorated rapidly" (*Solemn Covenant*, 218). Another account states that he "died of meningitis…after contracting a post-surgical inflammation subsequent to a chronic mastoid infection" (Richard S. VanWagoner and Steven C. Walker, *A Book of Mormons*, [Salt Lake City: Signature Books, 1982], 43).

[35] From the journal of Wilford Woodruff, 1 October 1896.

[36] *Collected Discourses* 5:191. President Woodruff here disclosed the reason why Elder Cannon died so young. It is a doctrine that is not commonly taught or understood in the Church. Many years later Elder Bruce R. McConkie of the Quorum of the Twelve was inspired to reveal "how the gospel is taught in the spirit world.... It is taught by a family, to their own family. We teach the gospel to our own progenitors" (Dennis B. Horne, *Bruce R. McConkie: Highlights from His Life and Teachings* [Roy, Utah; Eborn Books, 2000], 122).

[37] *George Q. Cannon: A Biography*, 410.

[38] Joseph Fielding Smith, son of President Joseph F. Smith, explained the apostasy of Frank J. Cannon in his father's biography:

One of the grave problems which confronted the Church at the time of this organization was the financial distress which had been brought upon it during the persecutions, when the property of the Church was escheated, and all that could be liquidated was confiscated by unscrupulous officials. The Church was mercilessly robbed and plundered and forced into the inconsistent position of paying exorbitant rentals for the use of its own property. The result of all of this was that the Church was heavily involved when peace was finally declared and its property—such as was left after the robbers got through with it—returned to the Church. President Snow took steps at once, with the backing of his brethren, to meet this condition by the issuing of bonds. Such steps had been under contemplation before the death of President Woodruff but were not consummated. Some of the enterprises which had been entered into at an earlier date, were also abandoned because of the financial distress. Thursday, December 1, 1898, the First Presidency and the Apostles met in council and President Snow reviewed the financial condition of the Church and said he deplored it, but it seemed necessary that the Church issue bonds in the sum of $500,000. The matter was put to a vote and unanimously agreed to by the brethren. Later it was determined that the bond issue should be double that amount and they were issued in two series, "A" and "B," each for $500,000. The first series to be redeemed December 31, 1903, and the second to be redeemed December 31, 1906. At this particular time a certain unscrupulous person who had the ear of some of the authorities and the possession of an oily tongue, tried to convince the brethren that these bonds could not be sold locally and would have to be disposed of in the east to certain financial firms. He volunteered his services to sell these bonds, but of course, with the understanding that he was to receive a very handsome commission. By his energy and flattering persuasion he almost accomplished his purpose and was able to convert many of the brethren to his way of thinking. To this proposition President Smith strenuously objected, taking the ground that there was no reason to fear that these bonds could not be sold at home and that too without paying any man a commission. "I opposed it," said President Smith, "and voted against it. I was opposed to giving a commission at all, and thought the bonds should be sold at home." Notwithstanding his strenuous objection, action was taken and it was agreed that this proposition should be accepted. Later, by earnest pleading, President Smith convinced President Lorenzo Snow that such a course was erroneous and it would be well to first try his plan, that of disposing of the bonds at home. The result was that the first issue was readily disposed of locally, and when the second issue was ready for the market it met with a like response, largely from the members of the

Church and others at home, and both issues were sold before the close of the year 1899, not long after they were issued. The blocking of the scheme of this individual, who hoped to become the agent of the Church in disposing of the bonds, brought down upon the head of President Joseph F. Smith the wrath of this particular individual, who in later times joined forces with the enemies of the Church in a campaign of bitterness and hate which in some respects surpassed any expression of bitterness ever before manifested against the Church....

The old editor of the anti-"Mormon" paper [the *Salt Lake Tribune*] was discovered to be too mild for this venture and the crowd which Mr. Kearns [senator from Utah] controlled, so he lost his place and it was given to this same apostate, who so intensely and bitterly hated President Joseph F. Smith. During the years of this anti-"Mormon" party, from 1905 to 1911, the columns of this paper were filled daily with the most bitter falsehoods, accusations and lying insolence. Editorials also appeared written in the same spirit until even the Gentiles became sick of it all, and even many of the enemies of the Church obtained their fill and asked for peace.

During these years this newspaper almost daily cartooned President Joseph F. Smith with a spirit of wicked and malicious vilification. These papers were scattered all over the United States, and naturally, appearing day by day and month after month, the people of the nation and even beyond the borders of the United States, reached the conclusion that the President of the Church, Joseph F. Smith, was the lowest and most despicable character in all the world. Missionaries out in the world were made to suffer and were persecuted and insulted in all parts of the earth. Yet during it all the Church continued to grow. This foul blot which was incubated in the spirit of greed and selfish desire, was not only hurtful to the interests of the Church and destructive of peace and happiness, but it cast its blight upon the entire State of Utah which also was made to suffer. It was largely because of this condition—the pocketbooks of the merchants being affected—that caused many to turn from supporting this evil condition which was a disgrace in the community and would not have been tolerated by any other community in the world.

While all of this vilification was going on and President Smith was being daily abused, he went about his affairs peaceably, making no answer to the vicious attacks. The only expression he made publicly was as follows:

"I feel in my heart to forgive all men in the broad sense that God requires of me to forgive all men, and I desire to love my neighbor as myself; and to this extent I bear no malice towards any of the children of my Father. But there are enemies to the work of the Lord, as there were enemies of the Son of God. There are those who speak only evil of the Latter-day Saints. There are those—and they abound largely in our midst—who will shut their eyes to every virtue and to every good thing connected with this latter day work, and will pour out floods of falsehood and misrepresentation against the people of God. I forgive them for this. I leave them in the hand of the just Judge." (Joseph Fielding Smith, *Life of Joseph F. Smith* (Salt Lake City: Deseret Book, 1938), 303-04, 350-51)

[39] "Reflections on the Remarks of President George Albert Smith at the Funeral Services of Grace Cannon Neslen," 2 October 1945, unpublished manuscript in scrapbook #1 in GAS collection, University of Utah Library (Box 124), 56; Cited in Glen R. Stubbs, *A Biography of George Albert Smith: 1870 to 1951* (Unpublished Ph.D. diss., 1974), 364-65.

CHAPTER ONE

◈

1882-1888

Wednesday, July 26, 1882:

After having supper at Uncle Angus', I went with him to the missionary meeting in the Council House. The subject discussed was the United Order, and a number of the brethren expressed their views concerning it. Uncle Angus in conclusion remarked that all who had received their endowments, had entered into that order. We should be prepared at all times to turn over all we possess to the Church. Many valuable instructions were imparted this evening, by which I hope to profit....[1]

Sunday, October 8, 1882:

I then accompanied Mina to meeting, and shortly after arriving there I was invited to the stand, where my name, together with that of Bro. F. B. Lewis, was mentioned by Pres. Woodruff before the conference, and we were selected to fill the vacancies in the Quorum of the First Seven Presidents of Seventies. I was chosen in Bro. Joseph Young's place and Bro. Lewis for John Hancock, both deceased. I was never more surprised in my life, as I had received no intimation of this appointment. Pres. Taylor gave an excellent discourse in the afternoon....[2]

---

[1] "[In the temple] we covenant with the Lord to devote our time, talents, and means to his Kingdom" (Boyd K. Packer, *The Holy Temple* [Salt Lake City: Bookcraft, 1980], 164; hereafter cited as *The Holy Temple*. See also James E. Talmage, *The House of the Lord* [Salt Lake City: The Church of Jesus Christ of Latter-day Saints, 1912], 100).

[2] At this time in the history of the Church, it was not yet common practice to inform men beforehand of the position they had been selected for (see *The Holy Temple*, 164). "The First Seven Presidents of the Seventy" was an early name for the First Council of the Seventy, now best equated with the Presidency of the Seventy.

61

Monday, October 9, 1882:

I was at my work until ten o'clock this morning, when I went to a meeting at the Council house. Pres. Woodruff there set me apart with an excellent blessing, and as he and the brethren were about to ordain Bro. Lewis, they learned that he was a High Priest and could not therefore be appointed to the office of a Seventy. A number of the missionaries were then set apart. I being mouth in setting three apart and in ordaining Leo Clawson to the office of an elder. The brethren then gave the missionaries some excellent advice in regard to their labors, and told them to be especially careful in their associations with women, so as not to commit themselves in any way. A good spirit prevailed....

Sunday, June 10, 1883:

In the morning I went with Pres. Taylor, Father, our Council and several other brethren to Centerville, were two meetings were held. In the afternoon meeting Bro. Thomas Grover testified to having heard the revelation on Celestial marriage read by Hyrum Smith in the high council previous to the death of the Prophet. All of the Council present excepting three accepted the doctrine, and those three soon afterwards apostatized. Bro. Nobles testified to having performed the first ceremony in Celestial marriage in this generation, he sealing his wife's sister to the Prophet Joseph.[3] Pres. Taylor, George Reynolds, C. W. Penrose and Father all testified of the same truth. The meeting was intensely interesting....

Sunday, April 6, 1884:

Father and Bro. Joseph F. Smith addressed the Saints at the forenoon meeting on the fulfillment of modern prophecy. At the afternoon services the authorities of the Church were presented and Pres. Taylor spoke. The

---

[3] At this time, "celestial marriage" was generally defined as "plural marriage." Plural marriage began in The Church of Jesus Christ of Latter-day Saints when the Prophet Joseph Smith was commanded by the Lord to marry plural wives, probably in the 1830s (see D&C 132 and B. H. Roberts, *A Comprehensive History of the Church of Jesus Christ of Latter-day Saints*, 6 vols. [Salt Lake City: The Church of Jesus Christ of Latter-day Saints: 1930], 2:93-110; hereafter cited as *Comprehensive History of the Church*). See also Appendix One: Plural Marriage Issues in the Abraham H. Cannon Journals.

following vacancies were filled. In the Twelve by the appointment of John W. Taylor; in the First Seven Presidents by C. D. Fjelsted, and as Presiding Bishop, W. B. Preston, the President of Cache Valley Stake was appointed. At a Priesthood meeting held in the evening (after the Hall was cleared of all those who were not worthy of being present by arranging the brethren according to Wards and Stakes) the strongest language in regard to plural Marriage was used that I ever heard, and among other things it was stated that all men in position who would not observe and fulfill the law should be removed from their places. The Spirit of the Lord rested powerfully upon the First Presidency each of whom addressed the meeting. All present felt the force of the remarks made.

Monday, April 7, 1884:

At 9 a.m. I went to the social Hall and assisted in setting a number of missionaries apart; was also present when the Twelve gave the brethren instructions. At 3 p.m. a meeting of the Presidents of Stakes was held in the Social Hall at which I was present. The revelation on Celestial Marriage was read and explained by Pres. Taylor in a clear and forcible manner, so that none could mistake its meaning. All were enjoined to obey this law....

Monday, June 9, 1884:

Called on Sister Eliza R. Snow Smith in the forenoon and in the course of our conversation she said she heard the Prophet Joseph once remark, "When the ten tribes were taken away, the earth was divided so that they occupy a separate planet from this." This was new to me....

Monday, March 23, 1885:

Father was indicted by the Grand Jury today for cohabitation.

Aunt Emily Little's house was searched today for Ella Little, but although she was secreted in a closet, her place of concealment was overlooked....

Saturday, June 20, 1885:

At 10 a.m. I attended a meeting at the President's office where a society was organized which could hold the Social Hall and prevent outsiders from seizing and confiscating it as Church property. After this meeting at which there were a number of young men in addition to the leaders of the Church in this city I attended another meeting at which the county and city Bishops were present to prepare for holding Church property....

Our enemies are now preparing to attack our property with a view to robbing us of our goods as well as our liberty.

Wednesday, August 11, 1885:

I went to Ogden on the morning train and was busy nearly all day in the office or rather store, where things seem to be brightening up a little....

...I went to see Father at the President's office, and had some talk with him. I made a proposition to buy the business in Ogden for $ 7,300 including the notes aggregating $2,325 which bear 1 and 1/2 % interest. Father talked with me about it and is inclined to accept my proposition....

From August 15 till September 5, 1885:

During this time I was engaged at the office, the store in Ogden and other places where my services were needed.... I also bought the business [bookstore] of Cannon and Sons in Ogden,...

From September 5 till October 25, 1885:

I was taken down with a severe illness tonight after being in the office all day. I arose on Sunday and in the afternoon went down to Bro. Jenkins' to see Sarah who is down from Ogden. I then returned and went to Mill Creek in Uncle Angus' buggy to attend a Seventies meeting. Mina accompanied me, but on arriving there I felt so miserable that I could not remain longer than half an hour. I ordained two presidents. On reaching home I endeavored to take an alcoholic bath but could not do so on account of weakness.

Monday Mina sent for Dr. Seymour B. Young who pronounced my disease a case of Typhoid fever. It proved to be very severe as I lay for seven weeks in bed, during part of which time I was delirious. It was only the faith of those who administered to me and others who knew of my illness that saved me, as I was several times at the point of death. Dr. Young was very attentive and kind. Many others rendered me kind service in sitting up at night and in various ways. Sarah and Mina nearly wore themselves out in waiting on me, though the latter had to be away several days as the Marshals were hunting her....

Sunday, October 25, 1885:

Today I was dressed and sat up part of the day. This is my first trial and it tired me not a little....

Monday, October 26, 1885:

About noon I went with Aunt Amanda out to the penitentiary to see Uncle Angus, I having received a pass to do so. We found him looking and feeling quite well. His striped suit, a garb worn now by all the prisoners, fits him quite well. He reports all the brethren as feeling healthy and happy. His time of imprisonment has expired, but as his case was appealed to the supreme court he is awaiting its decision before paying his fine of $300.

About eighteen brethren have been sent to the "Pen" during my sickness, because they would not deny their wives,...

Tuesday, November 10, 1885:

I went to Ogden on the morning train. There was a man aboard (Bishop Bills of South Jordan) who is trying to avoid arrest by U. S. officers, but he had on a wig and beard which everyone could see was false and thus made himself noticeable by everyone who saw him. I expected to see him arrested, as a number of outsiders watched him closely, but he got in the closet and took off his beard and then passed out with the crowd. He was very foolish to appear in such a garb....

Two U. S. deputy Marshals searched Moses Thatcher's house in Logan today. They said they were after Father, but it is supposed they wanted Bro. Thatcher.

A notice was published in tonight's *News* signed by all of the Apostles, except George Teasdale who is absent, stating that Albert Carrington had been cut off from the Church for lewd and lascivious cohabitation and adultery. These acts are said to have been mostly of recent occurrence. This action caused everyone to be surprised.[4]

Sunday, February 7, 1886:

After breakfast I went to the store for a few minutes and then to the train by which I went to Salt Lake. On my way home from the depot in the latter city I was met by Angus Cannon Jr., who told me that deputy marshals had raided Cannon's Home and aunt Emily Little's and arrested all the folks. I immediately went with him to get F. S. Richards to go and see to the matter and I then went to the court room where I found Aunt Emily and the girls…. After the arrival of Judge Zane and Attorney Dickson the former was placed under $2,000 and each of the girls under $500 bonds…. They were arrested as witnesses. After dinner Angus and I went to the farm where we learned that six marshals were there at 5 a.m. this morning and searched the premises three times in the hope, as they afterwards stated, of finding Father whom they had been informed was to be there today….

---

[4] According to the journal of Elder John Henry Smith, allegations of immoral conduct had been made against Elder Albert Carrington while on a mission to England in 1882. In 1885 Elder J. H. Smith learned that "a charge of adultery had been made against Bro. Albert Carrington." A few days later in Council, "Bro. A. Carrington got up and Confessed to guilt" with three women. "The brethren…could find no way to do but cut Bro. A. Carrington off from the Church. Bro. W. Woodruff decided that he be cut off and he was sustained by the vote of all present." In 1886 Elder J. H. Smith and Heber J. Grant visited Bro. Carrington and "he expressed an earnest desire to have the privilege of rebaptism and said he was willing to do whatever may be required of him." He was rebaptized in 1887. (Jean Bickmore White, ed., *Church, State, and Politics: The Diaries of John Henry Smith* [Salt Lake City: Signature Books, 1990], 92-93, 95, 141-142, 155; hereafter cited as *Church, State, and Politics*). This is an incident that refutes the charge from anti-Mormons that plural marriage was practiced so that Mormon men could indulge their appetites. If the charges were true, Albert Carrington would not have been excommunicated for doing the same thing the other brethren were doing. See Appendix One: Plural Marriage Issues in the Abraham H. Cannon Journals.

Monday, February 8, 1886:

About 4 o'clock this morning, the hired girl, Lucy Herbst, was awakened and on looking towards the setting room saw a light. She immediately arose, struck a light and dressed herself, supposing it was us who were up, but on coming from her room into the kitchen she found the back door wide open. She then came and called several times before she could arouse Mina, who then wakened me. By a bad taste in my mouth and our sound sleep I judged that we had been chloroformed. I immediately got my pants and found my purse and money missing, the former I afterward found in the hall with a check and dollar bill enclosed, but $6.50 in silver was gone. My necktie and a dressing case were also in the hall; fortunately my gold watch was under my pillow. I arose and looked through the house, but missed nothing else. Entrance was gained through the pantry window which was partly open and the flowers that were in front of it were pushed to one side. After this there was no more sleep for any of us, and Mina became quite nervous. Our lamp was left burning in the bedroom and therefore the burglar or burglars could easily see where my pants were hanging on the foot of the bed....

A posse of 20 deputy marshals with Ireland at their head made a raid on the Church offices today. The Gardo, Lion and Beehive houses, the President's and Historian's offices and Tithing yards and offices were all searched, but in vain, for the President, Father or others of the authorities. A large crowd assembled and there would doubtless have been trouble had any of the leaders been taken. Later that day the following notice was posted on the *Tribune* bulletin board: "$500 Reward. I will pay the above reward to any person for information leading to the arrest of George Q. Cannon, against whom an indictment is now pending in the Third District of Utah. The names of any person giving information will be held in strict confidence. E. A. Ireland, U. S. Marshall, Salt Lake City, February 8, 1886." Hand bills containing the same notice and a very good photograph of Father in one corner were also prepared and distributed....

I learned tonight that Bro. G. G. Paywater's house, the second one south of mine, was also visited by burglars last night, as he found his clothes scattered about on arising and the back and front doors of his house wide open. He, however, had no money at home, nor did he miss anything else.

Tuesday, February 9, 1886:

Returned home in the evening and found that my house had been visited by Deputy Marshals Greenman and Hurd this afternoon between 5 and 6 p.m. Mina was arrested and taken to the Marshal's office where she was put under $2,000 bonds to appear when wanted. Richard G. Lambert and Will James became her security....

Wednesday, February 10, 1886:

Last night there were three attempts at burglary in the southern part of the city....

Between 9 and 10 p.m. John Q. came for me and we went to the 19th Ward where we found Father. I took him and Aunt Emily down to John Q's, the latter following later. From here Father and I went to the farm where the folks assembled and learned that because of the wicked efforts of our enemies to entrap him, Father had decided to leave here for a season. He gave us all some good instructions to guide us while he is absent. He shaved off his beard which made him look quite funny....[5]

Thursday, February 11, 1886:

I slept until about 9 a.m. after which I got my buggy and took Arthur Winter to John Q's farm where we met Father, who gave the former some letters to write. I here bade him "God speed," and he went with John Q. in a close carriage to a box car which was to convey him and Apostle E. Snow northward....

---

[5] "The Federal authorities, considering him [President Cannon] a symbol of Mormon power and defiance, thought by capturing and imprisoning him, the rest of this people would be subdued and amenable. He was pursued all over the West, and seldom spent two nights in the same place. On one raid of the 'Farm,' the marshal, furious at not finding the elusive man, served subpoenas on his wives Sarah Jane and Martha and his daughters Mary Alice and Hester" (Beatrice Cannon Evans and Janath Russell Cannon eds., *Cannon Family Historical Treasury* [n.p.: Published by the George Cannon Family Association, 1967], 107; hereafter cited as *Cannon Family Historical Treasury*).

Sunday, February 14, 1886:

There was great excitement this morning which continued during the day, because of news published in the morning papers that Father had been arrested at Humbolt station on the C. P. R'y last evening by the sheriff of Winemucca. Notwithstanding all efforts no definite word concerning the matter could be obtained by our people, and at night the suspense was as great as it had been in the morning....

Monday, February 15, 1886:

While in Ogden today Frank and I arranged a plan whereby we hoped to rescue Father from the hands of his enemies should he so desire.

Frank was to go out to meet the train, and was to be met at Corrinne by a party from Ogden who were to hold up the train while the prisoner was being removed. Frank left on the C. P. a few moments after I had boarded the U. C. Train . A rescue party had also left Salt Lake on the same train with the marshal....

Tuesday, February 16, 1886:

With the expectation that Father was to be brought in on the morning train, I, with others, went to Ogden to meet him. On arriving there, however, we found a large crowd among whom the word was circulated that Father had jumped from the moving train at Promontory. I therefore returned to the city on the D. and R. G. train feeling overjoyed in the belief that Father had escaped. At the Salt Lake depot a very large crowed was waiting to see the prisoner, but most of them were glad when they heard of what was thought to be his release. A dispatch was however received just then from Marshal Ireland stating that Father had been re-taken and was considerably injured by his fall. He was going to meet his captors when found. All day long he was kept at Blue Creek station, Frank Cannon and Alonzo Hyde remaining with him. In the evening about 6:20 o'clock a detachment of 26 U. S. soldiers boarded a U. C. car and started north; it was soon learned that their duty was to bring Father down as a prisoner. For the whole night we were kept in a state of suspense not knowing at what time they would return....[6]

Wednesday, February 17, 1886:

A few minutes before 8 o'clock a special train bearing the soldiers and their illustrious captive rolled into the depot, where Father was placed in a carriage and taken to the U. S. Marshal's office. In a few minutes I was there and saw him lying upon a mattress on the floor with his head bandaged. I spoke to him and found that in spirit he was feeling quite well. Above his left eye he has a deep cut, his nose is injured and there are several bruises on his head and other parts of his body. After some little waiting Judge Zane and Attorney Dickson arrived when bail on the indictment for cohabitation was fixed at $25,000.00, John Sharp and Feramorz Little becoming sureties. Two other bench warrants were then served upon him for similar offenses at later dates. On each of these $10,000 bail was required. H. S. Eldridge and Frank Armstrong becoming bondsmen. The prisoner was then released and went down to the farm in a hack, several police and others going with him. I went part of the way down but was forced to quickly return for my trial. An immense crowd was around to see Father and not a few persons were in tears.

I reached the Court Room at 11:20 a.m. whither Mina and the other witnesses in my case had already gone. After receiving assurances through F. S. Richards from Dickson that if I would cause them no trouble my sentence should not be passed until March 17th, I went on the stand after pleading "not guilty" and testified in my own case. In answer to

---

[6] "President Taylor, deeply concerned for his First Counselor's safety, dispatched him to Mexico to negotiate a land contract for the Church. En route, the doughty apostle was identified and apprehended. On the return to Salt Lake the last possibility of escape seemed to be at hand; but as the train slowed down for Promontory, a brakeman and porter were on the platform, and Cannon gave up the idea. He recorded that 'as the train speeded up and was making full headway, it lurched and pitched him off the platform, where he landed full length on the frozen ground, breaking his nose, gashing his forehead…' and receiving other grievous injuries. He was immediately missed, the train was stopped and he was soon discovered walking in a dazed condition along the tracks. He presented a ghastly appearance, bloody, battered and not fully coherent" (*Cannon Family Historical Treasury*, 107).

Dickson's question whether Sarah and Wilhelmina were my wives, I replied, "They are, thank God," and I further admitted having lived with them during the dates mentioned in the indictment. A verdict of "guilty" was immediately rendered by the jury....

I took Mina home, had dinner and went to the farm where I remained until evening waiting on Father who feels quite sore from his fall....[7]

Thursday, February 18, 1886:

I then went to the farm and remained some time with Father who is steadily improving, but does not want his enemies to think but what he is very bad....

Frank informed me that the plans we laid on Monday, and which we thought so perfect for Father's escape utterly failed, and the men were not on hand as agreed. An escape could easily have been made had the men come on time....

Saturday, February 20, 1886:

In the afternoon I went down and visited Father whom I found feeling some better.

Frank came into the office today in a drunken condition and fell backwards, knocking over our stove and disgracing himself and family in the presence of several customers....

Tuesday, March 2, 1886:

Father was in town at the President's office today and is both looking and feeling much better than when I last saw him. He is keeping a little shady as he understands that efforts are being made to indict him now for polygamy and other offenses....

---

[7] Elder Cannon's usage of the word "fall" here grants credence to the insistence of President George Q. Cannon that he did not "jump" from the train as his enemies accused him of doing in an effort to escape, but that he did indeed fall. See *Comprehensive History of the Church,* 6:128-129.

Sunday, March 7, 1886:

At 2 p.m. I attended meeting at the tabernacle and listened to a very able discourse by B. H. Roberts on the attitude of the government towards the Saints....

Wednesday, March 10, 1886:

Sarah and the children came down from Ogden today to remain with Sister Jenkins while I am in the "Pen."

Thursday, March 11, 1886:

I was engaged at the office most of the day. In the afternoon was out for a short time making some purchases for my imprisonment. In the evening I drove to Father's farm where I met him. He called the family together and gave them instructions concerning their duties while he is away, if he goes; he then arranged some of his clothes and other things....

Friday, March 12, 1886:

Apostle Lorenzo Snow today voluntarily delivered himself up to the U. S. Marshal for confinement in the "Pen," so that his case, now pending before the U. S. Supreme Court, might be advanced on the calendar. His case is to test the validity of the segregating process now in vogue and to see whether a man must publicly announce that he is keeping the Edmunds law in order to avoid prosecution.

At 10 a.m. I was down to see Sarah at her mother's; she was not feeling very well, and at 12 o'clock she gave birth to a 10 lb. boy, a nice birthday present to me, I being today 27 years old. I did not learn of the event till 5 p.m. when I went down there and found Sarah feeling quite comfortable. During the evening I was writing up my journal and posting accounts....

Saturday, March 13, 1886:

In the evening I was busy preparing some things to take with me to the "Pen,' and also doing some little writing....

The deputy marshals again visited Father's farm this morning ostensibly to find Father's wife Eliza and Hugh, but most likely to see if

Father was there, as it has been reported that he has gone to parts unknown....

Tuesday, March 16, 1886:

In the forenoon I was around town attending to various matters of business. In the afternoon I went to see Father and others of the brethren who were with him. They were feeling very well and after conversing a short time Father gave John Q. and I his blessing. Among other things he promised me that I should be blessed with means, wisdom and fearlessness in the performance of my duties as a servant of God, and many other choice things did he pronounce on me....

Wednesday, March 17, 1886:

After arising which I did quite early, I went to John W. Taylor's with a commission and from there to the Warm Springs and had a bath. Returning to the city I went and bid the family "Goodbye.' I then went to the Federal Court House where at 10 a.m. I was called up to be sentenced. Upon Judge Zane giving me permission to speak I explained my position and stated that I had only sought to obey the law of God in doing as I had done, and if for doing that I deserved punishment I was prepared for sentence. He then sentenced me to six months imprisonment, to pay a fine of $300 and costs and stand committed till the fine and costs are paid. I immediately went into the marshals office under guard, and there remained until about 4 p.m., except for a few minutes when I went to a restaurant under guard, waiting for the Penitentiary wagon. Father's trial was set for today but as he did not appear, his bonds were forfeited. A great number of special deputies were sworn in for the occasion, a company of soldiers were held in readiness and all who entered were searched to see if they carried concealed weapons. All precautions were, however, unnecessary, as the prisoner did not come. Considerable money was lost by his not coming.[8]

---

[8] "As the district attorney gathered evidence for Cannon's prosecution, swaggering boasts were circulated by the federal agents 'that President Cannon would be imprisoned for the term of his natural life,' that 'he would be sent to a distant prison' where his condition would be 'unbearable.' President Taylor, ill and in hiding himself, had a deep conviction that George Q. Cannon must not be lost for life to the

About 5 p.m. after riding over a very rough road and wet, I arrived at the "Pen" in charge of Guard Jancy. I was ushered into the dining room where I sat while the guards and working trusties ate. I was offered food but did not care for any. The turnkey, Mr. Curtis, then came in and in a very gentlemanly way performed his duties. He took my name, age, height, weight, color of hair and eyes, occupation, crime for which sentenced, etc. He then took from me my knife, money and a newspaper, the other things in my pocket he permitted me to retain. I was then taken and measured for a suit of clothes (prison stripes). I was then put in the yard where I met a number of the brethren. Just as I got inside the prisoners received the signal to fall into line and I went in cell No. 3 where the most of the brethren were located. No. 1 is the cell in which all the worst characters are confined, No. 2 contains the medium class, among whom are some of our brethren. In our room there are 52 prisoners. It is 20 ft. 6 in. by 26 ft. 6 in. by 12 ft. 1 in. High. On three sides there are three tiers of bunks which should accommodate two persons each. There are only two bunks containing but one person each: Bro. Lorenzo Snow's and A. Miner's. On the top tier sleep the trusties who work outside. Shortly after I got in the room and the iron doors were locked, Bro. B. F. Due, who had been appointed floor-manager for the evening, came and told me that in order to be initiated as a member I must either…sing, dance, stand on my head or make a speech. I chose the latter and spoke a few words of greeting. We then had an impromptu concert in which all who were called took part. This, I was informed, was for my benefit, I being a new member. The brethren all crowded around me to get the news, as all local newspapers are prohibited them of late. At 9 p.m. the guard tapped on the iron door which was the signal for all talking to cease and the prisoners to retire. In a moment all was quiet. The guard passes the door every 15 minutes during the night and looks

---

Church—and a terrifying presentiment that if George Q. appeared for trial, he would forfeit his life! He implored his First Counselor not to appear, but to avoid the trap and 'jump his bond'! The jeopardized apostle recorded that this was the most painful decision of his life…. And yet, after much prayer, he submitted to President Taylor's request. When George Q. Cannon's name was called he did not appear. His $45,000 bond was forfeited (later reimbursed by an Act of Congress), and the entire community was staggered" (*Cannon Family Historical Treasury*, 108).

in to see that all is quiet. There are now 50 of the brethren in the "Pen" for conscience sake, and therefore it is not nearly as unpleasant as it might be or as I expected it would be. The warden, too, Mr. Dow, is said to be a fine gentleman, and does all he can to make it agreeable for the prisoners.

W. W. Willey, the first man convicted of unlawful cohabitation from Davis Co. first met and shook hands with me after I entered the "Pen."[9]

Thursday, March 18, 1886:

At 5:30 a.m. the guard rattled on the door when the trusties arose to go out to work. At six he rattled for us, but considerable leniency is shown the brethren and they are not forced to get up until about 7:30. I had a good wash, there being a wash and bath house provided. I then went for a little walk about the yard which was very wet from the snow which fell last night. At 8 o'clock we fell into line and marched to the dining hall, a building about 45 feet long by 20 ft. wide with stationary tables all around the sides and five movable tables down the center. We having first taken our cups in the dining room, those that had no water in them were filled with coffee. I sat at one end of the table where some

---

[9] I have chosen to include only a relatively small number of entries regarding Abraham's prison experiences. For further information see William C. Siefriet, "The Prison Experience of Abraham H. Cannon," *Utah Historical Quarterly* 53, no. 3 (summer 1985): 223-36. See also Abraham H. Cannon, "Mormons in Prison" *Voices from the Past: Diaries, Journals, and Autobiographies* (Provo, Utah: Campus Education Week-Brigham Young University Press, 1980), 97-100; and Stan Larson, ed., *Prisoner for Polygamy: The Memoirs and Letters of Rudger Clawson at the Utah Territorial Penitentiary 1884-1887* (Urabana and Chicago: University of Illinois Press, 1993). This compilation of the papers of Rudger Clawson, who served some of his prison time with Abraham, contains numerous notes and references from the A. H. Cannon journals, as well as some explanation about the other men incarcerated with them. The editor also used the A. H. Cannon journals to correct inaccuracies in the Clawson materials. Most of Abraham's time in prison was spent studying, writing articles and a book, discussing gospel doctrines with fellow Mormon polygamous inmates, holding meetings, and exercising. Through letters and visitors he managed to keep some degree of control over the family business interests. It is reasonable to conclude that Abraham's prison experience, though unpleasant, was not as harsh as what is normally understood to be involved in a prison term. It also helped that the warden's inmate rules and regulations were often more relaxed towards the Mormon inmates than the other prisoners.

brethren were and found there a large piece of tough meat, two potatoes and two pieces of bread waiting for me. Bro. George H. Taylor kindly gave me a small piece of butter which helped me out. I was hungry and ate very heartily.

I then returned to the bunkroom where I played dominoes for a short time and then wrote in my journal. At 12:15 we went in line to dinner when we had vegetable soup and two pieces of bread. Most of the brethren have a little honey, preserves or something of the kind which helps them out very much in their eating. After dinner, I was successful in purchasing the right to a seat on the side, for $3 for which I gave an order on the Warden who retains all money and keeps an account with each prisoner. Rudger Clawson made the purchase for me. A side seat is preferable because one can then use the small ledge on the side of the wall for standing his box, plates, cans, etc.

My pocket knife, purse and trunk with books, clothes, etc, were sent to me this morning, and my mattress last night.

At present there are about 150 inmates of the prison.

It snowed so hard today that one had to remain in the house or get very wet.

The buildings are all built of wood.

Just after dinner a number of the brethren were called to the door and asked by the Warden whether or not they would pay their fines. Those who did not are liable to have an execution issued upon their property if they have any, and if none can be found in their name, they must remain 30 days longer in prison, and then take oath that they have no means.

During the afternoon I commenced to prepare a catechism on the Book of Mormon for use in the Sunday Schools. I also spent some time in conversing with some of the prisoners.

At 4:45 we marched into supper which consisted of a cup of tea and two slices of bread. About 5:15 we fell into line and marched to our bunk rooms, where the evening was spent in reading, chatting, etc. The trusties in our room pick on B. F. Due and make a regular fool of him because he does not maintain his dignity as a Saint. While in the room at night pillows and other things were thrown at him until he became quite angry which only seemed to make the trusties more anxious to annoy him.

Quite a number of the prisoners are very ingenious workers in hair and wood; bridles, picture frames, small ships, etc, being manufactured in great abundance....

Friday, March 19, 1886:

Early this morning I got out and had a walk, though there was considerable snow on the ground which had fallen during the night. Bro. McHendrick is feeling quite well this morning and informs me that my speech to Judge Zane in court has been construed as containing the elements of treason and will be taken by Baskin to Washington to be laid before the government there as showing the feeling of the "Mormon" people. My expressions are sworn to by two witnesses....

It is remarkable with what eagerness any news from the outer world is devoured by our brethren inside. I never realized until now what a great blessing it is to have the news to read daily.

During the forenoon I was writing questions and answers on the Book of Mormon, and in the afternoon was busy preparing an article called "True Bravery" for the *Juvenile*. Just before dinner I was called outside the gate by the Warden, who asked me about what things I had in my box; he then permitted me to bring inside without examination my cake box with all it would hold....

Sunday, March 28, 1886:

Bro. Olson brought word in this evening that President Taylor had received a revelation from the Lord in which it stated that God was satisfied with the sacrifice made by the people in this crusade and that He would now turn their wrath aside. This word, he said, came from Bishop Allen of the 21st Ward, and, if true, we as a people can rejoice at it....[10]

---

[10] President John Taylor apparently received a revelation relating to plural marriage, which has been interpreted by some as meaning that plural marriage would never cease in the Church (see Appendix One: Plural Marriage Issues in the Abraham H. Cannon Journals). For the text of the purported revelation, see Fred C. Collier, comp., *Unpublished Revelations*, vol. 1, (Salt Lake City: Collier's Publishing Company, 1981), 145-46. From hindsight one thing is certain: persecution was not turned aside, but increased steadily until the 1890 Woodruff Manifesto, which became the point at which the nation's wrath declined, at least until the B. H. Roberts congressional hearings and the Reed Smoot senatorial hearings.

Arrests for cohabitation still continue to be made in Salt Lake and elsewhere.

Monday, March 29, 1886:

Just after breakfast I engaged in a game of football in the course of which I got hit in the face with the ball and was kicked in the ankle by another player....

In the afternoon I was engaged part of the time in writing catechism on the Book of Mormon....

We were informed today that three of the convicts in No. 1 are afflicted with loathsome diseases....[11]

May 11, 1886:

There have been two windows left out of the west end of the Salt Lake Temple through an error of the architect which will most likely necessitate the taking down of the wall for 20 feet. Order was given yesterday to stop laying stone now until a decision was reached about this matter. It is a most egregious error.

Tuesday, June 29, 1886:

In the forenoon Mattie Cannon and F. S. Richards came out to see me about my arranging to lift a note in the Ogden Bank for $250 for which A. H. Nelson and I went security for Frank, and also to see about drawing some little money along on the *History of Joseph Smith* which Frank is preparing....[12]

---

[11] This reference to loathsome diseases refers to the sexually transmitted diseases contracted by those non-polygamous prisoners serving time for actual criminal conduct and who engaged in homosexual practices. Abraham's journal for 16 July 1886 states: "Some of these [prisoners] are afflicted with loathsome venereal diseases." See also Stan Larson, ed., *Prisoner for Polygamy: The Memoirs and Letters of Rudger Clawson at the Utah Territorial Penitentiary 1884-1887* (Urbana and Chicago: University of Illinois Press, 1993), 145 and 163 n. 9.

[12] The authorship of the book, *The Life of Joseph Smith the Prophet*, which displays George Q. Cannon's name as author, has been questioned by some. A review of the A. H. Cannon journals, as well as other pertinent material, suggests that the work is something of a Cannon family collaboration, with contributions from Frank J. (who prepared a rough draft), Abraham H., John Q., George Q. (who extensively revised and

Saturday, July 10, 1886:

I timed myself today in writing shorthand dictation and I found that from the *Life of Nephi* I was able to report a little more than 50 words per minute.

Thursday, July 15, 1886:

In the evening Hud and I had a conversation with Bro. [Lorenzo] Snow about various doctrines. Bro. Snow said I would live to see the time when brothers and sisters would marry each other in the church. All our horror at such a union was due entirely to prejudice, and the offspring of such union would be as healthy and pure as any others. These were the decided views of Pres. Young, when alive, for Bro. Snow talked to him freely on this matter.

Bro. Snow believes that Jesus will appear as a man among this people and dwell with them a time before he comes in His glory. The Gentiles will hear of it and they will reject him, as the Jews did anciently, but they will have no power over him at all.

He says that if a man will place himself in a position where he is ready to sacrifice everything at the command of the Lord, he is then in a position to ask and receive Heavenly revelation.

Saturday, July 17, 1886:

During the forenoon I was studying Phonography [shorthand] and my lecture. I succeeded in writing nearly 60 words per minute today on a whole paragraph.

In the afternoon at 4 p.m. I commenced to deliver my lecture on "the German Land and People." I occupied about 55 minutes in treating upon the history, government, religion, language, habits, etc. and a great

---

added material), and even Joseph F. Smith. An entry from the journal of George Q. Cannon while in the Utah Penitentiary states: "Friday, September 1, 1888: I worked very hard at the message of my *Life of Joseph*" (see also 31 March 1888). President Cannon's biographer, Davis Bitton, wrote, "Of course George Q. Cannon had the final right of approval and was responsible for the final product" (Davis Bitton, *George Q. Cannon: A Biography* (Salt Lake City: Deseret Book, 1999), 296 and 511 n. 140; hereafter cited as *George Q. Cannon: A Biography*). See also AHC journals 29 June 1886, 7 November 1887, 11 February 1888, and 24 April 1888.

many complimented me on my effort, but if I succeeded in doing well the credit be to the Lord who aided me. Rudger Clawson then gave a select reading.... A vote of thanks was tendered us, and it was moved that I continue my lecture, as I did not have time to complete it, but I objected and the motion was overruled.

In the evening on my motion Rudger Clawson was appointed chairman of our exercises and we then had various exercises in honor of the early departure of Elders Morris, Willy and Nelson from our Midst, each of whom made a speech....

Tuesday, August 3: 1886:

I was studying during the morning and in the afternoon was busy writing some articles from Brother James Moyle's experience for the *Juvenile*....

In the evening...we had speeches of Bros. Bromley and Groesbeck,...and the valedictories of Bros. George H. Taylor, James H. Moyle and Jack Bryan who has been pardoned from serving his last three months in a five years sentence for burglary. These were interspersed with songs, dancing, speeches, etc., I making a few remarks.

Wednesday, August 4, 1886:

This morning Bros Taylor and Moyle were released, they having served out their sentences and paid their fines. Jack Bryan was also released.

After a bath I wrote letters to E. F. Parry and L. R. Rogers, of Ogden, on business. I was studying during the forenoon except for a short time when I with several other brethren was outside conversing with James Jack and C. P. Arnold. They report that in Monday's election the people's ticket was victorious everywhere. There is rather a dearth of news in town at present, though the Grand Jury are reporting a great number of indictments.

I was studying during the afternoon until about three o'clock when I wrote an article for the *Juvenile* from R. B. Young's experience. I also read and corrected part of the Book of Mormon Catechism. In the evening I corrected part of O. B. Huntington's manuscript....

Thursday, August 5, 1886:

I also finished revising the Book of Mormon catechism in the afternoon, and started to write the title page and contents....

During the evening I was busy correcting O. B. Huntington's manuscript.

Two new men were placed in No. 1 [bunkhouse] tonight—one, it is said, is accused of perjury, while the other, a lawyer, is said to have induced him to do so with a drink of whisky....

Friday, August 6, 1886:

During the forenoon I was busily engaged in study, and in the afternoon finished the preface to the Book of Mormon catechism and wrote an article for the *Juvenile* from Bro. Moyle's experience.

During the evening I was busy correcting Bro. O. B. Huntington's manuscript.

Charles Whitney, an younger brother of Orson's committed suicide day before yesterday by shooting himself through the head. The coroner's jury state that it was done during a fit of temporary aberration of the mind....

Saturday, August 7, 1886:

In the afternoon was engaged in writing up an article from Bo. Moyle's experience for the *Juvenile*.

In the evening I finished correcting Bro O. B. Huntington's manuscript....

Sunday, August 8, 1886:

During the forenoon I was studying from our Church works. In the afternoon the Episcopalian minister Mr. Miller, accompanied by two ladies held services. The sermon was a good moral one, the text being Christ's feeding of the multitudes with a small quantity of bread, which...he likened to the word of God to us. I was reading during a good part of the afternoon and evening....

Monday, August 16, 1886:

I was busy during the greater part of the day in settling up accounts, finishing up my writing, etc. In the afternoon I had a visit from W. M. Cannon and the children....

I had a settlement with Warden Dow in the afternoon and he said I had obeyed the rules of the institution and he was pleased to see me leave; he also hoped I would never return. I was pleased to know that my actions were worthy of his approval. And my feelings towards him are of the kindest. All of the brethren in the yard with whom I spoke expressed the kindest of feelings towards me. At night a sort of ovation was held in our room in honor of my expected departure. The speeches made were all made up of praises for me. M. Johnson, while acknowledging his prejudice against our people and religion, said that I would stand among the first on the list of those whom he thought were trying to approach the example set by our great Master. He made many other expressions of the highest praise. Mr. McConnell also expressed his pleasure at making my acquaintance, and said he wished from his heart that he could see and be as I was. Bros. Snow, Naisbitt, Lambert, Clawson, Foulger and others all gave me words of encouragement and praise. I made my valedictory in which I thanked all for their kind feelings. I do not believe there is a man in the yard but what feels kindly towards me.

I can truly say that I have tried to set a good example in study, work and morals, and the Lord has wonderfully blest me.

Tuesday, August 18, 1886:

At 5 o'clock, I was permitted to leave the yard with the trusties, who at that time went to work. I found John Q. waiting for me with a buggy, and, as Mr. Curtis did not desire to search my valise, I jumped in and we were soon in town. I called to see Sarah and the children at her mothers and then went to Aunt Sarah's, where I had breakfast, and met the rest of my folks.

I went to the office for a short time and then commenced to make some calls....

Thursday, August 19, 1886:

I was engaged at the office part of the day. In the afternoon I went down to the farm and visited the folks there and found all well. In the evening I accompanied Bro. S. Sudbury about 11 miles out of town in his buggy and was met at Bro. John S----'s by Charles Wilcken, who took me about seven miles further where I had the pleasure of meeting Father, whom I found both looking and feeling well. He was at the house of Bishop S----. Father seemed much pleased to see me and questioned me about matters pertaining to the "Pen."...[13]

Friday, August 20, 1886:

After breakfast we went out for a walk when Father told me that Bro. Moses Thatcher had preached that the people were to be robbed of all their political rights and brought into great bondage; and when it would seem as though there was no escape the people would cry unto God, who would then send to them the man like unto Moses of whom the Doctrine and Covenants speaks; this should be the Prophet Joseph resurrected. Bro. Thatcher claims no revelation for these things, which he says is all to occur within five years, but has made deductions from ancient and modern prophecies. Father says it has not been made known to him that this doctrine is correct, and he does not approve of its being taught.

Father told me of his deep financial embarrassments. Besides his bonds, which he feels he must in honor pay, he seems on the point of losing considerable in John Beck's mine, where he invested at Pres. Taylor's wish and suggestion. He says he sees nothing but ruin ahead, though he has faith God will yet relieve him.

During the day we were engaged in various business matters. We revised what Frank had written of the Prophet's *History*.[14] I took some short-hand notes from Father and transcribed them for the paper. We also talked over Cannon and Sons' affairs and I found that my ideas agree with Father's about the way in which it should be conducted....

This was a most enjoyable day to me.

---

[13] Evidently Abraham was so concerned with keeping secret his father's location that he withheld the exact names and location of those who were hiding President Cannon even from his journal.

[14] See AHC journals, 15 July 1886 note 12.

Saturday, August 21, 1886:

I was busy part of the day at the office. Went to the farm in the afternoon where I selected two hiding places so that Father could conceal himself should he be surprised when at home sometime….

Monday, August 23, 1886:

I was busy in the office most of the day reviewing manuscripts, writing, etc….

Sunday, August 29, 1886:

I went to Aunt Sarah Cannon's and changed my clothes and from there to the office where I wrote up my journal and read for some time….

Wednesday, September 1, 1886:

Wrote to Father in the afternoon concerning the amount Zion's Savings Bank owes me and urged him to use his influence to have a settlement made in some way. I also sent him D. P. Kimball's manuscript for review….

Thursday, September 2, 1886:

I was busy at the office most of the day. In the afternoon I was making some corrections in the Book of Mormon Catechism which Father suggested and preparing it for publication….

Saturday, September 4, 1886:

During the forenoon John Q. came to me at the office and after we had gone to the barn alone he made a most horrible revelation to me. It consisted of the information that sometime since he committed himself with Louie Wells and the result was that she had a miscarriage. Matters had reached such a stage that now he was forced to confess his sin to Bishop Preston and others. I am the first he says, to whom he has revealed it and he desired my counsel. I advised him to first tell it to Father and let him instruct him what to do. According to the present law of the Church he cannot retain his standing. He says he will place his resignation in the hands of Bishop Preston and, after hearing from Father will leave the country and try to build up a home elsewhere. He feels that he cannot live here and meet those whom he has known so long with the sense of shame resting upon him. He will send Louie to California to live with Belie Sears and if Annie is willing will leave her here with her mother until he can send for her. He desires to leave his business affairs in my hands so he says.

If I had heard of John Q's death the news would have been happiness compared with this. It will nearly kill Father. I felt sick at heart and for some time could not control myself. I have thought that of all Father's children John Q. was the least liable to fall. I have known my own weaknesses and follies, and supposed he was far from such. I fear pride is what caused the temptation to first enter John's mind. It is unaccountable to me, however, how he could so far forget himself as to fall when he might long ago have been joined to Louie in honorable wedlock.[15] O, God, preserve me in virtue and Thy truth! Permit me not to become proud and boastful of my own strength but to be humble and feel my dependence on Thee, that I may gain eternal and celestial glory!...

Sunday, September 5, 1886:

After breakfast I went to the office where Father sent for me about 10 a.m. and I walked to the farm. I then saddled up a horse and rode to town on errands, one of which was to see and tell Uncle Angus and John Q. to go to the farm, and the other was to see about a suitable place for Pres. Taylor and Father to stop tonight. Not being able to find John Q. I left a note for him, and then returned to the farm. Father communicated to Uncle Angus what had occurred and said he felt John Q. ought to get up before the public congregation in the Big Tabernacle this afternoon and confess his sins, and Uncle Angus should then propose and put it to vote that he be cut off from the Church. John Q. arrived there about 2:30 p.m. but he would not go to see Father. I therefore carried the latter's advice to John and he manfully agreed to follow it. He and Uncle Angus therefore went to town together and I took Bro. H. B. Clawson

---

[15] John Q. Cannon, older brother of Abraham, was also second counselor in the Presiding Bishopric.

up home in John's buggy. I reached meeting just in time to hear Uncle Angus put the motion to vote that John be cut off. It was unanimously sustained. Uncle Angus immediately left the meeting to again go in hiding. The affair created a great sensation because no idea was had by any, except two or three, of John's guilt, and the fact that Uncle Angus came out of his hiding to put the matter before the people that it might be a warning made a profound impression. Bro. John Nicholson having been interrupted in his remarks that this confession might occur, continued after it was done. He eulogized Father for the noble stand he had taken with his own son, and hoped the warning would be taken to heart by the people. I drove to the farm after meeting and heard Father tell the folks what had occurred. He began in this way. "John Q. Cannon has committed adultery and was today cut off the Church." The sadness of the scene which followed beggars description. All wept and felt their spirits wounded. I went over for John Q. in the evening and after giving solicitation, he went over and met Father and the folks. The former encouraged and advised him to remain right here and live down the sin he has committed as far as possible. John promised to do as told. He seemed to feel very penitent and humble, and will, I hope, try to live his religion hereafter. The blow has been a terrible one to us all as we all placed so much faith in John Q. He said he suffered a thousand deaths in telling Annie, Louie, and Sister Wells this afternoon of his fall from the Church....

Monday, December 13, 1886:

In the evening I attended the meeting of the 3rd Quorum of Seventies in the 10th Ward school house where I addressed the brethren on their duties and urged a faithful performance thereof. My remarks were heartily endorsed by several of the Presidents. Bro. Andrew Jensen was then sustained and I set him apart to fill a vacancy in the Presidency of that quorum....

I received a letter from Pres. John Taylor today in which he gives his approval to the circular prepared by our council calling upon all the Seventies to get their Bishops recommend and stating that those who failed to do this would after April 1st next be no longer considered Seventies....

Saturday, June 11, 1887:

I received word from Father today that he has been and is still suffering from sciatica. He thinks he is improving somewhat.

Thursday, July 21, 1887:

In the forenoon and afternoon I was with Father talking about some items of business. I also met Bro. Joseph F. Smith with him, he having just returned from the Sandwich Islands. He is both looking and feeling well. They report Pres. Taylor gradually sinking and think he will not last very much longer. His extremities are cold and his tongue is swelled; though he suffers no pain....[16]

Monday, August 15, 1887:

I then went to see Father with whom I spent a short time in talking over business matters. He said he has had to defend himself and me before the Apostles because of what was done in the matter of John Q's divorce and marriage, but Father said he assumed all blame for the part I took in the matter....[17]

Monday, November 7, 1887:

Was with Father a short time in the afternoon talking about various matters of business. I got his consent to get John Q. to revise the manuscript of *Joseph the Prophet*, which Frank prepared, after which Father and Joseph F. Smith will review it and we can then print the same....

---

[16] Under the same date of 21 July 1887 the journal of John Henry Smith records: "We received letters from Bro. Wilford Woodruff requesting Bro. Lyman and I to return home and saying President Taylor was very ill. Also from President G. Q. Cannon saying that President John Taylor was laying unconscious" (*Church, State, and Politics*, 173). President Taylor died 25 July 1887.

[17] For further explanation of this entry, see the A. H. Cannon journal for 4 and 5 September 1886; see also Thomas G. Alexander, *Things in Heaven and Earth: The Life and Times of Wilford Woodruff, a Mormon Prophet* (Salt Lake City: Signature Books, 1993), 243.

Wednesday, November 9, 1887:

Walter Lewis having returned from the East last night he gave in his report this morning, which was very satisfactory. The terms he made for a Hoe two-revolution #6 press were lower than we supposed he could get, and we have eighteen months in which to pay for it. We went to the farm and saw Father about the terms, size of press, etc., and he was well satisfied. I therefore telegraphed in the evening for the machine to be forwarded immediately, and also ordered a Thompson wire stitcher to come at the same time. We hope, when this machinery arrives, to do the nicest work in the west....

Saturday, February 11, 1888:

Part of the day I was at the office. About 11 a.m. Frank and I went down to the farm where we submitted a part of the *History of Joseph* copy to Father. He approved of it with a few exceptions and when these suggested alterations are made, we are at liberty to get the matter in type.

Friday, April 6, 1888:

After being at the office a short time in the morning, I went to see Father, who told me that the matter of the First Seven Presidents of the Seventies was mentioned in the council of the Twelve and the remark had been made that we did not fully tend to our duties. The proposition was also made to pay us a salary, which matter was referred to a committee, so that we might devote less time to business and more to our ministry. I told Father I would prefer to receive no salary, and as for neglect of duty I had tried to do my best. It would, however, please me very much if I could be honorably released from my position as it was very trying to me to go out and preach to the people. He then exhorted me strongly to battle against this man-fearing spirit and try to do my duty at all times.

Monday, April 23, 1888:

On Saturday we worked off two forms of laws, and today one form of laws and started on Joseph Smith's *History*, working off 2,500 copies of the first form.

Tuesday, April 24, 1888:

I was busy at the office nearly all day, where we worked off the remainder of the first form of *Joseph the Prophet* (a 10,000 edition) and one form of laws, though it was 1 a.m. before completing the latter....

Thursday, April 25, 1888:

Most of the day I was at the office where we worked off the second form of the *History*.

Sunday, May 6, 1888:

I went to the depot and met John Q. with his buggy, and told him that Pres. Woodruff, by and with the consent of the Twelve, had authorized Father to baptize John. At Father's request we took Bishop S. M. T. Seddon of the 5th Ward down to the farm, where Father spoke to him about the baptism, and asked if it would be agreeable to him which the Bishop said it would. John therefore took the Bishop home and then brought Annie over to witness the ceremony. About 1:30 p.m. Father's family and George Lambert repaired to the river, where I prayed, and, after John had expressed his desire to be baptized, Father immersed him in the water. After changing clothes we all assembled in the school house where father gave a most excellent discourse; he urged all to pray earnestly and often, to repent daily of weaknesses and sins and to seek at all times for the spirit of revelation which it was the privilege of each one to enjoy.

John Q. was then confirmed by Father a member of the Church and ordained an Elder. The sacrament was then administered and George Lambert added a few words expressive of his pleasure at being present on this occasion. A good spirit did indeed prevail, and I felt very happy....

Thursday, May 17, 1888:

Mina and I had a little spat today because of a remark she made that Pres. Young had "skinned" the Church for much of the property he owned. We parted angry this morning, but about noon she sent me a note asking my pardon....

Went with John Q. in his buggy to the races at the Utah Driving Park. A very pretty trotting race between "Bronco Jack" owned by Jack

Sagers and "Don Angus" owned by Matt Cullen was won by the latter in three straight heats....

A private dedication of the Manti Temple occurred today at which the Underground Apostles were present. I was invited to be present but owing to my lameness could not go.

We today worked off one form of laws and one of Tullidges History Biographies.

Wednesday, May 23, 1888:

Went with Frank to the Gardo House in the Forenoon where we had a long talk with Father about various business affairs. In the evening I remained at the office till 11:50 to complete the form of Tullidge's magazine which we put on the press after the laws were off this morning....

Friday, May 25, 1888:

I was out attending to some business, and among other things called to see Father with whom I had considerable talk about business. He desires me to learn the true condition of John Q's. affairs. He told me that at the dedication of the Manti Temple there were some remarkable manifestations of God's power. Various personages were seen. Phoebe Beatie saw a person standing behind D. C. Young while he was speaking. Halos were seen about the heads of several brethren, notably Apostle John W. Taylor. Voices were heard shouting "Hosanna", and singing was heard—Bro. John S. Lewis stating that he could distinguish the various parts. These were encouraging evidences to the Saints that God is pleased with the work done, and still lives to control His Church....

CHAPTER TWO

1889

Wednesday, February 20, 1889:

I went to the "Pen" in the forenoon and had a long conversation with Father about business matters, principally about Ogden Real Estate. He seems to feel inclined to invest some means there, but will consider it till tomorrow. I have prayed the Lord to inspire Father aright in regard to this matter. Father received word from Washington this morning that he had been pardoned by Pres. Cleveland, which act restores him to citizenship. He invited me to have breakfast with him tomorrow after his release from prison when his time expires.

During the afternoon I attended my Council meeting where I presided and assisted with the business....

Thursday, February 21, 1889:

Nice day overhead, but very muddy underfoot.

At 7 a.m. I went to the farm where within an hour I met Father and Pres. Woodruff. Uncle Angus and C. H. Wilcken were also there. We had breakfast together and then took a look at the stock and houses. Pres. Woodruff was delighted to have Father free again, and the latter was pleased to be so. The latter spoke in the kindest terms of the warden and guards at the "Pen."

Pres. Woodruff now decides to appear in public with Father.

Friday, February 22, 1889:

I then went to the D. and R. G. Depot to meet John Q. coming from Ogden, and we were met by Father and Charles Wilcken with carriages containing all mother's children. We all drove to the cemetery and looked at Mother's grave, and selected a style of coping with which Father desires to surround his lots. We then drove to the

President's office where the Tabernacle choir assembled—the largest number being together that I have for a long time seen—and serenaded Father and the President. After some singing Father and Bro. Woodruff feelingly addressed the company. As they dispersed the Sandwich Island choir also sang several pieces two of which were composed especially to honor father. He spoke to them in their language and Pres. Woodruff then spoke a few words in English which Bro. Robert B. T. Taylor interpreted. He told them they were of the seed of Israel of the tribe of Joseph, and they had a great work to do, for he had seen them in vision in the temples of God receiving their blessings. One Kanuka was present who is 95 years old. Father baptized him on the islands over 34 years ago.

After all had left Pres. Woodruff accompanied Father and us children to the farm where we had dinner. After dinner Pres. Woodruff made this remark to me while we were alone: "Bro. Cannon, your Father has yet the biggest brain and the best mind of any man in the Kingdom, without exception." Sometime since he remarked to Charles Wilcken that Father is the humblest man in the Church. John Q. left for the train about 4 p.m. He received word today from Pres. Woodruff that he might soon be called on a mission to Turkey. John expressed his willingness to go if it was desired. Through that country and Asia Minor it is believed the gospel will be carried into Arabia and to the Jews....

Father decided today to invest $5,000 in Ogden real estate, and will leave it to Frank and myself to take care of the investment for him....

Wednesday, March 6, 1889:

I was engaged at the office all day except while at my Council meeting in the afternoon, where I assisted Bros. Gates, Young, Roberts and Campbell with the business. This consisted principally of reading and amending an epistle to the seventies and a letter of questions to the Apostles which Seymour Young and I had prepared, and also the considering of missionary correspondence....

Sunday, March 10, 1889:

At 8 a.m. I drove to Father's farm and there met and accompanied him in his buggy to the East Bountiful Ward meeting house where the Davis Stake conference was to be held. The house was crowded. After Pres. William R. Smith had given a brief and good report of the condition of the people Father addressed the people. He spoke of the great blessings God had bestowed on us as a people even amid all our trials. He told the Saints that neither as individuals nor as a community could anyone injure them but themselves. Their own acts alone could do this. True, they might suffer temporarily through misrepresentation and slander, but by being faithful the Lord would bring them through all right. Concerning the coming of some great man to deliver Israel, he said there would be none save he came through the channel of the Priesthood. All the power of the Priesthood existed with as much force today as ever in the various quorums. He reviewed the conferring of the Priesthood on the Prophet Joseph and his receiving all the keys of the Gospel, and testified that he in turn had given them to others until now Pres. Wilford Woodruff held all the power necessary to the establishment and triumph of the Church and Kingdom of God....

In the afternoon Apostle F. D. Richards spoke on the duties of the Saints, and I also spoke for about 25 minutes in a confused way. I fear that I counted too much on my own wisdom in arising to speak, and I felt very much chagrined when I resumed my seat. I hope the lesson will not be lost on me.

As we drove home Father told me that all his success in life was due to his zeal for the work of God. Men gave him credit for much more ability than he possessed, but whatever talents he did possess he had tried to use to the glory of God. In his speaking he had never desired to be sensational but to be sound in doctrine.... I was very much instructed by the conversation and this day's services....

Monday, March 11, 1889:

After being a short time at the office I drove the carriage containing Pres. Woodruff and Father to East Bountiful. During the morning service some reports were read and Seymour B. Young then spoke for 20 minutes. Father then spoke on the love of God. He urged the Saints to love each other and to minister to each others wants, and not to feel that certain ones are unworthy of our aid because of their improvidence. He called to the Saints attention the fact that the men who were liberal of their time and means were apparently no worse off than those who were stingy with both in the work of the Lord. Speaking of the sacrament he said he believed considerable of our sickness was due to our partaking unworthily of these emblems. He called upon the Stake Presidency and Bishops to refuse the sacrament to those who they knew were unworthy to receive, and told them that if they did not follow this counsel the sins of the unrighteous individual would follow them. He fully explained the reparation required by the Gospel of those who do wrong. The confession must be as far reaching as the knowledge of the evil.

I took dinner at Bro. David Stoker's house. A little child belonging to Willard Call while playing in a swing between 11 and 12 o'clock became entangled in the rope and nearly strangled to death. It was black in the face when found and afterwards went into spasms. Seymour Young thought it would recover.

At 2 p.m. the house was full. Pres. Woodruff spoke for about _ of an hour: he urged the Saints to raise the best horses, fruit, vegetables, grain, etc.; to have the best houses, and to try and improve in all practical matters. He told the Saints not to go to Mexico, Canada or any other place, unless their circumstances required it, but to gather together. He told the men to make things pleasant at home for their wives and children, and for wives to look to the interests of their husbands. He particularly urged parents to instruct their marriageable sons and daughters in the laws of life, and not let them do themselves irreparable injury before gaining experience.

Pres. W. A. Smith urged the people to be careful of the water this season, which will undoubtedly be very scarce. He suggested frequent plowing among trees which would enable them to thrive without much water. He advised the building of reservoirs for water before another year....

Tuesday, March 12, 1889:

I am 30 years old today. How little I know for my age!…

Monday, April 29, 1889:

Bro. B. H. Roberts delivered himself up this morning and pled guilty to a charge of unlawful cohabitation. He will receive sentence on Wednesday.…

Tuesday, April 30, 1889:

It was a general holiday today, as per proclamation of President Harrison and Governor West, in honor of the centennial anniversary of the inauguration of George Washington as President of the United States. I attended the meeting at the tabernacle in honor of the event. The exercises commenced with an organ prelude by Joseph F. Daines, and then a song by E. Stephens' class of three hundred singers. Prayer was offered by Elias A. Smith. Another song by E. Stephens' class. Richard W. Young then delivered a 35 min. oration which he read from his notes. He reviewed briefly the scenes of a hundred years ago, and also the present condition of our great nation.

An organ solo followed the oration and then a quartette by Messrs. Whitney, Easton, Spencer and Goddard. F. S. Richards and Father then made brief speeches; Bro. Woodruff also added a very few words, all expressive of thankfulness for our good and great government given us of God through wise men.…

I took dinner at Aunt Amanda's and then went to the office a short time. At 2 p.m. went to see a baseball match on Washington Square between the Nationals and the Ogden Athletics. There was some very good playing done. In order to allow the Ogden boys time to get to the train the game ceased at 7-1/2 innings when the score was a tie at 14—the Nationals having two and the Athletics one inning to spare.…

Friday, May 31, 1889:

A sad affair is reported as having occurred in Provo a few days since: Joseph Smoot, a son of Pres. A. O. Smoot, who is wild and addicted to the use of liquor, went into a saloon and after getting a glass of whisky mockingly consecrated it, as is customary in the consecration of oil in the Church. No sooner had he finished this sacrilegious act than he was struck with paralysis and fell helpless on the floor. His Gentile companions were horrified at his act, and its result, and carried him home where he has since laid in a very precarious condition. A horrible warning to scoffers!

Sunday, June 23, 1889:

I spent the forenoon in conversing on the Gospel principles and reading. Father proved to my entire satisfaction this morning by passages from the Book of Mormon and Doctrine and Covenants that all men, even the sons of perdition, will be resurrected and stand before God to be judged. He believes…that under certain unknown conditions the benefits of the Savior's atonement extend to our entire solar system. Jesus, in speaking of Himself as the very eternal Father speaks as one of the Godhead, etc. Many obscure points of doctrine were made plain to me by the conversation of this morning….

Sunday, July 7, 1889:

At 3 p.m. the Sunday School Union met at the same place. The question was asked if partaking of the Sacrament would cause a forgiveness of sins. A question card used in the Sunday Schools said it would. Father said that partaking worthily of the Sacrament would gain for the Saint a forgiveness of sins, as well as a repentant spirit and humble prayer would bring the same blessing, yet this is not the ordinance instituted for the forgiveness of sins, and any question or answer which conveyed such an idea is incorrect.

Saturday, October 5, 1889:

I was in the office about two hours before meeting time. During that time Father came in and said the authorities of the Church had decided to appoint me to a mission, and he hoped I would round up my shoulders and take it….

At the close of the meeting I went to the "Gardo House,"[1] at Father's request, but as other parties who were to be there for the same purpose as I, did not come, I was excused till tomorrow at 9 a.m. I therefore went to the office till meeting time. At the afternoon meeting Apostle Snow spoke on our present condition and the improvements we would have to make before we would be prepared for the coming of Christ. He occupied 35 min. Bishop O. F. Whitney then spoke for 40 min. and related a dream he had just after arriving in his first missionary field 13 years ago. The dream was concerning the Savior's prayer in the garden of Gethsemane just previous to His betrayal when the Apostles slept while He prayed. Orson asked, in his dream, to be allowed to accompany the Savior to Heaven, but the latter would not permit it because his work was not yet done. The speaker then asked for an assurance that he might come unto the Savior when his work was completed; but the Lord replied, "That, my son, will depend entirely upon yourself." This dream roused the receiver to realization of his position and he never rested until he had a testimony of the truth of the Gospel....[2]

Returned to the Priesthood meeting at 7:30 and listened to good discourses from Father and Pres. Woodruff. The former told the brethren how revelation from God to the Church would be imparted—through Pres. Woodruff or his successor. If any apostle or other person should receive a revelation concerning new doctrine he had no right to preach or teach it until it had been submitted to and passed upon by the First Presidency or Twelve. Pres. Woodruff spoke upon Joseph E. Taylor's doctrine of the baby resurrection and said that such teachings unsettled the minds of people and made them

---

[1] The Gardo House (also called "Amelia's palace") was the official residence of the President of the Church, and where the Quorum of the Twelve Apostles met in council until construction was completed on the Salt Lake Temple in 1894. It was built in 1873 by President Brigham Young, acquired from his estate by the Church, and then occupied by President John Taylor in 1881. It was later sold by the Church and then torn down in 1921. (See *Encyclopedia of Latter-day Saint History*, 411.)

[2] A complete recitation of this experience is found in Orson F. Whitney, *Through Memory's Halls: The Life Story of Orson F. Whitney* (Independence, Mo.: Zion's Printing and Publishing Company, 1930), 81-83.

uneasy. In the resurrection whether babies grew or not, we will be perfectly satisfied with the arrangement....[3]

Sunday, October 6, 1889:

At 9 a.m. I went to the Gardo House where myself and Bro. Anthon H. Lund of Ephraim, Sanpete Co., were summoned into the presence of the First Presidency and Twelve Apostles. Pres. Woodruff then stated that Bro. Marriner W. Merrill and ourselves had been selected to fill the vacancies in the Quorum of the Twelve. Our selection occurred in this way: The apostles were asked to make suggestions to the Presidency in regard to this matter. Lists were prepared and submitted and among the names were ours. The subject was made a matter of prayer and the result was that we were unanimously chosen. We were asked as to our feelings in accepting, and though weak we both felt to accept the great honor and trust in the Lord to assist us in our labors. Bro. Merrill, through sickness was not present.

At 10 a.m. we went to meeting when the first business done was the presenting of the authorities. After the First Presidency and former Apostles were voted in Pres. Woodruff arose and spoke of the intention to fill up the latter quorum. He stated how the selections had been made, and said he had reasons for informing the people that neither he nor his counselors had made the selections proposed.[4] The names of Bros. Marriner W. Merrill, Anthon H. Lund and Abraham H. Cannon were then presented separately, and the vote on each was unanimous.

---

[3] Joseph E. Taylor (a counselor in the Salt Lake stake presidency) occasionally advanced speculative doctrines publicly. Apparently Church authorities had not yet formalized their position on this point. Nearly 30 years later, President Joseph F. Smith solidified the baby resurrection doctrine (that babies would first be resurrected and then grow to adult stature) for the Church in the *Improvement Era* 21 (1918): 567-73: "The first man I ever heard mention it in public was Franklin D. Richards; and when he spoke of it, I felt in my soul: the truth has come out.... Presidents Woodruff and Cannon approved of the doctrine and after that I preached it" (See *Gospel Doctrine* [Salt Lake City: The Church of Jesus Christ of Latter-day Saints, 1919], 574-77). See also AHC journals, 7 July 1893.

[4] President Woodruff probably used this tactic to help allay the charge of nepotism, since Abraham was the son of his first counselor. See AHC journals, 7 October 1889.

Father then spoke for the remainder of the forenoon on the cause and cure of disunion and the subject of the resurrection, proving from the Bible and our Church books that all mankind will be released from the bands of death, and upon the sons of perdition will pass a second death. In some places the idea has prevailed that these latter will never be resurrected.[5]

At the close of the meeting I received numerous congratulations and expressions of good will. Bro. Junius F. Wells said there was no man in the Church for whom he would more readily raise his hand than for me. Seymour B. Young said he knew two years ago that I would become one of the Twelve, and so wrote to Father. All the members of my Council gave me their most earnest good will....

Monday, October 7, 1889:

Early this morning I took Father to the Hot Springs in my buggy. Our conversation on the road gave me very great joy to see how happy he was at my call to the Apostleship without any suggestion from him. He said that the three men of all Israel whom he would have chosen had been selected....

At 10 a.m. I was present at a meeting of the Presidents of Stakes and their counselors, Bishops and their counselors and a few other leading brethren. Bro. Lyman was the principal speaker: His discourse was a fine one. He said among other things that this idea of looking for some great man who had been resurrected to come and deliver Zion was erroneous. No doubt God would raise up great men, but he believed they would be of flesh and blood as had been Moses, Joseph Smith and others. He did not encourage the idea of the world coming to an end in 1891....[6]

At 3 p.m. I attended a meeting of the Twelve at the Gardo House where Bros. Merrill, Lund and myself were set apart as Apostles in the order named. Pres. Woodruff set apart the first, Father the second

---

[5] This view usually results from an incorrect understanding of D&C 76:39.
[6] See D&C 130:14-17. Some Church members viewed this verse to mean 1891 would be the time of the Second Coming.

and Bro. Joseph F. Smith myself.[7] Our charge was first given us by Father at Pres. Woodruff's instance. The importance of our callings was portrayed, and our privileges were named. Among these were the privileges of having the ministration of angels, and of seeing the Savior Himself; of hearing the voice of God as audibly as we hear a man's voice; of continually being under the direction of the Holy Ghost; of being prophets and revelators; and of many other things of which I have a verbatim copy, as also of my blessing and ordination, in which I was promised everything my heart desired in righteousness if faithful. Oh, how humble and weak I felt! I feel the most unworthy of all my brethren for this exalted position. My sins rise up against me, but I pray God to keep my weaknesses continually before my eyes so that I may depend on Him and not on my own strength, and that I may never feel proud or haughty....

Tuesday, October 8, 1889:

Was at the office from 9 to 10 a.m. at which latter time I went to the Historians office and assisted in the setting apart of some missionaries. The instructions which were given thereafter concerning the care of the body and mind were most excellent. Among the others I spoke a few moments and encouraged the brethren to seek continually for the Spirit of God to direct them in their labors as well as in their speaking. I related how at one time in Germany I followed my own inclination instead of the direction of the Spirit in the appointment of a branch president and how I afterwards saw my mistake....

---

[7] Elder Marriner W. Merrill's journal of 7 October 1889 records: "I was ordained an Apostle under the hands of President Wilford Woodruff and Counselors George Q. Cannon and Joseph F. Smith and eight Apostles,...President Woodruff being mouth. This was done on Monday at the Gardo House after the close of the General Conference.... Brothers Anthon H. Lund and Abram H. Cannon were ordained Apostles at the same time. I did not attend the conference at this time on account of being unwell, but was telegraphed for by President George Q. Cannon and met this genuine surprise after arriving in Salt Lake City on Sunday evening, October 6th" (Melvin Clarence Merrill, ed., *Utah Pioneer and Apostle Marriner Wood Merrill and His Family* [n. p.: Marriner Wood Merrill Heritage Committee, 1980], 108).

Wednesday, October 9, 1889:

I was at my room for some time in the morning writing up my journal. Went to the office about 8 a.m. and prepared some articles for the *Juvenile,* and also looked over the correspondence.

At 1 p.m. I attended the meeting of my former Council and there gave my farewell address to the brethren in which I expressed my deep love for them and gratitude at their forbearance and kindness towards me during the 7 years, which it is today, that I have been a member of this quorum. Bro. Gates expressed himself in a very kindly way toward me, and Bros. Morgan and Young were appointed to draft resolutions of respect to present to me....

Thursday, October 10, 1889:

Between 9 and 10 a.m. was looking after work in the office. At the latter time I went to a council meeting of my Quorum in the Gardo House. Bros. Thatcher, Teasdale and Merrill were the only members absent. Pres. Woodruff desired the opinion of each member present as to whether we were suited with the present arrangement in regard to finance and as to whether or not he should have an office with clerks and books for the transaction of Church business. The present arrangement, which was adopted some time since on recommendation of a committee of the Apostles, places all funds in the care of the Bishop William B. Preston and they are to be expended only on an order from President Woodruff. Yet within the last month he had paid out several thousand dollars without any order. Of course these amounts were perfectly legitimate, and yet they were paid irregularly. The result of the present plan is that the Bishop has forbidden his agents to pay out anything except on a written order from his office, so that an Apostle in traveling through the country could not be allowed a feed of grain from tithing oats without an order from Bishop Preston. On the other hand the Bishop expends money on repairs and alterations at his office, while anything done for Pres. Woodruff would only by paid for on an order [from] Bishop Preston. Each of the brethren gave expression to his views and they were unanimous in feeling that the funds should only be expended on order from Pres. Woodruff, and wherein the

Bishop had done otherwise he should be reprimanded. Opinion however, was divided as to whether the funds should remain in Bishop Preston's care or be in the charge of Pres. Woodruff in his private office. I felt that the latter would be proper and Father's view agreed with mine. The First Presidency took the matter under advisement.

The matter of employing voters to work in this city then came up and after some little talk the subject was given into the hands of the Apostles for their decision as to plans and action. It was nearly 4 p.m. when we adjourned....

At 6 p.m. the Twelve met and spent about 3 hours in Council at the Gardo House. The following decisions were reached: That we start to build a Brigham Young College in this city to cost $200,000. Bros. John W. Taylor and John W. Young were appointed the committee to solicit subscriptions; That we build a $250,000 "Mormon" hotel, exclusive of the land; Bros. H. J. Grant and I were the committee to tend to the matter. Excavations and rock hauling are to be commenced within three weeks. These jobs will employ about 100 men. We then decided to ask the City Council to employ a number of men in cleaning the streets and water ditches until after election. It was the sense of the meeting that the resident Apostles be relieved from traveling in the country until after February next, and that they visit the Sunday evening meetings and political clubs in this city and rouse the voters for the 'Peoples Party." I acted as secretary of the meeting...

Friday, October 11, 1889:

At 10 a.m. we visited Pres. Woodruff to get his approval of our plans for a college and hotel, but he was so engaged that we adjourned until 4 p.m. I therefore returned to the office. At noon I drove to the farm and had dinner, and spent some little time with Mina who feels as though my duties in the apostleship would keep me away from her almost exclusively. This I assured her would not be the case.

At 4 p.m. I and other Apostles met with the City Council and talked over political affairs. The proposition to divide the city into separate districts was not thought advisable at present.

The members agreed to employ on city business a large number of workmen, and among other things they will get the proposed city and county building under way.

After this meeting Pres. Woodruff was told of our action last night, and he approved all we did....

Sunday, October 13, 1889:

Conveyances called for us about 7:30 a.m., and we went to Bro. William Black's where we had breakfast and put up during our stay here. At 10 a.m. a crowded meeting convened. Father spoke first on our duties to God and each other. I followed for about 25 minutes in urging the people to seek for the guidance of the Holy Spirit, and to seek by example as well as precept to teach the gospel. Bro. Hampton made a few closing remarks.

At 2 p.m. we again met when President Woodruff spoke about half an hour on the mission of the Prophet Joseph. Father then spoke a short time concerning the blessings which follow the faithful Saint; the performance of duty in no way is a detriment to him who is diligent in obeying the commands of God. For example the faithful tithe payer, or the missionary who leaves his business for two or more years, is no poorer than the man who devotes all his time to the accumulation of money....

Wednesday, October 16, 1889:

Sarah and I were married 11 years ago today. My happiness since that time has been very great.

We printed at the office today the first form of James A. Little's book *From Kirtland to Salt Lake City*. We bound the first copies of *Tullidge's History of Northern Utah and Southern Idaho*.

I was writing in my journal a short time in the morning....

Attended a meeting of the Scientific and Literary Association in the Assembly Hall at 2 p.m. where the proposition to sell the "Council House" or "Museum" property was discussed in order to raise funds for the erection of a suitable building for Museum, library and lecture purposes. The matter was finally left for the attention of the Board of Directors, and to be decided permanently by the members at some future special called meeting....

Thursday, October 17, 1889:

I answered some letters and read proofs until 10 a.m. when I went to the Gardo House where I met Heber J. Grant, and we two spoke to Pres. Woodruff about the hotel scheme. In view of other contemplated labors, he thought we had better drop this matter for the time being. We remained at a meeting with F. S. Richards, Mayor Armstrong, C. W. Penrose, W. H. Rowe, Frank Jennings and John W. Young to consider the matter of getting voters into this city. The latter agreed to furnish employment for 100 men in getting rock from his quarry from now until after the election, this accumulated material to be sold as soon as possible next year. The mayor was then asked if the city could not employ 200 men in putting shale on our streets, this material having been found better than gravel. He said that with the present finances the city could employ no more than the 300 they now have engaged on the sewers and other jobs, and unless the city Council stood by him and directed the employment of more laborers, he could not give another man a job.[8] We adjourned about 1 p.m. to meet with the Council at 3 p.m. today.

I went to the office for dinner and to look after the work, returning to the Gardo at 2 p.m. to our Council meeting. Pres. Woodruff, Father, H. J. Grant, John W. Taylor and myself dressed in our robes, and President Woodruff prayed to open and Father in the circle. This is my first meeting with a prayer circle, and I felt the solemnity of the occasion....[9]

---

[8] Church leaders were trying to bring as many Mormon men into Salt Lake City residence as possible, thereby enabling them to vote in the coming election. This was to counter similar moves by the anti-Mormon Liberal party, which was trying to use this tactic to take local government control from the Mormons.

[9] Traditionally, when the First Presidency and the Quorum of the Twelve Apostles meet in council to deliberate and direct the affairs of the Church, they first hold a prayer circle, invoking the blessings of the Lord upon their meeting: "We sing, kneel in prayer, and then join in a prayer circle at the altar, after which we

Friday, October 18, 1889:

At the latter time I went to the Gardo House where the Municipal Committee and City council were assembled. It has been discovered since last evening that the city's funds will allow the expenditures of between fifty and one hundred thousand dollars on the streets and in developing the water supply in City Creek Canyon, and it was therefore resolved that between two and four hundred men be immediately employed on public improvements until after an election. It was further resolved as the sense of the meeting that the Warm Springs be sold to Mayor Armstrong, Mr. McCune and Heber M. Wells for $26,000, it being the understanding that the latter would have the management of the same. The intention of these parties is to erect suitable buildings and immediately run an electric car line to these springs, and thus make them worthy of the patronage of the Salt Lake public.

Bro. John W. Young brought up his railroad schemes for discussion and spoke of the way his feelings had been hurt by the refusal of the City Council to grant him the franchise on 4th West Street for his proposed road to the shores of Great Salt Lake. It was claimed that this had been done because of his failure to get the approval of the majority of the property owners on the street in question. The majority present, however, favored his road providing he would keep the street on each side in proper repair and condition. This meeting adjourned about 2 p.m.

Some of the Twelve then voted with President Woodruff to have men employed to remove the Endowment House and erect a small building over the baptismal font; and also to have some forty or fifty men employed in other directions by the Church until after the election....

Thereafter I went to the office and read a proof of Dan Jones' book *Forty Years among the Indians*, of which we put the first form to press this evening At 5 p.m. I went to the Gardo House again and talked a short time with Father about various business matters.

---

change to our street clothes" (N. Eldon Tanner, "The Administration of the Church," *Ensign*, Nov. 1979, 47). Such an event took place at most of the Quorum meetings Elder Cannon attended throughout his tenure as an Apostle.

Returned to the office at 6 p.m. and waited there for Father till 7:30 when he came and I escorted him to the "Cannon House" where we remained....

Last night some person or persons tried to enter the window of my room at the corner house, but did not succeed. Two men were seen, however, between two and three o'clock this morning carrying away some books which they got from the bindery downstairs. I therefore took the precaution this evening to securely fasten the windows and doors in the basement....

Sunday, October 20, 1889:

During the forenoon I was reading from the Bible and other good works. After dinner I came to town and drove direct to the Tabernacle meeting. I there took my usual seat with the Seventies, but Uncle Angus called me to a higher seat among the Apostles....

Sunday, October 27, 1889:

I then drove to the farm, got Mina and went to the meeting in the Second Ward.... I occupied the remainder of the time—about 20 min. I urged the Saints to cease sustaining their enemies with their means or votes, and I was very unexpectedly led to speak about back biting and tale bearing and urged the people to cease their evil prejudices and to harmonize all differences among themselves. The place for reformation to begin is in the home and not on the public streets. Bishop Peterson said I was the second Apostle who has visited them since their new and very neat meetinghouse was built. After meeting I took Mina home and remained there all night. She complimented me on my remarks, and said they were the best she ever heard me make. I was certainly led by the Spirit in what I said, and if any good was done, to God be the glory.

Sunday, November 3, 1889:

I then went to the Theological class where I had promised to speak upon the subject of "Marriage and Procreation." I reviewed marriage from the beginning and explained the blessings which had followed the plural order. Also reviewed the revelation to us and told the class that none but those who had the divinity of this principle revealed to them should enter into its practice....

Saturday, November 9, 1889:

In the questioning of "Mormon" applicants for citizenship today before Judge Anderson, the oaths of the Endowment House were brought in, and it was stated by "Liberals" that Mormons took vows inimical to the government in that house. Witnesses will be summoned to try and prove this false statement.

U.S. Marshals arrested in Ogden recently several fast women. Yesterday one of them was tried before U. S. Commissioner Perrin when her "liberal" attorney made the statement that though there was a law against keeping a house of ill fame in this city and territory, yet it was like similar laws in Kentucky, Delaware and other states and was not intended for enforcement. In fact, the "legal voters" at the polls had so declared, which means that the "liberal" voter had declared for licentiousness and lawbreaking to suit their depraved taste.

Sunday, November 10, 1889:

At 2:20 p.m. today Frank D. Romayne was shot and almost instantly killed by Thomas M. Hughes. It occurred in front of the *Tribune* office, on Second South St., where both were employed as compositors. They are tramp printers, the former having arrived here about six months ago and the latter two months since....

Monday, November 11, 1889:

I went to supper at Sarah's and at 7:30 p.m. attended the Political Club meeting at the 20th Ward Hall. I spoke with considerable freedom for some time reviewing some of the acts of the "Liberal" party in Ogden and telling the people what they might expect if they turned over the offices and control to carpet-baggers. I received very hearty applause....

On the statement of Joseph Lipman, a *Tribune* reporter, that he expected to prove on Thursday next that an oath against the government was taken by every member of the Church who passed through the Endowment House, Judge Anderson refused to naturalize any "Mormon" until after the investigation. Yet he admitted men to citizenship who admitted their intercourse with other women than their wives—self acknowledged law-breakers....

Tuesday, November 12, 1889:

At 4 p.m. the Apostles who could be found at the Gardo house or in the city were called together. There were present Lorenzo Snow, Moses Thatcher, John Henry Smith, Heber J. Grant and myself. We listened to statements from James H. Moyle and C. W. Penrose concerning the efforts that will be made on Thursday to show that oaths have been taken against the government by those who passed through the Endowment House and therefore that "Mormonism" is in hostility to the Constitution and "Mormons" should not be admitted to citizenship. It was decided to rebut any testimony the opposite side might give by the statements of a number of polygamists and monogamists from among our people among whom were J. H. Smith, M. W. Merrill, A. H. Lund, A. H. Raleigh, H. M. Wells, W. W. Riter, John Clark, John E. Carlisle and others.

It was stated that the company of which I was one that asked some months since for a franchise on the streets of Salt Lake City were working in the interest of the U. P. railroad, and that if the franchise were now granted this latter company would immediately bring in 400 men and put them to work and allow them to vote and thus turn the scales to the "Liberal" side. I denied any knowledge of this assertion, but favored delay till the danger of registering the voters was past, and Bro. Grant and I called upon John Clark a member of the City Council committee which has this matter in charge, and urged delay. He promised to use his endeavors to this end. I went to the farm and spent my evening in reading and writing.

Wednesday, November 13, 1889:

About 1:30 p.m. I went to the Seventies Council meeting where reports and missionary letters occupied the attention of the brethren. I was presented with a letter expressing the kindest feelings of the brethren for me, and expressing their hopes and faith for me in the future, in my new appointment. After meeting I spent my time at the office in attending to business.

At 7:30, after supper at Sarah's, I went to the Gardo House where some of the apostles and other brethren counseled us to the best course to pursue in regard to the case which tomorrow comes before Judge Anderson, wherein the "Liberals" try to prove that all "Mormons" take oaths against the government when they pass through the Endowment House. As witnesses to disprove the assertion were selected J. H. Smith, M. W. Merrill, A. H. Lund, John Clark, James H. Anderson, Aaron Thatcher and perhaps one or two more. All were present and received some instructions in regard to their testimony, no advice being given, however, for them to deceive or tell any untruths....

Thursday, November 14, 1889:

Dickson and Baskin today conducted the examination on the "Liberal" side in regard to the Endowment oath. Silver, McGuffie, Cahoon, Bond and other bitter apostates testified that vows were made against the government because of the murder of Joseph and Hyrum, and they told many infamous falsehoods in their efforts to create prejudice against the Church. An adjournment was taken till tomorrow.

Friday, November 15, 1889:

The endowment oath examination continued today, the prosecution bringing in several new witnesses and reading abundantly from *Journal of Discourses* and the *Millennial Star*. The defense did not offer any testimony today, but doubtless will tomorrow.

Saturday, November 16, 1889:

Apostle John Henry Smith and John Clark were on the stand today in defense of the Endowment oath case, as also Apostles Lund and several other brethren.

Sunday, November 17, 1889:

As I was coming to Ogden this morning Apostle Merrill who was aboard told me that many people had received through beings from the spirit world the names of the dead for whom they desired to officiate in the temple.

One young lady who came to the temple to enter plural marriage wavered while there as to whether or not it was proper for her to take this step. She told her doubts to Bro. Merrill and he advised her to go home and make it a matter of faith and prayer. She decided to do this and her intended husband was informed of her resolution in which he acquiesced. She went home and after about two weeks told the Lord that she would neither eat, drink, nor sleep till He made known to her the path of duty. At the close of the third day as she was in her room two personages appeared to her dressed in temple robes, and told her the step she was about to take was right and she would find happiness therein, and blessed her. She sent for the man to whom she had given her promise and told him of her revelation, when he told her that the Lord had informed him that she was to be his wife even before he had made her acquaintance. Thus does God strengthen his people by His revelations to those who seek Him.

Monday, November 18, 1889:

After breakfast I spent some time in writing up my journal....

After dinner we returned to meeting, where I spoke for 50 min. on the succession in the Priesthood from the Prophet Joseph down to Pres. Woodruff, as it is said some apostates argue that after the death of Joseph the authority to administer the higher ordinances of the gospel ceased with the Church and all work done in the temple since his day is void.

I was quite free in speaking and at the close of my remarks Pres. Smith asked all who felt to accept my remarks as the word of the Lord to them to say amen, and a loud response followed....

Brother W. G. Smith related the following pleasing incident today: Once when the Prophet Joseph's life was in great danger in Nauvoo, he had a body guard stationed with him in his room in the Mansion, and there was another guard outside the door of the house. In the evening of a certain day he overheard two little children in an adjoining room earnestly pray that the prophet might by preserved that night from harm and rest in peace. He immediately went and dismissed his guards saying that he knew the Lord would have respect to the prayers of these innocent children and protect him from his enemies....

Our side in the endowment oath case today impeached the testimony of some of the witnesses for the prosecution. Even E. L. T. Harrison and other outsiders testified that no oath is ever taken by Mormons against the government. The sons and daughters of a man named Wardell, who testified that he saw a man named Green blood atoned for apostasy while crossing the plains, gave evidence that their father lied. In fact the man named Green to whom he refers, still lives at Wellsville.

Tuesday, November 19, 1889:

After arriving in the city I went to the Gardo House and reported myself. While there Bro. H. J. Grant came in to get some counsel about his family matters. Since he has been engaged in speaking at the Political Clubs, efforts have been made to get some charge against him, and several times spotters got on track of his plural wife. Now he desires to get her out of the country and he received some advice as to the best method of doing so....

The naturalization case still continues with our witnesses.

Friday, November 22, 1889:

At 7:10 a.m. I boarded the south bound train. Met Apostle F. M. Lyman and his daughter, Lucy, at Provo and we together rode to Juab,...

At 7 p.m. we attended a meeting that had been appointed, at which there was a very good attendance. Bro. Lyman spoke here for 55 min. on the proper method of presenting the Stake and Ward authorities and recommended that the latter be invariably presented before the people over whom they preside, and not before the Stake Conference. After he had finished I spoke for half an hour in regard to the charity we should feel for each other's weaknesses and also warned the people against the spirit of apostasy. I was afterwards informed that there were several apostates present.

Just before going to bed I had a few moments conversation with Bro. Lyman. He told me of a letter his father had written him when he was 15 years old. Amasa Lyman was not then an apostate but a faithful apostle. He warned his son of the follies of youth and urged him to good deeds, and after giving many good instructions told him that the "hopes and interests" of his father's house depends on him. Bro. Lyman paid very little heed to the letter, but his mother cared for it and after marriage handed it to his wife. Some years afterwards he discovered the epistle among some supposedly worthless papers and saw the prophetic utterance of his then dead father.

Friday, November 29, 1889:

About 2 p.m. I went to the Gardo House where I met Joseph Walter Dietrich, a German, who for many years was a Catholic priest and labored in Austria. He joined the Church some months ago being directed to our Elders by a part of a tract which he found in a restaurant when he stopped to procure a meal. Since his baptism he has converted to the gospel some 31 members, and he having received the Priesthood, baptized them. Sine his arrival here he has been working in "Liberty Park" at gardening, and though the work is pretty severe to one unaccustomed to labor in this way, he feels contented and happy. I introduced him to Presidents Woodruff, Cannon, Smith, Lyman, B. Young and others, and acted as interpreter between them and this Elder, who is still unfamiliar with the English language. I urged him not to take offense at the actions of men in Zion, for though called Saints many are guilty of great weaknesses and follies....

Parley McFarlane, who attempted to kill a "Mormon" sheriff of Sanpete Co. some months ago, and whose case was ignored by the Grand Jury, is now in jail awaiting trial for killing two men of the D. and R. G. surveying party a few days ago. Had justice been done this murderer would have been sent to prison for his first offense and thus saved the lives of two men....

Saturday, November 30, 1889:

In the application of some "Mormons" to become naturalized Judge Anderson today gave his decision. He refused them admission because he feels that they belong to an organization that is opposed to the U. S. government. His reasons for the denial are 1st: that the Mormon church teaches that it is the actual and veritable kingdom of God on earth with the authority thereof vested in the Priesthood. 2nd: that the kingdom is of a temporal and spiritual kingdom, and should rightfully control all affairs of men. 3rd: This kingdom will eventually overthrow the United States and all other governments. 4th: That "blood atonement" is a doctrine of the Church for certain sins. 5th: That polygamy is a command of God and will exalt all who obey it. 6th: [Mormons believe] That Congress has no right to interfere with the practices of the Mormon religion, and all enactments against the people are unwarranted.

Matters seem to be closing in around us, but God is still at the helm and truth will triumph.

Sunday, December 1, 1889:

William Green, the man whom the "Liberals" tried to prove by their witness Wardell was blood atoned by the "Mormons" while crossing the plains in Dame's company in 1862, now turns up in Spanish Fork, and makes affidavit that he crossed the plains at the time and in the company named and was the only man of that name in the camp; he knew Wardell, but knows that no murder was committed. This man does not now belong to the Church—Thus the fabrications of wicked men are being exposed.

Thursday, December 5, 1889:

At 2 p.m. I attended our Council meeting at which all the First Presidency, Bro. Lyman and John W. Young were present. Our prayer room being cold we did not dress in our robes, but had our prayers, Bro. Joseph F. Smith being mouth. We then considered the matter of the Church furnishing some sketches of events in our past history from which engravings can be made for H[ubert] H. Bancroft to use in a proposed new edition of his history of Utah. Bro. Young and I were appointed to see and arrange with Utah artists for some 13 sketches....

Friday, December 6, 1889:

At 2 p.m. I went to the Gardo House where several of the Apostles met with a number of the People's Party Central Committee when the matter of an appeal from Anderson's decision in the naturalization cases to the Territorial and U.S. Supreme Courts was considered. Most of those present were in favor of carrying the case to the highest court.

The best method of protesting against Anderson's ruling was then debated. The plan which seemed to meet with the most favor was for the First Presidency and Apostles to prepare and sign a dignified paper, without even mentioning the actions of the Courts, setting forth our doctrines, and denying the wicked charges of our murderous character and disloyalty to the government. Then another paper was to be signed by the "Mormon" business men of the city giving the lie to Anderson's statements. Following these mass meetings were to be called throughout the territory to protest against the vile political scheme to which Anderson has lent himself to rob a whole people of their franchise.

About 4:30 p.m. this meeting adjourned and was followed by a meeting of Presidents Woodruff, Cannon and Smith and Bros. Lyman and Grant. We here considered and made a few changes in a circular letter that is to be sent out to the Presidents of Stakes advising them to propose to the people of their Stakes to spend the 23rd of this month—the anniversary of the Prophet's birthday—in fasting and prayer that the Lord may interpose in behalf of His people and preserve them from the power of their enemies and incline the hearts of the rulers of the nation to us. We are also to pray for a righteous decision in the Church suits now pending before the U. S. Supreme Court, and also for other things which the Spirit may prompt.

In speaking of the recent examination before Judge Anderson Father said that he understood when he had his endowments in Nauvoo that he took an oath against the murderers of the Prophet

Joseph as well as other prophets, and if he had ever met any of these who had taken a hand in that massacre he would undoubtedly have attempted to avenge the blood of the martyrs. The Prophet charged Stephen Markham to avenge his blood should he be slain: after the Prophet's death, Bro. Markham attempted to tell this to an assembly of the Saints, but Willard Richards pulled him down from the stand, as he feared the effect of the enraged people.

Bro. Joseph F. Smith was traveling some years ago near Carthage when he met a man who said he had just arrived five minutes too late to see the Smith's killed. Instantly a dark cloud seemed to overshadow Bro. Smith and he asked how this man looked upon the deed. Bro. Smith was oppressed by a most horrible feeling as he waited for a reply. After a brief pause the man answered, "Just as I have always looked upon it—that it was a d--d cold blooded murder." The cloud immediately lifted from Bro. Smith and he found that he had his open pocket knife grasped in his hand in his pocket, and he believes that had this man given his approval to that murder of the prophets he would have immediately struck him to the heart.[10]

Sunday, December 8, 1889:

At 8:20 a.m. I took the north bound train and went to Kaysville. Father, F. M. Lyman and B. H. Roberts also went thither. Bro. Barnes kindly received us at his house until meeting time. A good congregation assembled in quarterly conference at the meeting house. Bro. Roberts was the first speaker; he referred to the very evil habit of swearing, and especially of taking God's name in vain; he warned the Saints against this evil. He also spoke of our disposition to find fault with the authorities, and to sustain in our feelings all evil accusations against them. He said the Lord would not sustain us in this course.

I followed him for 35 min. referring to the Lord's many favors to us and his preserving care.

Father briefly mentioned two cases with which he was familiar where men were killed in a violent way for the reason, as he believed, that they took the name of God in vain and were very profane....

---

[10] See "Blood Atonement," in *Encyclopedia of Mormonism*, 1:131.

Tuesday, December 10, 1889:

We are very much driven with our work. O. F. Whitney's book of poems we have promised by Christmas and it will work us very hard to get them out on time....

Thursday, December 12, 1889:

At 2 p.m. attended my Quorum Circle meeting at the Gardo House. Pres. Woodruff, being quite sick, did not dress in his temple robes, but Father, Joseph F. Smith, John Henry Smith, H. J. Grant and myself did. Bro. Grant opened with prayer and J. H. Smith led in the circle. A circular letter to all the world was then read and criticized by us and afterwards signed. It announces to the world that we do not believe in the shedding of blood for apostasy or for any capital offense except by the proper officers of the law. We deny the charges of disloyalty made against us, but claim the right to denounce unlawful acts committed by any administrator of the law. We ask a suspension of sentence on the part of all people until they have examined our side of the question. The First Presidency, Twelve Apostles, and their Counselors sign[ed] this document....

Friday, December 13, 1889:

I remained at the office until about 11 p.m. We are busy with Bishop O. F. Whitney's book of poems.

Monday, December 16, 1889:

Deputy Marshal Cannon came and arrested me on a charge of conspiracy to defraud the city. It arises out of the Hydraulic Canal business. Susa Young Gates was in the office at the time and proffered to go on my bonds. We therefore started for Commissioner Harmel Pratt's office and on the way met Nephi W. Clayton who was willing to act as another bondsman. The amount required was $1,500.

I worked at the office until about 11 p.m. and then drove to M.E.C's for the night.

Tuesday, December 17, 1889:

I was engaged all day at the office where our business was moderately good. We are driving Bishop Whitney's book of poems and also James A. Little's book....

Wednesday, December 18, 1889:

Arrests are daily being made of those who were connected with the hydraulic canal company.

Thursday, December 19, 1889:

At 2 p.m. attended my Quorum Circle meeting at the Gardo House. There were present who dressed in their robes Pres. Woodruff, Joseph F. Smith, Heber J. Grant, John W. Taylor, myself and John W. Young, and F. S. Richards. John Henry Smith who did not clothe. John W. Taylor was mouth in the opening and H. J. Grant at the alter. After prayers Bro. John W. Young brought up the matter of help for John T. Caine at Washington. He felt that a clerk should be sent from here to his aid, and perhaps others to counsel him. Pres. Woodruff then stated that it had been decided to call John Morgan and B. H. Roberts to take missions through the east to rent halls, lecture and also assist John T. as much as possible in his labors at Washington. Charles Nibley was also going to the latter city to work against the admission of Idaho as a state under its present constitution which contains some very un-American clauses regarding the Mormons. In addition to these Judge Jere Wilson, a man of the highest reputation as a lawyer, ex-commissioner A. B. Carleton, Gibson and another man, who is most intimate with Pres. Harrison and his family, but whose name for the present must be concealed, are retained by the Church to work for our benefit. It is said that to this latter person is due the credit for no mention of the "Mormon" question in the President's annual message to Congress. It is thought that these employee's are sufficient for the present.

During our meeting a revelation was read which Pres. Woodruff received Sunday evening, November 24th. Propositions had been made for the Church to make some concessions to the Courts in regard to its principles. Both of Pres. Woodruff's counselors refused to advise him as to the course he should pursue, and he therefore laid the matter before the Lord. The answer came quick and strong. The word of the Lord was for us not to yield one particle of that which He had revealed and established. He had done and would continue to care for His work and those of the Saints who were faithful, and we need have no fear of our enemies when we were in the line of our duty. We are promised redemption and deliverance if we will trust in God and not in the arm of flesh. We were admonished to read and study the Word of God, and to pray often. The whole revelation was filled with words of the greatest encouragement and comfort, and my heart was filled with joy and peace during the entire reading. It sets all doubts at rest concerning the course to pursue....[11]

Saturday, December 21, 1889:

In the evening I attended a meeting of the Hydraulic Canal Co. at the City Hall. We here decided by a majority vote to retain Dickson as one of our Counsel in the indictments against us providing we can get him. A committee was appointed to see and get from him his terms. J. S. Rawlins and LeGrand Young are already engaged to assist us. Myself, G. Y. Hampton and George M. Cannon were opposed to employing Dickson on any terms, but John Nicholson, O. F. Whitney, Mayor Armstrong and others strongly urged it and a majority voted for it. We agreed to stand united in our fight.

At 10 a.m. today we appeared in court and were arraigned on our indictments, but took several days to plead.

Sunday, December 22, 1889:

At 2 p.m. attended the Tabernacle services. John W. Young was the first speaker and occupied about 20 min. He bore his testimony to the loyalty of the Saints. John Henry Smith followed for about the same length of time, and spoke of that through which we have passed for our religion and denounced that person as a liar who said we were traitors to our country. Father occupied the remainder of the time—about 25 mins. He spoke of what the Lord has done for us in the past and His promises concerning the future, and then advised all

---

[11]   See Appendix One: Plural Marriage Issues in the Abraham H. Cannon Journals.

the Saints to read for their comfort and strength the 14th and 22nd chapters of 1 Nephi in the Book of Mormon. He referred to our fast which the First Presidency recommend should commence this evening at sundown. In our prayers we should not condemn our enemies but leave them in the hands of God; we should, however, pray for our own sins to be forgiven, and ask that the hearts of the nation's rulers might be softened towards our people....

Monday December 23, 1889, Salt Lake City:

This is the anniversary of the Prophet Joseph Smith's birthday, and has been set apart as a day of fasting and prayer for all the Saints throughout the Church. About 8 a.m. I had prayers with Mina and the children. I then drove to M.E.C's and prayed with her. At 10 a.m. met at the Gardo House with presidents Woodruff, Cannon and Smith, Apostles John H. Smith, H. J. Grant and John W. Taylor; Counselors J. W. Young and D. H. Wells. All but the two latter dressed in their temple robes. We then kneeled down, and commencing with Bro. Wells, each of us prayed until Pres. Woodruff had his turn. Bro. Joseph F. Smith was strongest in his prayer and urged that Baskin should be made blind, deaf and dumb unless he would repent of his wickedness.

In the prayer we all kneeled with our faces in.

Thereafter those who were clothed prayed in our circle with Father as mouth....

At 7 p.m. attended a Hydraulic Canal meeting at the City Hall. The committee in charge of the matter reported that they had engaged W. H. Dickson at $2,500, J. L. Rawlins at $1,000 and LeGrand Young at $1,000 to defend us in court against the charge of conspiracy. It is expected that all the indictments against the City and County offices and private citizens will be tried in four cases, and for each case that comes to the jury we must pay $250 additional. Dickson hopes, however, to get most of the indictments quashed before they come to trial. A committee was appointed to divide the attorneys' total fees equitably among the three sets of men indicted. We also agreed to incorporate the Canal Co., and a committee was appointed to prepare articles of incorporation....

It is remarkable how much interest this Fast Day has aroused. Persons who have been noted for their disregard of religious matters have, in many instances, fasted, prayed and attended the meetings which have been held in the various Wards in the morning and afternoon. Even little children have fasted. Everywhere the meetings were crowded, and a most peaceful and heavenly influence prevailed. Surely the Lord has blessed the Saints this day, and no doubt the results will continue to be seen.

Wednesday, December 25, 1889:

After breakfast I went to the office and remained about two hours writing my journal....

Thursday, December 26, 1889:

Attended my Quorum meeting at 2 p.m. at which there were present Bros. Woodruff, Cannon, J. F. Smith and J. H. Smith. We did not dress in our robes, but merely had prayers, Bro. Joseph F. being mouth....

Bro. A. O. Smoot desired some counsel in regard to the Temple Block at Provo. It was bought by the Church some years ago from a man named Bitton, and though a deed was received it was never recorded, and is now lost. This Bitton is now an apostate and when he found that the deed was unrecorded and lost, he refused to make a new deed, but offers to sell again to the Church for about $2500 for 12 Acres. Bro. Smoot was advised to obtain the land in the cheapest possible way either by purchase, compromise or law suit.

Charles Nibley stated that it would do his business (lumbering) great injury if he were called to immediately go to Washington to look after Idaho matters. Still he would do so if necessary. It was left for him and Bro. Budge to decide which of them would go....

We printed the last form today of O. F. Whitney's *Poetical Writings*. This is the quickest book that has ever been issued from the Utah press. It contains 208 pages and we did not receive the job until Nov. 22, 1889, after which we had to get the paper on which to print, which delayed us 12 days. The class of work also wins for us great praise.

Saturday, December 28, 1889:

I went to the office at 7:30 a.m. and spent two hours in reading the exchange and writing. We bound and delivered this morning the first copies of Bishop Whitney's book....

My afternoon was spent at the office in reading proofs, answering letters, etc. We today completed and bound James A. Little's book *From Kirtland to Salt Lake City*. It is a work of 260 pages.

CHAPTER THREE

⌒∞⌒

1890

Monday, January 6, 1890:

Pres. Woodruff today told Father he wanted him to prepare and go to Washington as soon as possible to labor for our people there during the present session of Congress.[1]

The U. S. Supreme Court today decided that the Governor of this Territory has the right to appoint the Territorial Auditor and Treasurer. Nephi Clayton and James Jack have held these offices respectively since 1879, when they were elected by the vote of the people. But Governor Murray claimed the right to appoint these officers and named Arthur Pratt and Bolivar Roberts for the positions. The elected officers, however, refused to yield until the matter was decided by the highest court. Now it is settled that the Governor with the legislative council can appoint these officials.

Tuesday, January 7, 1890:

In a fornication case tried yesterday before Judge Henderson in Ogden where the parties involved were not "Mormons," the prosecuting attorney said it had come to be thought and remarked that the law against this and kindred crimes in this Territory was to be applied in a different way when "Mormons" were defendants than when the accused were Gentiles; and the judge showed that this was his understanding, for when the female in the case refused to testify, instead of forcing her to testify by committing her to the penitentiary for contempt as he had done "Mormon" female witnesses who declined to testify, he permitted the case to be dismissed. How can

---

[1] President Cannon's difficult mission included trying to halt or slow efforts by anti-Mormons in Congress to pass legislation detrimental to the Mormons in general and plural marriage in particular.

we be expected to respect the law when such partiality is shown, and such manifest injustice is practiced? We at least must despise the law administrators.[2]

Thursday, January 9, 1890:

At 2 p.m. I went to Council meeting in the Gardo House. There were present, W. Woodruff, George Q. Cannon, Joseph F. Smith, H. J. Grant, John W. Taylor and myself. We dressed in our robes. I was mouth in the opening prayer and Father at the altar. After prayers the matter of the Literary and Scientific Association selling the old Council House corner on Main Street to enable it to build on the museum lot was discussed. I favored the sale but others were reluctant about it, but Pres. Woodruff favored selling and it was therefore understood that a purchaser should be sought.

I also brought up the matter of employment for Bro. Dietrich and it was finally decided that he should be employed in the Historian's office to correspond with German papers in Europe and America and do other writing. His letters, however, are to be submitted to me for approval before being sent away. This will be a blessing, I think, to this good man....

I was told today that Vandercook is after the appointment as city marshal, and he desires to make a record for himself in capturing prominent "Mormons" who have more than one wife. For this purpose he has engaged "spotters" to watch me among others. May the Lord frustrate him!...

Friday, January 10, 1890:

I fasted till 2 p.m. and prayed that the Lord would not let me fall into the power of deputy marshals....

Monday, January 13, 1890 {Wanship, Utah}:

In Ogden I met and had a short conversation with Father who is on his way to Washington.[3]

---

[2] See Appendix One: Plural Marriage Issues in the Abraham H. Cannon Journals

[3] See AHC journals, 6 January 1890 and note 1 above.

After reaching the city I spent several hours at the office reading the Hymn Book and *Juvenile* proofs. I also called on Pres. Woodruff and reported my labors and had some talk with him concerning Dan Jones' book *Forty Years among the Indians*, which we are printing. He had been informed that the author was censuring in his book the authorities of the Church in Arizona, and Pres. Woodruff did not approve of this. I told him that some features of this kind had been erased from the manuscript, and others would be if I found them, as I was revising the copy. This satisfied Pres. Woodruff. I told Bro. Jones of the President's inquiry, and he was willing to have anything objectionable withdrawn from the work....

Wednesday, January 15, 1890:

At 6 p.m. I went to a meeting at the Gardo House where a Legislative committee came to get the views of the authorities in relation to free schools in the Territory. It seems as though it will be necessary to amend the law to provide for free schools and compulsory education, and our brethren feel that we should introduce a bill of this nature and thus receive whatever credit is to be had from the adoption of such a measure. Pres. [Brigham] Young always opposed free schools because he feared it would pauperize the people and make them feel that the state owed them an education. My own feelings are in favor of free schools....[4]

Thursday, January 16, 1890:

I drove to the office in the sleigh at 8 o'clock and spent the forenoon in writing a cut article on "England's Queen" for the *Juvenile*. At 2 p.m. I went to the Gardo House where I met with Bros. Joseph F. Smith, Moses Thatcher, J. H. Smith and H. J. Grant. We did not dress in our robes but had prayer, Bro. J. H. Smith being mouth. Pres. Joseph F. Smith then stated that the First Presidency had decided to give Parley P. Pratt's family $6,750 as an offset to a claim of $13,500 which they make for the use which the Church has had of Apostle P. P. Pratt's books, *The Voice of Warning* and *The Key*

---

[4] See Stanley S. Ivins, "Free Schools Come to Utah," *Utah Historical Quarterly* 22 (Oct. 1954): 321-42.

to Theology. The Church does not, however, recognize or acknowledge the claim, but gives this sum as a donation to the family, and it is now understood that P. P. Pratt's heirs will hereafter control the copyright of these two publications....

Saturday, January 18, 1890:

At 2 p.m. I attended a meeting of our Quorum at the Gardo House. There were present, Presidents Woodruff and Smith, Apostles Thatcher, J. H. Smith, H. J. Grant, John W. Taylor, M. W. Merrill, myself and Pres. Lorenzo Snow; also the following brethren: James Sharp, F. S. and C. C. Richards, W. H. Seegmiller, C. W. Penrose, and Bishop Collett. The matter under consideration was as to free schools for the Territory. Each of the brethren spoke, and the majority were opposed to free schools, but in view of the present perplexing school laws which were enacted contrary to the advice of Pres. Young and others, and which are anything but good, it was thought best to go a little further and prepare the very best school law possible and then submit it to this council. The establishment of free schools by our people it is thought will have a good effect among the people of this nation in proving that we are the friends of education. Free schools will therefore be established....

Monday, January 20, 1890:

At 10 o'clock I went to the Gardo House where some members of the People's Political Party met with the Apostles to consider election matters. All the brethren present expressed themselves in regard to matters and favored, in view of our critical situation, a fusion with the outside element providing we can get several strong men to run on our ticket. It was proposed to give them the mayorship, Treasuryship and five members of the City Council....

At the close of this meeting Pres. Woodruff requested John W. Taylor and myself to remain with himself, Pres. J. F. Smith and Lorenzo Snow to talk about Bullion Beck mining matters. He did not approve of the course that had been taken in withholding from the California Company the amount of stock due them for their labors in effecting a compromise by which a protracted law-suit and perhaps the eventual loss of the property was avoided. John W. Taylor then went into a lengthy and detailed statement of affairs connected with the mine, and said he believed H. B. Clawson, S. W. Sears and Isaac Trumbo had formed a conspiracy to defraud the stock-holders out of 25% of their stock, and he for one did not feel like yielding either stock or dividends until he was convinced that there was a company in existence such as had a rightful claim upon the proceeds of the mine. I maintained that no matter whether or not the California Company was a sham, we had still pledged ourselves to yield 25% of our stock when an option held by California parties had expired and after a dissolution of such company. Now the proper time to fulfill our pledge had arrived, and because we might believe a fraud had been committed that did not justify any one in committing another fraud. Besides I thought that Pres. Taylor's heirs, John Beck and all others who had dedicated stock and then received it back from Father who was appointed by Pres. Taylor as custodian thereof, had broken a covenant with God, as I felt they had no more right to that which they had dedicated than to any property of Pres. Woodruff or any other man. Pres. Woodruff finally decided to bring the whole matter for adjudication before the Quorum as soon as Father returns....

Tuesday, January 21, 1890:

At 10 o'clock I went to the Gardo House where the Quorum met with some of the political leaders and talked over matters. It was decided to leave it with the Central Committee to meet with the delegates who were elected at the People's Primaries last night and prepare a ticket, after the committee has met with us and got our ideas about the men who should be nominated.

After this meeting I told Pres. Woodruff that we three boys thought of protesting to Moses Thatcher against his jeopardizing the interests of all the stock holders in the Bullion Beck mine by his failing to fulfill his agreement in delivering to the California Co. their share of the stock. For should they enter suit I feared that the whole property might be lost. Pres. Woodruff approved of this course.

While here, Miller, the crazy man from the 11th Ward, who walked through the Tabernacle in fantastic garb the first Sunday in the new year, came to see the President and I remained to hear his story. He tells of numerous visions, revelations and visitations he has had, and claims that he is the great latter-day Moses of whom the Scriptures speak who is to deliver the Saints from bondage and trouble. He says that Mormons have persecuted him and destroyed his property, which he does not like. Pres. Woodruff told him that it was wrong for anyone to persecute him and he should be left in peace. This seemed to satisfy the poor weak-minded man, and he went away....

Wednesday, January 22, 1890:

At 2 p.m. I was at the Gardo House with some bound volumes of the *Juvenile* and Books of Mormon for the brethren, who praised our work very much and were grateful for our presents....

Friday, January 24, 1890:

I agreed with Susa Young Gates this morning to become a half owner in her magazine, *The Young Women's Journal* on the following terms: She is to have full charge of the Editorial department and I am to control the entire business. All expenses are to be first paid from the proceeds of the business, and then the remainder, if any there be, is to be equally divided. Should there be a loss we share alike in that. I stipulated, however, that I am not to be known in connection with the business.

At noon Pres. Woodruff sent for me, and desired us boys to enter our protest with Moses Thatcher against the with-holding of the Bullion-Beck mining stock from the California company. He has had a talk with H. B. Clawson and I. Trumbo and they have apparently convinced him that the parties in California will certainly cause a great deal of trouble if their rights in this mine are not respected.[5] Bro. Joseph F. then went on to tell many of the things which Trumbo, Badlam and their party had done for the benefit of the

---

[5] For this date, President Woodruff's journal states: "I had an interview with Trumbo and Clawson."

Church and for which they had refused to accept any pay. They had traveled through the United States and had subsidized the leading newspapers and prevented their making any very hostile statements concerning the "Mormons" during their statehood movement. Of course the primary object of their visits to the newspapers was to protect the C. P. Railway interests, but in every case they had also made the "Mormon" question an object of their care.

They gained such control of Dyer when he was in office as to prevent him from making any very diligent search for certain offenders against the law, and they also checked him in his search for property that might be confiscated, and thus saved considerable means for the Church.

Isaac Trumbo succeeded in getting a bill passed by the Nevada legislature so as to prevent any prosecution of Father for "attempted bribery," which charge it was intended by bitter Utah officials to try and bring against him for trying to get the Nevada marshal to release him for $1,000 when he was captured some years ago.

And in many other ways have these people befriended us, and it would now be a most disastrous thing to make them our enemies. It is even said that they hold our present U. S. Marshal (Parsons) under their thumb, and are restraining him to our advantage....

Sunday, January 26, 1890:

I then went to Sarah's and spent the time till 2 p.m. when I attended the Tabernacle Services. Bro. James E. Talmage was the speaker. He gave a very pleasing discourse of one hour in which he spoke of the forces of nature and their control by God who also rules among men and will eventually work out all his purposes with regard to his children....

Wednesday, January 29, 1890:

The Liberals are performing the most devilish antics to prevent the members of the People's Party from voting. Contrary to the ruling of the Commissioners they place the burden of proof upon the accused when they are cited to appear to show cause why their names should not be stricken from the registration lists. Contrary to Judge

Zane's ruling they also strike from the lists the names of all men who ever had two wives regardless of the fact that the polygamous relation long since ceased which according to Judge Zane entitles a man to citizenship. No rights of the people are respected and no claims of their enemies ignored. It is a most unholy crusade that is now being waged against the Saints, and will one day be recognized as a great outrage....

Thursday, January 30, 1890:

At 2 p.m. I attended our Quorum meeting at which were present: W. Woodruff, Joseph F. Smith, John Henry Smith and myself. We did not dress in our robes, but had prayers in which the President was mouth. A petition from Edward W. Tullidge was then read in which he asks the Church to purchase 100 copies[6] of his history of Northern Utah for $500. The brethren were favorable to the purchase, but owing to the great lack of funds in the Church at present the First Presidency took the matter under advisement for the present....

Friday, January 31, 1890:

At this time I went to the Gardo House where the following brethren met: W. Woodruff, Joseph F. Smith, Moses Thatcher, M. W. Merrill, F. M. Lyman, H. B. Clawson, James Jack, George Reynolds, F. J. Cannon and myself. We were in session till nearly 2 p.m. talking about Bullion-Beck mine matters. Bro. Thatcher insists upon knowing who comprise the California Co., who demand and expect to receive 25% of the mine stock. On this being made known he expresses a willingness to give his proportion of the stock. Otherwise, however, he does not feel like giving a cent, but will do so if Pres. Woodruff requests it. H. B. Clawson feels unable to divulge the names of those he represents without their permission which up to the present he has not received. Most of the brethren felt that these California stock-holders should be known to those resident here, but Frank and I maintained that this information has nothing to do with our agreement to deliver 25% to them. They fulfilled their agreement

---

[6] It appears that a one (1) has been written over a five for this number.

and it now only remains for us to do as we agreed—turn over the promised stock, and then we can demand and secure an investigation of the whole proceeding, and if fraud has been committed we can have recourse of law on the guilty parties.

Presidents Woodruff and Smith made a statement as to what our California friends had done for us in allaying prejudice and restraining Utah officials and other prominent men when they were inclined to attack us and they felt it would be very wrong for us, on account of this mine, to antagonize these men and thus jeopardize our interests in various parts of the country.

A better feeling prevailed at the close of the meeting and it was left for the brethren of the company to settle the matter....[7]

In a case brought before Judge Zane today where a voter tried to prevent the removal of his name from the registration list, the judge decided that he had no right to interfere, which means that the decisions of corrupt registrars are supreme as to who shall be allowed to vote. It is one of the greatest infamies ever perpetrated under a free government.

At the Gardo House the question arose this morning as to whether the face of a woman who has had her endowments should be veiled or not when her coffin is closed on her dead body. Pres. Woodruff did not decide in the absence of any written law on the subject, but Bro. Joseph F. thought the face should be covered as this was the course pursued in early days of the Church, and it was doubtless done in accordance with some instructions of the Prophet.

Saturday, February 1, 1890:

At 11 a.m. I went to the Stake Priesthood meeting in the Assembly Hall. After the usual business Dr. Isaacson, at his own request, then made a few remarks in which he bore his testimony to the truth of the work and its final triumph. Pres. Samuel R. Bennion of the Uintah Stake then spoke; he spoke of the county where he lived and encouraged those who desired to move away from this county to go to Uintah. I followed him and urged our young folks to

---

[7] For this date, President Woodruff's journal records: "I met with the Beck Mine Com. Not a pleasant meeting." See AHC journals, 28 January 1891.

remain here and build up homes in this valley instead of scattering out. I then urged the Priesthood to use their influence to prevent the Saints from dealing with those not of our faith which course will do more than any other thing in our power to relieve us from the oppression under which we suffer. I also proclaimed against the encouragement which is given to the feeling that we must go into bondage in order that the Lord may send "a Moses" to deliver us. I feel that if we will only do as God has commanded, we need go no further into bondage....

Sunday, February 2, 1890:

I occupied the whole day at the farm in reading and study. I was not feeling the very best....

A new invention: Leonide Aposteloff, a Russian engineer of considerable experience and considered an authority on all matters pertaining to submarine navigation, claims to have invented a vessel in which the Atlantic Ocean can be crossed in 28 hrs.—the whole distance—3000 miles—to be made under water. His assertions are entitled to some consideration. He asserts that he can travel 110 miles in less than 50 minutes....

The main idea is the simple but effective application of the spiral movement to a metallic boat so shaped as to offer the least resistance to hydraulic pressure. This is achieved by the construction of a long oval boat or craft of iron and steel with spiral groovings and a fish tail propeller. It will only be necessary for the vessel to come to the surface once in every 34 hours and this merely for the renewal of the air. Light is obtained through a belt of heavy glass which is about midway between the ends of the boat....

This invention greatly reminds me of the barges which the Lord commanded the brother of Jared to build as recorded in the Book of Mormon, Ether 2:16.... The end was also pointed. But the ancients had no power for propelling their barges, and it required the wind 344 days to drive them from the place of embarkation in Asia to the promised land on the western coast of North America. No doubt the plan given by the Lord to Jared's brother was very excellent for such barges.

Monday, February 3, 1890:

I was interrupted considerably during the day by persons coming in to talk with me about various matters of business. Among these were Sisters Susa Gates and Ellen F. Jakeman, the latter of whom I engaged to write for the *Juvenile*. Also Sister Julie Richards came to see about the prizes we have offered for articles and I explained to her that we proposed to pay for all articles we used whether they gained the prizes or not. This pleased her and she promised to contribute some articles to the paper....

The U. S. Supreme Court today decided that the Idaho test oath, which disfranchises all Mormons, is constitutional. According to this oath no man who believes in plural marriage or who is a member of our Church can vote or hold office. This decision will doubtless have the effect to eventually debar every Mormon in the whole United States of the rights of free men. Speedily are the safeguards to religious liberty in this republic being swept away, and the time is fast approaching when the Saints will be called to fulfill their destiny and save the Constitution from being trampled underfoot....

Monday, February 17, 1890:

Until about 10:30 a.m. I was engaged in writing my journal and an incident of faith for the *Juvenile*.... I then went to meeting....

Bro. John W. Taylor then spoke strongly on the Word of Wisdom, the law of tithing, etc., and strongly urged all the Saints young and old to cease using tea and coffee, tobacco, liquor, and other things which are forbidden. His remarks were very interesting and instructive.

At the close of this meeting we called the Presidency of the Stake and High Council together and had a plain talk with them. Bro. Taylor advised them to build a vestry to their meeting house and use the upstairs room of it for a prayer circle. He then urged the brethren to be exemplary in all their habits and whatever they desired the Saints to be they should themselves set the example in their own lives. After advising them in regard to their duties he made the prediction that all who would follow his advice from that time should prosper both temporally and spiritually, while those who neglected these duties should go backward.

I also spoke to the brethren and told them to stand at the head of their families and not allow their wives to govern and rule over them....

At 2 p.m. the meeting house was filled and I spoke first for about 40 min. I advised the Saints to deal only with our people and build each other up. The results of disobedience to this advice I pointed out. I also spoke upon the education of the hand, head and heart which we should always encourage....

Bro. [John W.] Taylor then spoke for three-quarters of an hour on the mixture of the races in the Southern States where the whites cohabit with the blacks and have children of various colors; he also referred to the killing of unborn children in the north and said he did not know which of these evils was the worst, but because of these awful crimes the Lord would pour out his judgments on this nation. He proclaimed loudly against unchastity and drunkenness

Our meeting closed about 4:30 p.m. and we went to Bro. Francis' home where we had supper and spent the evening in pleasant conversation. Bro. Taylor related considerable of his missionary experience in the Southern States which was very interesting. He told of the following *Prophecy and its fulfillment*: He was laboring in Kentucky when one day as he was walking through the woods two men, delegates from a mass meeting which had been held in the neighborhood met and told him that they had decided he must leave the state. He asked the reason of this decision and was told it was because he was ruining the neighborhood by his strange doctrines. He commenced to tell them about Paul, the apostle, when one of them spoke up and said "We don't care a damn for Paul, but you have got to leave the state." He then told them he would not leave, because as an American citizen he claimed the right to remain where he desired so long as he broke no law. He continued his labors and one day in a public meeting a man and his family arose and asked for baptism. They were taken to a pond and baptized and there on the edge of the water Elder Taylor predicted that many more would be baptized shortly in that place. Elder Taylor and H. W. Bigler his companion therefore commenced to labor in that neighborhood, and in a very short time they had converted a number of families. One evening they called at a house and Bro. Taylor told the proprietor that they were ministers of the gospel and desired a meal and bed. He then promised the family that the angels of God would visit them that night and give them testimony as to the real character of their guests if they would entertain them. They were received and provided for. In the morning the lady arose early and prepared breakfast after which the brethren took their departure without once thinking of the previous night's promise. As they were passing out of the front gate John W. remarked to a little girl who had followed him from the house that there would be a storm that day, though at that moment the sky was clear and there was no indication of bad weather. In that country a storm indicates a hurricane and not merely a little rain. The girl ran back to the house and told her parents what had been said. The father began immediately to nail up his windows and doors, and he had scarcely done so when a most violent wind swept over the place utterly demolishing the orchard and nearly capsizing the house. After the storm was passed the man hitched up his team and went to find the elders, but failed. Elder Taylor felt urged, however, in a few days to return to this gentleman's house, and on doing so found the family ready to receive baptism. They then related how the angels had visited them on the night of the elders' first visit and given them such visions as convinced parents as well as children that these men were servants of God.

Friday, February 28, 1890:

At the latter hour [10:30 a.m.] I went by invitation to the Gardo House. There, where we usually hold our prayer circle, the following brethren met: Presidents Woodruff, Cannon and Smith. Bros. John R. Winder, B.Y. Hampton, F. Armstrong, J. W. Fox, Jr., N. V. Jones, George Reynolds, Arthur Winter and myself. Before the business of the meeting commenced we were all placed under obligation to keep the matter entirely secret. Pres. Woodruff then stated that his mind had been considerably exercised of late in regard to the prospect of our people being taxed under "Liberal" rule to such an extent as to ruin them. After thought and prayer on the subject he felt impressed that we should carefully begin to sell our surplus property at the exorbitant figures now being paid by outsiders for real estate, and reinvest our money on good security, thus shifting the burden of taxation from our shoulders to those of our enemies. All the brethren expressed their approval in general of the plan, and Father expressed the idea that he believed the Lord was, for some good purpose, turning the tide of Gentile wealth in our direction, and he felt that we should take advantage of the event. The necessity of perfect secrecy and the utmost care in this movement was apparent to all, for should it once be known among the Saints that it would not meet with disapproval to sell their property to speculators a great panic would immediately ensue. Bros. Winder, Armstrong, Hampton, Fox and Jones and I were appointed a committee to take this matter in hand and work it up. We accordingly met at 2:30 p.m. and after considerable discussion adopted [the] following recommendations: That two or more real estate agencies be organized under the management of B. Y. Hampton and Co., and Jones, Fox and Co. Also a loan agency be organized under the direction of Armstrong, Winder and Co. These businesses to be under the control absolutely of one Board of Directors, though ostensibly owned by the parties named. Further, that the First Presidency form part of the Board of Directors. That we rent the Amussen building (containing six rooms besides the store) at a monthly rental of $300 for 5 years. It was found that the brethren present could immediately list over one and one half million dollars worth of property. Our recommends were approved and the bargain with Amussen was ordered closed.[8]

About 6 p.m. we adjourned,…

A few days ago John Q. got me to let him have my check for $1650 for which he gave me his check for a like amount in return. This latter, however, when sent to Ogden was not honored, on account of lack of funds, and it was thrown back on my hands. It placed me in a very awkward position. John Q. telephoned me that he would meet the amount as soon as he could. I am being taught some very severe lessons by favoring him in a financial way.

---

[8] See AHC journals 9 October 1890.

Saturday, March 1, 1890:

I had to borrow $5000 of Father this morning to tide us over a few days.

Pres. Woodruff is 83 years old today....

At 2:30 p.m. I attended our Real Estate Committee meeting at the Gardo House where we matured our plans more minutely for the conduct of our business. I placed the 20 Acre piece on the list of Bro. Hampton to sell. We reported to the Presidency that we recommended the opening of our places of business immediately, and they approved of the plan....

Monday, March 3, 1890:

At 2 p.m. I met with our Real Estate Committee where satisfactory reports of progress were made. The necessity of crowding on the market Father's low land and other suburban property where the price is liable to decline was shown, and the promise was given by the brethren to push these pieces to the front....

Tuesday, March 4, 1890:

I then went to the B. B. & C. mine meeting, where Father's stock was virtually cut off from representation in the Board of Directors, and the excuse for this unjust policy is that our views in regard to the dues of the California Company are at variance with those of the majority of the stock-holders—one very great [reason] in my opinion why we should be represented. Frank, myself and George Reynolds were each in turn voted down, and the following were elected as a Board for the ensuing year: Moses Thatcher, William B. Preston, John Beck, Alonzo Hyde and Richard J. Taylor. I told the brethren that all their pretensions in regard to desiring minority representation were vain as was apparent by their injustice in today's election. The following officers were elected: Moses Thatcher, Pres.; John Beck, Vice Pres.; George J. Taylor, Secretary; William B. Preston, Treasurer; and William B. Preston and Frank J. Cannon an auditing committee. The meeting then adjourned and I hastened to the Gardo House to meet the Real Estate and Loan committees. There being no particular business we adjourned. At 4 p.m. the B. B. & C.

stockholders met at the Gardo House where we were in session three hours. Bro. Joseph F. Smith at Pres. Woodruff's request, sought to act as peacemaker, and prevent the mine affairs from being taken into court. But there was no disposition manifested on the part of Thatcher, Hyde, Preston and the Taylor boys to yield to the demands of the California company. They persist in the belief that the strong California men who were ostensibly the owners of the expected 25% of stock own but a mere pittance, while Alex Badlam anticipates receiving the great bulk of it. With this belief they refuse to yield a single share of stock. Hyrum Clawson stated that he held receipts for the disbursement of all the dividends heretofore paid to the California people and these he would produce at the proper time. We adjourned till tomorrow....[9]

Wednesday, March 5, 1890:

I then went...to the Gardo House where our B. B. and C. meeting of last evening was continued. The brethren were determined to prevent Badlam or Clawson from receiving any stock in the mine. The question was then put direct to each one present, "Will you give to Pres. Woodruff, to be used as he may see proper, 25% of the stock in the mine, which you own?" Father's stock, William B. Preston, Frank, George Reynolds and Alonzo Hyde (personally) voted in the affirmative. Moses Thatcher, John W. and George J. Taylor evaded the question, though the former positively stated last night that he would give a quarter or the whole of his stock to Pres. Woodruff.

About 2 p.m. the meeting adjourned....

Thursday, March 6, 1890:

We did not hold our circle meeting today because of the fact that the Court holds that Receiver Dyer can obtain higher rent than is now being paid by the Church for the Gardo House, Historian's Office and Tithing offices and yards, for which cause bids have been called for and visitors are daily inspecting the premises with a view to

---

[9] For this date President Woodruff's diary states that "Joseph F. Smith met with the Board of Beck mine. They had a bad spirit."

renting. Therefore our altar has been removed from our prayer room....

It is remarkable how high the prices are becoming on Salt Lake Real Estate, both in and near the city. Acreage which could have been bought 3 years ago for $300 per acre now commands $2,000 or upwards per acre. Business and residence property are correspondingly inflated....

Friday, March 7, 1890:

At 2 p.m. I met the real estate and loan committees at the Gardo House where we talked over the situation. At present there is much more property for sale than there are buyers, and unfortunately none of our poor property is yet disposed of,...

Saturday, March 8, 1890:

I went to the office at 8 a.m. and spent the forenoon in reading proofs and writing a cut article on the Russian naval station, Cronstadt, for the *Juvenile*. Frank and I secured from Alonzo Hyde, the Trustee of the Bullion-Beck and California Co. mining stock, an order for the transfer to Father of that to which he is entitled. This order we obtained this afternoon and it is directed to the Secretary (Badlam) of the California Company....

Sunday, March 9, 1890:

At Father's request I went to the Davis Stake Conference today which was held at East Bountiful. I went on the 8:10 train to West Bountiful where Israel Call met us with a conveyance and took us to his Father's—Anson Call—where we remained until meeting time. The forenoon services consisted of remarks by Seymour B. Young and Anson Call. The former occupied an hour and ten minutes in speaking of how God has dealt with wicked men who have opposed truth and righteousness. Bro. Call occupied ten minutes in relating an incident of the Prophet Joseph's life. Joseph was once summoned to appear before Judge Stephen A. Douglas at Carthage on a trumped up charge. Having good reason to fear that his life would be in danger he selected 50 firm and trusty men from the Nauvoo legion to enter Carthage unsuspected and to be near to protect him with their side arms in case of danger. He and some of his friends then went openly to court. As he entered the place of judgment Judge Douglas stepped down from his seat, greeted him cordially and gave him a comfortable place to sit. At this mark of esteem from the Court the crowd hissed, but the Judge took no notice of this except to call order. Joseph's case was not reached in the forenoon, and when court adjourned Douglas locked arms with the Prophet and walked across the square to the hotel. Here he seated Joseph at the head of the table and called on him to say grace. At the conclusion of the meal he returned to the Court House locked arm in arm with Joseph. The trial in the afternoon resulted in the acquittal of the accused. As soon as the 50 who had been called to be near Joseph saw how he was treated by the Judge they felt that his safety was assured. When Mr. Douglas was subsequently taken to task by some of his acquaintances for his friendliness to the "Mormon" leader, he said, "Joseph Smith is the only independent man I ever saw. We are always wondering what effect our actions will have upon our constituents or friends, but he does what he thinks is right regardless of what people think or say of him."[10]

At noon I went with a number of others to dinner with Bro. Anson Call....

Monday, March 10, 1890:

At 12 o'clock Frank and I visited Father and talked with him in relation to his mining stock. We urged him to sell and thus be free from an uncertain thing. Frank urged that I go to California and receive in person Father's certificate of stock in the Bullion, Beck and California Company.

I went from the Gardo House (which has been rented by John R. Winder for $450 per month) to a directors meeting of the State Bank. We voted to increase our capital stock to$500,000, but before proceeding further in the business H. J. Grant and myself were appointed a committee to wait on the First Presidency and see if we

---

[10] This seems to be another account of an incident found in *Comprehensive History of the Church* 2:79-82.

could effect a consolidation with Zion's Savings Bank increasing its stock and paying its stockholders a fair price for their investments and good will. We saw the President and his counselors in the afternoon but they received our proposition with coldness, and promised to consider the matter. I personally think a union of the two banks would be advantageous....

Tuesday, March 11, 1890:

After this meeting Bro. Grant and I called on the Presidency to receive their answer in relation to the proposed bank amalgamation. They did not look favorably upon the union, as they expressed a fear that the stock which our bank proposed to take would so greatly out-value theirs that young Utah would have a big majority and could run it to suit themselves. They contemplate however, an increase of Savings Bank stock but it will be then too late for the purposes of our proposition. I was disappointed at the decision, because I can see many advantages which a union would make for both banks....

Thursday, March 27, 1890:

At 2 p.m. I went to my Quorum meeting where there were present W. Woodruff, Father, Joseph F. Smith, H. J. Grant, John W. Taylor, John W. Young and myself. We all dressed in our robes, and Joseph F. Smith was mouth in opening and John W. Taylor at the altar. After prayers Bro. J. W. Taylor asked that he might go, after conference, to visit his family in Canada. Permission was given him.

Bro. John W. Young also asked that he might be permitted to go on a mission to Palestine before very long. To this all the brethren assented, but Bro. Joseph F. insisted that he should first settle in full all his debts, and put himself straight with the world....

Saturday, April 5, 1890:

From 8 till 10 a.m. I was engaged at the office in writing a cut article for the *Juvenile* on Charlemagne. At the latter time I went to meeting. John W. Taylor was the first speaker: he felt that our failure to receive revelation from God is due to the fact that we are too much engaged with the affairs of this world and our efforts are to accumulate wealth that perishes instead of eternal riches. He occupied 15 min.

Heber J. Grant followed for the same length of time, and bore his testimony to the truth.

John Henry Smith spoke 20 min. and strongly advised the people against neglecting the commands of God in relation to the Word of Wisdom. He felt that as soon as we were in a position to refrain from the use of tobacco alone we would be more free than we ever yet have been.

Francis M. Lyman followed in a similar strain, and counseled the abstaining from meat in large quantities, and also advised all to frequently visit the meetings and partake of the sacrament, and be sure to have the proper spirit when we thus ate and drank.

Moses Thatcher followed for 20 min. and referred to financial affairs. He hoped the day would soon come when the apostles would be relieved of financial affairs connected with the community and be permitted to devote themselves exclusively to the ministry. As for himself it would be the happiest day of his life if the Presidency would today relieve him of his positions in various businesses and call him to go abroad or labor at home in his Priesthood.

At noon we went to the Gardo House, the First Council of the Seventies (Jacob Gates, S. B. Young, John Morgan and B. H. Roberts) meeting with us. I was requested to act as secretary which I did.

The first matter considered was the filling up of the quorum of the First Seven Presidents of the Seventies. Job Pingree, Joseph W. Summerhays and George Reynolds were suggested and after some little consultation the latter was selected without a dissenting vote.

Next the advisability of the Saints uniting with either the Republicans or Democrats in politics was considered. It was discussed pro and con for some time and finally Pres. Woodruff announced that he did not feel otherwise than that we should hold ourselves aloof from both parties. This feeling agreed with the ideas of all present. Bro. John Morgan suggested that we state to the two parties in this Territory that "we are now out of politics, but you gentlemen bring forth your best men, and we will vote for those who best suit us." This was adopted as our feeling by unanimous vote....[11]

Sunday, April 6, 1890:

I took dinner at Aunt Amanda Cannon's and at 2 p.m. was at meeting in the Tabernacle where I opened the same with prayer. Father spoke for an hour and 10 min. on the beauty, comprehensiveness and symmetry of the Gospel. His sermon was a strong testimony of the divinity of Joseph Smith's mission.

Pres. Woodruff made a few closing remarks asking the blessing of God to be upon the people. Conference then adjourned till October.

An overflow meeting was held in the Assembly Hall this afternoon and was crowded.

At 4 p.m. the First Presidency and Twelve Apostles met at the Gardo House where the matter of selling Salt Lake Real Estate was considered. All voted to approve the advice already given in regard to this matter, but the arrangement of the details was left for further arrangement.

At 7 p.m. I attended a Sunday School Union meeting in the Tabernacle. The building was well filled....

Bro. James E. Talmage next gave his ideas concerning the grading of S. S. classes. He felt that more care should be exercised in the placing of children in classes suited to their capacity, and that proper books for exercise should be obtained.

Bro. John Morgan spoke of the use of the leaflets and Father made a few closing remarks. The latter urged the teaching of good manners in our schools. In our meeting this evening there was a great deal of

---

[11] Church-state issues frequently came before Church leaders; political opponents constantly charged them with interference in government while others worked to curry their favor in hopes of winning the Mormon vote. From Elder Cannon's diaries, it becomes evident that while Church leaders sought to distance themselves from political activism, sometimes they couldn't resist influencing matters that they felt strongly about and that could impact the Church. This created what sometimes appeared to be hypocrisy, but is probably better explained by a variety of factors bearing on a complex situation. Most importantly, Church leaders knew they couldn't surrender political power to the anti-Mormons.

running about thus causing considerable disturbance which was the reason for this reproof in regard to manners....

Wednesday, April 9, 1890:

At the latter time [10 a.m.] I went to the Historian's office where all the brethren met who were present last evening. After the singing of two hymns and prayer Pres. Snow arose and expressed his pleasure at our fasting (which we all did this morning) and our meeting.[12] He said: Every one of us who has not already had the experience must yet meet it of being tested in every place where we are weak, and even our lives must be laid on the altar. Brigham Young was once tried to the very utmost by the Prophet, and for a moment his standing in the Church seemed to tremble in the balance. William Smith, one of the first quorum of apostles in the age had been guilty of adultery and many other sins. The Prophet Joseph instructed Brigham (then the President of the Twelve) to prefer a charge against the sinner, which was done. Before the time set for the trial, however, Emma Smith talked to Joseph and said the charge preferred against William was with a view to injuring the Smith family. After the trial had began Joseph entered the room and was given a seat. The testimony of witnesses concerning the culprit's sins was then continued. After a short time Joseph arose filled with wrath and said, "Bro. Brigham, I will not listen to this abuse of my family a minute longer. I will wade in blood up to my knees before I will do it." This was a supreme moment. A rupture between the two greatest men on earth seemed imminent. But Brigham Young was equal to the danger, and he instantly said "Bro. Joseph, I withdraw the charge." Thus the angry passions were instantly stilled.[13]

---

[12] John Henry Smith's journal states: "The Council of the Twelve apostles met yesterday as a separate Quorum from the First Presidency for the first time in many years.... We were together about 10 hours. We all spoke in turn confessing our sins and expressing our determination to live nearer the Lord in the future. We administered the Sacrament after the early order, eating our fill of bread and drinking the wine" (Jean Bickmore White, *Church, State and Politics: The Diaries of John Henry Smith* [Salt Lake City: Signature Books, 1990], 235).

[13] The parallels between this story and the following related by former BYU professor Truman Madsen are striking: "This is a story still carried in the family

John Taylor also was similarly tested by the then Pres. Brigham Young at the time the St. George temple was dedicated. The United Order was then a favorite theme of Pres. Young, but in his views John Taylor did not fully coincide. Because of this the latter was most terribly scourged by the tongue of Pres. Young in the temple before all the people. Bro. Taylor was then President of the Twelve. It looked for a time as though these two great men would separate in anger, for Pres. Young had forbidden John to travel through Kanab and Panguitch Stake and organize them with Bro. Lorenzo Snow as had been intended and said he had better return home and make wagons until he knew what was right. Bro. Snow saw the danger and knew the disposition of the two men. He therefore visited Pres. Taylor and after considerable argument induced him to go and visit Pres. Young. They were coolly received at the latter's house, but as soon as Pres. Taylor said, "Bro. Brigham, if I have done or said anything wrong I desire to make it right," every feeling of anger vanished and these two men were reconciled. Thus the Lord will try us wherever we seem to be strong and those who today seem to be very prosperous financially may meet constant reverses until they will be forced to acknowledge that in and of themselves they are nothing. Thus it becomes us to be humble in every particular.

Apostle F. D. Richards spoke next. He said: When some of the brethren in Nauvoo were sent out to collect funds for the building of the temple part of their collection stuck to their fingers. Because of this Bro. Joseph said he thought it best to put the brethren under bonds to make correct returns, and this plan would be commenced

---

lore of Brigham Young's descendants but, so far as I know, never recorded. It says that in a meeting the Prophet rebuked Brigham Young from his head to his feet for something he had done, or something he was supposed to have done but hadn't—the detail is unclear. And it may well have been that the Prophet was deliberately putting Brigham Young to a test. When he had finished the rebuke, everyone in the room waited for the response. Brigham Young rose to his feet.... In a voice everyone could tell was sincere, he said simply, 'Joseph, what do you want me to do?' And the story says that the Prophet burst into tears, came down from the stand, threw his arms around Brigham, and said, in effect, 'Brother Brigham, you passed'" (Truman G. Madsen, *Joseph Smith, the Prophet* [Salt Lake City: Bookcraft, 1989], 87-88).

with the apostles. Bro. Brigham arose and said he did not propose to be thus treated. If the brethren could not trust him he would not go out to collect. Nothing further was said in this forenoon meeting concerning the subject, but in the afternoon when the assembly again met Bro. Brigham took a seat in the congregation. Bro. Joseph after going on the stand looked about and not seeing Bro. Young in his accustomed place, inquired for him. On being told that he was seated below, the Prophet called out, "Oh, Bro. Brigham, come up here, we want you." Improper feelings were soon allayed, and the brethren were sent out under bonds, Bro. Brigham among the rest....

Bro. F. M. Lyman was the next speaker: he felt that he had failed in many particulars to do as he ought, but he desired to improve. He had felt very anxious to do something for his father who had died out of the Church. He had labored very hard and for years before he succeeded in releasing his own mother from the errors into which she had fallen by the teaching of his father in regard to Spiritualism. Now, however, he had succeeded in winning nearly all the family back to the Church. He wept in talking of his father.[14]

At this juncture Pres. Snow arose and said he had been thinking last night before retiring as to the condition of Amasa Lyman, and he felt convinced in his own mind that he would be permitted to associate with the Prophet Joseph to whom he was a true and devoted friend during his life. Of course he would be required to pay the penalty for his sins, but this being done he would be rewarded for his good deeds.

When Bro. Lyman completed his remarks it was 2:15 p.m. Bros. Thatcher and Grant were now excused to attend a Z.C.M.I. directors meeting which occupied 1 1/4 hrs. The remainder of us stopped in the room.

---

[14] Amasa M. Lyman, father of Francis M. Lyman, was an early member of the Quorum of the Twelve Apostles and associate of the Prophet Joseph Smith who was dropped from the Quorum in 1867 and then excommunicated three years later for apostasy (denying the need for the atonement of Christ for personal salvation in his public preaching). See Andrew Jenson, *Latter-day Saint Biographical Encyclopedia*, vol. 1 (Salt Lake City: The Andrew Jenson History Company and the *Deseret News*, 1901), 96-99.

When these brethren returned we clothed in our robes and Franklin D. Richards prayed as we knelt and Pres. Snow at the altar. We then dressed in our usual clothing and prepared to eat the Lord's Supper in the same manner in which the Prophet Joseph said it was eaten by the Savior and His disciples at Jerusalem, and as Joseph and the brethren did occasionally at Nauvoo: we had several loaves of bread and bottles of wine. The former was broken and we ate and drank till we were fully satisfied. I took a very small quantity of wine.[15]

About 5 p.m. our speaking was resumed. Bro. John Henry Smith and Heber J. Grant each spoke concerning their financial and family affairs and expressed their love for the members of the quorum. It now being 7 p.m. an hour's intermission was taken for exercise. When we again convened Bro. Merrill spoke second: He related how wonderfully God had preserved and guided him in youth and watched over his advancing years, so that he was able to remain as the only representative of his stock in the Church.

John W. Taylor spoke first: he related how he received a testimony of the divinity of the work while engaged at his father's saw mill some years since in Summit County. In a vision he saw the place where he had been at work cutting logs gradually lit up by a brilliant light which seemed to emanate from the east. This light continued to increase in intensity and with the increase he seemed to be pushed further away from its source. Finally he clasped his arms around the stump of a tree for the purpose of keeping himself in position. He saw the Son of God appear in the brilliance of the light, and then his hold upon the stump began to slip, and he knew that should he release his grasp he would be thrust back with such violence that he would be dashed to pieces . As he was holding with grim desperation he awoke. His father told him that the interpretation of the dream was that the bright light was the truth which would banish all truth-haters from before it, and the tree stump to which he was holding was a similar representation to that of the rod of iron in the Book of Mormon.[16] Bro. Taylor related several

---

[15] See D&C 27:2-4.
[16] See 1 Nephi 8 and 11.

other manifestations of God's goodness to him in answer to his prayers.

Monday, July 7, 1890:

At 3 p.m. the S. S. Union Board met at the same place. The question was asked if partaking of the Sacrament would cause a forgiveness of sins. A question card used in Sunday Schools said it would. Father said that partaking worthily of the Sacrament would gain for the Saint a forgiveness of sins, as well as a repentant Spirit and humble prayer would bring the same blessing, yet this is not the ordinance instituted for the forgiveness of sins, and any question or answer which conveyed such an idea is incorrect.

Pictures on Book of Mormon subjects which had been submitted by C. C. A. Christensen and E. F. Darling were submitted and selections were made from which to have S. S. charts made. They were mostly very crude, the perspective and figures being poor....

Sunday, July 20, 1890:

I returned to John's and started to eat my dinner, but had to leave the table and go outside to vomit. After lying down a short time I felt better, and went to a meeting of the 77th Quorum of Seventies in the 5th Ward meeting house. In addition to the brethren who are here from Salt Lake City Apostle F. D. Richards was present. There is contention in this quorum which needs adjustment. Firstly, some of the Presidents hold that partaking of the Lord's supper will gain a forgiveness of sins, and quote as authority a card which was printed some years ago at the *Instructor* office. Secondly, the authority of the Presidents to preside was in question, some feeling that one President had no more authority than another to preside. Thirdly, the jurisdiction of the Bishop over Seventies was discussed, some considering that he had no control over them at all. Bros. Roberts, myself, F. D. Richards and F. M. Lyman spoke on these points, after Presidents Moench and Nye had made brief statements concerning their troubles. In answering the first question the brethren were told that the Lord's Supper was not instituted for the forgiveness of sins, though after being baptized our minor failings could be and were forgiven on sincere repentance and petitions to the Lord. Father's recent article in the *Juvenile* on this subject was read.

The second subject was settled by telling the brethren that the senior president in point of ordination always presided in the meetings of the quorum. Though all the Presidents hold the same or equal authority, yet order must be maintained by the senior always acting as the leader.

The third answer was that the Bishop does not preside over seventies in a quorum capacity, yet he presides over them as members of his ward, and as such they should ever be willing to render him obedience.

All agreed by lifting their hands, to discontinue these profitless bickerings.

Tuesday, August 5, 1890:

Bro. F. D. Richards: If there are differences between the members of our quorum this is the place where we should settle them, and then we can partake of the influence of the Holy Spirit which will cause us to see and speak alike, and when we go among the Stakes all will give like counsel on like subjects. The Lord intends to make us great in the earth, not only among the Saints, but also in the world in directing governmental and other affairs. I feel to respect and heed the counsel of Pres. Woodruff and would as soon think of fighting against God as to oppose His mouthpiece.

Bro. Brigham Young Jr.: I feel that very important events are at our doors, and we apostles should be prepared to perform the labors which will be required of us. The people need our counsel and instruction and I feel that we will not have the full influence of the holy Spirit until we lay aside much of a temporal character that now occupies our time, and devote ourselves more to spiritual things. I know that we may receive the ministering of angels and many great gifts if we will but live for them. I believe we will soon see better times and then perhaps worse times again. Our own foolishness as a people is apt to bring trouble upon us. Down in Mexico I found apostates and Gentiles associating with our people and learning all about their private affairs, thus placing weapons in the hands of our enemies which they may hereafter use to our great injury.

Bro. Moses Thatcher: It is necessary that the union desired among the people should begin at the head. A revelation was given some time ago in which the Elders were told to wash their feet against the wicked of this nation., but no sooner did they begin this labor than Satan raised a terrible storm of persecution against us. For some reason this command is now held in abeyance, but when it is fulfilled we will no doubt see great trouble. We will some day, if faithful, be required to testify that we have seen the Lord Jesus, and perhaps the Prophet Joseph in his resurrected state. Such testimony may endanger our lives. We should not permit evil reports concerning our brethren to find credence in our hearts, for by these means divisions are created.

Wednesday, August 6, 1890:

I was at the office by 7 a.m. and studied until 9 o'clock. At this time I went to the Gardo House and met with the Quorum. In addition to those present yesterday we had with us John W. Taylor, Anthon H. Lund and Daniel H. Wells. Opened by singing, "God moves in a mysterious way," etc. Prayer by D. H. Wells. After Pres. Snow had explained to the brethren who were absent yesterday the object of our meeting, Bro. F. M. Lyman spoke: I have full fellowship for all my brethren, and desire to learn my duty and then do it. To me it seems that nearly all our temporal business should be laid aside, and our time should be spent among the Saints counseling them and answering such questions as continually arise. All the people seem anxious to know the will of God as it is revealed through His servants. We should move around among the Saints wherever we see that good can be done, and not wait to be commanded in regard to every little item.

Bro. John Henry Smith: I think the apostles should visit as much as possible among the Stakes. I find that there are some places where they are scarcely known. By changing the places of our visits we will become acquainted with the whole people. In these meetings of our quorum we can blend our spirits and become one in doctrine and feeling. I had the experience on one occasion of giving directions in regard to an ordinance on which point Bro. F. D. Richards had already given other instructions, but without my knowledge. This gave occasion to the man who had asked the question to find some fault, because the apostles were at variance, but the matter was finally referred to the First Presidency who settled it.

Anthon H. Lund: I feel that as far as possible two of the Apostles should be together in visiting the Stake Conferences, for intricate questions often arise which it is difficult for one of inexperience to answer. He had met such a case at a recent conference, but the spirit of the apostleship had rested upon him, and he had been able to make a satisfactory settlement of an intricate situation....

Daniel H. Wells: When I entered this Church it was with the determination to cut loose from everything that was likely to retard my progress in the work of God. Position or honor I have never sought, but have endeavored to do my duty as I understood it. I feel that the special duty of the Apostles is to open the door of the gospel to all nations, to learn languages, translate the Book of Mormon, and do other things which are necessary to warn the world before the Savior comes.

When Bro. Wells had finished all, excepting the latter, dressed in their temple robes. Heber J. Grant then prayed, and J. H. Smith was mouth at the altar. We then dressed and partook of the Sacrament after F. D. Richards had blessed the bread and wine.

While seated at the table Pres. Lorenzo Snow stated that it was the privilege of each member of this Quorum to live upon the earth just as long as he desired providing he would keep the commandments of God, and be ready at all times to make such sacrifices as Abraham made. He felt to suggest that at our meetings we bless each other. He spoke as follows after the table and things had been removed.: "I feel that the Lord is bringing our hearts together, because we are learning the feelings and peculiarities of each other. We will yet have to see Jesus so as to be able to give the testimony to the world which he will require us to bear; and our testimony will cause some people to reflect and repent of their sins.[17] As apostles we should seek to know where we can do the most good and there our time and attention should be occupied. Our ears should be dull in listening to slanders concerning each other, and our eyes should not be seeking evil."

The whole quorum now laid their hands upon my head, and Pres. Snow pronounced a blessing. Among other things he told me I might live to see the Savior, the triumph of Zion and many other great events connected with the latter-day work. In fact, every righteous desire of my heart he promised me through my faithfulness. I was then mouth in blessing him.

Sunday, August 24, 1890:

I also told the congregation [Richfield, UT.] that when the Lord had any great work to do connected with the last dispensation He would reveal it unto His servants, the prophets, and He will not cause any irregularity in the selection of His servants or the performance of great missions.

Monday, August 25, 1890:

Pres. Peterson [Richfield, UT. Stake] told of an incident which he often heard Zebedee Coltrin relate. One day the Prophet Joseph asked him and Sidney Rigdon to accompany him into the woods to pray. When they had reached a secluded spot Joseph laid down on his back and stretched out his arms. He told the brethren to lie one on each arm, and then shut their eyes. After they had prayed he told them to open their eyes. They did so and saw a brilliant light surrounding a pedestal which seemed to rest on the earth. They closed their eyes and again prayed. They then saw, on opening them, the Father seated upon a throne; they prayed again and on looking saw the Mother also; after praying and looking the fourth time they

---

[17] To live worthy to "see Jesus" was a recurring theme of President Snow's, who received this privilege himself at the time he became President of the Church. See N. B. Lundwall, comp., *Temples of the Most High* (Salt Lake City: N.B. Lundwall Publishing, 1944), 145. See also Dennis B. Horne, *Called of God, by Prophecy: Spiritual Experience, Doctrine, and Testimony from Church Leaders Reveal How God Chooses His Servants* (Roy, Utah: Eborn Books, 2002), 192-93.

saw the Savior added to the group. He had auburn-brown, rather long, wavy hair and appeared quite young.[18]

Wednesday, September 3, 1890:

I then returned to town and went to the Gardo House where I waited until two a.m., when I accompanied Father, Presidents Woodruff and Smith to the D and R. G. train which they boarded and started for California. They desire to avoid being subpoenaed as witnesses before Stone in the Receivership investigation....

Monday, September 29, 1890:

I was at the office a good part of the day writing the minutes of our last Quorum [of the Twelve] meeting when I acted as Secretary.

Tuesday, September 30, 1890:

I was at the office by 8 a.m. and was copying our Quorum [of the Twelve] meeting minutes nearly all day until noon.

At 2 p.m. our Quorum meeting was held There were present Lorenzo Snow, Franklin D. Richards, Moses Thatcher, Francis M. Lyman, John Henry Smith, Heber J. Grant, John W. Taylor and myself. J. W. Taylor was called to act as clerk. Opened by singing, "Come let us anew," etc. Prayer by John H. Smith. Pres. Snow was pleased to meet and felt that if we really deserve a blessing we will get it as the Lord is willing to bestow light and wisdom upon us, and in these meetings it is our privilege to receive great knowledge.

Referring to Pres. Woodruff's late manifesto[19] concerning plural marriage Pres. Snow said: The Lord will not permit any faithful Saint

---

[18] For an alternate account of this experience, see Hyrum L. Andrus and Helen Mae Andrus, comp., *They Knew the Prophet* (Salt Lake City: Bookcraft, 1974), 28.

[19] The Manifesto is dated 24 September 1890, just six days before this council meeting of the Apostles, so this was probably their first opportunity as a Quorum to discuss its tremendous implications. Elder Marriner W. Merrill's journal records the substance of a meeting with three of the Quorum of the Twelve held the same date as the Manifesto: "I went to Salt Lake and met in council with President Woodruff, George Q. Cannon, Joseph F. Smith, F. D. Richards, and Moses Thatcher, where President Woodruff had an article read he had prepared for the press of the country declaring to the world that we did not celebrate plural

to lose blessings through the acts of the wicked, or because of circumstances over which the individual has no control. Elder Lorenzo Barnes who was a faithful missionary many years ago in England, was at the time in correspondence with a young lady in Philadelphia, whom he expected to marry, but he died while in the performance of his duty. Now, though he died without any wife he will not be the loser thereby for the Lord will supply all that is necessary to give him the salvation he merits. So also will it be with those who are prevented by no act of their own from fulfilling all the requirements of the gospel. A faithful man, though he may have wayward wives or children, will doubtless have the power hereafter given him to bring them up to a plane of happiness and to exaltation, even though he may have no influence with them here. God has a right to suspend His law, as He has done in the inspiration under which Pres. Woodruff wrote the manifesto, and as the Savior did when He suspended the law of Moses and permitted the disciples to pluck corn on the Sabbath day when they were hungry. The very important law concerning baptism is at times suspended as in the case of married women whose husbands are opposed to the gospel, or minors whose parents object to the baptism of their children. I can see great good and no inconsistency in this matter. Many honorable men in this nation have been opposed to us because they believed we were disloyal, but this declaration will remove stumbling blocks from the paths of such persons.[20]

Franklin D. Richards: In the issuance of this manifesto I see good, and those who possess the spirit of revelation will understand and appreciate it. Before the War of the Rebellion slaves were refused

---

marriages now in the Church and that he counseled the members of the Church not to break the law in relation to plural marriage. The article was approved by all the brethren present, including myself, which seems the only way to retain the possession of our Temples and continue the ordinance work for the living and dead, which was considered more important than continuing the practice of plural marriages for the present" (Melvin Clarence Merrill, ed., *Utah Pioneer and Apostle Marriner Wood Merrill and His Family* [n. p.: Marriner Wood Merrill Heritage Committee, 1980], 127). For the text of the Manifesto, see D&C, Official Declaration 1.

[20] See D&C 124:49-50.

baptism unless their masters consented, and because of the refusal of the latter to permit such things the gospel was withheld for 25 years from the Southern states. When Pres. Woodruff prepared his manifesto it was without the aid or suggestions of his counselors. He took a clerk and went to a room alone. There under the spirit of inspiration he dictated the declaration he desired to make, and there was only one slight change made therein when it was read to Counselors Cannon and Smith. Therefore I feel it is from the Almighty. The Lord is causing the wisdom of men to fail. The Supreme Court held the case of the Church property under advisement for over a year and then rendered so foolish a decision that when they began to consider the result, they vacated their own order, and in some matters will give a decision later. Thus the highest tribunal in this land is confused and disgraced when it seeks to do wrong to the Saints.

John W. Taylor: When I first heard of this manifesto I felt to say "Damn it," but on further thought I felt it was not right to be so impulsive. I do not yet feel quite right about it. My father when President of the Church sought to find a way to evade the conflict between the Saints and government on the question of plural marriage, but the Lord said it was an eternal and unchangeable law and must stand. Pres. Woodruff lately received an encouraging revelation in regard to this principle and now I ask myself, "Is the Lord a child that He thus changes?" Yet I feel that the Lord giveth a law and He can also take it away.[21]

Moses Thatcher: In 1885 Pres. Taylor made a public statement in the Tabernacle that he had taken a course to place himself outside the

---

[21] Elder John W. Taylor never fully accepted President Woodruff's Official Declaration, or Manifesto, shielding his non-obedience behind the revelations of his father, President John Taylor. Because he continued performing plural marriages into the administration of President Joseph F. Smith, he was eventually dropped from the Quorum (1905) and then excommunicated (1911). Elder John Henry Smith's journal account of this same meeting states: "[The Quorum] spoke upon the President's Manifesto in regard to the solemnization of Plural marriages and endorsed it. John W. Taylor was somewhat mixed but acknowledged the hand of the Lord in it" (*Church, State, and Politics*, 241). See also Appendix One: Plural Marriage Issues in the Abraham H. Cannon Journals.

reach of the law, and many persons then felt and do feel that he was seeking to evade the issue, just as many now feel concerning Pres. Woodruff's declaration. Yet I feel that both of these brethren acted exactly right. The law of God is not abrogated, but in order to try this nation which has long called us traitors because of the practice of this principle, this cause of offense is removed, so that the law makers and people may be left without just excuse in their prosecution of the Saints. This manifesto will doubtless have the effect however, to make the attacks upon us in other directions more bitter, and we may have to suffer greatly at the hands of the wicked yet it is satisfying to my feelings. It may force us to make friends with the "battle axe" of the Lord in Canada and Mexico, and we will yet become the saviors of the Constitution of our country.

In support of Pres. Snow's statement that the Lord will amply provide for His faithful servants, I will mention the case of Feramorz Young who died on the ocean, when about 21 years old, while returning from a mission to Mexico. When he went to the latter country he had no testimony of the gospel though he believed it to be true. While there the Lord convinced him of its truth and included a knowledge of the principle of plural marriage. Of the latter he wrote in his journal that he would obey it if he had the opportunity even though he should be required to sacrifice the love of Hattie Hooper, whose love he had gained and appreciated, but who, he feared, did not believe in the principle. After his death she married his brother Willard. Subsequently a young unmarried lady who died in this city approached her mother and requested that she be sealed to Feramorz and it was done. Some time thereafter a young lady who died in Philadelphia, and who was not a member of the Church and had never seen Ferry so far as known, appeared to a Gentile acquaintance in this city and requested her to call on Ferry's mother, and get permission to have her sealed to him. Three times did this girl appear to her friend and threw her arms about her neck and would not be dismissed until her friend had promised to do as requested. The lady called on Sister Young and related the affair, adding that she did not believe in any such ordinances, and the work was done as the dead girl desired.

Francis M. Lyman: "I endorse the manifesto, and feel it will do good. I design to live with and have children by my wives, using the wisdom which God gives me to avoid being captured by the officers of the law." He gave a brief account of his recent labors.

We then adjourned till tomorrow at 10 a.m. Benediction by John H. Smith.

Wednesday, October 1, 1890:

Was at the office by 6:30 a.m. and occupied the time until 10 in posting up the books.

At the latter time I went to my Quorum meeting in the Gardo House. In addition to the brethren of yesterday Anthon H. Lund was present today. Singing: "O my Father." Etc. Prayer by Lorenzo Snow in which he asked that if it was the Lord's will, we might be permitted to see his face even as Joseph and Oliver, and Moses of old did.

John Henry Smith: I cannot feel to say that the manifesto is quite right or wrong. It may be that the people are unworthy of the principle and hence the Lord has withdrawn it. I cannot consent to cease living with my wives unless I am imprisoned.

Heber J. Grant: I approve of the manifesto and feel that it is merely a public announcement of the course which we had already decided in our private councils to adopt, and this being the case I do not know why we should not receive any possible benefits which may arise from a public declaration. Yet I believe greater troubles will follow the prominent Elders in the Church through the adoption of this policy. If this plan had been accepted in the beginning of this crusade the nation would not have been tried as it has been, and would not be worthy of condemnation such as it now merits, hence I feel this has come at the proper time.

Anthon H. Lund: Sickness prevented my being here yesterday to my sorrow. I feel that the manifesto will result in good. I gave my approval to what had been done.

Moses Thatcher: I think the brethren should so arrange their families that women bearing children shall not be in constant fear of capture. For this feeling is bound to affect the offspring both in mind and body to its injury. The troubles will perhaps cause us to seek refuge in Mexico where there are twelve millions of Lamanites to whom we can then turn our attention, and when they are converted they will form the battle-axe of the Lord, and we will help them to redeem and build up Zion.

Lorenzo Snow: I am pleased at our unanimity of feelings, and know that the Lord will direct us aright.

We now clothed in our Temple robes, and Anthon H. Lund opened by prayer, John W. Taylor was mouth at the altar. We changed our clothing and Moses Thatcher then blessed the bread and wine, and we partook of the Sacrament. While at the table some choice remarks were made. Pres. Snow said that the Savior will undoubtedly come to visit His servants many times appearing as an ordinary man before He appears in glory and with his angels. On one occasion fourteen Elders, including the Prophet Joseph, were engaged in prayer when a personage passed through the room. He glided past about five feet above the floor. Next came a man in ordinary dress who walked through. The first, Joseph said, was the Father, and the second the Son.

When Oliver Cowdery in Joseph's presence gave the charge to the first Quorum of Apostles in this age he told them they should pray to see the Savior, for this was their privilege to see and know Him.[22]

If we are faithful we will yet have a similar power to that possessed by the Savior to make and save worlds, but we will also have to pass through a similar experience. He was begotten by the Father, who overshadowed Mary, just as our earthly fathers beget us.

Pres. Brigham Young once told Bro. Snow that the reason Negroes could not receive the Priesthood was through the exercise of their own agency before they came to this earth. Cain and Abel were princes in the first estate and stood at the head of a vast body of

---

[22] Each man who has subsequently been called to the Apostleship has been given a similar charge. It usually consists of three elements: To seek the face of the Lord Jesus; to make the call highest priority in life; and to support the decisions of the Twelve and First Presidency, even if those decisions are not in agreement with your own. For the text of Oliver Cowdery's charge to the Twelve, see Joseph Smith Jr., *History of the Church of Jesus Christ of Latter-day Saints,* 7 vols. (Salt Lake City: The Church of Jesus Christ of Latter-day Saints, 1948), 2:192-98.

spirits for whom they were to beget bodies. Cain knew this and in slaying Abel he realized he was doing injury to all who acknowledged him as prince. Hence when Cain was cursed his subjects were given the privilege of selecting some other medium through which to be born, but rather than select another prince they decided to be born of Cain and become partakers of his curse. For this reason wherever Negro blood exists it will at times show itself in the offspring, and not until all of Abel's royal family have received bodies will the curse be raised from Cain's posterity.[23]

F. D. Richards: I feel that a history of the Apostles of this dispensation should be written, and with the help of God and my brethren I will undertake to prepare one from the time the revelation was first given concerning the organization of the Quorum.[24]

The proposition was heartily approved.

John Henry Smith said he heard Pres. B. Young once say in St. George that the Presidency of the Church would devolve in regular succession upon the Apostles, with the exception of Orson Hyde and Orson Pratt who had forfeited their rights through faithlessness before the Saints came to these mountains.[25] About 3 p.m. we adjourned.

---

[23] In 1978 President Spencer W. Kimball received a revelation that granted to all worthy men—regardless of race—the right to hold the priesthood. See D&C, Official Declaration 2. See also Dennis B. Horne, *Bruce R. McConkie: Highlights from His Life and Teachings* (Roy, Utah: Eborn Books, 2000), 151-67.

[24] As subsequent journal entries attest, this Apostles' history was written and periodically read to the Twelve in their meetings. It has never been published, but a senior employee with the LDS Family and Church History Department, when contacted by the editor, affirmed that while it is no longer housed in the department archives "it has been in the possession of the Church and there is no reason to believe that it is no longer in the possession of the Church."

[25] In his journal, Elder John Henry Smith wrote: "I related to the brethren an answer made to me by President Brigham Young to the Question 'In case of your death to whom should I look to lead the Church?' His answer was. To any one of the Council of the Apostles in the order of ordination, baring Orson Hyde and Orson Pratt, who had forfeited their right. This was in the spring of 1874" (*Church, State, and Politics*, 241).

Thursday, October 2, 1890:

The manifesto was next discussed, and finally on motion of F. M. Lyman, all voted to sustain and approve it. The question as to whether or not it should be presented to the Saints for their approval or rejection at our Conference was discussed at some length. Some felt that the assent of the Presidency and Twelve to the matter was sufficient without committing the people by their votes to a policy which they might in the future wish to discard. Joseph F. Smith presented the view that it would lack much force and would not bring the desired results unless accepted by the vote of the people. The manifesto had already been the means, he was convinced, of preventing the enactment of [the] Edmunds bill, which passed the Senate, confiscating the Church personal property to the school fund. Now if we could convince leading men of the nation that it is the bona fide intention of the people to have no more plural marriages in this country in conflict with the laws, it would no doubt bring some concessions on the part of the government towards those who have already entered into the plural relation. The matter of presenting the manifesto to the Conference was left open for the present. It was, however, resolved that "we use our private influence at present to prevent our brethren from going into Court and promising to obey the law; and as soon as possible we take steps to get some favors from the government for those who already have more wives than one."

Saturday, October 4, 1890 [general conference]:

Wilford Woodruff: The Lord has never revealed to any man when the Savior will come. I have seen and conversed with Joseph, Brigham and others of the brethren. Once I saw Joseph and he was in a very great hurry. Afterwards he told me that the cause of his haste was that the work of this dispensation was being crowded, and while other former dispensations had plenty of time in which to do the necessary work, the present had no time to spare.[26] He said that the Father alone knew the time set for the coming of Jesus....

---

[26] See G. Homer Durham, comp., *The Discourses of Wilford Woodruff* (Salt Lake City: Bookcraft, 1946), 288-89.

George Q. Cannon: "It would be well for us to do more missionary work at home than is now being done. In the case of our children we are not as perfect as we should be. Where religion is not taught to young people they are apt to drift into infidelity, especially where science is studied and its harmony with revelation is not shown to the youthful mind."

Sunday, October 5, 1890:

Father spoke 1 hour and 19 min. in a very powerful discourse. "All of our elders have told the people to whom they preached that they might have to lay down their lives for the truth as did the ancients. There is a living testimony in the hearts of the Saints concerning all counsel and advice which are given. For this I thank God. If the people are in doubt in regard to any policy which is adopted, they can go to God, and He will clear the minds of those who seek instruction. The Presidency of this Church have to walk as you do; they cannot see the end from the beginning, but must seek for light just as you do. They seek for revelation and when it comes they must do as directed whether or not it agrees with their views or wishes. It is just as necessary that our faith should be tried and exercised as that yours should. Whenever we take a step we know that it is the right one. The course which the Saints have taken in the last 5 years will yet be recognized as one of the brightest pages in history. We will yet show the nation that the Saints are a people of truth, loyal to God, to this country and in all the relations of life.

There is no greater cause of apostasy in the Church than unchastity. You can predict the result of an unvirtuous man's course as easily as you can that darkness will follow the setting of the sun. He that looketh upon a woman to lust after, shall lose the faith. A man from Massachusetts was telling me lately that after a 10 years absence from his home he revisited it, and in one school he found only 4 American born children, the remainder being European importations, and two of these were darkies. This tells a terrible story of crime. Women have ceased to desire children and commit murder to prevent their being born. Thus the race is being exterminated. God will judge the nation because of these evils. I am told such things are not unknown here. The curse of God will rest upon the man or woman who is guilty of such crimes.

Concerning 1891 I will say that the Savior will not then come in glory. Judah must rebuild Jerusalem, Zion must be redeemed and Jacob must be restored before this event occurs."…

After meeting our Quorum met the First Presidency at the Gardo House where we agreed that John T. Caine would suit us as Delegate to Congress if he was acceptable to the Convention which meets on Tuesday. A telegram was read from J. T. Caine concerning an interview with Secretary of the Interior Noble. The latter felt that he could not accept Pres. W. Woodruff's manifesto without its acceptance by the conference as authoritative, against the statements of the Utah Commission and Gov. A. L. Thomas. It was therefore decided to present the matter tomorrow for the vote of the people. [27] It was said that Gov. Thomas had overreached himself in his zeal, and this thing would break his influence.

Monday, October 6, 1890:

I was at the office till 10 a.m., and then went to the Tabernacle. The Church authorities were presented and sustained. O. F. Whitney then read the Articles of our Faith and on motion of Franklin D. Richards they were accepted by the Church as its rules of guidance. Pres. Woodruff's manifesto was then read, and Lorenzo Snow moved that recognizing Pres. Woodruff as the only man who now holds the keys of the sealing ordinance upon the earth, we sustain him in his action in this matter. The vote was unanimous. [28]

---

[27] This entry would seem to indicate the main reason the Manifesto was presented to the people for sustaining vote. The Manifesto was published in the *Latter-day Saints Millennial Star* on Monday, 13 October 1890.

[28] Elder Marriner W. Merrill's journal for this date records: "Singing, after which President George Q. Cannon presented the Authorities of the Church, who were unanimously sustained. Bishop Orson F. Whitney then read the Articles of Faith, when they were adopted by the Conference by vote. Then President Woodruff's late Manifesto regarding the cessation of plural marriages in the Church was read, and on motion of Apostle Lorenzo Snow President Woodruff was declared by the Conference as the only man in the Church holding the keys of the sealing power; hence has the right to issue or put forth such Manifesto to the people, and it was

George Q. Cannon: Then spoke 30 min. He read from a revelation given Jan 19, 1841, where the Lord releases his people from obligation when their enemies come upon them and prevent their fulfillment.[29] He then gave a comforting discourse to the Saints on the new position we have been forced to assume, and showed that this course was not possible some years ago, for thereby the nation would not have had the opportunity of showing itself. Now, however, the responsibility rests with the nation for the suspension of this law.[30]

Pres. Woodruff: expressed his gratitude to the Saints for the support they had given him. He knew God would over-rule this act for the good of His Saints. His course had been taken under direction of God, and rather than do anything contrary to the will of God, he would allow himself to be taken out to his death.

Tuesday, October 7, 1890:

I was busy at the office attending to business. I then went to the Gardo House where the majority of the First Presidency, Twelve, First Seven Presidents of the Seventy, Presiding Bishopric and Presidents of Stakes were assembled.

George Q. Cannon: "Our financial affairs merit our earnest attention. The calls upon the Church are numerous and pressing, and we are constantly going deeper in debt. A defense fund should exist in each Stake and collections should be made from the Saints on this account. Now we are compelled to divert tithing from its proper

---

carried by a weak vote, but seemingly unanimous; after which President George Q. Cannon spoke on the plural relations for 30 minutes. Then President Woodruff spoke on the necessity of the issuing such Manifesto and said it was the impression of the Spirit of the Lord to him" (Melvin Clarence Merrill, ed., *Utah Pioneer and Apostle Marriner Wood Merrill and His Family* [n. p.: Marriner Wood Merrill Heritage Committee, 1980], 128-29).

[29] See D&C 124: 49-50.

[30] See *Comprehensive History of the Church*, 6:222. This general conference address of President Cannon's would be viewed by many as one the most important and powerful ever delivered to the Saints. See Davis Bitton, *George Q. Cannon: A Biography* (Salt Lake City: Deseret Book, 1999), 315-16.

channel and use it for political purposes and in various ways, because the Saints have failed to properly donate for defensive purposes.

"A strict system of Home Missionary labor should be instituted in the various stakes. I favor a plan similar to that which has been adopted in some places of calling men on missions to devote their whole time for a certain season to visiting and living with the people. Thus they can become acquainted with their daily life, and correct evils which exist.

"Where Bishops or other officers in the Church are incompetent or too aged for active labor, they should be relieved in a kind manner, and their places should be filled by abler men."…

George Q. Cannon: "I feel like saying, 'Damn the law.' We can expect neither justice nor mercy in the administration of the law with the present corrupt administrators. Women should be encouraged for some feel as though they had been betrayed, and a man who will act the coward and shield himself behind the manifesto for deserting his plural wife or wives, would be damned. I will prophesy that in our action at conference yesterday lies safety; the Lord has revealed this much to me. I believe that before long you men will be allowed to vote. If it were not for my public duties I would not live a day in my present condition, but my family understands that my liberty depends on refraining from visiting them in their homes and they are contented."

Wilford Woodruff: "This manifesto only refers to future marriages, and does not affect past conditions. I did not, could not, and would not promise that you would desert your wives and children. This you cannot do in honor."[31]

---

[31] Elder Marriner W. Merrill's journal for this meeting records: "Much valuable instruction was given by the Presidency on the relations of men and their families. President Woodruff said brethren must not abandon their plural families, but be more kind than heretofore if it was possible, and also to children of such relation, and if they did not God would hold them responsible. It was also decided to raise means in the different Stakes to help the Church defend the rights of the people, as the tithing was not sufficient after doing other things" (Melvin Clarence Merrill, ed., *Utah Pioneer and Apostle Marriner Wood Merrill and His Family* [n. p.: Marriner Wood Merrill Heritage Committee, 1980], 129).

Wednesday, October 8, 1890:

Judge Zane, influenced doubtless by advice from Washington, yesterday rendered a decision that he would not now bar Mormons from admission to citizenship simply because they are Mormons. He felt bound to take judicial notice of Pres. Woodruff's manifesto and to respect the same unless some future event should prove that it was a false statement. This is quite a victory for our cause, and the news being brought to our meeting yesterday just after Father had prophesied that good would result from what had been done, it was a partial fulfillment of the prediction, and was quite marked.

Thursday, October 9, 1890:

I then went to the Gardo House where we held our Real Estate meeting. Present: W. Woodruff, George Q. Cannon, J. R. Winder, B. Y. Hampton, N. N. Jones, G. D. Pyper, F. Armstrong and myself. Since the brethren were called together some months ago and it was decided to sell our real estate at high figures, the boom has declined and no business to speak of has been done. The result is we find ourselves in debt. It was decided to no longer continue our organization, but to rent the Amusson building to the State Bank, find out the amount we owe and take means to pay our indebtedness. Bros. Hampton and Jones have permission, however, to carry on their real estate business as a private affair.[32]

At 2 p.m. I went to our Council meeting at the Gardo House. We did not dress in our robes, but I was mouth in prayer. C. W. Penrose submitted the People's Party platform, and resolutions, which were corrected and then sent to the Convention now in session. While together the fate and treatment of suicides were discussed. The feeling is that such criminals should be denied Christian burial, and their crimes should be held up to public execration. It is affirmed on the authority of reputable physicians that the three young men who have of late suicided in this Territory were diseased through improper associations with the opposite sex. Uncle Angus stated that he has positive evidence from physicians who saw the body, that Jeremiah Kimball, who was called on a mission at the same time as Louis, but

---

[32] See AHC journals, 29 February 1890.

was killed by the train while en route, was diseased, and the belief is that he committed suicide.

It is thought wrong for young girls whose betrothed ones die before marriage to go and be sealed to their dead lovers, and thus bind themselves to those to whom they never belonged. Their earthly prospects are thereby in a measure blighted, as young unmarried men in the Church desire to marry their wives for time as well as eternity.

Friday, October 10, 1890:

I was told today that in a Relief Society Conference held since our General Conference a sister spoke in tongues, and the interpretation being given it contained comforting words to the sisters. It was said that the Lord approved of all that had been done by the authorities at Conference and urged the sisters to be firm, quiet and steadfast. What will occur among the Saints before next April had best not be told, the Spirit said, and on what will happen in the world, the curtain had better not be drawn.

Monday, October 27, 1890:

I next spoke for 50 min. [to the Brigham City stake conference] on tithing and the dangers which threaten the nation in the fight between capital and labor, and the organization of secret societies. F. D. Richards also spoke a short time on the subject of tithing.

At noon I accompanied Pres. Snow to his room where he lives separate and apart from his family because of the law. His meals are sent to him by his wife Minnie, who lives opposite. It made me feel sad to see him thus banished. I took dinner with Minnie J. Snow.

At the afternoon meeting Pres. Woodruff spoke about an hour. He told of the great financial embarrassments of the Church, and told the people they would be blessed abundantly in paying their tithes.[33] Told of many of the manifestations of God to him, and among others of a dream or vision he had before these valleys were discovered by the Pioneers in which he saw the Salt Lake Temple

---

[33] From this and other AHC journal entries, it is clear that tithing was strongly and commonly taught to Church members long before President Lorenzo Snow's revelation affirmed the principle as the solution to the Church's indebtedness.

completed and he with many others entered therein. The Savior appeared there and sent out the Elders in this and other nations to bind up the law and seal up the testimony so that the judgments of God might be poured out upon the wicked without measure. He hoped to still live to see that day.

Wednesday, November 26, 1890:

A rough spirit: Pres. Joseph F. Smith today told the following: Henry C. Rogers, counselor to Pres. Robson of the Maricopa Stake, became quite friendly with a Judge Hagan of Arizona, and the latter frequently invited Pres. Rogers to visit him. One evening the latter complied with the request and at the Judge's house a number of Gentiles were assembled and agreed to hold a spiritualistic séance. For some time Pres. Rogers prevented any manifestations by the exercise of his faith, but finally his curiosity was aroused to see the result of the spirit's works, and he drew up and placed his hands on the table with the others. Now the tapping of the spirits could be heard. Two taps indicated "No", and three taps "Yes." The Judge now began to ask who the spirit was—George Washington, Joseph Smith, Brigham Young and so on through a long list of noted persons, but the taps for "No" were heard invariably. Finally Brother Rogers suggested that he ask if it was Gadianton (the noted robber of Book of Mormon fame). The Judge had no sooner done as requested than the spirit seized him, and danced him around the room at an alarming rate. Chairs and tables were overturned, while the visitors, looking on in alarm and astonishment moved out of the way of the afflicted medium. Finally when thoroughly exhausted he fell in a swoon on the floor, Pres. Rogers and Mrs. Hagan then began to rub him vigorously with liquor and cold water, and the former did some of his most earnest praying that his host might not die. After some time the Judge opened his eyes, and his first expression was: "My God, I don't want anything more to do with Gadianton."[34]

---

[34] Elder Bruce R. McConkie related the following experience to a Church Educational System religion class at BYU in 1967: "There was one of these séance's (this is a true story). It was going on and two Mormon elders walked in, and this happened to be an instance where the medium actually had power to call back

Pres. Rogers believes that around in Maricopa Stake are located some of Gadianton's ancient strongholds. The ruins would sustain the theory.

Tuesday, December 2, 1890:

At 2 p.m. I attended my Quorum meeting. There were present, Lorenzo Snow, F. D. Richards, Moses Thatcher, F. M. Lyman, J. H. Smith, H. J. Grant, M. W. Merrill, A. H. Lund and myself. Pres. Snow opened by prayer. We then spent nearly two hours in interesting and instructive conversation on various points of doctrine. The subject of the Josephite Church[35], its authority and gifts, was discussed, in the course of which John Henry Smith read a letter to him from the head of that Church, Joseph Smith [III], dated Nov. 7. The people and authorities here [in Utah] are congratulated therein for their abandonment of plural marriage, and the writer suggests that this matter could not have originated with the Lord or it would

devils and was doing it. But when these Mormon elders got inside, the medium couldn't do it. The priesthood was there and the devils weren't responding. But one of the devils said to this medium, 'Those two fellows back there, get them out of here and then we can go on.' And so the medium comes back and says to the Mormon elders, 'Would you please leave our meeting? We can't operate while you are here.' And these Mormon elders said, 'No, we are staying.' And the medium was trying to go on, a little desperate. Sort of by…instinct, the medium said, 'Well let us call somebody back for you then.' Then one of the elders said, 'Alright, do it.' 'Well, who would you like to have come back?' The elder said, 'Gadianton.' Well, the medium goes to work and shortly the medium is picked up off the ground and thrashed down on the floor and whipped and beaten severely and finally when this medium gets control and possession of his faculties again, all he can say is, 'Who in the hell is Gadianton?'… Now, I don't know who the missionary was, but President Smith told me this. [Student question] Well, don't they put it on Joseph F. Smith? [B. R. McConkie answer] No it wasn't Joseph F. Smith, but he told the story, President Joseph F. Smith. But I don't know who the missionaries were. There is an instance where President Joseph Fielding got into this meeting and the mediums couldn't work and they [the devils] did say to the medium this same thing.… It is those fellows back there and the mediums couldn't work, but he didn't have that experience" (Taken from "Miracles" [unpublished lecture transcript, summer 1967], 10).

[35] The Reorganized Church of Jesus Christ of Latter-day Saints, now called the Community of Christ.

have remained unchanged. This man is certainly not sincere or he would have accepted the truth long ago, as he has had abundant evidence given him that his father, the Prophet, had more than one wife.[36]

The question was asked if Temple work could be done for people who were once in the Church, but gradually grew cold and moved away. The answer was "Yes." This, of course, when they have not sinned against light and truth. By special permission of the President cases have even occurred of living wives who are in the Church being sealed to their husbands who died out of the Church.

The question of forgiveness for the sin of adultery was considered at some length, and examples were given of the views entertained by the various Presidents who have led the Church. All consider it a most grievous sin, but the strictness with which the law of excommunication has been enforced has varied. There seems to be more leniency in this regard at present, and some of the brethren seem to feel that this laxity is doing injury among the people by causing them to look upon this sin as being of no very grave import. Bro. Snow said he expected to see the day when a man's blood will be shed for the crime of adultery.

Wednesday, December 3, 1890:

We clothed in our robes at first in our meeting and I opened by prayer. Bro. Merrill was mouth at the altar. We next dressed and listened to F. D. Richards read some matter which he has prepared to enter in a record of the Apostles of this dispensation. He began by making extracts from the revelations concerning the calling and duty of the Twelve, then recorded the appointment and ordination of the first apostles and the organization of the Quorum. The blessings pronounced upon the head of some of the early apostles were also read together with the charge of Oliver Cowdery to them. It was

---

[36] Emma Smith, first wife of the Prophet, taught her children that their father had not entered plural marriage, and even when presented with testimony from living witnesses, they refused to believe it. For further information on this subject, see Gracia N. Jones, *Emma and Joseph: Their Divine Mission* (Salt Lake City: Covenant Communications, 1999), 351-56 and xiii.

resolved that the blessings of all the brethren be recorded as far as they could be obtained.

Thursday, December 18, 1890:

At 2 p.m. I attended my Quorum meeting. There were present Presidents Woodruff, Cannon, and Smith, F. D. Richards, F. M. Lyman, and myself. Bros. Woodruff and Richards did not dress in robes as did the rest of us. Joseph F. Smith was mouth in opening and F. M. Lyman at the altar. Thereafter we had a long conversation in regard to sealings and adoptions. The question was asked if a married couple having parents who died out of the Church could be sealed to the same parents. The answer was in the affirmative. Bro. Joseph F. Smith rather held to the idea that children should be sealed to their parents even when the latter died without a knowledge of the gospel, and thus the connection with our ancestry should be extended as far back as it was possible to reach, when the link should be made with the Prophet Joseph who stands at the head of this dispensation and he will form the connecting link with proceeding dispensations. Father holds that we who live on the earth now and are faithful, will stand at the head of our lineage and will thus become Saviors as has been promised us. Pres. John Taylor was not sealed to his parents though they died in the Church, as he felt that it was rather lowering himself to be thus sealed when he was an apostle and his father was a high priest; but this is rather a questionable proceeding.

Chapter Four

1891

Wednesday, January 28, 1891:

I then went to the Gardo house where I gave Father a report of the *Juvenile* business which was satisfactory to him. Our debts are pretty heavy, but with the continuation of our present business and the blessing of the Lord we will be able to work along and gradually reduce our obligations.

At 11 a.m. the Quorum of the Twelve met with the First Presidency in the upper room of the Gardo House to counsel together. Present: W. Woodruff, George Q. Cannon, Joseph F. Smith, Lorenzo Snow, Franklin D. Richards, Moses Thatcher, F. M. Lyman, J. H. Smith, H. J. Grant, J. W. Taylor and myself. Pres. Woodruff opened by stating that he desired to consult with the brethren in regard to the sugar industry which we are seeking to establish. He felt that while the Apostles are at home they should engage and direct in temporal affairs and he desired the brethren to speak freely on this subject.

Pres. Snow read from two revelations concerning the will of God in regard to temporal matters as given to the Prophet Joseph in Kirtland and Far West (Sec 104:78. Sec. 115:13). He believed the Spirit of God inspired the movement which we are now considering and good would result from it. In order to insure success, however, the Brethren assembled must become united in spirit and object, and then the blessings of God would attend us, and seeming insurmountable difficulties would be overcome. He felt that we should lay aside the matter in hand, and first reconcile all differences between the First Presidency and Twelve, and then our business matters could be more easily settled. He was anxious to see perfect union between the two leading quorums, and when he beheld this he was ready to be taken from the earth at any time.

Pres. Woodruff approved of the suggestion and also felt the necessity for union. The First Presidency were united with each other and worked in perfect harmony. Personally he had seen things in Moses Thatcher which he did not like, especially in his actions with regard to the B. B. and C. mine, but these things he had now laid aside, and he felt nothing but blessings for his brethren. He desired the forgiveness of any whom he had offended.[1]

Pres. Snow desired a full and free expression from each of the brethren so that we might now bury all enmity once and forever.

Moses Thatcher had felt for a long time that the President had entertained feelings against him, and he was glad to have the opportunity of a full explanation of his actions. He then explained how he became connected with the B. B. and C. mine which was not of his own volition, but at Pres. John Taylor's request. He also explained some of his recent action in connection therewith. He then said he was now in a condition to lose all his worldly wealth with his brethren than to gain the whole world without them.

George Q. Cannon: "I have yearned for the confidence and love of my brethren, but since Pres. Young's death it has seemed to me

---

[1] The Bullion-Beck and Champion Mine would occasionally be a source of ill feeling between Moses Thatcher and other members of the First Presidency and Twelve. While the various accounts are confusing, apparently the Church and some of the Brethren had invested in mine stock at the instigation of President John Taylor, who designated it as "dedicated" and to be under the control of the First Presidency and then President Cannon specifically. Misunderstanding and confusion arose over control and ownership of the stock and outside (California Co.) interests. See AHC journals 20, 21, 24, 31, January; and 4, 5, 8, March 1890. See also Davis Bitton, *George Q. Cannon: A Biography* (Salt Lake City: Deseret Book, 1999), 286-87 and 510 n. 102 and 104; see also Thomas G. Alexander, *Things in Heaven and Earth: The Life and Times of Wilford Woodruff, a Mormon Prophet* (Salt Lake City: Signature Books, 1993), 244-45, 284-85; and Philip F. Notarianni, "Symbol of an Era: Bullion-Beck & Champion Mining Company Headframe and the Tintic Mining Company"; and "Faith, Hope and Prosperity: The Tintic Mining District," Eureka Utah; both available from the Tintic Historical Society, 1982; copies used by editor found in the University of Utah Marriot Library Special Collections. A journal account of Elder Merriner W. Merrill's visit to the mine can be found in Melvin Clarence Merrill, ed., *Utah Pioneer and Apostle Marriner Wood Merrill and His Family* (n. p.: Marriner Wood Merrill Heritage Committee, 1980), 143-44.

that I have done something deserving of censure from my brethren, for they have singled me out as an object for their attacks. I love you all and desire God to give you the same gifts which He bestows upon me, and I desire your love and confidence. I did feel that Bro. Thatcher and others were unjust in B. B. and C. matters in refusing my stock representation on the Board, but that is now a thing of the past.

Moses Thatcher explained that the reason for this refusal was that the Company expected trouble with the California company with whom Father was in sympathy, and hence he and colleagues did not desire their position weakened by the election of Father's representative.

Joseph F. Smith spoke concerning the morals of Isaac Trumbo and others who compose the California company. "Their morals are not good it is true, but they are equal in that respect to all Californians. At any rate they have been our friends and we should feel grateful for their labors in our behalf. Even the good and well-beloved Stanford, now Senator, is not free from illicit intercourse. But these men have done much for us politically. When I visited San Francisco Col. Trumbo took me around to the U. S. Marshal's office and introduced me, as one for whom arrest papers might be forwarded from Utah. I being under indictment for cohabitation, but the marshal said he had a capacious waste basket to which he would consign them if they did come, and he assured me that as long as I remained in San Francisco I was perfectly safe. The only feelings I have had against any of the brethren has been because I thought Moses Thatcher, John W. Taylor, William B. Preston and Alonzo Hyde had not shown proper respect to the counsel of the First Presidency. When the effort was made to settle differences existing between the California and Bullion Beck stockholders, Moses stood out against it and said he had $100,000 which he would spend in fighting these Californians. Now, there is trouble started among the interested owners in California, and I believe that the dissatisfaction was created by people from this Territory who felt chagrined at the necessity of giving 25% of their stock, as per agreement, to the California people and now desire to institute strife between them.

Should the case come into Court I greatly fear the result, as the Church is bound to be exposed in some manner, and the result may be a confiscation of stock." Quite a chat on mine matters followed. Notice has been served on the Western Union Telegraph Co. for all dispatches which have passed between California people and us, and as there was much Church business connected therewith, no telling what trouble may ensue. John W. Taylor thought that if the trouble in the west had its origin with any person in this city the matter could be checked. Moses Thatcher felt that all business rivalries should cease among the brethren.

About 4:45 p.m. we took an adjournment till tomorrow at 11 a.m.

Thursday, January 29, 1891:

At 11 a.m. our meeting convened and we all attended without having broken our fast. In addition to those present yesterday A. H. Lund was here. Prayer by Joseph F. Smith.

Lorenzo Snow asked that the Apostles have the privilege of expressing their feelings towards each other and the Presidency. This opportunity was given.

F. M. Lyman said his feelings towards all of the brethren were of the very best. He loved them all and knew the power of God accompanied them.

J. H. Smith: "If the Brethren have anything against me they have never said so, and if I had anything against them I would have said so."

H. J. Grant: "I have none but the best of feelings now for all the brethren, though a short time since I felt hard towards Pres. Cannon because I thought he was the cause of a number of humiliations which I received in the Quorum. I also was hurt deeply by remarks which Moses Thatcher made about me, but he has made ample apology for all these. I have felt at times that the brethren have misunderstood my business motives and intentions, but I can truly say that my greatest ambition has been and is to see Zion prosper and all her institutions flourish. Any success I have had either here or on my recent trip east was due alone to the blessings of God upon me."

George Q. Cannon said the remarks of Bro. Grant were a great revelation to him. He had not been conscious of injuring him in any way, and as for failing to confide fully in his brethren if he failed to tell them many things it was because he thought it Pres. Woodruff's place to say what he felt led to do to the brethren. "Why" he asked, "should I be blamed for keeping secrets, when Pres. Woodruff knows them and could tell if he desired." He said he had perfect confidence in the brethren.

Moses Thatcher explained away the differences which had existed between him and others. Now he was in full accord with all the brethren.[2]

F. D. Richards, John W. Taylor, A. H. Lund and myself expressed our perfect harmony with all the Quorum and First Presidency.

Pres. L. Snow: It has been the rule of the past with me to honor and reverence the Priesthood. I may and do see things in the leaders which are not in exact harmony with my views, but that does not affect my faith in the least. I may criticize the actions of our leaders, but never do I question their authority. I saw Joseph the Prophet do, and heard him say, things which I never expected to see and hear in a Prophet of God, yet I was always able to throw the mantle of charity over improper things. I feel like David of old who would not raise his hand against the anointed of God even though Saul had sought to take his life. We have got to submit to things that do not agree with

---

[2] These occasions of full accord seemed to last but a short time. As the months and years passed, Elder Thatcher's position became increasingly tenuous, until by early 1896 the Brethren concluded to drop him from the Quorum. He differed politically from the First Presidency; his stomach ulcers caused him acute pain whenever he ate until he became addicted to the morphine he took for the pain; and he largely quit attending his quorum council meetings, basically becoming inactive in the Apostleship. Upon losing his position, he used the newspapers to justify his conduct. This became known as the "Thatcher Episode," and these events were written up by Charles W. Penrose and published under that title by the Church. See *The Thatcher Episode: A Concise Statement of the Facts of the Case* (Salt Lake City: The Church of Jesus Christ of Latter-day Saints, 1896). After being dropped from the Quorum of the Twelve, Elder Thatcher came very close to excommunication by his stake's high council. See Kenneth W. Godfrey, "Moses Thatcher in the Dock: His Trials, the Aftermath, and His Last Days," *Journal of Mormon History* 24 (spring 1998): 55-88.

our ideas if we remain true to God, and Bro. Grant will yet live to see the day when his name will be honored among men, and again when he will be cursed to his face because of failures which will follow his enterprises. Thus will the Lord teach him and all of us to rely on Him.

Joseph F. Smith: "I have sometimes felt that Presidents Woodruff and Snow have not shown me that confidence and love which I was entitled to receive, but I often felt that I was to blame, and hence I determined to try and be worthy of their esteem. I feel that there is not the humility and contrition shown by the apostles which once characterized them, nor is proper reverence for the Priesthood and sacred things always shown. Personally I have no complaints to make, for no matter what course a man takes or however much he may injure me, if he will keep the faith and be true to the brethren I can forgive him. I love and honor men who are true to God and I look upon Franklin D. Richards and George Q. Cannon with love and admiration because they were faithful when the devil seemed determined to kick them out of the Church; when their brethren turned upon them and sought occasion against them they were true to God and their religion.

"I believe that John D. Lee who in his fanaticism committed murder will receive a far greater glory than some of those who executed him, because he paid the penalty of his crime, and was true to God and his brethren."[3] Pres. Smith closed with the motion that "we seek to live so humbly before the Lord that we may get the Spirit, so that we may place His will uppermost and make everything subservient thereto, and that His kingdom may be first and foremost with us. We also agree to bury all ill feelings and past differences and henceforth be united in all things and forgiving to each other. If we will do this all our troubles will sink into insignificance and we will accomplish all we desire." This motion was unanimously carried.

---

[3] John D. Lee was a central figure in the Mountain Meadows Massacre, which is considered one of the most tragic incidents in Mormon history. He was later executed by the state for his part in the slaying of troublesome California-bound immigrants passing through Southern Utah. See also AHC journals, 11 and 13 June 1895.

Presidents Woodruff and Snow expressed their love for and confidence in Pres. Smith.

We now partook of the Sacrament after the bread and wine had been blessed by Lorenzo Snow. Bro. George Reynolds, our secretary, took part with us in this blessing.

Sunday, March 15, 1891:

At 2 p.m. I attended the Tabernacle services. Heber J. Grant was the first speaker. He occupied about a half an hour in speaking about union and the causes thereof among the Saints. Father then spoke for 40 minutes in relation to our duty in sending abroad the printed word and in warning those whom we meet of the restoration of the gospel and the judgments which are to follow its proclamation.

Monday, March 30, 1891:

I then went with Father and all my brothers down to Willard, over to Savage's photograph gallery where we had our picture taken in a group. Father, John Q., Frank and myself also had ours taken together. I had mine taken alone at the request of the photographer as he desired to keep it on sale....[4]

Wednesday, April 1, 1891:

I posted the office cash book in the morning, and then was running around considerable to try and arrange a loan for Father to pay his Cannon & Sons stock debt. At noon I assisted F. D. Richards set apart four young ladies to act as midwives. They have studied and graduated under Dr. Ellis R. Shipp.

At 2 p.m. I attended the meeting of the Twelve in the prayer room of the Gardo House. Present: Lorenzo Snow, F. D. Richards, F. M. Lyman, J. H. Smith, H. J. Grant (he came in a little late) J. W. Taylor, M. W. Merrill, A. H. Lund and myself. Moses Thatcher could not be present today.

Opened by singing three verses of "Oh my Father," prayer by M. W. Merrill. Pres. Snow felt glad to meet again in this capacity. He

---

[4] Charles R. Savage was perhaps the most famous photographer of early Mormonism.

felt that we would be privileged to receive much light and revelation in our future meetings. "I feel that we will do all that God expects of us, and all that we were sent here to do. When I feel the spirit of my brethren, as I have done, I know that they will perform a mighty work. I believe these apostles were chosen before they came to this earth to do the labor to which they are now called, and perform the duties of apostles."[5]

F. D. Richards now read the continuation from the History of the latter-day apostles from the point where he discontinued at our previous meeting. Today's reading, in which H. J. Grant assisted, contained an account of the meetings and duties of the Quorum in 1835 and down to the martyrdom of David W. Patten, the apostle "who laid down his life for his friends."[6] About 4:30 p.m. we adjourned till tomorrow. We met for a few moments with the Presidency thereafter to consider the wisdom of John Henry Smith acting as the President of the *Standard* Publishing Co. of Ogden, a position to which he has been recently elected, he being a republican in principle. Father explained in detail the political move in Weber County and then further consideration of the subject was deferred till tomorrow....

Thursday, April 2, 1891:

At 11 a.m. I was at the Gardo House where all the brethren of yesterday were present, and about an hour after commencing Moses Thatcher came in. Meeting was opened with the hymn, "Come let us anew," and prayer by John Henry Smith. I was asked to take the minutes, which I did.

Pres. Snow spoke briefly: "If we are engaged in any business that is not in accordance with God's will we will not prosper therein. I believe you apostles will yet be blessed with the presence of Jesus in your midst, and He will lay his hands upon your heads. This, too,

---

[5] For an explanation of the LDS doctrine of foreordination, see *Called of God, by Prophecy*, 25-37.

[6] John Henry Smith's diary records that "the time was spent in reading some notes made by Bro. F. D. Richards on the early history of the Twelve" (*Church, State, and Politics*, 251).

before He comes in great glory. The apostles should desire and pray for this blessing, and also to live till the end of time.

"I do not know but what Joseph and his co-laborers on the other side of the vail have the privilege of calling brethren from this earth to assist them, but you need not go. You should live above sin and without pain, except the pain caused by seeing the sins of others around you."

Heber. J. Grant: "I am convinced that those who have died in the faith exert an influence upon those who live on the earth. When my brother George accidentally shot and killed himself I felt very sad, because he was a most faithful Latter-day Saint. I brooded over his death until the Spirit impressed me that my father desired his services on the other side. I then felt easy.

"When I was called to the apostleship I felt so unworthy that I desired to decline the honor. Even after my ordination this feeling continued until about three months later while on a mission with Brigham Young Jr. in Arizona. I was one day riding alone and thinking of my unworthiness, when the Spirit impressed me just as though a voice had spoken, 'You were not worthy but the Prophet Joseph to whom you will belong in the next world, and your father, have interceded for you that you might be called, and now it remains for you to prove yourself worthy.'[7] I certainly desire to live and do good."

At this juncture the Presidency entered, and the matter of John Henry Smith accepting the Presidency of the Ogden *Standard* Company was discussed. Each of the brethren spoke on the subject and none favored it. The fear of division and antagonism in our quorum was manifested; also the step might cause a loss of influence on the part of Bro. Smith. The feeling was general that we should hold ourselves aloof from politics. If the *Standard* can sell out to advantage there will be no objection thereto, though it is realized that the paper can do a vast amount of good if controlled by our people, even if ostensibly managed by Gentiles. After Pres. Woodruff

---

[7] Some particulars of Heber J. Grant's account of his call to the Apostleship have been disputed by some historians but are clarified here. See *Called of God, by Prophecy*, 79-80, 90 n. 8.

expressed himself as opposed to J. H. Smith acting in the capacity mentioned, the latter said he would inform the stock-holders that he could not accept the proffered position.[8] Father in his remarks, spoke strongly on the political move in Ogden. He knew the Lord's hand was in it, though what the result will be I cannot say. "I feel more and more how little is my wisdom when contemplating the works of God. When the manifesto was issued it shattered many of my fondest anticipations, yet I know it was inspired by God. So, too, in our political moves they do not agree with my desires or ideas, still I knew God is controlling and directing them, and this is the great comfort I have that he will bring triumph to His work."

It being after two o'clock we partook of the Sacrament (bread and wine) after it was blessed by Joseph F. Smith. Thereafter Pres. Woodruff spoke: "In the name of Jesus Christ I say that God has not forsaken the Presidency or Twelve. He inspired me to issue the manifesto and if he had not done so I should never have taken that course even though all ordinances for the living and the dead had ceased, and our temples had fallen into the hands of our enemies. The principle of plural marriage will yet be restored to this Church, but how or when I cannot say.[9] God will hold this nation responsible for the wrongs done this people.

"The Presidency and apostles will be organized when Christ comes to the earth."

Friday, April 3, 1891:

I accompanied Frank to the Gardo House to see the Presidency about John Henry Smith acting on the *Standard* board. They gave permission for him to qualify as President so as to avoid confusion in

---

[8] For 2 April, John Henry Smith's diary records: "The Ogden Standard matter was talked over and spoke upon it. It was concluded I better not enter the Political field." (*Church, State, and Politics*, 251).

[9] This statement of President Woodruff's affirms that the Manifesto was given him by revelation. Some writers have used his expression "will yet be restored" to infer that issuance of the Manifesto was a strategic tactic to preserve plural marriage in the Church—that President Woodruff would soon rescind his Manifesto. This interpretation seems unwarranted when placed in context with his other statements. See the introductory essay.

the calling of another stockholder's meeting, and then he is to resign the Presidency, though he may act as a director if he so desires....[10]

Monday, April 27, 1891:

We then went to meeting where F. D. Richards occupied the time in an able manner. Encouraged the Saints in their singing, to pay their Fast offerings promptly and liberally, and then spoke on how the testimony of the gospel has gone through this nation by means of the cases which have been considered and deliberated before the Supreme Court, and the questions about us which have been debated in both houses of Congress....

Pres. L. Snow then spoke strongly against the marriage of Saints with outsiders. This course is sure to bring unhappiness sooner or later....

Joseph W. Summerhays and I spent about 2 hours with Rudger Clawson and family where we had supper, and listened to his interesting recital of Joseph Standing's murder.[11] We then went to Sister Minnie J. Snow's and spent some time very pleasantly. The boys' drum corps serenaded us while at the latter place. The manifesto was the principal topic of conversation with Sister Snow, and she said that there were over 25 unmarried ladies of her age in Brigham City alone, who would now most likely be left as old maids. There is no doubt but many of the young people sincerely regret the issuance of the manifesto....

Thursday, May 14, 1891:

At 2 p.m. I was at my Council meeting where were present, W. Woodruff, George Q. Cannon, F. D. Richards, Moses Thatcher, J. H. Smith, H. J. Grant, J. W. Taylor, M. W. Merrill and myself; George Reynolds, clerk. Bro. Merrill offered prayer, and then the

---

[10] For 3 April, John Henry Smith's diary records: "Presidents Woodruff, Cannon and Smith asked me to go to Ogden and qualify for a Director and President of the Standard Publishing and Printing Co. I did so and will resign the Presidency at once and remain a Director" (*Church, State, and Politics*, 251).

[11] For further information about the murder by a mob of Elder Joseph Standing, see David S. Hoopes and Roy Hoopes *The Making of a Mormon Apostle: The Story of Rudger Clawson* (Lanham: Madison Books, 1990), 1-31.

Conference appointments were made. John W. Taylor reported satisfactory progress on the defense fund business.

I asked concerning a young man who some years since passed through the endowment house and was sealed to his wife without having been ordained to any Priesthood. Is it necessary for him to pass through the Temple or can he be ordained now as an Elder? The latter course, it was said, is all that is necessary.

Bro. Merrill said his son had a similar experience, and Pres. Young directed that he merely be ordained.

John W. Taylor asked what he should do in the case of numerous women who applied to him for the privilege of being sealed to his father. None of them are such as he would personally desire to take. The brethren felt it is not right to allow any and everyone to be sealed to the dead, and felt that John W. should not consent to having any sealed to his father except such as he could take himself after considering the disparity in ages. Bro. Merrill said Pres. Taylor felt to protect the interests of Pres. Young in this matter after his demise, and he thought each President of the Church should look after his predecessor's rights in this respect.

The question was asked if the apostles were at liberty to perform marriage ceremonies for such persons as are unable for any reason to go to the temple for the time being. The answer was in the affirmative.

Saturday, June 6, 1891:

At 11 a.m. I attended the Priesthood meeting. After the usual business H. J. Grant spoke strongly on the principle of tithing and donation. I also spoke about 15 min. on the duties of teachers, and told the Priesthood not to address the Saints unless the Spirit of the Lord prompted the remarks. The necessity of continuing the monthly Free Will Offerings was urged. It was advised that our meeting houses be not used for the holding of political meetings....

Monday, June 8, 1891:

Bro. Grant and I went to the Gardo House and reported our labors, and in the course of the conversation the Whitney *History of*

Utah and Dr. Williams management of its issuance were discussed. The brethren felt fearful, from reports that reach them, that there is a chance for a big swindle of the Saints in this affair, and, at any rate, the Presidency do not approve of the way their names are used to secure subscriptions to the book. Bishop Whitney was sent for, and asked in relation to the work. He seems to have confidence in the integrity of John Williams, but feels desirous that a committee should give the matter attention, and so arrange the affair that we all feel secure. I was appointed a member of such committee....

Tuesday, June 9, 1891:

I then went to the Gardo House where Father, J. H. Smith, John Morgan and others were talking about politics. The danger of our people all becoming Democrats through the influence of the *Herald* which is widely circulated is feared, and the results of such a course would doubtless prove most disastrous to us, for we would have a repetition of the persecutions which we have endured for 5 or 6 years past. It is felt that efforts should be made to instruct our people in Republicanism, and thus win them to that party. The influence of the *Tribune* thus broken, we may look for good results to follow this division.

I met with the building committee of Young University where Willard Young submitted a preliminary draft for the building,...

It was thought best to try and purchase the interests of all of Pres. Young's heirs to the square where the building is to be erected, who will not sign the deed without pay, and to build the south east corner of the structure first....

At 4 p.m. I was at a meeting of the committee on publication of Whitney's *History of Utah*. The members present were, John R. Winder, Chairman, F. S. Richards, O. F. Whitney, George Reynolds, C. W. Penrose and myself. We considered the charges made against Williams and his agents which come from various parts of the Territory, and Bishop Whitney said that whenever complaints had reached Dr. Williams they had been investigated and corrected. He had made personal visits to settle some feelings which had been created by an agent in Sanpete County.

To allay our suspicions concerning the honesty of Dr. Williams a number of letters were read testifying to his good character, and the bond of $25,000 which he has furnished as security for the faithful performance of his labor has been fully verified.

It was finally resolved to have Bishop Whitney get an extension of time on his bond for the completion of his part of writing the history. The history was to be completed within two years from it commencement, or about one year from today, the bond for which is $5,000, but the author has only done about one half of the first volume up to the present. An extension of time was, however, proffered him. This done we decided to invite the publisher, Dr. Williams to be present at a meeting and hear the charges made against him, after which we will request him to increase his bond to $50,000 as he originally agreed to do.

My fears concerning this matter are very much calmed by the conversation of today....

Wednesday, June 10, 1891:

At the latter time I went to the Gardo House where a number of the apostles met with the Territorial People's Party delegates who met today and disbanded that Party thus leaving the people free to unite with either of the National parties they may select. Joseph F. Smith, Father and Wilford Woodruff each spoke to the brethren, and while they desired the Saints to join the different organizations, they did not want them to go en masse to either party. If we can divide about evenly between the parties, leaving an uncertain element to be converted to either side, it is thought the best results will follow....

Friday, June 12, 1891:

I wrote some letters at the office for a short time in the forenoon, and then had a conversation at my room with Bishop O. F. Whitney concerning the *History of Utah*. He says that Dr. Williams has become so annoyed at the numerous reports which have been circulated concerning his trustworthiness, and his character has been so maligned, that he is determined to get out of the business if Bishop Whitney can find someone who will be congenial to him to buy his interest, which is 45 % of the whole enterprise; 5% is owned by F. S. Richards, who is the attorney, 25% by O. F. Whitney, who receive $200 per month as an advance on his share for writing the work, and 25% by Mr. Webster, who is the secretary. The Bishop thinks there is big money in the enterprise for anyone who will buy it. He thinks the Dr. will take $10,000 for his share of a business which he feels is worth $30,000. Orson is very anxious for George Q. Cannon and Sons' Co. to take the business, and thus reassure the doubting people of the certainty of the issuance of the work. We together laid the matter before Father and then before the First Presidency. After considerable talk on the subject, on suggestion of Pres. Joseph F. Smith it was decided that O. F. Whitney and F. S. Richards make another effort to get Dr. Williams to continue in the business, but if he refuses to do so, then I had better investigate the matter, and if the results warrant it, buy out his share....

Monday, June 15, 1891:

At 9 a.m. I met O. F. Whitney and Dr. Williams and had some conversation about the *History of Utah*. The latter is very desirous that we purchase his interest and thus reassure the people of Utah that it will be issued, though he expresses a desire to continue with the thing and work to make it a gigantic success. I presented the matter to the First Presidency who told me to investigate the affair, and if everything was satisfactory to engage in it. Two of Dr. Williams' agents, Waterman and Clark, called to see me in the afternoon, as they had heard rumors of the pending sale, telling me of claims which they hold against the concern for canvassing services. The former spoke as though Mr. Williams is a rogue, but he was very desirous that I should not tell the latter of his visit to me. Mr. Clark said Mr. Webster had always treated him in the best possible manner. Their claims are really not due until the first volume is issued and delivered. Father's principal objection to the enterprise is the length of time required by Bishop Whitney to complete the manuscript—5 years from the time it was commenced....

I was invited to a Republican council with the Presidency this morning, where it was felt that this party must arouse itself or Democracy will sweep the Territory....

Tuesday, June 16, 1891:

At 11 a.m. Frank and I met with Dr. Williams, Mr. Webster and O. F. Whitney. We spent several hours in looking over the accounts of the Utah Historical Society and inquiring into the details of the publishing arrangements. The proposition finally made was that the Dr. remain with the business and receive 33-1/3% commission on all orders for books and pictures, and that he sell us 70% of the business with his already accrued commissions for $15,896. The actual orders taken for the book amount now to over 2,500 at $30 per set. Available notes would be turned over to us in this deal to the amount of seven or eight thousand dollars. As pictured by Williams and Webster there is big money for us in this undertaking, but it also means a considerable outlay before returns are had. We presented the matter to the First Presidency and they decided to consider it for a day or two....

Friday, June 19, 1891:

I also wrote a letter to Dr. John O. Williams making him a proposition in regard to the purchase of his interest in the *History of Utah*. I submitted the letter to Father and Joseph F. Smith before sending it and they approved it. The offer is that we give him $12,000 for all his right, title and interest in the work to date. He is then to receive 33-1/3% commission on all book and picture orders. The amount is to be paid as follows: $6,000 cash down; $3,000 when the first copy of the first volume is issued, and the remaining $3,000 when 2,000 copies of the first volume are issued. In the afternoon he came in the office and accepted our offer with these changes, that he be engaged as canvasser for at least three years, and that a certain date be fixed for the payments of the two latter notes, at such a time as we think the conditions of our proposition are fulfilled. We agreed to these modifications....

Sunday, June 21, 1891:

We spoke about the political situation [to the southern Utah stake presidencies] and urged the brethren to start the agitation in their respective counties, but to see that each party had a fair show. The Presidency of the Stake would use their endeavors to have the two parties about equally divided as to strength. Our counsel given to them was to be kept secret, but they were to act as if from their own volition.

Wednesday, June 24, 1891:

About five hours of today I was engaged in my room with Dr. Williams and Mr. Webster checking up the *History of Utah* business. I found that about 2,700 bona fide contracts for the work have been obtained. Notes for about $7,500 are on hand. There are time commissions due agents when the books are delivered to the amount of about $7,000. Judging from what appears on the books the business is in a very good condition. We agreed to meet F. S. Richards tomorrow to prepare the legal papers necessary to the transfer....

Thursday, June 25, 1891:

At 11 a.m. I met Dr. J. O. Williams and Mr. Webster at F. S. Richards' office where we talked over with the latter the terms of our agreement in regard to the publishing of Whitney's *History of Utah*, and instructed him to prepare the necessary papers for the transfer....

Saturday, June 27, 1891:

F. S. Richards, Frank Cannon and I had a conversation with him in relation to the Utah History, and read him the papers in relation thereto. He approved of them with two or three slight changes. At 2:30 p.m. F. S. Richards, O. F. Whitney, Dr. Williams, Mr. Webster, Frank and myself met in the office of the first named and consulted about the agreements for the transfer of the Utah History business. We had considerable talk about their receiving their full commissions out of the first collections on the books, and finally compromised by their agreeing to accept _ of their commission out of collections on the first volume, and the other _ when the second volume is delivered and paid for.

We adjourned till Monday to finish the business, as we could not do it today owing to the changes to be made in the papers....

Sunday, June 28, 1891:

At two p.m. I attended the Tabernacle meeting, where Charles W. Penrose spoke an hour and ten minutes on the text from the Doctrine and Covenants where God says what He appoints shall endure, but everything else will be shaken and destroyed Among other things he spoke of matrimony and our views concerning it. He could not imagine what our young people were thinking about when they were married by those who united them only for time, when the authority is here and can be exercised to seal for time and eternity....

Monday, June 29, 1891:

I was engaged in the office till 10 a.m. at which time Frank and I met Dr. Williams and the others of Saturday's meeting and made final arrangements for the payment of the money ($6,000) and notes ($6,000) this afternoon and the transfer of the business to us. This was done at 4 p.m. when all the papers, etc., were completed and properly signed, and with the very best of feelings we started out on our new venture.

At 11 a.m. I met in council with W. Woodruff, George Q. Cannon, F. D. Richards, M. Thatcher, F. M. Lyman, J. H. Smith, H. J. Grant, M. W. Merrill, A. H. Lund and clerk George Gibbs. The political situation was discussed and it was deemed advisable for us to do our utmost to keep the two political parties about evenly divided in this Territory. It was also thought best for our people to refrain from accepting nominations, except where they are thrust upon them, and to rather seek for honorable Gentiles to fill the various positions....

Tuesday, July 7, 1891:

At 2 p.m. I met in the Gardo House with my Quorum. Present: L. Snow, F. D. Richards, M. Thatcher, F. M. Lyman, J. H. Smith,

H. J. Grant, J. W. Taylor, M. W. Merrill, A. H. Lund and myself. Singing: "Come let us anew, etc." Prayer by Moses Thatcher. Pres. Snow then said: "I feel safe in saying that no twelve men since the days of Adam have had greater responsibilities resting upon them than we now have. We live in the flood of intelligence, and also in the midst of supreme wickedness, and hence the necessity for superior intelligence. God will, however, assist us if we live aright, as He did Enoch, and cause us to become powerful among the children of men. I desire all the brethren to be united in whatever labors we have to perform.

"I would like to have the brethren express themselves in regard to the political situation, and what is best for us to do in this condition of affairs. I feel that the Lord will eventually bring good out of this movement."

Moses Thatcher after detailing at considerable length the political situation here, said: "In a council of the First Presidency and Apostles held a short time ago we were united in saying John Henry Smith should not actively engage in politics, and yet he has done so, doubtless with the sanction of the Presidency. If he goes into politics I do not know why other Apostles should not seek to make converts to their principles. I am opposed to the Church using any influence to turn the people to one party or the other, and if we play with these things it will bring ruin to us. We will never become a strong people until we act conscientiously in politics." He referred to the disaster in Idaho by which 175 of our people withdrew from the Church in order to vote, and through this act they lost privileges which have never yet been regained.

Franklin D. Richards: "I have never taken very much interest in politics, but I am anxious to labor to prevent our disfranchisement. Efforts will be made to catch the Priesthood influencing people in their political affairs, and such a hue and cry will then be raised as we have never yet heard. I have not yet had any manifestation that we will become a State, but I do believe the Lord will bring good out of this movement."

Francis M. Lyman: "It has seemed quite proper to me for the people to divide on party lines, and I would like to see as near an equal division as possible. Still I believe the people are mostly Democrats, though I am a Republican and expect to work for my party. I do not think bitterness between brethren will result from this political division."

John Henry Smith having withdrawn in order to fill a political appointment in the north, Heber J. Grant was the next speaker. "I would like to see the 'Liberal' ring broken up, but do not believe it can be accomplished by a fusion of Republicans and Democrats. John Henry Smith's actions in the Republican party make it almost necessary for some Democratic apostles to take the stump. Already Judd, Dyer and others feel that the Church is restraining me from making speeches so that the Republicans can get a good start in the Territory. I am not sure but what it would be best for Bro. Thatcher and myself to make some speeches for the Democrats." At this point Bro. Grant made some remarks in favor of protection in connection with our sugar industry which called forth opposing remarks from Bro. Thatcher and a brief colloquy ensued. Pres. Snow reproved them for their disputation and both apologized.

John W. Taylor: "I believe the Lord is in the present agitation, and He will cause it to bring us relief as individuals and as a Church. The apostles should, however, in my opinion, keep out of politics as much as possible. I fear if we make ourselves too prominent in these affairs, traps will be set for us, and trouble will follow. One or several brethren from Cache valley suggested to the First Presidency a few days since that as Bro. Thatcher and Merrill had difficulties years ago with each other, it would now be quite proper for them to be opposed in politics. The suggestion gave me sorrow."

Mariner W. Merrill: Bro. Thatcher will agree with me in saying that we have no unsettled difficulties between us, and have for years worked together in the most perfect harmony. Being engaged in the Temple I have not engaged in politics to any extent, yet I do feel that the Church should not attempt to manipulate one or both of the parties. The last time I met Pres. Taylor he said to me: "I may never see you again and I want to tell you that I have seen the Prophet Joseph, who said the Lord did not want His people to be concerned about the raid or inquire when it would cease. 'It will stop in mine own due time,' said the Lord. Joseph, however, said it made him sad to see his own son (Joseph Smith Jr.[III], who was then traveling through the territory preaching against this Church) trying to tear down what he had given his life to establish. 'Now' continued Pres. Taylor, 'you will be blessed in devoting yourself to the work in the temple.' And this I have tried to do."

Anthon H. Lund: "I have not been very actively engaged in politics, and any influence I have used in Sanpete County has not resulted in making many Republicans. I believe those who have taken sides are firm, and this is as it should be. I favor this division on National party lines, as I believe it will prevent a division on clerical and anticlerical lines which has been the tendency of late years and would be very disastrous to us as a people."

Abraham H. Cannon: "I fear that animosities may result from this division, but if not I heartily favor the movement. I do not like to see John Henry made the object of the jeers and insults of his political opponents, and would feel much better if he and all the apostles could keep free from politics. I favor the non-interference of the Church in these matters. I have joined neither party."

We now adjourned till 10 a.m. tomorrow....

Wednesday, July 8, 1891:

At 10 a.m. went to Council meeting in the Gardo House where all the brethren of yesterday were present except Moses Thatcher, who started east this morning on some public business, and John Henry Smith who was in attendance at the Salt Lake County Republican Convention. Opened by singing, "O, my Father, etc." Prayer by F. D. Richards. The Presidency being unable to meet with us today we decided to postpone partaking of the sacrament till tomorrow with them. We therefore spent the time today in listening to the history of the apostles of the latter-days as prepared by F. D. Richards. The period of time covered in today's reading was from the death of David W. Patten till the return to America of the Apostles whom the Lord sent to preach the gospel in Europe in the year 1839-40-41. Many interesting items were presented in this manuscript.

Thursday, July 9, 1891:

At the latter hour [10 a.m.] I went to the Gardo house where our meetings of yesterday were continued. We had with us today, in addition to the brethren of yesterday, George Q. Cannon, Joseph F. Smith and John Henry Smith. Pres. Woodruff was so sick as to be unable to attend. Singing: "God moves in a mysterious way," etc. Prayer by F. M. Lyman. Pres. Snow told what we had done in former meetings. "We desire to be united in all things with the Presidency, and whatever they wish done in political or other matters we will try to accomplish." John Henry Smith felt anxious to do only that which would advance the work of God. He thought when this political division occurred and all seemed to be turning to Democracy that he could see great danger to us; hence he announced himself a Republican and began working to make converts. He had not been counseled by the Presidency to take the course he did, but felt to be guided by the Spirit of God. "I have tried to disprove the theory that this Territory belonged to the Democrats by divine right."

Pres. Snow said the question for us now to determine was whether or not we approve of the apostles making public acknowledgment of their political faith. If the brethren do engage in politics they should not indulge in personal remarks, but be as Dr. Franklin was who conducted a paper for 30 years and never gave offense to any person. "I feel that Bro. John Henry is taking the proper course, but hope no more of the brethren will be under the necessity of taking the stump."

Joseph F. Smith: "We have received the strongest admonitions from our Republican friends that we must not allow this Territory to go strongly Democratic. We favored John Henry's going on the stump so as to convince the people that a man could be a Republican and still be a Saint. I wish more of the apostles belonged to this party and would sign the roll. The Republicans will stand by their friends, which the Democrats have not done, and I believe they will yet grant us amnesty if we encourage them to believe this may become a Republican state. I know many prominent men of this party who are today our friends and are working in our interests, but I do not know a single Democrat who is helping us...."

George Q. Cannon: "We have approved John Henry's course...." He referred to the labors of Judge Estee and Col. Isaac Trumbo, whose hearts h ad been touched by the Lord, and softened towards us. Especially has the latter been interested and he has spent large sums of money and a great deal of time to do us service, and this without any hope of pecuniary reward. He has, however, acknowledged the blessing of God on his labors.... "Whatever may be the result of our labors, if we do all we can, the issue we can then safely leave in the hands of the Lord. If the First Presidency and Twelve are united there is no power that can hurt them or prevent the success of their labors. The clouds which seem to obscure John Henry's reputation will soon pass away. The legislators which are soon to be elected should be opposed to disfranchisement and in favor of statehood for Utah and their pledges should thus be taken. My idea would be for good Gentiles to be nominated for these offices in this and a few other counties." F. M. Lyman said the Twelve would always be united with the First Presidency when they were informed of matters which were occurring, but being sometimes left in partial or total ignorance, they did not always act with that unanimity which should characterize them. Father said he had felt at times that the Twelve lacked confidence in the Presidency but the latter had never concealed anything because of fear of the apostles, but in order to protect our friends.

It was explained that the duties of the proposed secret committee to act in political matters was only to try and prevent the people going overwhelmingly in either direction, and not to influence or coerce them contrary to their desires....

Monday, July 20, 1891:
The afternoon services were occupied by F. M. Lyman in a very practical sermon. He testified that God had never permitted the authorities of the Church to mislead the people and He never would permit the President to lead them away from the truth.

Saturday, July 25, 1891:

At the time mentioned [3:30 p.m.] I went to the U. I. depot where I took the train for Preston. Father and Bishop Whitney traveled on the same train as far North as Brigham City. Bro. L. F. Moench traveled from Ogden to my destination where we arrived at 9:45 p.m. and were met by Bishop William C. Parkinson and Presidents George C. Parkinson and Mathias F. Cowley. We were entertained at the home of the former. His wife here told me that when I was here last in blessing her new born babe I had promised it should live to manhood. Several weeks thereafter it was taken sick with pneumonia and while in this condition the Elders who administered to it promised it continued life. Yet it died and being their first and only son out of several children the blow was a severe one. I could not account for the failure of our promises that it should live except that sympathy instead of the Spirit of God prompted the utterances.

Sunday, July 26, 1891 [Preston, Idaho]:

At 10 o'clock the Stake Conference convened and there was a good attendance. Apostle M. W. Merrill, who came up yesterday with a plural wife, was the first speaker. He urged the Saints to be punctual in keeping all their appointments of whatever nature they might be. They should be punctual at all meetings, in keeping promises which they make relating to business or religion....

In the afternoon meeting I occupied nearly an hour in referring to the conditions which will hereafter exist in the Church because of the purity of its members. We should seek to overcome all our weaknesses and set such an example to the world that they will desire to follow it....

At the close of this meeting we met with the Stake Presidency and Superintendency of Secondary Schools to try and settle some differences which exist particularly between Bro. C. Parkinson and William Webster, which caused the former to say one or the other must be relieved of his position. We listened patiently to the unpleasantnesses which are all of a financial nature, but which are not so serious but what we think they can be overcome. We therefore advised them to get together and settle them between themselves, as they are both too energetic and faithful in their callings for us to feel that we can spare either. They expressed their willingness to accept this counsel though Bro. Parkinson had very little faith in its lasting benefits, as the same course had been followed so frequently in the past. He was told, however, to continue making the effort even until he had forgiven his opponent seventy times seven in one day. After we adjourned these brethren therefore met and settled the matter between them....

Thursday, August 6, 1891:

It was about 2:30 when I arrived at my Council meeting. There were present, the First Presidency, F. D. Richards, J. H. Smith, H. J. Grant, J. W. Taylor, and myself; George Gibbs, clerk. F. S. Richards was present and read a number of questions prepared by himself and W. H. Dickson to give an idea of the inquiries which will be made in relation to the manifesto and the abandonment of polygamy, when the matter of disposing of the Church property is considered by the Master of Chancery. Some of these questions it will be hard for any of the brethren to answer satisfactorily. It is thought likely that Lorenzo Snow and F. D. Richards will be the best men to act as witnesses....

Sunday, August 9, 1891:

I went to the farm where I remained until time for the afternoon meeting when I went to the Tabernacle. I was the first speaker and occupied 40 min. in a discourse on the plan which the Lord has prepared for the redemption of His children. He will save those who have died or do die without hearing the truth, and even those who reject the truth will be rewarded for all their good deeds.

Heber J. Grant spoke 20 minutes in enlargement of some of my remarks upon the work for the dead.

When meeting closed Heber said that before coming to meeting he had thought of a subject which he felt anxious for Mr. Aubertin, who said he would be present, to hear, and that was the very one I handled, quoting one passage concerning the sons of perdition which he had read just before coming to meeting, and which he thought of mentioning were he to speak.

Rabbi Brown came to the stand after meeting and expressed his pleasure at the doctrines he had heard. He felt that the Mormons should be left alone to work out the problem they have undertaken. He was formerly much prejudiced against us, but on seeing and hearing us he feels that he was hasty in his judgment. He is a noted Jewish Rabbi from the east who is traveling through the country during his vacation.

A young man appealed to me to know more about our doctrines. He is a recent arrival from England and the States, and expects to find work on the D. and R G. Line as a telegraph operator. He said he was impressed by my remarks and was anxious to converse with me. I spoke to him on the principles of the gospel, and then took him to the office and gave him a *Voice of Warning*. I urged him to read it, and pray to God for guidance, and I could assure him that he would be led to join the Church. He seemed to be very anxious to know what course to pursue in order to please God....

Wednesday, August 12, 1891:

For the afternoon I had a long talk with Susa Young Gates in relation to the story she proposes to have published in the East which gives a glimpse of life among the Mormons, and also names some of their principles. We also conversed about Sister Jakeman's proposition to take half the paper and attend to the business management while Susa does the editing. I advised Sister Gates not to let her have a one-half interest, but to retain the control in her own hands. I expressed a belief that it would not be long before Sister Jakeman would possess the whole thing if she were given so good a start. She said she felt as I did about the matter....

A scandal has just been unearthed concerning ex-deputy marshal, now Detective E. A. Franks, by which it is discovered that he has been married at least four times—once in Georgia, once in Alabama, once in Nebraska and once in this city. Though a bigamist it is feared he cannot be prosecuted because of the time which has elapsed since his crimes were committed. He was most vigorous at one time in trying to abolish Mormon polygamy, by hounding honorable men and their faithful and acknowledged wives....

Thursday, August 20, 1891:

At 2 p.m. I attended my regular Council meeting where all the Presidency and Twelve were present excepting Brigham Young, John Henry Smith and George Teasdale. George Gibbs was clerk, and Franklin S. Richards was present. The matter to be considered was what to do in the Church property case which is soon to be brought before the Master-in-Chancery. The government expects him to suggest some plan by which some $400,000 of property can be disposed of to satisfy the persons who contributed the same. After prayer by Lorenzo Snow, F. S. Richards read a "scheme" which the Church attorneys prepared and proposed to submit to the Master, by which the property can be turned over to the Presidency of this Church, and be invested by them according to their best judgment to bring in the largest returns, and all the profits of these investments are to be used for the benefit of the poor of said Church. The Presidency are then to be required to file annually with the Court a statement of all business connected with this fund.

If it were only to secure these funds the brethren all seemed to be inclined to let the matter drop without any protest from us, but it is felt that the situation here demands the saying of something in regard to the Manifesto and our future intentions in regard to polygamy, and hence it is expected that we will prove that the latter is really abandoned. Written questions, which it is likely will be asked in Court, have been sent to all the Twelve for their replies, but only Bros. Snow and Lund have thus far answered them. Some of these are very searching, and almost make us, if we answer them the way it is desired, deny the principle of plural marriage for all time. We all believe that this suspension is merely temporary, and, that God will open the way for his divine revelation to be established, but judging from a human standpoint plural marriage is forever stopped.[12]

---

[12] Use of this statement to support the charge that the Manifesto was but a strategic move to keep plural marriage alive is unwarranted. Yet it is also true that the Brethren began to realize that suspension of the principle would

The questions and answers of Bros. Snow and Lund were then submitted and in general approved, and after considerable discussion it was decided by unanimous vote that Father, L. Snow, M. Thatcher, Bro. Lund and any others whom the Presidency may select, receive our support in going on the witness stand to answer any questions which may be propounded.

It was also decided that the "scheme" presented be accepted by us with such modifications and changes as the First Presidency may see proper to make. John W. Taylor was the only one who did not vote on these propositions, he feeling that we had better take no action whatever in the matter.

It was decided by vote of all present, that we approve of the plan of erecting a monument in this city to Brigham Young, and that the sculptor, C. E. Dallin be employed to prepare the design and figure. The cost is to be $25,000 which amount can be raised by popular subscription. The statue of Pres. Young is to be 8 ft. high, and stand on a base embellished with entablatures containing scenes from our history. Meeting adjourned....

Friday, August 21, 1891:

I answered today for F. S. Richards the questions which were yesterday under discussion....

Monday, August 31, 1891:

I went with Father to Provo on the 7:10 a.m. train. We were a few moments at Pres. Smoot's before going to meeting.

Father spoke about an hour on the teachings of the Savior to the Nephites, when He presented the same doctrines as are contained in the Sermon on the Mount. He showed the difference between the law of Moses and the higher law established by Christ, the latter requiring the subjection of our fallen natures to the will of God in all things. He spoke strongly on adultery and warned the Saints against the committing of the same in our hearts which will lead to darkness and apostasy. His whole sermon was beautiful and convincing.

---

probably last much longer than they had at first thought. See Appendix One: Plural Marriage Issues in the Abraham H. Cannon Journals.

I spoke 20 min. about the marriage of our young people and the pure lives they should lead....

In the afternoon Bro. Lyman spoke about half an hour on the perfection for which we should aim in all things....

Tuesday, September 8, 1891:

A telegram from Washington today announces that Pres. Harrison has pardoned Joseph F. Smith of the crime of polygamy for which he was indicted some years ago since which time he has been on the "underground." This is good news to all the Saints....

Sister Davis, a wife of Theophelus Davis of the 19th Ward, came to me today with a strange tale. She has two daughters named Mary, aged 22, and Martha, aged 20. The latter is married. In the first Sunday School Union meeting I attended after returning from my mission these girls were present, and the older said to the younger when I arose to speak, "When I grow up, I am going to marry Brother Cannon." Her sister was not impressed with the remark and has, perhaps, never thought of it since; but Mary has continued to the present time to believe that she is destined to be my wife. Her fasting and prayers have only confirmed her in this belief. All advances from young men she has resolutely repulsed, and of late she has so brooded over this matter as to make herself sick. Her mother only comes to me now in the hope that I can say something to relieve the stress upon her daughter's mind. Mary says she is willing to wait for me all her life, if she can only be sealed to me for eternity.

I told her mother to say to her that the Manifesto will prevent any marriages of a plural character, and for her to cease worrying about this thing, for if the Lord has destined that we shall be united, He will direct and arrange the same in His own time and way.

She should therefore be content to leave the whole affair in the hands of God, and not make herself sick by worrying about it.

I promised to call some day and tell Mary my views and feelings in relation to this event.

Friday, September 11, 1891:

About 2:30 p.m. I went to the home of Sister Davis who visited me a few days since in regard to the strange infatuation of her daughter for me. I was introduced to this young lady named Mary. She is a tall, spare girl, with large eyes and rather pleasant countenance though seeming to lack force. She was very bashful and said but little. I told her that it was useless for her to think of me, as I am a married man, and under the present law of the Church, cannot think of such a thing as to encourage her. I told her to cease thinking of this affair and to turn her attention to the recovery of her health.....

Monday, September 21, 1891:

My youngest child, Gene, 7 days old, by Mamie, died a few minutes after 7 o'clock this morning. I had scarcely expected it to live. After receiving word of its death I went down to Mamie's and talked about its burial. I also saw Joseph E. Taylor and arranged with him to have the body deposited in my cemetery lot under the name of "Gene Crawford from Farmer's Ward." It is thought best to dispense with funeral services, as such would place me in jeopardy....[13]

At 9:30 Joseph E. Taylor brought a coffin and after placing Gene's body in it, took it away. He will see to its burial tomorrow. I remained at M.E.C's all night.

The Amnesty papers granted Pres. Joseph F. Smith by Pres. Harrison have been received by the former. He is granted a full and unconditional pardon, and is therefore again a free man. The Saints will rejoice with him in this good fortune.

Saturday, September 26, 1891:

I was in the office most of the day, where I read proofs, wrote letters, and attended to other matters of business. I visited F. D. Richards in the morning and got his ideas in regard to the best form

---

[13] These measures were necessary to protect Elder Cannon and his plural wives from law enforcement officials who could use official death records as a means of proving relations with plural wives in court.

of a family and temple record. We think of issuing one for general sale....

We set the first type today on Whitney's *History of Utah*, Vol. I. We have obtained a new font of Pica type, and nearly two cars of paper for the job....

Sunday, September 27, 1891:

At 2 p.m. I attended the Tabernacle services. Pres. Joseph F. Smith was the first speaker. He occupied about 25 minutes, but found it somewhat difficult to speak because of his emotions at again meeting with the Saints in public after a separation of over seven years, he having been that long in seclusion. Still, he bore a very strong testimony to the divinity of the Work, and its final triumph. Father followed him and spoke of the power which unites and holds this people together. If it were not for the spirit of God we would soon be disrupted and scattered. Neither man nor any set of men could hold this people together unless inspired of the Lord. He also gave a strong testimony....

Thursday, October 1, 1891:

Attended my Quorum meeting in the afternoon where were present Presidents Woodruff, Cannon, and Smith; Apostles Snow, Richards, Lyman, Grant, Taylor, Merrill, Lund and myself; L. John Nutall, clerk....

John W. Taylor desired to know how to act in selecting Bishops and other presiding officers. Shall the Priesthood nominate and the people accept, or shall the people nominate? The conclusion reached in the discussion which followed was that it is always the right of God through His Priesthood to appoint, but it is quite proper for the brethren before making appointments to consult with the local authorities and be sure to select men for position whom the people will be glad to sustain. Father said we should treat the people as we do our families—make them think that the thing we do is the very thing they desire. If we try to force matters contrary to their will, a rebellion is apt to ensue. We should never over-reach our influence, or disaster will result....

Friday, October 2, 1891:

At 10 a.m. I attended my quorum meeting at the Gardo House where those of yesterday were present excepting Joseph F. Smith and John W. Taylor, who were in attendance at the funeral of W. G. Collett, who died two days ago from typhoid fever....

We spent the forenoon in reading that part of the History of the Twelve which F. D. Richards has prepared since our last meeting. We had a recess of about two hours at noon and then were in session till 5:30 p.m., during part of which time I read from the History. We also considered somewhat the matter of the brethren going before the Master in Chancery in the Church property cases, and testifying in regard to the Manifesto and the suspension of plural marriage. It was thought best for the brethren to meet alone and unite upon their testimony, and then to meet Dickson, Richards and LeGrand Young and receive their suggestions in regard to the desired testimony.

We also decided unanimously to tender the use of our Tabernacle next year for the purpose of holding therein the National Educational Convention....

I subscribed $200.00 today to an association which designs to help young men of our faith to get an education by loaning them means to meet the expenses of their time in school, they being required to repay the amount they borrow with interest. Benjamin Cluff Jr., of Provo is the President, and the Directors are all Provo men for the present, though the benefits of the association are to be extended to all the settlements of the Saints.

Saturday, October 3, 1891:

I attended to a little business at the office and at 10 a.m. met with the Presidency and Twelve at the Gardo House. I first read the remainder of the History manuscript to them, and the subject of the vacancy in the quorum of the First Seven Presidents of the Seventies was considered. George Reynolds was called in who said that their quorum had talked about this matter some little, and the brethren whose names were mentioned in this connection were Joseph H. Dean, Joseph W. Summerhays, O. H. Berg of Provo, and Ben E. Rich of Ogden. It was decided to have the First Seven Presidents meet with us during Conference and then decide on the proper person.

The Twelve now withdrew and went upstairs. Bro. Merrill opened our meeting with prayer, and we then considered the case of John W. Young. There was a fear expressed that if his name is presented to the Conference there will be some vote against him, and many will refuse to vote in his favor. The brethren were then called in turn to express themselves concerning him…. F. M. Lyman had felt condemned in his heart for years whenever he voted to sustain John W. Young as counselor to the quorum, because of his utter indifference to his Church duties, and his financial difficulties which have brought reproach upon the Saints. He favored his removal. H. J. Grant felt that it might be best to hold on to him a while longer and not to add to his troubles by withdrawing our support when he might be in a position to need it most to consummate his financial plans. He once felt to remove John W., but now that he was in difficulty he did not know but what it would be best to keep him in his position. Bros. Merrill and Lund offered no decided opinion either way, though the former had refused for some time to vote in favor of John W. when he was counselor to Pres. Young because of his improper acts; now, however, he had nothing in his heart against J. W. Young.

I felt that the most we could do in the matter and what I thought would be proper, to suspend John W. and so state to the Conference, till he gave some satisfactory explanations concerning his conduct of late in the matter of his financial obligations, it being even said that he is liable to indictment in Provo for embezzlement for his dishonesty in connection with the disposal of the street railway bonds of that city.

Pres. Snow was just about to give his views when the Presidency entered, and upon hearing what was under discussion Father read a letter which he received yesterday from John W. who is in London. Therein he expresses his faith in the success of his plans, but regrets that unforeseen difficulties prevented their consummation at an earlier date. He expresses a wish that his name be withheld at Conference, and that for the present he be relieved of his position. It was therefore unanimously decided that this course be taken and a statement be made that at his request his name is not presented.

We next spread the table for our sacrament. Before partaking Father offered prayer, Pres. Snow blessed the bread and the wine and Pres. Woodruff made a few remarks in which he expressed his great joy at seeing so much union and harmony among the brethren. While eating and drinking, the brethren related many interesting incidents concerning the early days of the Church.

After our sacrament the Twelve were together a short time. As Joseph F. Smith was leaving the room he turned and said he believed Brigham Young and George Teasdale could regain their freedom by taking the course he had pursued. He had promised to obey the law as expressed in the Manifesto, and through the assistance of friends he had been granted a full pardon. He promised to suggest to these brethren in writing a plan whereby they may be freed.

Pres. Snow said he desired our meetings to be used generally in gaining spiritual strength. He felt that we will receive great blessings in these meetings if our faith and love are strong. We are now having a breathing spell; but before long the burdens of the kingdom will rest heavily upon our shoulders. The sacrifices which the brethren have made have won his love.

F. M. Lyman made some quite lengthy remarks the substance of which was that the Saints living in the various Stakes and Wards should be more often visited by the living oracles. The lesser Priesthood should receive more attention from those in authority and young men and boys should be encouraged to join the Priests', Teachers' and Deacons' Quorums....

Monday, October 5, 1891:

I was at the office attending to business until 10:00 a.m. when I went to Conference. F. M. Lyman spoke for 35 min. on the requirements of the Gospel, which will make us perfect men and women capable of exercising all the gifts and graces of the Lord. He spoke of the great missionary work which can be done at home among the young.

Heber J. Grant next spoke about the temporal labors of himself and some of the brethren. All that he has undertaken has been with the consent and approval of those over him, and he can and will lay down everything of a temporal nature any time his brethren desire it.

M. W. Merrill spoke for 35 minutes on the purity of lives and actions which should characterize the Saints. He also referred to the duties of the lesser Priesthood and urged them to act diligently in their callings and under the direction of the Lord....

Attended meeting again at 2 p.m. Moses Thatcher spoke first for about half an hour on the accumulation of wealth. He felt that it is proper for us to make efforts to obtain riches so long as we do not set our hearts upon such things. He does not know but that the Lord will in this way give us influence and power among men of the world. The mountains are full of precious minerals and it may be that the Lord will pour it into our laps.

President Woodruff felt that it is right for the brethren to engage in temporal labors if such things do not blind them to the work of God. Such things are necessary to the establishment of the Kingdom. He testified that there was no member of the First Presidency or Twelve who would not give his life for the Work if it was needed, and many Saints would do likewise. So long as we felt this way there is no danger if we engage in financial matters.

Father referred to the blessings which have attended all the Saints who have sought and followed counsel. In early times when allurements were presented for the Saints to go to California Pres. Young counseled them to remain here, promising them more ultimate blessings in this land. Results have proved the correctness and wisdom of his instructions. So in many other things wherein the counsel of the leaders has seemed contrary to human expectations the future has disclosed the inspiration of their teachings. He spoke of our prosperity, and the duty we owe to our co-religionists to see that employment is provided for all, and that there is no suffering among men or animals for the necessities of life....

Tuesday, October 6, 1891:

At 9:15 I went to the Gardo House and met the Presidency, Twelve, First Counsel of Seventies and some other brethren. The recent report of the Utah Commission, the full text of which just came during the night, was discussed. In it they make a number of false statements: that 18 polygamous marriages have been performed since the Manifesto was issued; that the Church rules the State in Utah; that the political move in the Territory is a trick of the Mormons, etc. It was felt that some public denial of these falsehoods should be made. Charles W. Penrose therefore read quite a lengthy document which he had prepared; it was very good but it was felt that to have a spontaneous demand from the people for a refutation of these charges would be better than to present to them a long document for their acceptance. It was therefore decided to use the forenoon in showing up the inconsistencies of the Commission's (four of them) statements.

We next considered the vacancy in the First Council of Seventies. There were named in this connection, Joseph H. Dean, Joseph W. Summerhays, Ben E. Rich, George D. Pyper and Golden Kimball, as also Willard Young. Some discussion followed as to the merits of the men, but was not concluded when the time for meeting arrived.

At the meeting Charles W. Penrose spoke first for half an hour. He reviewed the statements of the Utah Commission and showed how utterly false they were.

Pres. Woodruff arose and said that as an evidence of his interference in politics he could say that he had very much desired to see some Republicans sent to the Legislature, but not one had been elected. Bro. Lund, one of the Apostles, was a candidate but he did not win.

Moses Thatcher spoke of the opposition he had long felt to the union of Church and state, and he knew their was no disposition here to unite them. He testified to the fidelity of the people to this government.

Franklin S. Richards said we had met every suggestion made us by the commission concerning our political affairs, and he could not understand what more was needed or desired.

John T. Caine thought that their salaries was one great inducement to them to lie about us, so that the necessity of keeping them in office might be felt. He knew of the falsity of the Commission's majority report.

As this point John Clark arose in the congregation and moved the appointment of a committee of five to prepare resolutions against this lying report. He came to the stand and explained his feelings about it. There were a number of seconds to the motion, and it met with a unanimous "aye" from the congregation. The committee appointed were John Clark, W. H. Rowe, C. W. Penrose, John T. Caine and F. S. Richards. They were unanimously accepted by the congregation and ordered to report at 2 p. m.

Meeting adjourned and we went to the Gardo, where we considered the vacancy in the First Council of Seventies. The nominations were now reduced to three—Joseph H. Dean, Ben E. Rich and Willard Young. The first named was the favorite and would very likely have been selected but for Father arising and saying that his mind was not clear in relation to any of those mentioned, but if those present were satisfied he would vote with them. As perfect unanimity in the selection was desired it was thought best to leave the place vacant till we all see alike in the matter.

I went to the office for a short time and then to meeting.

Bro. A. H. Lund spoke a few moments urging the Saints to carry out the instructions they have received.

I then spoke 10 min. and testified that I had never heard a word from the Church leaders or my parents against this government. I expressed the hope that our young people would not draw off from this gathering place of the Saints, but strive to build up and strengthen Zion.

The committee on resolutions having entered they were called on to report. They presented a Preamble and Resolutions wherein they denounce the statement that the Church dominates or tries to influence in the affairs of State; that plural marriages have recently been performed, or that we were not sincere in the acceptance of the Manifesto. After the document was read by John T. Caine its adoption was moved and seconded. At this point Charles Ellis arose and inquired if "a Gentile and a sinner" might make a remark. Permission being given he came to the stand and proposed as an addition to the paper read a resolution to the effect that as the "Mormon" people have conceded every demand made upon them by the government, therefore they demand that fair play and equality before the law be guaranteed to them. (Loud applause) B. H. Roberts read from the Doctrine and Covenants wherein the Lord commands the people to protest against the slanders and falsehoods told about them. He felt that we had silently submitted to misrepresentation sufficiently long, and now we should make ourselves heard in our own defense.

By request John T. Caine now read an announcement of the First Presidency wherein they deny that plural practices have been taught or marriages solemnized since the issuance of the Manifesto.[14] Both documents were heartily accepted by raising the right hand and saying "aye" at the same time.

On motion of John T. Caine, Mr. Ellis' sentiments were also adopted.

The Church authorities were next presented and sustained, John W. Young's name being omitted, after Father had explained the reasons why Bro. Young desired his name withheld.

Elders Jacob Gates and Lorenzo D. Young next bore strong testimonies to the truth and to the divine mission of the Prophet Joseph with whom both were intimately acquainted. The latter said that Hyrum Smith prophesied in his house in Kirtland in 1834 that the Saints would yet find a home in the Rocky Mountains.

Father referred briefly to the chasm which has existed between Mormons and Gentiles in this Territory, and he felt that we ought to take all proper means of bridging the same so that harmony may exist between all citizens or residents. He said when any of us desire to make an important move we should counsel together in regard to it, and then act according to the best wisdom of all. Parents should counsel with their children, as well as the latter doing so with their parents.

---

[14] See Appendix One: Plural Marriage Issues in the Abraham H. Cannon Journals.

Pres. Woodruff made a few closing remarks expressive of his pleasure at the good attendance of the Saints during this Conference, and he prayed for blessings on all the people. Conference adjourned for six months by Pres. Woodruff pronouncing the benediction....

Wednesday, October 7, 1891:

I spent two hours in work at the office and at 10 a.m. attended a meeting of the Presidents of Stakes, their counselors, the Bishops and their Counselors, the Presidency, Twelve and First Council of Seventies, held in the 18th ward chapel.

After the usual opening exercises Pres. Joseph F. Smith spoke. Among other things he said, "God will not justify you in kicking out your families and stultifying yourselves in the eyes of all good men. We do not want you to leave your wives because of the manifesto. Tell your people to take care of their families just as they have always done. What, cohabit with them? I would advise them not to do it in the United States. Take them where they will be safe and where you can live with them without violating the law. The time will come when those who endure faithful in this practice will receive a full, complete deliverance and be more exalted. All the principles are just as true as they ever were, and if they have been withdrawn it is because the people as a rule are unworthy of them."

He referred to the political situation and showed how necessary it is that we divide on national party lines in order to be preserved from expatriation by both parties. He spoke a few words in encouragement of the Deseret Hospital.

Moses Thatcher made a few remarks concerning the Company which has been formed with Father as President and R. C. Chambers, F. H. Auerbach, himself, F. L. Webber and others as directors whereby the people can now begin to save their money to attend the World's Fair at Chicago in 1893. For the sum of $110 or thereabouts the Company provides railway fare, 6 days hotel accommodations there, entrance to the grounds for six days, a competent guide and meals to and from Chicago.

Judge Coburn, the general manager of the Company, was introduced and explained the details of the scheme.

Charles Ellis announced that he was willing and ready to travel and lecture in any places where his presence was desired.

Pres. Woodruff said among other things: "I never would have issued the Manifesto had it not been for the inspiration of God to me.

"I want to see the Salt Lake Temple finished, and poor as I am I will donate $500.00 towards this work. The Lord also wants it completed, and I ask you brethren to try and collect enough for this purpose."

Heber J. Grant spoke with earnestness concerning the Sugar factory and urged the brethren to subscribe stock. He told of some of the difficulties it had met and overcome. He felt and promised that though the means which any of the Saints might invest there should be lost, the Lord would return to them in other ways to a far greater extent.

F. M. Lyman related a vision he had while in the "Pen" concerning the Salt Lake Temple. He saw it in a finished condition and Pres. Woodruff, George Reynolds and many other brethren were there as well as a large number of Lamanites. His feelings were so joyful as to be beyond expression.

Pres. Woodruff told of manifestations he had received 50 years ago concerning the Temple. Before the material for its construction had been selected, he knew it was to be constructed of cut granite. Before Pres. Taylor's death he dreamed for two nights in succession that he received the keys to the Temple from Pres. Young; and at its dedication he beheld a large number of elders called and sent forth into the world to bind up the law and seal the testimony to the Gentiles.

Elias Morris spoke concerning the sugar industry, and Bishop Preston about the Temple. We all voted to do our utmost in collecting and donating means for the completion of the Temple which will require about $100,000.

Bishop O. F. Whitney spoke of the *History of Utah*, explaining its origin and progress, as also the plan of the work.

Political matters then received some attention and the Monthly Free Will Offering Fund.

About 3:15 p.m. we adjourned, and the Presidency and Twelve went to the Gardo House where we had some dinner, and then had a council meeting concerning the replies we shall give concerning polygamy and cohabitation when the Church cases come before the Master in Chancery in the near future. There was considerable discussion with the result that we all got to the point where we realize that polygamy is no longer a law of the Church, and as far as our present families are concerned we must support and honor them, though if we live with them it is at our peril....

Friday, October 9, 1891:

About noon Maria Y. Dougall and Ellen Jakeman came to the office and in my room we had a long talk about the *Young Woman's Journal* business. Sisters Gates and Jakeman, who had arranged to become equal partners in the affair, had some disagreements and now Sister Gates feels, and quite properly so, that Sister Jakeman is not entitled to half the business, as the latter has received her monthly salary for all her labors, while the former has received nothing. I told the Sisters that I felt that Sister Jakeman had received already in her salary all to which she was entitled, but in view of the promises which Sister Gates had made her I did not know but what she should receive something additional....

Saturday, October 10, 1891:

Early this morning I went to M. E. C's piece of land, whereon I contemplate building for her, and with a forked stick located a spot for an artesian well....

Sunday, October 11, 1891:

Attended the Tabernacle services at 2 p.m., and listened to a very good discourse by Joseph F. Smith on the qualifications a preacher of the Gospel should possess. He showed that the learning of the world is not sufficient, but the authority to preach and the testimony of the truth will enable any man however weak and unlearned, to become an efficient minister of Christ....

Monday, October 12, 1891:

At 11:00 a.m. attended a meeting in the Gardo House of the Presidency and our Quorum where attorneys Richards and LeGrand Young propounded some questions to Pres. Woodruff concerning the attitude of himself and the people in regard to plural marriage. We all understand that polygamy has ceased in good faith, and as to the course we will take if it is ever revealed anew, we cannot say, though there is no human probability of its restoration. Considerable talk was had on the question until about 1:30, when we adjourned till 2:45 to meet William H. Dickson, and consider this matter further, in the office across the road. We met as per our adjournment, and Mr. Dickson put some very pointed questions to Pres. Woodruff and the others. After hearing us testify that polygamy had indeed ceased, he said he believed the best way to meet the thing was to say in substance: We believe God revealed the principle of plural marriage, and hence we practiced and maintained it in the hope that the sentiment of the nation towards it would change when they became convinced that it was a religious principle with us. As the opposition to it increased, however, instead of abated, we became convinced that it was useless to further oppose public sentiment. Then the Manifesto was issued and we are relieved of further obedience to this principle.

If any are questioned as to what we should answer if plural marriage were again commanded of God, he said we could only reply that we do not know. There was considerable discussion on these matters, but the result was an acceptance of Mr. Dickson's theory.

In the after conversation Mr. Dickson said the law had no intention of preventing a man from providing for his family and of seeing to their necessities.

All the First Presidency and several of the Twelve will act as witnesses in the Church cases before the Master in Chancery....

Thursday, October 15, 1891:

In the afternoon at 2 o'clock I attended my quorum meeting in the Gardo House where was present Pres. Woodruff, Father, F. D. Richards, F. M. Lyman and myself; George F. Gibbs, clerk. Father was mouth in prayer. It was then reported that A. H. Lund had been appointed and set apart as President of the Manti Temple, with John Maiben as his assistant….

Father presented to us some very confidential communications from Judge M. M. Estee of California. The first was the draft of a petition to the President of the U. S. (Harrison) which is to be signed by Gentiles of the Territory, as far as their signatures can be obtained, asking this officer to grant amnesty to all Mormon polygamists for the reason that they are now trying to obey the law.

The next was the copy of a letter which Judge Estee sent to General J. S. Clarkson wherein he urges this gentlemen to use his influence as the chairman of the National Republican Committee to check the Liberals in Utah and prevent their interference in the organization of the Republican party here. He holds out the hope to Mr. Clarkson that if the Mormons are now properly handled they will make of Utah a Republican State, and he speaks in high terms of our fidelity and virtues.

It was told us also by Father that there is a possibility of Judge Estee going into the President's Cabinet as Attorney General which, if he should do, would be a great blessing for our people, even though he dare not publicly announce himself as our friend….

Sunday, October 18, 1891 [Nephi City, Utah]:

I accompanied Pres. Paxman to the Prayer Circle which he directs. Bro. Maiben and I each spoke a few words to the brethren after they had clothed in their robes and had prayer. I urged all the members to avoid hard feelings towards each other and towards any of the Saints when they meet for the purpose of prayer. Unless all bad feelings are overcome before they assemble their unity is impaired….

At 2 p.m. [Nephi City Stake] Conference convened and after the authorities of the Church and Stake were presented, I spoke nearly _ of an hour on the union in temporal things for which we should seek, the love which should exist in families and the charity which should be characteristic of all Saints.

George Goddard then sang "Who's on the Lord's side, who?" and at the last verse he requested all to arise who are on the Lord's side, and those who preferred to remain in sin and iniquity to keep their seats. Naturally all eyes turned to James Clinton who kept his seat, and I felt that Bro. Goddard's last remark was improper and unnecessary....

Monday, October 19, 1891 [Nephi City]:

I went directly to the office where I read the final Doctrine and Covenants proofs, *History* proofs and answered some letters....

I received word today through Deputy Marshal Cannon and Charles H. Wilcken that the former was questioned by the Grand Jury last Friday as to why I was not arrested under the Edmunds law. Some woman had given testimony that Mina was at the Fair with a girl carrying a baby. Broman Cannon said he would serve the papers if some person would swear to the complaint.

The case of Joseph F. Smith was also called in question, and the feeling seems to prevail that the U. S. Marshal (Parsons) is not doing his full duty.

I hope the Lord will deliver me from arrest.

The Church cases came up before the Master in Chancery today, to hear evidence and devise a scheme for the disposition of the Church property which was seized. Three Gentile attorneys from Ogden intervened in behalf of the 5 northern counties, and asked that they receive a portion of this fund, to be used as a Charity Board may direct. Their application is made at the instance of a number of Gentiles and with the consent of no Latter-day Saint.

Attorney Dickson, in behalf of the Church, asks that it be turned over to the First Presidency to be used by them for charitable purposes.

Father and Pres. Woodruff were placed on the witness stand and questioned as to the uses to which Church funds received from tithing and donations had been put. They were also examined as to the meaning and intent of the Manifesto. They gave it as their views that plural marriages had ceased in the Church and cohabitation was discountenanced. In fact, Pres. Woodruff said that he intended in the Manifesto to cause men who had plural wives to cease associating with them. This was in reply to Dickson's inquiry.

The examination was very critical, the prosecution being represented by C. S. Varian, Joseph L. Rawlins and J. A. Marshall, the defense by F. S Richards, W. H. Dickson and LeGrand Young.

Tuesday, October 20, 1891:

In the afternoon Sisters Gates, Jakeman, E. S. Taylor, and M. V. Dougall came to my room where we talked over the *Young Woman's Journal* affairs, and tried to get Sisters Gates and Jakeman reconciled to each other. The former offered to take the latter into the business as a third owner, and to make the Y. L. associations per Pres. E. S. Taylor owner of the other third besides her own. Or she offered to pay Sister Jakeman a monetary consideration for any loss she has sustained in moving from Sanpete Co. to Provo to become an equal partner in the business of the *Journal.* She would accept neither of these offers, but held that as Sister Gates once promised her half the business, she felt that it should be given her. Still she affirmed she would not continue to work with Sister Gates on any terms whatever. My view was that Sister Jakeman had received full value for all services rendered, yet in view of the promises made her by Sister Gates the latter should pay her some money or give her an interest in the magazine as a remuneration. Sisters Taylor and Dougall took the same view as I did, but after considerable talk Sister Jakeman took offense and left the room in tears, and said she would have nothing more to do with the matter. She said she always would feel that Sister Gates had done her an injustice.

She having left so unceremoniously, the sisters desired me to crowd the canvassing ahead as best I could and see to the business....

Bro. Joseph F. Smith, Lorenzo Snow, and Anthon H. Lund were on the witness stand today in the Church cases, but the testimony of the first two was not as straight as it should have been in order to suit the prosecution; in fact their expressions are likely to injure our case.

Wednesday, October 21, 1891:

Sister Jakeman came into the office today and apologized for her unceremonious conduct of yesterday. She still feels to refuse any remuneration for her loss, and says she cannot consent to longer labor for or with Sister Gates....

Wednesday, November 11, 1891:

Heber J. Grant, who just returned from a pleasure jaunt in California and elsewhere, came in to obtain my views this afternoon concerning the recent testimony by the Presidency before the Master in Chancery. He feels that according to their statements made under oath none of us who have plural wives can live with them any place on the earth. He thinks therefore, that the brethren should issue another manifesto commanding polygamists to cease cohabiting with plural wives, at least within the jurisdiction of the United States, otherwise some of us will be watched and captured with the result that we will nullify the testimony of the Presidency and brand ourselves as a set of base deceivers. The testimony which they gave is opposed to what was decided should be given, at a former council of ours. Heber will bring the matter up for discussion in an early council....[15]

The office was today awarded the job to print the report of the recent Irrigation Congress. The Chamber of Commerce are responsible for its issuance. We received the first installment of copy.

Judge Zane today rendered his decision in the case of the U. S. verses the Church for some real estate which had been seized. He decides in favor of the government, for the reason that he thinks the Temple block did exceed in value in 1862 the sum of $50,000, which

---

[15] Journal entries regarding the Manifesto and related matters serve notice of how complex the plural marriage issue had become, as a continually evolving situation sometimes exasperated and confused even those in the highest quorums. As the 12 November entry makes clear, the Brethren were forced to walk a very fine line—they must keep their marriage covenants, yet they must also try to obey the laws enacted by the government, which forbade them living with their plural wives. This conflict only served to maximize the trials and suffering endured by plural families, including Elder Cannon's. See also Melvin Clarence Merrill, ed., *Utah Pioneer and Apostle Marriner Wood Merrill and His Family* (n. p.: Marriner Wood Merrill Heritage Committee, 1980), 147-48 (1 November entry).

latter was the limit of Church possessions as then established by law. The case will be carried to the higher courts....

Thursday, November 12, 1891:

At 2 p.m. I attended my Council meeting where were present all the Presidency, F. D. Richards, F. M. Lyman, John H. Smith, H. J. Grant, John W. Taylor and myself; George Gibbs, clerk. Bro. Richards was mouth in prayer, after which appointments for Quarterly Conferences were made. The matter of the Manifesto and the extent of its meaning was then discussed. Pres. Woodruff said that he was placed in such a position on the witness stand that he could not answer other than he did; yet any man who deserts and neglects his wives or children because of the Manifesto should be handled on his fellowship. Our talk resolved itself into this—that men must be careful to avoid exposing themselves to arrest or conviction for violations of the law; and yet they must not break their covenants with their wives.

The Presidency have decided to vacate the Gardo House, inasmuch as it appears as though the government was determined to hold on to it, and they will occupy the offices on the opposite side of the street. This will save considerable to the Church....

Thursday, November 19, 1891:

During the afternoon I was employed in reading proofs except when at meeting.

At 2 p.m. I went across to the Bishop's General Storehouse and reported myself at a meeting of the Deseret Investment Co., but excused myself immediately to attend my regular quorum meeting. At the latter were present all the Presidency, John H. Smith, Heber J. Grant, John W. Taylor and myself; George F. Gibbs, clerk. Charles W. Penrose submitted an article which he had prepared for publication in answer to an inquiry as the proper words for use in a case of rebaptism. In this article he states that the words "for a renewal of your covenants," should be inserted in the regular form. Considerable discussion which followed resulted in the conclusion that except where the President of the Church directs otherwise the regular form given us in the written revelation should be strictly followed.

H. J. Grant was mouth in prayer. He then submitted the question as to whether or not some ordinations of Bishops and counselors were valid, which have occurred in the Rexberg Stake within a week, wherein Seymour B. Young, a President of Seventies, was mouth. The latter told him he had been called to do similar acts by Moses Thatcher, John Henry Smith and John W. Taylor. For this reason Heber asked him to assist him, though he did not feel right about it all the time Seymour was officiating. The brethren decided that it was improper, and instructed that those whom Seymour was mouth in ordaining, by ordained over again....

Thursday, December 3, 1891:

In the afternoon I attended my Quorum meeting at which were present all the First Presidency, Franklin D. Richards and myself; George Gibbs, clerk. This was our first meeting held in the recently prepared room opposite the Gardo House.

Bishop Orson F. Whitney was present to obtain information concerning the object in settling this Territory when the Pioneers came here, as he desires to make a statement concerning it in the *History of Utah*. He had prepared something in which he affirms that the Mormons came here to found a new state for the United States. This is incorrect, as it was the expectation when the people arrived here to establish an independent state, and it was only when this western tract of land was ceded to the United States by Mexico in the treaty of Guadelupe Hidalgo (February 1848) that the Mormons began to seek for admission into the Union as a State, and saw therein their success and destiny.

The matter of a form to be used in baptisms was considered, but no decision was reached, it being desired to first send to the various temples and see what forms they use and why they do so....

Tuesday, December 22, 1891:

At noon I was requested to go to the President's office where I met the *Deseret News* Co. Board of Directors of which Father is the

President. He requested me to state for the information of the brethren my reasons for printing the Church Works. I said it was because we lost money by carrying the *News* publications, they gave us so small a percentage; because their books were frequently out of print; because they refused to let us have books when we needed them and they had a stock on hand; and because we believe our facilities for distributing books at home and in the east are better than those of the *News* Co., and we supposed it was desired to circulate these books as widely as possible. There was considerable talk about our action in this matter, but when all desired inquiries were answered by me I withdrew....

Chapter Five

1892

[Elder Cannon began typing his journal on 1 January 1892]

Saturday, January 2, 1892:

Dismissed: The indictments which were found in 1888 against nearly 100 Mormons in Idaho for illegal voting, were today dismissed in the courts of that State on motion of United States Attorney Woods. These indictments were found because some of the Saints withdrew from the Church for the purpose of escaping the effects of the Idaho Test Oath, which was framed and passed for the express purpose of preventing Mormons from voting. When they had taken the oath they were arrested, some for perjury and others for illegal voting. The dismissal of these cases shows that a better feeling is beginning to prevail in our neighboring state.

Sunday, January 3, 1892:

At the Tabernacle services Father and Pres. Joseph F. Smith were present, but I was called to speak, which I did for 40 minutes. I spoke of the weakness of the instruments which God chooses for the accomplishment of His purposes and stated that a man's usefulness in this Work is at an end when he imagines that its progress or development depends upon him or his efforts.

John Morgan followed me for about half an hour, and treated upon the remarkable change which the religious sentiment of the country has undergone since the Prophet Joseph Smith introduced the Gospel. Then it was publicly taught that as a person died so would he be judged, and the idea of a possibility of repentance after death was unheard of; but now this doctrine is accepted and believed by all progressive preachers and religious people. So is it also with other principles which were new in the early rise of the Church....

Thursday, January 7, 1892:

At two o'clock I attended the meeting of my quorum at the President's office, where all the Presidency were present as well as F. D. Richards, Francis M. Lyman, John W. Taylor and myself; George Gibbs, clerk. The manner of clothing the dead sisters who have had their endowments, was first considered. It was agreed that when the coffin is closed containing the body of a sister who has been through the Temple, her veil should be placed so as to hide her face, so that when her husband meets her on the other side he may lift the same from her countenance. This is in accordance with the instructions which President Young gave during his life. The carelessness of the Saints in regard to their Temple clothing was talked about, and it was voted that instructions be sent to each Temple that those who receive the ordinances of the House of God be told especially to be careful not to expose their clothing to the public gaze. This clothing is as sacred as the ordinances themselves.

Tuesday, January 12, 1892:

I was at the office at eight o'clock and spent the most of the forenoon in filling orders, writing letters, etc. Sister E. S. Taylor was in to make some inquiries concerning the business of the *Young Woman's Journal*, in which she today became, as Trustee for the Y. L. M. I. Associations of Zion, an equal partner with myself and Susa Y. Gates by signing the articles of co-partnership.

At two o'clock I attended the special meeting of my Quorum at the Historian's Office, in the upper room. There were present, Pres. Lorenzo Snow, Franklin D. Richards, Francis M. Lyman, John Henry Smith; John W. Taylor and Moses Thatcher both came in late, M. W. Merrill, Anthon H. Lund and myself. Pres. Snow called the meeting to order, and Bro. Richards opened with prayer. Pres. Snow then spoke: "I know that the Lord is pleased with our meeting together, as are also our brethren of former quorums who have lived and died. I hope that we will be able to keep from us any such spirit as that which took possession of the Apostles and people in Kirtland, when half of the quorum apostatized and the Prophet scarcely dared to go upon the street for fear of being killed. Still the same beginning is being made in our midst today as then existed; the spirit of disrespect for the Priesthood and of disregard of its teachings. If this continues it will lead to apostasy and trouble. We should use our influence to check it. We should never allow ourselves to listen to remarks which are made against any member of this quorum without seeking to check the same. I know the day is not far distant when you brethren will be clothed with great power from God, and you will do things that will astonish yourselves and those who witness them. In view of these glorious things, how careful we should be to do just as near right as we possibly can."…

Apostle Moses Thatcher said that the cause of his tardiness in coming to meeting was because of his illness, which causes him the utmost pain in his stomach after nearly every meal, and is sometimes so bad as to be almost unendurable. He spoke as follows: "We should never use the pulpit for the purpose of rebuking those of the Saints who may have done wrong or offended us. In Kirtland at one time Sidney Rigdon took occasion to reprove Father John Smith in a public meeting for having spoken in favor of a certain brother who had been excommunicated from the Church. Father Smith desired the Saints to exercise charity for the fallen soul. He had, however, been one of the Council that had cut him off. Brother Rigdon therefore took it upon himself to speak against Father Smith for thus acting. The Prophet was present, but said nothing. Some days afterwards, however, he told Brother Rigdon of his wrong, and admonished him never to be guilty of chastising any person from the public stand again. We too often give ear to false reports about our brethren. This we should avoid, and never encourage the Saints to come to us with hard stories about one or the other of the Apostles. Also if we know that one of the brethren has been unwise we should speak to him personally about the matter. All kinds of plans will be laid to divide us up as a quorum. I am reminded of a dream which Brigham Young [Jr.] had just before he went to England on his present mission: He dreamed that he saw a large enclosure wherein a vast number of the Saints were gathered. Within this concourse of people was a small tent wherein were gathered a few men whose conversation was audible to the people who were outside. These men were plotting for the division of the Mormon people. After some talk one arose among them and said: 'It is useless to try and divide the people till we cause division among the leaders. Let us therefore try to divide them!' I believe this political movement is tending to our division." He then spoke rather discouragingly of John Henry Smith's labors in politics and seemed to feel that he was doing wrong in the course he had been taking in politics.

Pres. Snow said it was a question which we could discuss as to whether or not we approved of the course Bro. Smith has been taking in political matters, and which we would not approve in all the members generally. For his part he felt to approve of what he had been doing, for he felt sure that the Presidency were pleased with his actions. He said he would like us to speak on this subject, and also upon the manner in which we are to treat our wives under the present condition of affairs. He felt that God will never approve of our forsaking our families, and we must each live as the Spirit dictates.

John Henry Smith next told of the way in which he had become mixed up in politics, and of the work he had been doing. If it had not been for his labors he said we might every one have been disfranchised by this time. It seemed to me that he took considerable honor to himself for the present mildness which is shown towards us. He then spoke of the principles of his party in such a partisan spirit that it caused several interruptions from Bro. Thatcher who is as strong a Democrat as John is a Republican. Bro. Snow had to interfere and check the Spirit which was starting. He said he had been called by the Lord to this work, and he knew the Lord would eventually vindicate him. After some further talk as to what he had done and was doing Bro. Lyman moved that we approve of the course which John Henry has been taking. At this juncture Bro. Richards arose and said he could not vote for that without first telling his mind upon the matter. He knew of times when Bro. Smith had caused great offense by calling those who did not believe as he did some pretty hard names. Many people felt insulted at his remarks, and he for one did not approve of such talk. He gave Bro. Smith a rather severe rebuke. Bro. Thatcher also felt somewhat opposed to the motion and Pres. Snow therefore decided to withhold it from vote. If John Henry is doing any good, however, we all felt to give him our blessing.[1]

John W. Taylor next spoke and told of some of his movements in Canada. He told of his being called to Canada by Sir Alexander Gault, and his receiving from him an offer of several hundred thousand acres of land at a very low figure. This he disposed of to some of the brethren here and in Canada, and received as his bonus for affecting the sale 120,000 acres of choice land, of which he had given George M. Cannon $500 worth amounting to 30,000 acres, because the latter had loaned him this sum at one time last summer when he was in a pinch and no other person would help him. He told of his financial difficulties which of late have given him much anxiety. He made it a matter of fasting and prayer. One day he came in town when he was thus supplicating the Lord, and a messenger came saying that Mr. O. J. Saulsbury desired to see him. At first he said he would not go, but as the Spirit urged him to do so, he went and Mr. Saulsbury said he understood that he had been looking for money the day before. John told him that his information was correct. Mr. Saulsbury then asked what sum he desired and was told $20,000. "You can have it," said the gentleman. On being told the security Mr. Saulsbury said that would be satisfactory, and that John could have the money for as long a time as he desired it. This was a direct answer to his prayer, for which he felt to thank the Lord....

Wednesday, January 13, 1892:

I then went to my quorum meeting. We met in a fasting condition. John W. Taylor sang a hymn, and M. W. Merrill was mouth in prayer.

Pres. Snow said we had now arrived at that point in our history when if we injure the feelings of another it hurts us more than it does the person whom we attack. We should therefore try to refrain from anything that will cause the least unpleasantness between ourselves. I

---

[1] See Jean Bickmore White, ed., *Church, State, and Politics: The Diary of John Henry Smith* (Salt Lake City: Signature Books, 1990), 267 and note for 12 January 1892; hereafter cited as *Church, State, and Politics*.

do not feel that we should rebuke each other even when we are in the wrong, because we are all equal in authority. Pres. Young once told Erastus Snow that he did wrong in rebuking Almon W. Babbit, who had done some wrong, for they both held the same Priesthood, and it was not proper for two brethren of equal position to chastise each other. Of course, when we see wrong doing in each other we should call each others attention to the same, so that our weaknesses may be overcome.

A telegram was read from Heber J. Grant who is in San Francisco, excusing himself for his absence on account of the sickness of his wife. He desired to have her prayed for.

John Henry Smith asked forgiveness for anything he had said yesterday to give any one offense.

We next listened to the reading of the History of our Quorum which F. D. Richards had prepared since our last meeting. It was concerning the brethren and their labors in the days of Joseph.

Bro. Thatcher was taken so ill about 11:30 that he had to leave the meeting, after we had administered to him, Pres. Snow being mouth.

We continued the reading of the history till 12 o'clock, when Father and Joseph F. Smith of the Presidency came in and partook with us of the Sacrament. Bread and wine had been provided, and we all ate to our satisfaction. Joseph F. Smith offered a short prayer, and John H. Smith asked the blessing on the bread and wine.

While at table we were told by the brethren of the work that is being done for our emancipation. To our astonishment it was said that Gov. Thomas, P. H. Lannan, C. C. Goodwin and other strong and bitter Liberals are in favor of amnesty for the Mormons, and of the political division which is now taking place. It will not do, however, for the *Tribune*, which these men control, to change its position suddenly, as it would result disastrously to the Republican cause, but they will gradually work to assist in the great work of making this a Republican State.

The brethren of the Presidency having an appointment at 1 p.m., withdrew, but sent us some correspondence from Judge M. M. Estee of California, who is working in our interest, though it is under the utmost secrecy, so that his national influence may not be injured when he speaks in our defense. He sent to Father a copy of a letter which our Gov. Thomas sent him concerning his desire to see amnesty granted to the Mormons, and also a letter which Estee sent him giving him some good advice concerning the mild course he should pursue with regard to the Saints. This correspondence shows that we have a strong friend in the person of Judge Estee.

After hearing this we continued the reading of the history till all was read that is prepared amounting to 40 pages of Manuscript.

Bro. Lyman next spoke and expressed his good feelings for all the brethren, and his pleasure at being at this meeting. He also gave a brief synopsis of his travels since we last met as a Quorum.

M. W. Merrill gave an account of some trouble he has had with Fred Turner of Logan, for which the latter threatens suit for slander unless Bro. Merrill makes a statement through the papers that he has injured Fred's character, and makes public amends therefore. This Bro. Merrill will not do, as he has not done anything to require it.... [Bro. Merrill] says the real cause of the trouble is that Fred owes him a thousand dollars and interest for several years, which Bro. Merrill borrowed for him. Still the latter has no hard feeling towards him or any other person in the world.

Bro. Lund expressed his pleasure at being here and in listening to the instructions which have been given. He felt well towards all.

I next told of my feelings and desires. I related about how I have managed my family affairs since I have had more than one wife, and the brethren approved of the same, but desired me to be cautious so as not to be caught. I expressed the view that a vast amount of good should result from this political movement, for it is spoiling a large number of good young men....

Thursday, January 14, 1892:

In the afternoon I was at the Presidents office to see Father. He spoke to me about rumors that he had heard that I was not treating Mina with that consideration that I should. He advised me to be very careful of the feelings of all my folks in these troublous times, so that their affections might not be alienated from me, and that they might feel that I was just in my attention to them. We had some talk about the *History of Utah* which is to be issued on the 1st of March. Bishop Whitney the author, is breaking down. The Bishop coming in at this time we spoke to him about the matter, and he feels that he cannot get out the work by the time named unless he has help. This I promised to try and find for him....

Monday, January 18, 1892:

At noon I went to the President's office to see about John Q. [Cannon] beginning his labors on the *History of Utah* in connection with Bishop Whitney. The brethren approved of his undertaking the same, and he accordingly received his instructions from his co-laborer, and will begin his active work tomorrow....

Sunday, January 24, 1892:

I went to the U. P. depot where I took the train for Brigham City to attend the Box Elder Stake conference. Seymour B. Young also went along. We arrived at our destination about 1:20 o'clock and went directly to Sister Minnie J. Snow's where we were most kindly received and entertained. We had a bite to eat and then went to the meeting with Pres. Lorenzo Snow. The attendance was very good, and a most excellent spirit prevailed. Pres. Rudger Clawson was the first speaker. He occupied about 50 minutes in telling of some of the improper things which exist in the Stake, such as fault-finding, back-biting and a desire to fail to seek counsel or to follow it when it is given. I then spoke for 25 minutes on the lack of appreciation we show towards some of our brethren and sisters. We should remember that the Lord has sent some of his choicest spirits to the earth in these last days, and we should treat even the humblest person with the greatest consideration, for we do not know but he or she may be one of these valuable spirits....

We went to Sister Snow's after meeting, and were visited by Brothers Hoskins, Gibbs and Ward from the Malad Stake, who told us of the condition of the Indians at Washakie, who belong to the Church. The brethren do not know what counsel to give them concerning the marriages which are performed among them, but have referred that matter to Pres. Woodruff. These brethren think it will be best at the present time to have them continue to marry Indian style; for they are as yet so unreliable that if they desired to separate from their wives they would do so regardless of whether they were married by the Bishop, in the temple, or in any other way. Their marriages are nothing more than the swapping of blankets. When a young man sees a girl whom he wants, he first gets the consent of the parents, and the girl seldom refuses. In the meantime he purchases a nice blanket which he gives her, and this completes the marriage ceremony. When either desires a separation, he or she just takes his or her belongings and leaves the wick-i-up. Sometimes the girls are promised when they are very young, in which case the youth to whom she is thus betrothed can come and get her at any time when he is grown. Recently there was a girl married in the tribe who had been promised in her childhood to a young man, but as he had gone away the girl's father supposed he had given her up, and he therefore gave her to another. But when the youthful buck heard of his girl's marriage he came a long distance and claimed her, and no person interposed an objection. She accompanied him to his home.

The visitors to the conference were divided up to attend the evening Ward meetings. I went to the Second Ward, being accompanied by Bro. Clawson. I occupied the whole time of the meeting—about an hour—in speaking upon the heed we should give to the counsel of those who preside over us, and the respect we should show to them. Also urged families to live in peace and with love and harmony ever present in their homes....

Monday, January 25, 1892 [Brigham City, Utah]:

In the afternoon Pres. Snow addressed the congregation for about three-quarters of an hour on the spiritual things belonging to the Kingdom, and presented some ideas which were very exalting. He said that the Prophet Joseph was once asked who he was; the Prophet smiled kindly upon his interlocutor and replied, "Noah came before the flood; I have come before the fire." The Saints were urged to as nearly approach the example set us by the Savior as it is possible for us to do, and to always remember the high calling to which we are appointed. I next spoke for 25 minutes upon the present condition of the people, and told them of my faith that the Lord would soon work out our deliverance, and give us a hundred fold of joy for all the suffering we have undergone. Seymour spoke a few minutes telling the Saints to respect and honor the Priesthood that is placed over them. He felt that it is not proper for men to assail the authorities of the Church who do not happen to agree with them in politics. At the conclusion of Seymour's remarks we withdrew from the meeting and were taken by Roy Snow to the train which started for the south at 4:10....

Tuesday, January 26, 1892:

In the afternoon I went to the President's office where Father told me of the inconvenience under which he was laboring because he had no buggy. I therefore proffered to buy him one, and we went down to the Co-op Wagon and Machine Co. and selected a Miller Concord buggy, costing $210.00, which I had charged to myself. He will therefore be no longer dependent upon others for a buggy in which to ride....

Wednesday, January 27, 1892:

I went with Father at noon to see the buggy which I bought for him last evening, and as we were returning we came to the State Bank where the Cashier, Heber M. Wells, told me that we must immediately reduce Cannon & Sons overdraft, which now amounts to over $6,000. I promised to do the very best I could to reduce and then fully pay the amount....

Thursday, January 28, 1892:

I was at the President's office in the morning to see if the Church would pay about $80.00 for some valuable information which a man named Wilden in the south where Andrew Jenson is collecting matter says he possesses concerning the Mountain Meadows Massacre. After some talk it was decided that nothing except a set of the *History of Utah* should be given him for what he has, and I so telegraphed Andrew Jenson.

At two o'clock our Council met. Present: Father, Joseph F. Smith, F. M. Lyman, John H. Smith and myself; George Gibbs, clerk. F. D. Richards was excused because of some pressing work on the History [of the apostles]. Joseph F. Smith was mouth in prayer.... Whether or not a High Council is a legal body to transact business when only six of the Councilors are present and alternates are drawn for the remainder, was considered. The feeling of those present was that it was legal, and the case was cited in support of this view where Pres. Young once had the High Councilors and Alternates all presented to the conference in this Stake for their votes and called them High Councilors. John Henry Smith reported that Gov. Thomas today told him that our petition for amnesty is now in the hands of President Harrison....

Monday, February 8, 1892:

At 2 o'clock I was at the Historian's office where Brother B. H. Roberts and myself set apart and instructed four missionaries for the States. I then went to the President's office where I remained a short time listening to the political talk of several of the brethren. I was surprised to see the warmth of feeling in John R. Winder when his Democratic principles were assailed, and he did not hesitate to oppose the expressions of Joseph F. Smith in favor of Republicanism. I very much fear that the politics which are being introduced among us will lead to a spirit of disregard and disrespect for the Priesthood. Such a feeling is already beginning to make its appearance in some places....

Thursday, February 11, 1892:

...At 2 o'clock attended my quorum meeting. There were present all of the First Presidency, Lorenzo Snow, John W. Taylor, M. W. Merrill and myself; George F. Gibbs clerk. Bro. Merrill was mouth in prayer. We had some talk as to the correct form to be used by the person who administers the ordinance of baptism, and President Woodruff expressed himself in favor of adhering to the words used in the revelations of the Lord as contained in our church publications, except in the case of baptism for the health, when the object of the ordinance might be mentioned.[2] The final decision in this matter, however, was laid over for future consideration when more of the Quorum are present....

Friday, February 19, 1892:

The remainder of the day I spent in the office attending to work which has accumulated since I left. I found that the manuscript of the first volume of the *History of Utah* has been finished by O. F. Whitney and John Q., and the most of it is now in print. The reading matter will occupy 720 pages. I am now doing my utmost to crowd ahead the plates so that the binding may be done without any delay. We desire to deliver the book during the next month.

Saturday, February 20, 1892:

George C. Lambert today took me to task for having issued an edition of the Ready References which he prepared while on a mission in England. I told him we did so because the book was out of print, and we did not like to have orders coming to us without our being able to fill the same. If he felt that we had infringed on his rights, however, we will pay him whatever he thinks right in the matter. In the evening I was engaged at the farm in writing up my journal on the type-writer....

Sunday, February 21, 1892:

Went to the tabernacle services at 2 o'clock....

I spoke for the remainder of the time—about half an hour, but did not feel at all well in doing so. I could not get the spirit of speaking, and therefore indulged in considerable noise without much substance. I was perhaps not sufficiently humble in commencing, and

---

[2] Baptisms for health were practiced in the earlier days of the Church, and historical sources relate many occasions where someone had faith sufficient to be healed. "The earlier practice of rebaptism to manifest repentance and recommitment, or for a restoration of health in time of sickness, is no longer practiced in the Church." (Carl S. Hawkins, "Baptism"; cited in *Encyclopedia of Mormonism* 1:94.)

hence the Lord left me to myself that I might realize how incompetent I am....

Tuesday, February 23, 1892:

We had a car loaded today with the printed sheets of the *History of Utah*, which we are sending to Becktold & Co. of St. Louis to have them bound, as we are unable to get them gilded and bound in time for delivery this month, and hands cannot be found in this country in sufficient number to do the work....

Thursday, February 25, 1892:

I was at my quorum meeting where were present Pres. Woodruff, Joseph F. Smith, F. D. Richards, F. M. Lyman, John W. Taylor and myself; George F. Gibbs, clerk. Bro. Richards was mouth in prayer. It was decided to lay the top stone of the Salt Lake City Temple on the 6th of April next, and to commence the Conference on the 3rd.

Bro. F. D. Richards gave our office the privilege of issuing an edition of 1,000 copies of the *Compendium*. The order was handed us today. The cost of printing is to be $.10 per copy; for binding we are to receive $.15 per copy cloth, and leather $.30 per copy....

Friday, February 26, 1892:

We today commenced to set the type for the *Life of President John Taylor*, which we expect to issue during the spring....

Saturday, February 27, 1892:

I had to borrow from the Deseret Bank today the sum of $2,000 to meet notes of the office which fall due on Tuesday in connection with the *History of Utah*. I got it for seven months. I hope we will get financial relief when we begin to deliver the first volume, for if we do not I do not know what we will do to meet our engagements. I had hard work today to get enough money with which to pay the workmen....

Sunday, February 28, 1892:

I...took the...train for East Bountiful to attend the funeral of Elder Daniel Davis... The Bountiful tabernacle was crowded, and the leading men of the Stake and Ward were in attendance. Pres. Joseph F. Smith, Elder George Reynolds and George Goddard of Salt Lake were also present.... After the opening exercises and the passing of the Sacrament, the Bishop (Chester Call) made a few remarks in which he told of some of the excellent qualities of the deceased. I then spoke for 15 minutes and told of my acquaintance with Bro. Davis and the very great esteem in which I held him. Bro. Joseph F. Smith occupied an hour of the time after George Reynolds had spoken for 10 minutes on the death of the Savior and the redemption He wrought out for us by His suffering. Bro. Smith said he felt that Bro. Davis had not taken proper care of himself or he would have lived longer, though he was 83 years old last December. In his remarks he then told the assembly of how they can secure for themselves the blessing of eternal life. The books will be opened in the great hereafter, and we will be judged therefrom. The books which are kept here on the earth, as well as those in heaven will help to make up the account against us or in our favor. It does not matter how limited our means or opportunities have been upon the earth, if we have only improved them to the utmost we will be crowned with that crown which is fadeless, and be given those blessings which will endure throughout eternity. If we lose our faith our punishment will be awful. Having received the Holy Ghost and then sinning against the light which God has bestowed, we become the sons of Perdition, and upon us the sentence of a second death will be passed. Those who have never received the truth cannot sin against the Holy Ghost, and they will be redeemed in the due time of the Lord. But for the sons of Perdition it is not revealed that there will ever come a time of redemption, but they are dead to all hope, to all glory, and are eternally shut out from the presence of God. Can you imagine how great will be their punishment? Having a full knowledge of what they might have enjoyed, they are still without hope of ever receiving the same, and all because of their sins. In this place of torment there will be indeed weeping, and wailing and gnashing of teeth. It is a place where the worm dieth not and the fire is not quenched. Beware of it, all ye Saints!...

Tuesday, March 1, 1892:

In the evening I took Sarah with me to President Woodruff's farm to celebrate his birthday, and to be present at the dedication of his new house.... President Woodruff is eighty-five years old today. Heber J. Grant was the first speaker; then followed in the order named the following brethren; William B. Preston, M. W. Merrill, Anthon H. Lund, F. D. Richards and L. Snow. All wished the President many happy returns of the day, and the firm conviction was expressed by several that he would live to see the Salt Lake Temple finished and to dedicate it. Pres. Woodruff made some remarks at the close. He said it is marvelous how the Lord has preserved his life, he having passed through enough to kill a whole regiment of ordinary men. Nearly every bone in his body has been broken. When he was a child he fell into a kettle of scalding water, only his head and feet escaping immersion, and when he was lifted out all his skin fell from his body. Twice he passed though a water wheel when it was in motion. But through all his dangers and misfortunes he has been remarkably preserved for some purpose which he was unable to understand.[3] He hoped to live to dedicate the Temple in this city, for he dreamed on two occasions that he would be given the keys for this edifice by President Young and Taylor also had preceded him. He believed that he would live to accomplish this labor....

Saturday, March 12, 1892:

I am 33 years old today....

In the evening I went to the farm where Mina had prepared for me a dinner, to which she had invited Patriarch John Smith, for the purpose of giving me a Patriarchal blessing, her Father, Nora, Lewis and Mamie, David Sylvester and Eugene. Emily was also invited, but

---

[3] See also "A Chapter of Accidents" in Preston Nibley, comp., *Faith Promoting Stories* (Independence Mo.:Zion's Printing and Publishing, 1943), 14-22.

did not come. We had supper about 7 o'clock, and thereafter Patriarch John Smith blessed me, and then gave Claude a blessing also. The following are copies of his words which were taken by my brother David: "Brother Abraham Hoagland Cannon, by the authority of the Priesthood I bear I place my hands upon thy head and pronounce and seal a blessing upon thee as the Spirit shall indicate. Thou art numbered among the sons of Zion of whom much is expected. Thou art born under the covenant, thus an heir to the blessings, gifts and privileges thereof, and I say unto thee, reflect upon the past and present, and thou shalt realize that the hand of the Lord has been over thee for good, that His eye has been upon thee from thy birth, and that He has given thine angel charge concerning thee, and that He has watched over thee by day and night thus far on thy journey; that many times He has preserved thee from evil which has been placed in thy way. He has also delivered thee from thine enemies, warded off many times the shafts of the adversary which have been hurled at thee, and preserved thy life. It is also a decree of the Almighty that you should live to a good old age, and see much of the world, and assist in gathering scattered Israel. It shall be thy duty to travel by land and water, and to preside among the people, to guide the minds of the youth, to reclaim the wayward, to exhort the Saints to faithfulness, to become a savior among thy kindred, to strengthen the weak and to provide for widows and the fatherless, that thy fame may go forth as a father in Israel far and near, for the Lord has heard thy petitions. He knowest the secrets of thy heart. He has accepted thine offerings, and will reward thee for the trials through which thou hast passed. Look forward to the future with a prayerful heart and an inquiring mind, and thou shalt comprehend the blessings promised unto the faithful, and as you learn to listen to the whispering of the Spirit, the vision of thine understanding shall be opened that thou shalt see things as they are, for the angel of thy presence will whisper in thine ear in time of need, warn thee of dangers by dreams of the night, and by the prophetic vision of thy mind thou shalt see events to come, and if necessary thou shalt prophesy, for this shall be one of thy gifts, and another shall be the gift of discernment. Thou shalt detect error, and evil-disposed persons shall be made to fear and tremble at thy gaze. The honest-in-heart shall rejoice in thy teachings. Therefore I say unto thee, be prudent and listen in obedience to the whisperings of the still small voice of the Comforter, and thy pathway shall be made clear, peace shall be in thy circle and thou shalt have joy in thy labors, spiritual and temporal, for thou shalt ask the Father in faith, and thy petitions shall be heard and answered. Thou art of the lineage of Ephraim, and thine inheritance hereafter is among those who shall stand upon Mount Zion, Saviors of men. Thy name is written in the Lamb's Book of Life, registered in the chronicles of thy fathers with thy brethren, and shall live in the memory of the Saints, and be handed down with thy posterity in honorable remembrance from generation to generation. Therefore I say unto thee, be always cheerful in thy deportment and guarded in expression, and the blessings of the Lord shall attend thee, and direct thy course, and all shall be well with thee both here and hereafter. It shall be thy privilege, also, in thy journeyings, when it shall be necessary, to command the elements by which life shall be preserved, both upon the land and sea. Thou shalt acknowledge the hand of the Lord when friends shall be raised up unto thee among strangers. Therefore look forward to the future with pleasure. This blessing, with the blessings of Abraham, Isaac, and Jacob, I seal upon thee in the name of Jesus Christ, and seal thee up unto eternal life, to come forth in the morning of the first resurrection a savior in thy father's house, even so, amen." …

Tuesday, March 29, 1892:

I asked Joseph F. Smith why it was that Ham's son Canaan was cursed instead of Ham for exposing his Father's person. He said that the Prophet Joseph is credited with saying that the sin of Ham consisted in trying to castrate his father, Noah, and kill his brothers, Shem and Japheth, so that he might become the head of the nations of the earth. Ham had married a daughter of Cain, and by him the curse was carried through the flood. The seed of this union is the Egyptians, which are not black, but after Ham's curse, his seed were entirely black. Hence the difference between the races who now inhabit Africa.…

Thursday, March 31, 1892:

At 2 o'clock I was at the meeting of our Quorum. Present: Presidents Woodruff and Smith, F. D. Richards, F. M. Lyman, J. H. Smith, H. J. Grant and myself; George F. Gibbs, clerk. Joseph F. Smith was mouth in prayer. A letter was then read from Joseph Dameron, who is on a mission in Tahiti, one of the friendly Islands in the Pacific Islands. His companion is William Seegmiller. An account is given of their efforts to open the gospel door in that place. The Josephite church has gathered into its fold nearly all those people who once belonged to the Church, but it was thought that if a man could be sent who has had experience in the Church, and who had been a preacher on the islands of the Pacific, a great many can be reconverted. It was proposed to send James S. Brown, who was there in early years. He told Joseph F. that he is willing to go, although he is about 65 years of age. We all voted that he had better go and see what he can do....

Friday, April 1, 1892:

At 2 o'clock was at the meeting of my quorum in the upper room of the Historian's office, where, after waiting about three-quarters of an hour, we got seven of the brethren together. They were, Pres. L. Snow, F. D. Richards, Moses Thatcher, F. M. Lyman, H. J. Grant, John W. Taylor and myself. After prayer by Moses Thatcher, Pres. Snow arose and expressed his dissatisfaction at our lack of promptness in attending these meetings, and our neglect of them. He felt that we should always be on time, and never allow anything to interfere with our being present at the times appointed. He then continued: "As for myself I would like to get rid of all financial matters and devote myself to the spiritual affairs of the work. This might not do for my brethren, but I believe we will yet have to take positions which we do not now understand. When the Manifesto was issued we had no idea that it was to effect our cohabitation with our wives, but Pres. Woodruff and his brethren who were on the witness stand before the Master in Chancery, were forced to go further in their testimony than we anticipated, or we would have been placed in a worse position than we were before the Manifesto was issued.

"It is the privilege of you brethren to see the Savior, and thus testify of Him, and that you know He lives."

Heber J. Grant said: "I remember Pres. Woodruff saying that the Manifesto would never apply to our living with our wives, and he would see them damned and in hell before he would agree to cease living with his wives or advise any other person to do so. Still we have been led to our present position by degrees, and I believe it is all right.

"I would like to be relieved of financial matters if it were possible and in accord with the minds of my brethren, and go upon a mission so that I can get those great spiritual blessings of which the brethren speak but which I have never enjoyed. I find that dissensions are growing to some extent among my brethren engaged with me in business, and this I do not want. I have tried to do my daily duties to the best of my ability, but wish I could now have a relief in this way. Concerning the living with our wives, I believe that if we had taken the manly stand and had said we will continue to live with and honor our present wives but will cease marrying in the future, we would have fared better; but now I cannot see any chance of our ever being permitted to live with our wives in freedom again."

Moses Thatcher: "I have yet to meet the first man among all the eminent men with whom I have conversed upon our question who feels that our past family relations should be disrupted. They did not want this, and therefore I must believe that the Lord had some other object in permitting us to make the promises we have concerning the relations with our wives. I think it is the duty of every Latter-day Saint to place himself in such a position that he will not bring reproach upon the Church for any of his actions, and we should especially do nothing with our wives that would give the lie to the testimony of the brethren in the Court." He then spoke of the union of Church and State, and protested against our interference in political matters….

At this point Pres. Joseph F. Smith entered with a dispatch from Judge Williams of Washington saying that if an urgent dispatch were sent tonight to Pres. Harrison, he did not know but that the Amnesty petition would be signed in time to present to the approaching conference. The following was therefore presented: "Could Amnesty come before our Conference, we believe the boon would be profoundly appreciated by our people." All of us excepting Moses Thatcher and John W. Taylor authorized our names to be attached to the telegram. Another dispatch will be sent signed by prominent Outsiders in this city. Moses said he believed it was for political effect that this was proposed at this time, and he did not propose to be led into any such trap. We all feel that this was probably the object, but were still willing that it should occur. John W. did not want to sign it or anything else without having time to consider it. Pres. Smith then started with the message to President Woodruff's house to obtain his signature to it. We continued our meeting. Pres. Snow said he felt that when any question came up among us on which the majority were clear, should there be one who did not see as the others, that one should be willing to yield his views to those of the majority, and leave the responsibility of the course pursued with them.

John W. Taylor spoke in relation to the Manifesto: "I do not know that that thing was right, though I voted to sustain it, and will assist to maintain it; but among my father's papers I found a revelation given him of the Lord, and which is now in my possession, in which the Lord told him that the principle of plural marriage would never be overcome. Pres. Taylor desired to have it suspended, but the Lord would not permit it to be done."[4]

At the close of John W's. remarks our meeting adjourned till tomorrow at 10 o'clock....

Saturday, April 2, 1892:

At 10 o'clock our quorum met, and in addition to those present yesterday we had John H. Smith and Anthon H. Lund. Prayer by F. D. Richards. Pres. Snow spoke of cohabitation and said though our sisters were in great trouble they were not enduring worse things now than the female Saints had endured in the past. They should be

---

[4] See Appendix One: Plural Marriage Issues in the Abraham H. Cannon Journals.

willing to put up with inconveniences and troubles in order that the Church and the brethren may not be brought into trouble.

F. D. Richards said: "I met and talked with Pres. Cannon just before coming to this meeting and he told me that it was only a question of a short time before we would have amnesty, as Pres. Harrison had decided to issue the proclamation, but was only considering the terms and phraseology of the same. He has a desire to make it as broad as possible. The feeling in the east towards us is very kind. Pres. Cannon succeeded in getting his bonds released, which is quite an important thing for him. Concerning cohabitation I think we should use the utmost care. We should refrain from living with our wives until a better feeling is created towards us, and then we will be permitted to give them our attentions as we formerly did. Amnesty will only apply to past offenses, and will not relieve us of future misdemeanors."

I then arose and explained the position I occupied and my manner of living. I wanted the brethren to counsel me if I was doing wrong, but hoped they would not tell me not to live with my families.

It was a marvel to my brethren, as it is to me, how I have escaped arrest and conviction, but it is only through the blessing of the Lord that I have been thus preserved.

The brethren had not any censure for me, but felt that we should all be very careful so as not to bring trouble upon the Church by our actions. All of the brethren spoke upon this subject with the result that it was left for each person to do what he felt to be right, and as the Lord might inspire. John Henry felt that all should take their plural families over the line. As a parting counsel Pres. Snow told us to keep our own affairs to ourselves in such matters. We now adjourned subject to call, Bro. Lund dismissing with prayer.

At 1 o'clock I was at a meeting of the trustees of Young University where the question of making Young University the Church University and changing its name was discussed. It was felt that so many contributions would not be made to the institution if it bore the name of any man, as if it were a Church institution. This view was entertained by quite a number of those present, and it was therefore decided to try and make the change, and Willard Young was appointed to see the heirs of Brigham Young and see if they would all consent to the change in the name. It is designed, however, to name different departments after our prominent men, so as to perpetuate their memories....

Sunday, April 3, 1892:

At 10 o'clock our general conference convened in the large Tabernacle. There was a very large attendance of officers and members, and a very good spirit prevailed. After the usual opening exercises Father spoke for about half an hour giving a very good and extended report of the various missions of the Church and the work that was being done among them. He expressed his gratitude to the Lord for all His mercies unto His people, and felt that we all have cause for thanksgiving for the manner in which the Lord has blessed us.

Franklin D. Richards spoke for a short time on the principle of revelation, and urged all the Saints to cultivate it so that they may receive instruction from the fountain head of all light.

Heber J. Grant and John W. Taylor each spoke for a few moments on the duties we must perform in order to retain the Spirit of the Lord.

In the afternoon the large congregation in the Tabernacle was addressed by Joseph F. Smith for about an hour. He spoke of the punishment which will be meted out to the wicked who receive not the testimony of the Elders, but said that the Saints who turned away from the truth when once they had received it would receive a far greater punishment for their sins. He referred to our professions which do not always correspond with our acts, for we do things of which Saints should be ashamed. We must keep all the commandments of God if we expect to receive the highest exaltation. He read from the Doctrine and Covenants to show that we must be willing to sacrifice everything for the work of the Lord.

Pres. Woodruff testified briefly to the work which the Lord is doing in these last days, and spoke of the officers which will exist in every Church which God establishes among the children of men....

Monday, April 4, 1892:

After the opening exercises of the Conference this morning James E. Talmage read the general circular of the Church Board of Education concerning the nature of the Church educational system, and the manner of conducting the schools now organized. It also mentions the intention of organizing a Church University. This reading finished, Willard Young presented a resolution to the effect that the Presidency of the Church name a committee of five persons to consider the matter of a University, and to report their labors to this Conference. This motion was carried.

Pres. Lorenzo Snow spoke for about 35 minutes on the blessings which God has bestowed on us through our obedience to the gospel, and said we must seek to be perfect; though we may today fail in our aims to perfection , we must try again tomorrow, and so continue till we do become as God desires us to be—a righteous people.

Moses Thatcher spoke for 25 minutes on the subject of education, which he felt should be encouraged among us so that the bright minds of children may be trained for the great labors which will hereafter devolve upon them in a Church capacity, as well as in the government under which we live. Meeting adjourned.

At one o'clock the Presidency and Twelve met to consider the program for the exercises at the laying of the cap-stone of the Temple on the 6th. H. J. Grant, J. W. Taylor, A. H. Lund and myself were appointed a committee to examine the scaffolding around the tower to see how many persons it will hold, and to see where a stand can be erected for the choir and speakers so that the people can hear what is said and done.

In the afternoon meeting the Presidency named the committee on University as follows: Willard Young, Karl G. Maeser, James E. Talmage, James Sharp and Benjamin Cluff, Jr. These nominations were unanimously sustained.

Father then spoke for nearly an hour, and with such power as has seldom been witnessed in the Tabernacle. He kept the attention of the people riveted to his remarks, and several times the tears sprang to my eyes while he was speaking. He first read from the prophecy of Enoch in the Pearl of Great Price, concerning the kind of people who will prepare to meet the Lord when he shall come, and said we are to be that people. He told of our weaknesses, however, and said we must overcome them. Referred to politics, and the bitter feelings they have caused, and said that the Presidency held it to be their right to counsel the Saints in these as in all other things, and if they (the Presidency) were to keep quiet and allow evils to grow unreproved, the sins of the people would cling to their skirts. Therefore they would tell of sins and leave the Saints to accept their counsels or not, as seemed good to them.[5]

Presidents Woodruff and Joseph F. Smith both testified that what had been said was the word of God to us, and we will be condemned if we reject it.

After meeting adjourned I went with the committee to examine the Temple and grounds. We ascended the scaffolding to the top, and had an excellent view of the Country. After giving the matter consideration we decided that the best place for the people to stand and for the platform to be erected was on the south side of the Temple....

Tuesday, April 5, 1892:

In this mornings meeting the first business was the reading of the report of the Church University committee. They recommended the adoption of a resolution to the effect that the Presidency and Twelve found and endow in the best manner they can devise a Church University of high grade at the earliest possible date. This resolution was adopted by the Conference.

Francis M. Lyman spoke for half an hour in an able manner on the support we should give to the authorities of the Church, and told that when Pres. Woodruff was not present he felt it to be his duty to listen to his first counselor, and in the absence of they two, he should accept the counsels of the second counselor. He spoke of the duties

---

[5] For this date, President Woodruff's journal records: "Then President George Q. Cannon spoke 50 minutes in the power of God, followed by Wilford Woodruff in the same power and spirit. J. F. Smith spoke 15 min. and much of the power of God was with us."

which we owe to the world to preach the gospel, and the duty we owe to God to live our religion.

John Henry Smith spoke for about 10 minutes principally on the subject of the statue which is to be erected in honor of Pres. Brigham Young, and urged all to do something towards this thing.

Marriner W. Merrill spoke on the subject of temple building and the work to be done therein, urging the Saints to do their duty in this direction, and Anthon H. Lund spoke on the subject of education.

Father then added a few remarks on the matter of the statue to be erected in honor of Pres. Young, and said it had the approval of the authorities of the Church.

At one o'clock the Presidency, Twelve and First Seven Presidents of the Seventies held a meeting in the President's office, where it was decided to erect the platforms for the services of the laying of the capstone of the Temple to the south of the building, and to lay the stone by means of electricity. The vacancy in the Seventies was considered next.... After some little discussion and consideration it was decided to appoint Jonathan Golden Kimball to the position. He received the unanimous vote of the brethren.

There was an overflow meeting held this afternoon. I was the first speaker in the Tabernacle. I occupied about 25 minutes on the necessity of our people providing employment for those who come into our territory, and also to find something for our own boys to do at home instead of allowing them to spend their time in idleness or in seeking for homes elsewhere.

Abraham O. Smoot of the Utah Stake next spoke for a few minutes, and bore his testimony of the truth. He said among other things that if half the stories which were told by the political parties against each other were true about half of each party should be in the penitentiary....

Wednesday, April 6, 1892:
Meeting convened at 10 o'clock and the building was crowded. Father spoke in behalf of the Presidency and Twelve, and said we accepted the charge laid upon us in regard to the establishment of the Church University.

Pres. Lorenzo Snow then instructed the congregation in regard to the shouting of Hosanna, when the top stone of the Temple shall have been laid. The Priesthood were arranged in their various orders in the body of the building, and thus left it to march to the place where the ceremonies are to occur. At 11:15 we began the march, and by 12:30 all was ready for the services. Held's band played the Capstone March which had been prepared by C. J. Thomas, and then the choir sung the Temple anthem, the words of which were composed by C. L. Walker and the music by Evan Stephens. Father then exhibited a polished brass plate which was to go beneath the cap-stone. It contained the names of the authorities of the Church at the time the corner stone of the temple was laid—April 6, 1853, and the names of the present authorities. Also the names of the architects. The engraving was done by David McKenzie. There were placed in the cap-stone also a full set of our Church Works, photographs of Joseph and Hyrum Smith, Brigham Young, John Taylor, Wilford Woodruff, George Q. Cannon and Joseph F. Smith. Also a picture of the Temple in its present condition.

The prayer was then offered by Joseph F. Smith, and then the cap-stone of the structure was laid by Pres. Woodruff touching the electric button by means of which the stone was dropped into its place.[6] Under the direction of the President of the Apostles, Lorenzo Snow, the assembled multitude, numbering perhaps 40,000, shouted "Hosanna, Hosanna, Hosanna to God and the Lamb, Amen, Amen, Amen." This was done three times, each shout being accompanied by a waving of handkerchiefs, except when the names of God and the Lamb were uttered. The choir, band and congregation then rendered the hymn, "The Spirit of God like a fire is burning." The Union Glee

---

[6] President Woodruff's journal records for this date: "This was the most interesting day in some respects the Church has ever seen since its organization. The temple capstone was laid today with imposing ceremonies with electricity by President Wilford Woodruff. It was judged there were 50,000 on the temple grounds." John Henry Smith's journal records: "At 12:30 President W. Woodruff touched an electric button and the stone dropped into place. I believe that sixty thousand people witnessed the ceremony. Bro. Lorenzo Snow led the Hosanna shout and the waving of handkerchiefs. It was indeed a grand sight" (*Church, State, and Politics*, 274).

Club next rendered a selection prepared specially for the occasion. Apostle F. M. Lyman then offered the following resolution: "Believing that the instructions of President Woodruff, respecting the early completion of the Salt Lake Temple, are the word of the Lord to us, I propose that this assemblage pledge themselves, collectively and individually, to furnish, as fast as it may be needed, all the money that may be required to complete the Temple at the earliest time possible, so that the dedication may take place on April 6, 1893." All responded to this resolution by raising the right hand and shouting "Aye." Bro. Lyman then headed the subscription list with an offer of $1,000. After music by the band and singing by the choir, Father dismissed with prayer, and Conference was adjourned for six months. The figure of the angel Moroni in the act of blowing the gospel trump, which is to surmount the cap-stone, was unveiled in its position at 3:10 today. It is a beautiful figure of 12 feet five and _ inches high, and is made of hammered brass after a model by C. E. Dallin of this city. It is covered with the best gold leaf, and has an electric jet in its crown of 100 candle power....

Thursday, April 7, 1892:

At 10 o'clock I was at a meeting of the Presidents of Stakes, Bishops, High Councilors, and others in the Assembly Hall. After the opening exercises Father spoke for a short time, and referred to the changes which have occurred in our surroundings within the last ten years. It was just about 10 years ago that the legislation of so terrible a character began in Congress against us, but the Lord has overruled it all for good. "I feel to say that there is a still better day dawning for the Saints, if we will but do as the Lord directs. You men have it in your power to hasten or retard the glorious day, for if you will lead out in doing right, the people will follow you. Your acts will influence your posterity till the latest generation, and they will also influence the Church of God. How much you cannot now tell, but you will know some day. I desire to do what is right, and if I have hurt the feelings of any man or woman in the Church I desire their forgiveness, and now ask it of you who are here, if I have done you any wrong. We should love the work of God more than we do wife or child, or anything that is upon the earth."

Pres. Woodruff spoke of the spirit which had prompted him to issue the Manifesto, and said it was of God. He also spoke of the heavy expenses under which the Church is laboring, and hoped we would get relief soon....

Pres. Lorenzo Snow spoke of the duty which devolves on us to feed the sheep of the Church, and we should never do anything to disgrace our calling as the servants of God.

Joseph F. Smith spoke in favor of the sugar factory and said it was started with the view to give our people employment. We should give it our support. He also spoke of tithing and said we should be faithful in attending to this duty because of the blessing it will bring to us. A poor woman who receives assistance from her Bishop should pay her tithing so as to have her name on the book of the Church.

Heber J. Grant spoke strongly in favor of the brethren taking stock in the Sugar factory, and said he knew the Lord would bless all who would do so, and even if the business paid no dividends it could still prove a blessing in the end to us.

John W. Taylor moved that we consecrate all our surplus property to the work of the Lord, but Pres. Woodruff felt that the proper time for that had not yet arrived....

Tuesday, April 19, 1892:

Father and I had a talk with Bishop O. F. Whitney today in regard to the second volume of the *History of Utah*. We urged it upon him to hurry the work along, and he promised to do so with the help of John Q. Cannon.

Wednesday, April 20, 1892:

I was at the President's office with Mr. Webster for a short time in the afternoon trying to obtain from the Church an additional subscription to the *History of Utah* of 300 volumes or less; but our efforts were not very successful, though it was not said that the Church would not take more than already ordered....

Thursday, April 21, 1892:

We received from the binders in St. Louis (Becktold & Co.) a sample copy of the first volume of the *History of Utah* today. It makes a most excellent work, both in the contents, printing and binding, and one which pleases and astonishes every person who sees it. The Presidency are highly pleased with it. It is bound in full morocco, embossed in gold and gilded on the edges.

At 2 o'clock I was at my Quorum meeting where all the Presidency were present and F. M. Lyman and myself; George F. Gibbs, clerk. Pres. Woodruff was mouth in prayer. We considered the matter of appointing a day of fasting and thanksgiving because of the blessings the Lord has bestowed upon us. In this meeting we are to supplicate the Lord to continue to favor and deliver Zion, and subscriptions are to be taken for the completion of the work upon the Salt Lake Temple. A circular letter was prepared for issuance in the papers, in which the desires of the Presidency in this matter were expressed....

Sunday, April 24, 1892:

Was at the Tabernacle services at two o'clock....

I then spoke for about 35 minutes on the care we should exercise in the calling of men to perform various labors, so as to be sure to get those whose talents and education have fitted them for the duties devolving upon them. Also spoke of the responsibility of the Saints concerning the work for the dead, and urged all to do their utmost to assist in the work on our temple that it may be speedily completed so that the work may commence there for the salvation of those who are gone....

Thursday, April 28, 1892:

Attended my Quorum meeting in the afternoon, where were present all of the Presidency, and Bros. Richards, Grant and myself; George F. Gibbs clerk. Father was mouth in prayer. The matter of the Young Men's M. I. Associations of this Stake holding a conference in May was discussed. It is desired to occupy a Sunday for this purpose, but Father objected to the interruption that would thus be given to the Sunday Schools. Considerable spirited discussion followed between Father and Pres. Smith, with the result that it was decided that for the present there would be no conference held for this Stake, inasmuch as the General Y. M. M. I. A. conference will meet in this city in June next....

Letters were next read from Senator A. G. Paddock to C. C. Goodwin, and from Judge Estee to Father concerning the amnesty, and from their statements it does not seem likely that we will receive the benefits of such an act, as Pres. Harrison is so afraid of injuring his chances for re-nomination that he will not do anything that he thinks will offend any of his party. We feel, however, to now leave the matter in the hands of the Lord, feeling sure that He will control matters for the good of Zion....

Friday, April 29, 1892:

At 3:30 I was at the meeting of the Deseret S. S. Union Board, where the usual reports were rendered and other business had attention. The matter of paying the tithing on the S. S. Union funds was then raised by myself, and was the cause of considerable discussion. The views of the brethren vary as to what is required by the Lord, but that which is generally accepted as correct is for a man to pay the tenth part of all profits which arise from his labor, or the tenth part of his annual salary....

Thursday, May 5, 1892:

At two o'clock I was at my Quorum meeting where were present all of the Presidency, also Bros. Lyman, John H. Smith and myself; George F. Gibbs, clerk,. Bro. Lyman was mouth in prayer. There was no business of importance considered except to talk some of political matters in Wyoming, whither Father felt that Bro. Smith should go to see that our people do not become traitors to the Republican party which has helped us so much....

Friday, May 6, 1892:

I was at the office most of the day attending to the delivery of the first installment of the *History of Utah*. We succeeded in getting rid of nearly 150 volumes, and the general feeling is one of satisfaction on seeing the volume, though we have had one or two subscribers who tried to get out of taking the work....

Saturday, June 25, 1892:

Father went to St. George with President Woodruff last week, and returned this [week]. They had a good time. During their absence we held none of our Quorum meetings as only Pres. Smith and myself were in town....

Saturday, July 2, 1892:

The Territorial school convention today adopted "Domestic Science" as a text book for use in the District schools of the Territory. This means that we will have to issue immediately a large edition of the work inasmuch as we are the publishers of the same, Dr. James E. Talmage being the author....

I today bought through John Q. from Newton Farr of Ogden a one-sixth interest in the "Blue Bird" mine located in the Deep Creek country. All the reports go to prove that this is a valuable piece of property.... I gave my check for $612.50, and my note payable in 60 days for a like amount, for my one-sixth interest, and I have promised the Lord, and here record my covenant, that if the Lord will bless me in this venture I will give to Him one-fifth of all the profits I receive from the property after the return to me of the amount I have thus invested, and which is already tithed. I hope and pray He will bless me in this venture. In the evening I was at Mina's for supper, and then spent the evening in type-writing.

Tuesday, July 12, 1892:

At two o'clock I was at the Historian's office where our Quorum met in the upper room according to appointment. There were present Pres. Lorenzo Snow, Moses Thatcher, Francis M. Lyman, John Henry Smith, Heber J. Grant, John W. Taylor, M. W. Merrill, Anthon H. Lund and myself. I was appointed to act as secretary in the absence of Pres. F. D. Richards, who has gone to Alaska with his son Franklin for his health. Singing, "Come let us anew," etc. Prayer by M. W. Merrill. Singing "God moves in a mysterious way," etc. It was decided to postpone the reading of our History till the return of Bro. Richards. Pres. Snow said he felt very happy to meet with the Brethren today. It is our privilege and duty to seek for the mysteries of the Kingdom, and to be in advance of those who are around us. It is our labor to bring about the immortality of man, and the more earnestly we are engaged in this labor the more we will be blest in all our affairs. He referred to politics and said the position taken by Bros. Thatcher and Smith had made him think seriously about our condition. He was determined, however, not to let the actions of the brethren divide our Quorum. It is the privilege of the brethren to enjoy the spirit of prophecy and to be guided of the Lord in all the labors required of us. He requested all who engaged in politics to be very careful of the feelings of the brethren. If there are any hard feelings existing among us, this is the time and place to make them known so that they can be settled. Nothing that occurs here should be carried further.

Several of the brethren expressed themselves as having the very best of feeling for each other, and in this sentiment all the others present acquiesced.

Moses Thatcher: "I was drawn into politics by a train of circumstances which I could not control. We were being suspected by those of the Gentiles who had divided, and it was necessary in my opinion that something should be done by the leading men to establish confidence in the minds of all. I believe that great good will result from this political movement in the relief from oppression, and we will soon learn to differ on politics and still entertain no animosities in our hearts."

John Henry Smith: "I am entirely free from bad feelings towards my brethren. The events that are taking place will tend to make us more tolerant of the feelings and views of others."

Heber J. Grant: 'McCormick, Dooley and such men who oppose the division movement pursue this course for the money there is in it to them. The little rift between the Bros. Smith and Moses Thatcher in the papers will do more towards satisfying the people of the world that we are sincere than a great amount of talk would do."

Francis M. Lyman: "I am pleased at the way in which politics have been going of late, and believe the result will be greater liberty for our people. I am not offended at any of my brethren. I am pleased at the progress being made on our temple. I hope all the Quorum will be able to attend the dedicatory services. Bro. Teasdale has felt at times as though he was not appreciated by the brethren of the Quorum, but I know we all love him. I feel sorry that he could not be with us in our meetings."

Bro. Lyman was appointed to write a kind letter to Bro. Teasdale and express the love and good feelings of the brethren for him.

Meeting then adjourned till tomorrow with prayer by John W. Taylor....

Wednesday, July 13, 1892:

I was in my Quorum meeting from 10 a.m. till 2 p.m. All the brethren who were in attendance yesterday were also here today. Singing, "Come all ye sons of Zion," etc. Prayer by F. M. Lyman. Pres. Snow: "I love all my brethren of this Quorum, and I desire to see them united. Before I die I want to see us all unalterably and immovably fixed in the unity of the gospel. If such a spirit was in us we could work wonders, and with the help of God could manage His work as He desires. We should never get into positions where we forget the respect due from one of us to the other. We ought to always cultivate the spirit of kindness and love for our brethren and be careful of the feelings of those around us." He referred to the story of David who would not lift his hand against the Lord's anointed even though that man had sought his life. Also the case of Noah's sons who covered his nakedness though Noah had been in great sin and was uncovered because of his drunkenness. The son of the latter who made sport of his father's condition was cursed, while his brothers were blessed. The lesson he desired to teach us by these examples was that we should not expose the weaknesses of the Priesthood which is over us, if they have weak points, we should try to shield them from the gaze of the unbelieving or scoffing attitude. He especially mentioned the newspaper controversy between Bros. Joseph F. and John H. Smith, and Moses Thatcher. He said that when Pres. Woodruff asks for our views upon any subject, we should express the same fully, but if his advice is contrary to our views we should follow his counsels in opposition to our own feelings if necessary.

John W. Taylor: "I believe but few of the people are injuriously affected by the controversy in the paper on political matters, and as for me I do not care which party is victorious, for I believe God will overrule all these matters for our good. I often wonder if we as Apostles are doing our duty in the preaching of the gospel. The world is not being warned as it should be, and here at home many of the people are becoming careless and indifferent. Perhaps the Lord is waiting for the world to become ripened in iniquity before sending us out to preach. It seems to me necessary for us to arrange our temporal matters so that the poor may share in our blessings temporally. If this is not done we will have troubles in our midst such as exist in the world."

M. W. Merrill: "I have no ill-feelings towards any of my brethren, nor have I heard much complaint against any of the brethren. The Lord will lead His servants in the way that will be most profitable to his cause. In my labors among the people I have tried to select men for positions who have kept the law of God, for I believe such will be more abundantly blessed. In politics I have not been active, because I think I should not take sides in the position I am called to fill in the Logan temple."

Anthon H. Lund: "I believe the Lord will control all our mistakes for the good of His cause. It would be bad for the idea to get out among the people that we are not sincere in our political affairs; such a feeling would do us irreparable injury. I believe it would have been better for us to have divided more nearly equal, yet I believe all will yet come out right. I feel well towards all, and pray that the Lord will bless us in His work."

Moses Thatcher: "At a recent conference of Cache stake Pres. Woodruff said it was the will of God that we should divide on the national party lines, therefore I have worked earnestly to have an honest division occur. Good men should study the political questions so that they can direct in these matters, and not leave it to the common people to direct, and thus commit sometimes very grave mistakes."

Abraham H. Cannon: "I feel that before we arrive at the point that we can be united in all things we will have to first learn to strictly pay our tithes and offerings." I then told of remarks which I had heard against Bros. Lyman and J. H. Smith, concerning their injustice in Arizona towards Bro. L. Brown, and of their partisanship in Manassa for Silas Smith. The brethren disclaimed these charges, and fully and satisfactorily explained them.

Pres. Woodruff came in about one o'clock, and after some time spent in making appointments for Quarterly conferences Bro. Thatcher offered prayer for the health of Heber J. Grant's wife, and we partook of the sacrament after it had been blessed by John H. Smith. While at the table Pres. Woodruff made a few remarks concerning the times in which we live. He said the Prophet repeatedly prophesied that this nation would have all the mobbings and blood it desired because of its inhuman treatment of this people. "The hand of the Lord has been visible in our preservation from the evils which have threatened us, and we should labor to do the will of God, and to establish His work upon the earth. The Lord and His angels are with us and will bless us in our labors."…

Thursday, August 4, 1892:

I was busy at the office till 11 o'clock when I went to the President's office, where my Quorum was requested to meet with the Presidency. The matter of dedicating the Salt Lake temple next April was considered, and it was decided after all the brethren had spoken to hold the exercises in the temple each day until every worthy member of the Church should have the privilege of entering into the building and taking part in the dedicatory exercises. The decorating of the building will not be fully done, but no impropriety could be seen in dedicating the structure at the time appointed—April 6th. This decision being reached the meeting adjourned till two o'clock.

At the latter time the brethren met. There were present this morning as well as this afternoon all of the Presidency, L. Snow, Moses Thatcher, Francis M. Lyman, John Henry Smith, Heber J.

Grant, M. W. Merrill, A. H. Lund and myself; George F. Gibbs, clerk. Pres. Woodruff expressed a desire for the brethren to be united in all things, political and otherwise, and for this reason he desired to have this meeting so that we may be brought to see eye to eye. Bro. Joseph F. Smith arraigned Moses Thatcher for his actions politically, and said he had felt hurt at the course Bro. Thatcher had taken. He enumerated the occasions when he felt Bro. Thatcher had been in error, and in opposition to the advice of the Presidency in the course he had taken. Bro. Thatcher responded in a mild and humble manner to what had been charged, and explained his reasons for doing as he had done. He felt sorry if he had done wrong, and was willing to be guided by the counsels of the brethren. He said that the Gibbs letter had never been placed in his hands for safe keeping, and this he could very easily prove if it was desired. Considerable talk was indulged in by the brethren, and then Father arose and explained the course the Presidency had been trying to take, and which had for its object the good and deliverance of the people. He felt that the Twelve had not given the Presidency the support they should have done. He spoke with considerable warmth, and when he had finished it was unanimously voted that we endeavor to carry out the wishes of the Presidency in regard to politics, as well as everything else. The meeting adjourned about 6:30 with the very best of feelings prevailing....

Wednesday, August 10, 1892:

Father came in about 2 o'clock and wanted to buy some of my stock in Cannon & Sons. I told him I did not want to sell, but if he desired more to divide among his other children I would part with some of mine. I do not like to sell, but under the circumstances will do so.

At 3 p.m. Bros. George Reynolds and T. C. Griggs came in, and we considered the subjects for pictures for the next Book of Mormon chart for the Sunday School Union. We were agreed as to most of the 24 needed. At 3:30 I went to the Sunday School Board meeting where the correspondence was read, the reports heard, and the price of the new music book considered. Bro. Griggs favored selling it at

$4.00 per dozen, but I favored the same price as that of the old book—$0.50 each, or $4.80 per dozen. The latter view prevailed and the price was fixed accordingly. It has double the number of pages that the old book had, though it is a little smaller in form....

Thursday, September 1, 1892:

In the afternoon John Q. and I had some talk with Father concerning the leasing of the *Deseret News*. We told him we thought of offering for a 20 years lease the sum of $60,000. He had in his mind the sum of $5,000 per year, but did not think the office would be able to pay that much. He told us to try and get our offer ready to present to the meeting of the Company tomorrow....

Friday, September 2, 1892:

In the afternoon I was at the President's office where the Presidency desired the opinion of the brethren as to whether it would be right for the sisters to lay the corner stones of their relief society buildings without the assistance of the brethren of the priesthood. All of the Presidency, and Apostles F. D. Richards, J. H. Smith and myself thought it scarcely the proper thing to do.

After this meeting I remained at the office some little time with John Q. to get an answer if possible to our proposition to the *Deseret News* Co. to lease their plant for the term of 20 years for the sum of $60,000; we did not, however, receive our reply, but the matter was referred to the Executive Committee. They will doubtless act on the matter very soon....

Wednesday, September 8, 1892:

I went to the [Logan] Temple with the folks at 7:30 o'clock, and after the names of those who desire to work for themselves and their dead had been registered, I spoke, by request of Bro. Merrill, to the Saints, and sought to impress upon them the importance of the step they were about to make. I then went to Bro. Merrill's room where he gave me the marriage service to study so that I could perform the same, it being to officiate in the case of Amelia and her husband that I came to Logan. After having dinner I went to the sealing room and sealed for time and eternity fourteen people in addition to William H. Chamberlain, Jr., and my sister Amelia. In their case I laid my hands upon their heads, as Father had suggested I should do, but in the case of the others I merely repeated the ceremony....

When all the sealing was done Bro. Merrill said I had done the best of any person who had sealed in the Temple for the first time.

It was about 2:30 o'clock when I left the Temple....

Monday, October 10, 1892:

At 10 o'clock I attended a meeting of the Presidency of the Church, the Apostles, the Seven Presidents of the Seventies, the Presidents of the various Stakes, the High Councilors, the various Bishoprics and a few others. It was held in the assembly room of the Temple, which had been temporarily fitted up with seats for this occasion. There was a good attendance and the spirit which prevailed was heavenly. The necessity of finishing this building by April next was strongly urged and after some little talk on this subject subscriptions of means were called for. The result was the promise of $50,000 from those present towards the sum of $175,000 which will be needed for the completion of the building alone not to mention the amount necessary to the furnishing of the same. All present agreed to use their energies and means to finish the structure. Pres. Joseph F. Smith made a few remarks concerning the change which has occurred in the business of the *Deseret News*. He said it was still the Church organ.

Father, Joseph F. Smith and Pres. Woodruff then spoke each for a few minutes. Such glorious instructions as they gave it has never been my privilege to hear before. They were filled with the spirit of God, and told the brethren how they should act towards God and their brethren. It was told us that if we would follow the counsel of the Presidency of the Church we would soon see a brighter day dawn upon Utah, and our deliverance would soon come. We were urged to love each other and never be guilty of betraying our brethren nor our God. When Bro. Smith was speaking on the subject of love there were many eyes wet with tears. My heart was moved and my eyes were wet.

After the speaking we were all shown through the Temple and saw the fine workmanship which is being done. I subscribed another thousand dollars for the work on the Temple, and Father went as high as $3,000. Several of the brethren gave $2,000. A very liberal feeling was manifested....

Thursday, October 13, 1892:

At 2 p.m. I was at my Quorum meeting at which were present all of the Presidency, Bros. F. D. Richards, F. M. Lyman, J. H. Smith, H. J. Grant and myself. George F. Gibbs was present a part of the time as clerk. Pres. Woodruff was mouth in prayer and he made a very strong appeal to the Lord in behalf of Mrs. Harrison, who is afflicted with some lung disease. The President of the United States had asked that we pray for his wife. The telegram which Pres. Woodruff had received and which he read to us assured us that amnesty would be granted to the Mormons within a week. It is very evident that the Lord has moved upon the hearts of influential men in the nation to favor Zion. May He still continue to bless His people until we are perfectly free is my prayer. Bros. F. D. Richards and F. M. Lyman were appointed to go to Wyoming and try to have our people there favor the Republican side in that State because of the kindly feeling which that party has there manifested towards us....

Monday, October 17, 1892:

...I received the following telegram from Jacob Schaerrer, the president of the Swiss and German mission in Berne: "Hugh telegraphs David died this morning 9 o'clock." For a few minutes this news stunned me, but recovering myself I went and told John Q. and then went to the President's office and broke the sad news to Father. He received it very composedly, but it was evidently a very severe ordeal for him. It was a most terrible and unexpected blow to us all, as we had received no intimation of his illness. I hired a buggy and went to the farm and told Mamie and the folks. The former was overcome with grief, and all felt very badly. At Father's request I cabled Pres. Schaerrer, "If permissible send Hugh home with body." The *News* of today publishes his last letter to Father which shows how interested and earnest he was in the missionary work to which he was assigned, and by his words he seems almost to have had a premonition of death. He was 21 years old on the 14th day of last April, and was perhaps the smartest and best son Father had. He was always of a most lovable nature and made friends with all people with whom he came in contact. We will all miss him very much, and yet we must feel resigned to the will of God....

Bro. Brigham Young, who presides over the European mission, cabled his condolence this afternoon to Father, and said he had ordered the body embalmed....

Tuesday, October 18, 1892:

From 11 to 2 o'clock and from 3 till 4 o'clock I was engaged in committee with Heber J. Grant, John R. Winder, L. John Nuttall, D. McKenzie and Robert L. Campbell in apportioning to the various Stakes the amount each should raise for the completion of the Salt Lake Temple. In order to arrive at a just and equitable assessment we considered the population, the amount of tithing paid, the amounts already donated and the financial condition of the people. We did not complete our labors today....

Wednesday, October 19, 1892:

From 9 till 2 o'clock I was engaged with the apportionment committee in preparing the list of amounts for each Stake to raise for the completion of the Temple. We first selected from each stake the names of those persons who in our estimation should pay $500 or more. To these, special letters will be sent soliciting the amounts we think they should pay. It will then be left to the Stakes to make their own apportionments to the various Wards....

Thursday, October 20, 1892:

At 2 o'clock I was at the President's office to my Quorum meeting. There were present in addition to the Presidency only Bro. Grant and myself. Father was mouth in prayer. The committee on Temple apportionment came in at 3:30 o'clock, and we laid our business before the brethren and it received their approval. We were requested to prepare the necessary correspondence concerning the matter....

Sunday, October 23, 1892 [Franklin, Idaho]:

Pres. Smith and myself started for Preston in a buggy at 6:45 a.m. Arriving at this place we found that George C. Parkinson had started for Oxford, and we therefore had to find our own way across the country. We had quite a time getting there, as we lost our way, and found some difficulty in going over some gullies, around wire fences, etc. We did reach our destination, however, at 10:45, and found Pres. Parkinson addressing the Saints of whom there were a goodly number present. When we had finished Milo Andrus spoke for a few minutes, and bore a good testimony to the truth of the gospel. Pres. Smith followed for a half hour and told of his testimony, and his experience in the Church.... In the afternoon I was the first speaker. I occupied about 50 minutes in talking upon the love and union which should characterize the Saints. Joseph Nelson then bore his testimony to the truth in a brief but forcible manner. Pres. J. Smith followed for 50 minutes in a most powerful discourse in which he told the Saints to be true to the gospel, to each other and to the servants of God. His exhortations were strong and convincing. When the meeting adjourned he called the Bishops together and gave them some political advice. He urged them to divide on party lines, and those who are Republicans should not flop over to the Democratic side because of the recent decision of the Supreme Court of the State by which Mormons are prohibited from voting. As soon as the Republican party is sure that there is strong representation of Mormons who are Republicans they will restore to us our rights. He expressed the hope that a goodly number of the people would become Republicans. I confirmed his remarks, and testified to the brethren that Pres. Smith had given them the will of the Lord. I told them that when they saw the Twelve and First Presidency at variance they should always take the counsel of the Presidency in preference to that of the Apostles....

Wednesday, October 26, 1892:

Our *News* press failed to work satisfactorily this evening, and as a result our paper was two hours behind time in being issued. The paper we are using is home-made, and was very poor stuff. We are very busy at present printing Republican campaign literature. This matter keeps the *Juvenile* presses going nearly 15 hours per day. The fight between the two parties is waxing very hot. I fear great trouble in the Church over these political matters....

Thursday, October 27, 1892:

At 2 o'clock I went to my Quorum meeting at the President's office. There were present all of the Presidency, Bros. F. D. Richards, F. M. Lyman, John H. Smith and myself. Bro. Richards was mouth in prayer. We had considerable talk about politics, and in the course of the conversation Father told it as a secret that our newly-appointed marshal, I. A. Benton, had been instructed from Washington that he must do as he was directed by the heads of the Mormon Church if he desired to retain his position as Marshal. He had expressed his willingness to do so, and had sent such word to the Presidency....

Thursday, November 17, 1892:

I was at my Quorum meeting at two o'clock, where Bro. Joseph F. Smith offered prayer. All the Presidency were present, and Bro. Grant and myself. No other business was done.

The Presidency awarded to the *News* Pub. Co. yesterday the contract for printing the German Book of Mormon for $3,100 for a 10,000 edition. The binding is to be paid for as the books are wanted.

Father talked to me today about the *History of Utah* and Mr. Webster's dissatisfaction concerning its affairs. He blames me for the slowness of delivery, but I explained matters to Father's satisfaction....

Saturday, December 17, 1892:

At my Quorum meeting on Thursday the brethren were told that our success in the Church suits was in a great measure due to the fact that we have a partner of Justice Field of the Supreme Court of the United States in our employ, who is to receive a percentage of the money if the suits go in our favor, and the property is returned to us. It was decided at this meeting that we would dispense with the services of the Church attorneys at the end of the year. Those now employed are F. S. Richards and LeGrand Young. The former receives $5,000 per year, the latter $3,000. The latter has felt some reluctance at accepting his pay for the work now being done, but the former has felt it was his due.

Thursday, December 29, 1892:

I went to my Quorum meeting at 2 o'clock. There were present all of the Presidency, F. D. Richards, F. M. Lyman, H. J. Grant, J. W. Taylor and myself. George Gibbs was clerk. John Henry Smith was also present. The Board of Trustees for the Church University was submitted and approved. I was omitted from this list, as was also J. H. Smith and some others whose names were on the old board.

For some time there were various points of doctrine discussed which were called out by a question which was asked as to the reason for the baptism of those who come to Zion from abroad. The Josephites object to our common use of this doctrine. It was done by the Prophet Joseph in Nauvoo, and by Pres. Young and those who succeeded him in this Territory. The subject in its various phases was given to the Historian, F. D. Richards, and John H. Smith to investigate and prepare an article upon it. The latter said in very strong terms that the authorities of the Church must meet the various questions of doctrine which are continually arising or the people will lose confidence in us.

It was decided to use the old organ which stood in the old tabernacle for the large room of the Temple, after the instrument has been repaired by Joseph J. Daynes.

It was decided by vote that Brigham Young shall be released from the Presidency of the European Mission to return home as soon as the Presidency can find some person to take his place....

Saturday, December 31, 1892:

I closed with Junius F. Wells today in behalf of Cannon & Sons Co. for the purchase of the 10,000 edition of the *First Book of Nature* which he published for the schools. We take the plates, edition, cuts, etc., for the sum of $2,300 of which $500 goes as royalty to the author—Dr. Talmage. The rest of the amount is payable in three, six and nine months. The book was published in New York....

I closed a contract with the Graham Paper Co. this evening through their representative, Mr. Tirrell, for them to supply the *News* office with print paper for the term of one year at 4 cents per pound on the track in this city. We are under the necessity of doing this because our local mill upon whom we have been depending has failed to get us the color or thickness required, and just now are unable to furnish us any kind of paper of the proper size for our Semi-Weekly paper.

CHAPTER SIX

1893

Tuesday, March 21, 1893:

I feel ashamed for my neglect of the past few weeks in regard to the writing of my journal, but I have been so extremely busy in various ways that it has been impossible for me to find the necessary time in which to do so. During this time I have attended to my usual labors in the offices, and it has kept me very busy to meet the heavy financial drains which have been made upon me. Money has been very close, and business dull [slow]. I have acted during the time on the committee with Bros. Joseph F. Smith and Lorenzo Snow to see that the temple in this city is finished ready for dedication on April 6th. Our duties in looking after the workmen has kept me visiting the building with the other brethren and alone nearly every other day....

Today at 2 o'clock my Quorum met in the upper room of the Historian's office, where every member was present excepting Heber J. Grant, who is detained in Washington City through the illness of two of his children with diptheria, he having taken them to that place on a visit to be present at the inauguration of President Grover Cleveland. Both Pres. Brigham Young and George Teasdale are well. We spent the afternoon in talking, and also in listening to the reading of a portion of the History of the Twelve which Pres. F. D. Richards is preparing....

Wednesday, March 22, 1893:

Our Quorum met this morning at 10 o'clock. Eleven of us were present. We took turns in talking until noon when we adjourned for two hours. The brethren expressed their feelings one towards the other, and it was found that they were of the very best. At two o'clock we met again, and shortly thereafter the Presidency joined us. They then occupied the most of the time. They expressed themselves very freely on the disunion which has existed among us, and desired to know from all present whether or not we considered they had a right to dictate to us the policy we should pursue in politics, as well as in all other things, temporal or spiritual. The brethren all agreed that this was the right of the Presidency, and Bro. Thatcher, to whom the remarks were specially directed, said he not only admitted this, but wherein he had failed to show proper respect to the counsels of his superiors, he was willing to make it right....

Thursday, March 23, 1893:

I was at my meeting at 10 o'clock at which all were present excepting Bro. Thatcher, who went home this morning quite sick. The Presidency each spoke of Bro. Thatcher and his actions, and felt to condemn his course during the past few months, especially in regard to political matters. They felt, and all present shared in the feeling, that it would be necessary for him to make acknowledgement of his improper course and ask pardon for the same before he is permitted to enter the Temple.[1] Pres. Snow said that if any of the apostles stood out in opposition to the Presidency the Lord would cause such persons to repent, or he would remove them out of the way. All of the brethren present felt of one heart and mind, and in the spirit of perfect union partook of the sacrament, after it was blessed by President Woodruff. The latter made some few remarks in the course of which he said that he felt to prophesy that none of the brethren present would go into darkness or lose the faith. We had a very happy time together. It was decided to leave the case of Bro. Thatcher to his Quorum for settlement, and several other similar cases of quite prominent men were left for the judgement of their respective Quorums....

---

[1] For a summary of the discussions of the First Presidency and Twelve concerning Moses Thatcher that occurred before late March and are therefore not found in the A. H. Cannon journals, see Melvin Clarence Merrill, ed., *Utah Pioneer and Apostle Marriner Wood Merrill and His Family* (n. p.: Marriner Wood Merrill Heritage Committee, 1980), 160-64.

Monday, April 3, 1893:

At 2 o'clock our Quorum met in the Historian's office, where all were gathered excepting Bros. Thatcher and Grant. We had some conversation with each other to see that our feelings were right before commencing our conference. It was found that nothing but the best of spirit prevailed with us. We learned by telegraph that the other brethren expect to join us before the dedication of the Temple. In the case of Bro. Thatcher we hope he will set himself right.

Thursday, May 18, 1893:

The period which has elapsed since I last wrote my journal on April 3rd has been to me a very eventful one. The general conference began on April 4th and lasted two days, during which time some very choice instructions were given. The attendance of the Saints was unusually large.

On the night of the fifth my quorum met to consider the case of Bro. Moses Thatcher. At first he strongly opposed the brethren in their efforts to reconcile him with the Presidency, but after each one had spoken, and all were unanimous in their statements that he was in the wrong, he yielded, and asked the forgiveness of the brethren, and promised to seek the forgiveness of the Presidency on the morrow before entering the Temple.

On April 6th the dedication services in the temple were held at 10 a.m. All of the Presidency and Twelve with their families were present, and quite a large number of the Priesthood. The wives of deceased apostles were also present. The assembly room was filled to its utmost capacity. Pres. Woodruff offered the dedicatory prayer. Remarks were then made by himself and counselors. During the time of the services the wind outside blew a perfect hurricane, doing considerable damage throughout the city, and in various parts of the country.

The first service was the pattern for all the other services which were held in the temple, consisting of two sessions a day, and one day three. Also when the Sunday schools were admitted on two different days, three sessions per day were held, at each of which each of the apostles spoke briefly. During the other services the Apostles were called to speak once or twice, and also to read the prayer. I did each of these on two occasions. The instructions were of a character to teach forgiveness and purity of life. The promise was made that if the Saints would sin no more their past sins would be forgiven of God. It was also said that our enemies would never have so much power over us again as they have had, if we will only be faithful. Many remarkable things were seen and heard in the Temple. Andrew Smith, Jr., said he saw on the stand with the brethren President Young, a number of the Twelve who are dead, and several other brethren whom he did not know.

A little nine year old boy also told his mother that he saw angels in the room and on the stand. Numerous parties saw brilliant lights, and heard singing and instrumental music. One rough young man from Brigham City, a son of the late Judge Wright, and the leader in the escapades of the young men at his home, said he saw a bright halo about the head of Pres. Woodruff, and the spirit of the Temple was so strong in him that he went to his home and started a reformation among his companions, which Pres. L. Snow thinks will affect great good.

Our Quorum held two evening meetings in our room in the Temple in which each of us spoke.

Bro. Thatcher was so seriously ill at one time that we expected every moment to hear of his death. He returned to his home in Logan within a few days after the Temple services commenced. Pres. Woodruff was also taken very sick, and got very low, so that on two different occasions arrangements were being made for his burial. Both of the brethren gradually recovered.

A two day meeting was held with the general authorities and the Presidents of Stakes and their counselors on April.[blank] and [blank]. There were 115 brethren present. On the latter day we dressed in our priestly robes, formed a circle in the large celestial room, and had prayers. Father was mouth in the circle, and Pres. Snow in the opening.[2] We then partook of the sacrament in our

---

[2] Elder Marriner W. Merrill wrote the following of this occasion (20 April): "I met with the Priesthood, First Presidency, Twelve, Presidents of Stakes and Counselors, and Presiding Bishopric, in the Temple at 10 a.m. today, all fasting. We remained

robes in the room of the Presidency. It was a very happy and never to be forgotten time. Our first day of meeting, and part of the second were spent in speaking, each man being asked to express his feelings towards the authorities of the Church, and the Saints generally.

During the conference we have held numerous meetings, at all of which I have been present. Rulon S. Wells was selected and set apart to fill the vacancy in the Quorum of the First Seven Presidents of the Seventies. Because of my numerous meetings I have had to neglect some of my business, though I did considerable at night and early mornings. I have, however had a very happy time.

Saturday, May 20, 1893:

At one o'clock I went to the Temple, and assisted in the setting apart of the Temple workers. There being six of the Presidency and Twelve present, we divided into three parties of two each, I being with Pres. Joseph F. Smith. Thereafter we went through the various rooms, and listened to the ceremonies and dialogues of the same....

Tuesday, May 23, 1893:

I was at the President's office for about two hours today, where I met Bro. A. H. Lund who is on his way to England to take charge of the European Mission. Some matters of Temple ordinance work were considered, and also as to how it could be arranged for us to reach our new U. S. Marshal, Nat M. Brigham, who has just arrived from Washington, and has not yet assumed the duties of his office. It is desirable to arrange with him to be fair in his treatment of us, and not arrest people at the request of spotters. I stated that I had endorsed his application for the office, but am not personally acquainted with him....

---

in the Temple until 6 p.m. All joined in the Prayer Circle clothed (115) in the
Celestial Room, the largest Circle ever convened or got together in the Church. All
of the Twelve present and Presidents Cannon and J. F. Smith spoke today,
President Woodruff and Apostle Moses Thatcher both being sick and not able to
be there. We had a glorious time and all felt well and all testified at these meetings
to sustaining the First Presidency in all things, political as well as all other matters"
(Melvin Clarence Merrill, ed., *Utah Pioneer and Apostle Marriner Wood Merrill and
His Family* [n. p.: Marriner Wood Merrill Heritage Committee, 1980], 165).

Wednesday, May 24, 1893:

I spent the most of the day in the offices attending to business. I read some proofs of the German Book of Mormon, thus completing the body of the book itself. I also read proofs and prepared copy for the *Contributor*....

Thursday, May 25, 1893:

I started David Wilcken to work delivering and collecting for the *History of Utah*,...

The *Deseret News* Pub. Co. bid for the issuance of a 5,000 edition of the German Doctrine and Covenants at $2,100 for the work and a set of stereotype plates, was accepted, the binding to cost in full cloth 25 cents per copy, leather 40 cents, full roan 75 cents and full leather gilt $1.10 each additional....

Sunday, May 28, 1893:

At 2 o'clock I attended the services in the Tabernacle, which was well filled with an attentive congregation. Pres. Woodruff was there for the first time in several weeks and spoke a few words of thankfulness that he was again able to be out. He attributes his recovery to the faith and prayers of the Saints in his behalf. Father spoke for about an hour on the similarity of our organization and experience to those of the Former-day Saints, and predicted in strong terms the ultimate triumph of Zion....

Tuesday, May 30, 1893:

Until 8:30 I was at home posting the office books and reading the copy for a brief life of Pres. Brigham Young which Edward H. Anderson is writing for us, and which we propose to issue from the *Juvenile* office.

I then went to town and spent some little time at the *News* office. Bros. Joel Ricks and H. E. Baker of Logan called in and told me of a trip they propose to take, if the Church Authorities are willing, down into and through Arizona, old Mexico, and perhaps into South

America, in search of antiquities and evidence of the divinity of the Book of Mormon. They will continue their journey till their money is exhausted or until they have accomplished the object of their journey. They will take their own team and outfit, and are prepared to remain away for several years if necessary.

At 11 o'clock I attended the funeral of the wife of Henry Pearson....

I then spoke for 20 minutes on the influence which a good wife can exert over a man. Said I believed that the dead have great power in our behalf in their supplications to the Father in their spirit state. Urged the living to be more kind to those who remain, and not reserve all their praise till our dear ones are dead....

Thursday, June 1, 1893:

At 2 o'clock I attended my Quorum meeting in the Temple. Present: All of the Presidency, though Pres. Woodruff had to leave because of weakness before the meeting dismissed; Pres. L. Snow, F. D. Richards, F. M. Lyman, John W. Taylor and M. W. Merrill, as well as myself; George F. Gibbs, clerk. Bros. John D. T. McAllister, Nephi W. Clayton and James Jack were also in attendance a part of the time. We first had some talk about the ordinance of adoption in the temple. Joseph F. Smith said Pres. Young had told him to follow in ordinance work for the dead the rules which will ordinarily govern similar work for the living. Pres. John Taylor had ruled that no person could represent another who is dead in the receiving of any ordinance which the living person had not already received. The conversation lasted for some time but was finally dismissed for future consideration, when we could devote more time and thought to the subject. The custom was, however, approved of giving endowments to children over 8 years of age if they are dead, and of sealing to parents only one generation beyond the one [already] in the Church....

The question was asked by Bro. Lyman whether or not it was necessary in setting apart a Bishop to ordain as well as set him apart. Father read three passages from the revelations which proved to our satisfaction that an ordination as well as setting apart is necessary....

Friday, June 23, 1893:

At 3:45 I went to the Temple to a meeting of the workers. Presidents Woodruff, Smith and Snow, and Bros. F. D. Richards, Young and myself were also present. The object was to talk to the workers, and dispel any wrong feelings which might exist. Bro. Snow told them not to impose on the cook by inviting their friends to eat who do not work in the temple. They are not to go out of the door and leave it unlocked in the absence of the door-keeper, and under no circumstances are they to invite strangers into the building....

Pres. Woodruff also spoke for some little time, and expressed his pleasure at the work being accomplished in this structure....

Friday, July 7, 1893:

...I went to the farm to the funeral of Lewmar Q. Cannon. There was a large gathering of friends and acquaintances. I conducted the services. Music was rendered....

Bishop Preston offered prayer, and Bro. Joseph F. Smith delivered a very excellent discourse. In the course of his remarks he said that the parents of the child would receive it back in the same size and condition, except for its mortality, as when they laid it down. It would then grow and develop into perfect manhood. John Q. dismissed the meeting....[3]

Saturday, July 8, 1893:

...I went to Bro. Wilcken's to the funeral of his daughter. Uncle Angus spoke first on our belief concerning the future. I followed for 15 minutes and told of instances where our evil genius seems to control us, notwithstanding all our efforts to resist him.... Pres. Joseph F. Smith also spoke for 35 minutes. He spoke against the use of fireworks, and said we as Saints should cry down this infamous practice of buying and shooting them....

---

[3] See AHC journals 5 October, 1889, note 5.

Tuesday, July 11, 1893:

At two o'clock I went to a meeting of my Quorum in the Temple. Present: Pres. L. Snow, F. D. Richards, Brigham Young, F. M. Lyman, J. H. Smith, M. W. Merrill and myself. Pres. Snow made a few remarks after the opening exercises. He spoke of our present financial difficulties, and though our lack of wisdom may be blamed for some of our troubles, he felt that we will be delivered this once therefrom, and prosperity will shine upon us. His words were very encouraging for us. John Henry Smith, who had to attend a funeral, spoke a few words before leaving. He said that though he was in great financial difficulty himself, and knew that the Church was also, he had not felt any very great concern, but knew that all would turn out well.

I told them some of my troubles, but hoped they would not lead me to complain or murmur at whatever results might follow. I knew that Zion would be alright eventually, and hoped I might be able to stand with her.

Bro. Merrill said he was out of debt, and had always followed the plan of living within his means. This is a safe course to pursue, and he therefore always felt comfortable at the thought that he could not be pinched because of his obligations.

We now adjourned till tomorrow at 10 o'clock....

Wednesday, July 12, 1893:

Was at the Temple at 10 o'clock, where the same brethren assembled as were present yesterday. After the opening exercises Bro. Lyman spoke. He felt very well as far as the gospel is concerned, but had some financial trouble in common with the other brethren. Still if the Lord sees fit to take all his means, he will feel well about it. He referred to some of John W. Taylor's business matters, and said there was a hard feeling against him in some parts. He read a letter from Charles L. Anderson of Grantsville, in which he shows his hard feelings towards Bro. Taylor for some of his improper business matters.

John Henry added a few words expressive of his feelings, and then Brigham Young spoke. He owes but very little, and is therefore much composed in these times. He felt that our failure as a Church to get money in the East and in England would enable us to develop our strength at home, and therefore this would be a blessing to us. He felt that we might get something for our pay in protecting the country from the Indians in early days. We should also get something from [the] government for their seizure of Fort Bridger, in which location the Church had quite a heavy interest. These things are at least worthy an effort.

We now adjourned till 2 o'clock. The sacrament was had in the afternoon, Presidents Woodruff and Joseph F. Smith partaking of the same with us, after it had been blessed by Pres. Woodruff. Before partaking of it Pres. Woodruff decided, and we all sustained him in the decision, that where young unmarried men or women, who have had their endowments, desire to stand for their dead relatives in receiving the sealing ordinances, they can do so, even though the persons officiating have not been married themselves. It has been the rule in the Logan temple, and this was done by order of Pres. Taylor, that no person could stand for another in the sealing ordinance unless he or she had been themselves sealed in life....

It has been the rule to not seal women to their dead husbands unless those husbands were in the Church. It was today decided that where men are dead who would likely have joined the Church, their wives may, if they so elect, be sealed to them.

It is also proper for children to be sealed to their parents, and then have those parents sealed to the Prophet Joseph....

After the sacrament F. D. Richards gave us a little of his past experience, and the faith he has gained makes him feel quite easy in the present condition of things, knowing full well that God will bring things around according to His wise purposes. He is out of debt. Bro. Snow now gave us his blessing and we adjourned....

Thursday, July 20, 1893:

At 2 o'clock I was at my Quorum meeting. Present: Pres. Woodruff and Smith; L. Snow, F. D. Richards, F. M. Lyman, J. H. Smith, and myself; George F. Gibbs, clerk. We first had prayers, Bro. Lyman being mouth in the opening, and Bro. Snow in the circle.

Thereafter we had considerable talk about the financial situation. It was proposed that a hundred or more men of the Church be asked to loan to the Church from one to five thousand dollars apiece to meet the bills which are continually falling due. I felt that this course would be unwise, as such men as have money would draw the same from our needy institutions, and thus cripple them if they agree to loan the money on these terms. I expressed my views and others of the brethren coincided with them. I felt that an appeal for the prompt payment of tithing should be made, and that men be asked to assume the Church debts, instead of asking them to raise the money. The matter was finally postponed for future consideration....

Thursday, July 27, 1893:

At 2 o'clock I was at my Quorum meeting. Present: Presidents Woodruff, Smith and Snow; F. D. Richards, F. M. Lyman, and myself; George F. Gibbs, clerk. We dressed in our robes, when Pres. Woodruff opened by prayer and F. D. Richards was mouth in the circle. We thereafter had some talk about the financial situation. It has been found best to drop the plan of raising funds which was proposed last week. There is great destitution in this city at present because of lack of work. In the temple I had a young lady named Walker today sealed to me, she being dead, and her Father desiring this to be done. Sister Harriet Barrow Cox stood as proxy for her....

Thursday, August 10, 1893:

At 2 o'clock I went to my Quorum meeting at which all of the Presidency were present, and of the Twelve, L. Snow, F. D. Richards, J. H. Smith, H. J. Grant, M. W. Merrill and myself; George F. Gibbs, clerk. Father prayed in the opening, and Bro. Merrill was mouth at the altar. Thereafter Pres. Woodruff arose and said he desired the brethren to keep up their courage, and not lose hope, faith and spirits concerning our financial matters. All the Lord requires of us is to do the very best we can, and he will then take care of the remainder. He predicted that we can and will come out of our present difficulties with credit to the Church. Father, Joseph F.

Smith, L. Snow, F. D. Richards, J. H. Smith and H. J. Grant bore testimony to the truth of Pres. Woodruff's remarks....

Saturday, August 12, 1893:

I...had a talk with the Presidency concerning the *History of Utah*. I told them of our inability to meet our bills to the author, Bishop O. F. Whitney, and told them we would like their authorization to pursue our own course with regard to its continuance. Feeling this labor of issuing the work to be a mission on us, I did not feel at liberty to discharge him without the consent of the brethren. They did not decide about it at this time but will give the matter more consideration. Bro. Smith said quite warmly that he considered this work a private enterprise, but Father combated this idea with equal warmth.

At 1 o'clock the Presidents of a number of the stakes in close proximity to this city met in the President's office, where the financial condition of the Church was clearly stated to them by several of the brethren, and they were asked to use their influence to obtain relief for the Church by the collection of tithes, offerings for the temple, and also by making loans for the Church at the rate of 10% per annum. All present held up their hands in token that they will do their best to relieve the Church, and help it to pay its debts....

Thursday, August 17, 1893:

I...went over to Father's where he had a meeting with his family in which he took measures to cut down his expenses by keeping the boys out of school to do the work, thus releasing the hired help, and by the abandonment of the kitchen plan of living. Hereafter each family will cook for itself....

Saturday, August 19, 1893:

I...had a talk with Father concerning his affairs, and he decided to transfer to his folks all his unencumbered property, so that in the case of the failure of Cannon, Grant & Co. no more of his property will be taken then he has already pledged, which amounts to $100,000....

Sunday, August 20, 1893:

At 2 o'clock went to the Tabernacle services, and heard Prof. J. Baldwin of the University of Texas speak for half an hour on the subject of "What is Truth?" He was followed by Elder James E. Talmage on the same subject, the latter giving some of our views about truth....

Thursday, August 24, 1893:

At 10 o'clock I was at the President's office and met with the Presidency and Bishop O. F. Whitney. We had a talk about the *History of Utah*, and I told the brethren that we would be unable to continue the work in our present straightened financial condition. The question they should decide is whether the Church can carry the load of paying Bishop Whitney while he completes the work, and then let us pay for it as soon as we are ready to print it, or if he shall discontinue his labors altogether. During the conversation over the matter Father and Joseph F. Smith had some very heated words over the matter, because the latter disclaimed as one of the Presidency any responsibility in connection with the matter, while Father correctly maintained that the Church had called Bishop Whitney to do the work, and was morally responsible for its completion. We all admit the Church has no financial responsibility in the affair. We adjourned without reaching any conclusion in the matter, until tomorrow.

At 2 o'clock I was at my Quorum meeting. There were present all of the Presidency, and L. Snow, F. D. Richards, B. Young, J. H. Smith, and myself; George F. Gibbs, clerk....

Father reported that there was a probability of a raid being made on polygamists in the near future. He felt to warn the brethren to be careful. It was also voted that a little money be used if necessary to pacify Prosecuting Attorney Judd, and the marshals so that they will not vigorously prosecute cases under the law against cohabitation....

Friday, August 25, 1893:

At 10 o'clock I met with the Presidency and Bishop Whitney, and after some discussion it was decided that the Church will pay him $2,700 for the finishing of the third volume of the *History of Utah*, and then when we desire to publish it, we are to repay the Church this amount. Pres. Woodruff told me that part of his pay would be in tithing orders, which the Bishop said he would accept....

Tuesday, October 3, 1893:

At 2 o'clock I went to my Quorum meeting in our room in the Temple. There were present Pres. L. Snow, F. D. Richards, B. Young, F. M. Lyman, John H. Smith, H. J. Grant, M. W. Merrill and myself. We sang, had prayers, and Pres. Snow then spoke for a few minutes. He said it is our privilege to receive great revelations in our meetings, and we should seek for knowledge and instruction whenever we come together. We may not get any very great physical manifestations, but we can enjoy the things of the Spirit. God will try us till He knows our hearts, and finds us worthy to suffer all for His sake. Jesus was tried till it became necessary for an angel to come and strengthen him. We must be prepared for all things.

Heber J. Grant next gave a report of his labors in the east in the obtaining of money. He had to pay as high as 20% for $200,000 which he succeeded in borrowing, but it was this amount which had saved the State and Zion's Savings banks from closing their doors before this time. He obtained it through the kindness and efforts of John Claflin, at a time when no prospect of relief was at hand. The Lord helped him or he would have failed....

Wednesday, October 4, 1893:

At 10 o'clock I went to the temple, where the brethren who were together yesterday met again. After singing, and prayer by John H. Smith, Pres. Snow gave a few introductory remarks, and Brigham Young then told of his trip through the north country, where he found in Jackson's Hole in Idaho a very good country which he thought our people should occupy. He organized in one end of the valley a ward of 40 families calling it South Park Ward. He proposed to take a trip after conference through the south, and spend the winter in Mexico if the brethren were agreeable. He felt that Bro. George Teasdale should be recalled from Mexico, and be at headquarters where his labors can be utilized for the good of the people.

Bro. Richards said that evangelists as mentioned in the [New] Testament were represented in the patriarchs of the present time. So said Pres. Young. Pastors were appointed in the early English mission to preside over several conferences, and might well be likened now to the Presidents of Stakes. These responses were given in reply to a question from F. M. Lyman. Bro. Richards further gave a strong testimony to the truth, and to the value of our meetings.

F. M. Lyman said he felt that the apostles should be out among the people, as they greatly need instruction. This is our particular calling, and we should fill it. When the brethren do not go out among the Saints they are apt to get false ideas about various matters, and thus go astray. He saw this on his recent trip in the south. The Stayner doctrine of the transmigration of souls found some believers in the south, but he had denounced the doctrine wherever he found it. He felt also that the Patriarch of the Church, John Smith, should travel more, and should keep a full record of all the patriarchs in the Church.

We now took an intermission till 3 o'clock, at which time Bro. Moses Thatcher was with us feeling some improved in health, but still very weak and feeble. John H. Smith felt well in the work and said he would do all he could in the way of visiting among the Saints.

Bro. Merrill spoke of his labors being condensed in the Logan Temple, and yet he meets very many people from all parts of the country, with whom he has an opportunity to talk. He said the crops in Cache Valley are only about half their usual size, and the financial condition of the people is very bad.

Bro. Thatcher spoke of his severe sickness, and felt it was only through the goodness of God that he was restored. He felt thankful to the brethren for their prayers and faith in his behalf.

Four doctors had given him up for incurable, but he was spared for some wise purpose known to God.

We now adjourned till tomorrow, after dismissal by myself....

Thursday, October 5, 1893:

We went to our Quorum meeting fasting. After singing and prayer by Bro. Merrill I was called to speak. I said that I had not done my part in visiting among the Saints, but is had been because of my labors in the offices at home. I enjoyed such labors, and hoped to do more of it in the future. I thought a committee should be appointed to see to the introduction of the written word at expositions of the people in various parts of the world, and every means should be employed to make ourselves better known than we now are. I hoped the day is not far distant when the Presidency will not be so burdened with care as they now are, but will have more time to devote to spiritual things, so that we may receive the great knowledge which the Lord has in store for us if we are faithful.

John W. Taylor, who met with us this morning, next spoke. He feared that one result of the present stringency will be to make the people stop improvements, and their great ambition will be to get a little money and loan it out, instead of using it to furnish employment for those who now have nothing to do. He expressed a desire to be faithful.

We then had some desultory conversation on various matters. It is now allowed under certain conditions to have temple work done for suicides. Permission is also given for women who desire it, to be sealed to their dead husbands, though the latter did not join the Church in life, but were good people. These are instances where changes in the rule have lately been made.

Bro. Thatcher asked if plural marriages which had not been solemnized over the altars in the temples could now be performed in renewal. It was thought best that this be not done, because it might jeopardize the buildings. We joined in a discussion of financial matters. And then Pres. Snow said he felt sure that the Lord would help us out of our present difficulties, but we must be careful to avoid them in the future. We must learn to keep secrets, and to not tell all we know.

About this time the Presidency came in, Father having returned this morning from San Francisco. We partook of the Sacrament, after it had been blessed by Father. After doing so Father said he desired to say a few words to the brethren. He promised us in the name of the Lord that we would come out of our present financial difficulties without loss of credit, and in a better financial condition than we were when we entered upon the stringency, if we will only keep putting our trust in God, do His will, and not lose our courage. This prophecy was a great comfort to me. It was about 2:30 when we adjourned by prayer from Pres. Snow....

Friday, October 6, 1893:

There is but very little money being brought in, and everything is extremely dull [slow] for Conference. The attendance is also very small, there being scarcely more at the meetings than we usually have at our Stake Conference. All the general authorities were present excepting George Teasdale, A. H. Lund, Golden Kimball, and Rulon S. Wells. Bros. Teasdale and B. H. Roberts were present at the evening meeting. Father was the first speaker. He gave a general review of the condition of the Church at the present time. Told of the progress of the missionary work in the various parts of the earth, and advised the young men to study languages, and to prepare themselves to carry this gospel to the ends of the earth. He gave much other excellent and timely advice. Pres. Snow and F. D. Richards each spoke for about half an hour on spiritual matters. Bro. Snow said that he believed that power would be given to every faithful father in Israel to draw his children to him and save them either in this world or in the world to come. He did not know how this would be done, but felt that it would occur. Bro. Richards confirmed this doctrine.

In the afternoon services Heber J. Grant was the first speaker. He spoke of the manner in which the Lord is changing the feelings of people in this nation towards this people. He also referred to the hard times, and said the money stringency was due to the lack of confidence in the country, and also because there was insufficient money. He advised the people to seek for the riches of the kingdom of God, and then all other things would be added unto us.

John W. Taylor referred humorously to the hard times, and urged the people to leave their money in the banks instead of drawing it out to hide away.

Bro. Merrill spoke for 25 minutes on the advisability of the Saints keeping out of debt, and to live within their means.

In the evening I attended the Priesthood meeting, and heard some very good instructions. Joseph F. Smith spoke first and occupied nearly an hour. He said we should try to divest ourselves of all animosity, and hard feelings towards all men, and bring ourselves in complete subjection to the will of God. He was trying to reach this happy condition, but finds himself far from being as he should....

Saturday, October 7, 1893:

I was in the offices all the time when the conference was not in session. In the morning meeting Bro. Lyman spoke and advised the Saints to place themselves in a condition to receive the counsels of the Priesthood, and to carry the same out. We should be careful of the reputations of our co-laborers, and do unto others as we wish them to do unto us.

Bro. George Teasdale was the next speaker. He reported the condition of the Saints in Mexico and said they were doing all they could to assist in the work of God. He bore his testimony to the truth of this gospel, and invited all people to receive the same testimony, and thus obtain salvation.

I spoke next and said that the Saints had always done things in a different way to that which is common in the world, and it was thus that the Lord intended we should act in the future. We will take a different course to that common to men in our financial, social and religious affairs.... I bore my testimony to that which had been said during this conference, and was very much pleased to hear the prophecy that if we are faithful the Lord will deliver us individually and collectively from debt, without loss of credit.

In the afternoon the authorities were presented, and several reports were read. Brigham Young then spoke. The men at the head of the Church are worthy of the confidence and support of the

Saints. He said we should be more careful in the cultivation of the soil than we now are, and make it yield more abundantly.

Moses Thatcher followed him, and spoke of the financial situation. He believes in a short time there will be more money scattered through the country than the people will be able to use, because one extreme follows another in all things. We must be wise in the use of those things which God places in our hands, and He will then bless us abundantly....

Sunday, October 8, 1893:

In the forenoon meeting Bro. Joseph F. Smith spoke. He said we have been greatly blessed of the Lord, and we should show our appreciation of his blessings by keeping His commandments. He advised economy in the households of the Saints, and told of how his mother used to keep him out of mischief by having him learn to knit and sew. He was able as a child to knit suspenders and socks, and he now urged his family to knit his socks. He felt that every boy and girl ought to learn to be industrious, and earn something by the labor of their hands. Every Latter-day Saint should be industrious, and then we can hope to become self-supporting, until which time we will be in bondage, for the community or individual that spends more than it earns will finally land in the midst of poverty....

I went to Heber J. Grant's house to lunch with several brethren.

In the afternoon I was asked by Pres. Woodruff to take charge of the overflow meeting in the Assembly Hall. This building was also crowded. After the opening exercises John Morgan spoke on the waste which is shown in our midst of fruit, vegetables, etc., and urged the Saints to be careful with their property, and to use any surplus they may have in providing work for the poor.

Seymour B. Young next spoke on the history of the Church, and the drivings of the Saints, comparing their present happy surroundings with that which they had to endure in the past. He also urged that the Saints attend to their temple work.

Rulon S. Wells spoke against the evils of back-biting, and other little sins common among the people, and advised the Saints to be more careful in regard to their conduct.

I spoke for about half an hour on the promise given us by Bro. Snow during this conference that the children of faithful parents will all eventually be brought into the fold and receive salvation. This should not place any premium on sin, for those who sin will have the penalty to pay sooner or later. I spoke of the evils which are growing up in our midst by which the virtue of the people is being attacked. We must guard against such terrible vices, and protect our families from the wiles of the adversary. Confidence should exist and be encouraged in families, and love also.

In the Tabernacle Pres. Woodruff bore a brief testimony to the truth, and was followed by Father in a strong sermon against Spiritualism, Christian Science, Transmigration of souls, and such other false doctrines and evils which are seeking to make their way in the midst of this people.

After meeting I went to the farm and had supper, returning to town in time for the German meeting in the Assembly Hall at six o'clock. Rulon Wells spoke a few words in German, but because of long absence from the country of the Germans, was unable to say much, and that little was very imperfect. Bro. Maeser spoke fluently and freely to the Saints on the principles of the Gospel. I occupied about 60 minutes, and surprised myself at the fluency with which I spoke. It was only by the blessing of the Lord that I could speak. The words came to me without trouble. I urged the brethren to prepare themselves for the work of preaching the gospel to people speaking their language, and told those who had friends and acquaintances in the old country to write to them, and thus spread abroad the truth. I said that a very great work is yet to be done among their countrymen....

Monday, October 9, 1893:

At 10 o'clock I went to the meeting at the Church University Building on first North street where a meeting of the Literary and Scientific Association was held. The roll was called and an adjournment was taken. The President of the Church University, Willard Young, then gave a statement of the manner in which this building had been erected, which was by means furnished by the

Church as part of the $100,000 with which it has endowed this institution, but the whole of which it is not now able to advance. It was also narrated concerning the gift of Pres. Brigham Young of a piece of valuable land in the 18th Ward for University purposes, and which the heirs have agreed to give for the benefit of the Church University. It is designed to eventually teach in this place the highest branches of human learning, so that our young people will not need to go east to acquire the best information pertaining to every branch of education. After W. Young had finished his remarks Father was mouth in dedicating the building. We then had some singing, and the meeting was resolved into a gathering of the Presidents of Stakes, Bishops and their counselors, together with the general Church authorities. Prayer was offered by Pres. Joseph F. Smith.

Pres. Woodruff told the brethren they are not to use the Relief Society wheat unless the sisters desire them to do so, and in this case they are to be sure and return what they borrow…. He spoke of the judgments of God which are being poured out upon the nations, and said there would be many terrible things occur in the world before very long.

George Reynolds urged the brethren to be careful and prompt in making out their reports of statistics. These reports will thereafter only be required yearly.

Father spoke next on various subjects. He urged the brethren not to become heated in politics, but to be calm in all they do. Presiding brethren were advised to refrain from accepting office, and thus place themselves in a position to be arbiters among the Saints. It is proposed to hold Sunday School conferences once a year in the various stakes of Zion, and thus give the presiding brethren an opportunity of visiting the various parts of the country in the interest of these important organizations. The Presidents of Stakes should interest themselves in this great labor. He spoke further against the false doctrines which are being introduced into our midst, and advised the Saints to be on their guard against them. He said we have all the power in this Church which any body possesses, and if we will follow the lead of God's servants we will always be safe. He said men should not join secret societies, for they had sufficient protection in the Church for all their conditions. He believes the time will come when marriages will occur in the temples under the Aaronic Priesthood, instead of giving to young and inexperienced men all the blessings belonging to the Higher Priesthood. It is frequently the case now that unworthy persons go into the temples on recommends, which they should not receive, but it cannot well be prohibited to them to enter, because of their family connections. He hoped this change would occur soon. The brethren should pay their tithes and offerings promptly and fully, and thus aid the Church in its difficulty. Men should not sell their honor, their wife's virtue or their inheritances. We should hold all of these sacred.

Pres. Woodruff and Joseph F. Smith approved of all that had been said, and the latter spoke at some length on the false doctrines which are now being circulated. He said he measured everything by the standard of the gospel, and what did not fully agree with it he immediately rejected.

Pres. Snow said there was a perfect union among the Twelve, and he hoped the same condition would prevail among the Saints....

Thursday, October 12, 1893:

At 2 o'clock I went to my Quorum meeting in the temple. Present: All of the Presidency, L. Snow, F. D. Richards, B. Young, F. M. Lyman, J. H. Smith, H. J. Grant and myself; George F. Gibbs, clerk. Also George Teasdale.... After some discussion it was decided to counsel all the Presidents of Stakes with their counselors, and Bishops with their counselors to decline nominations for political offices in either of the political parties....

Sunday, October 15, 1893:

The Weber Stake conference is to be held today and tomorrow. Meeting convened at 10 o'clock, and after the opening exercises Father spoke for 65 minutes on the class of men whom God chooses to perform His work, and the manner in which he accomplishes His purposes. He also told us to not become discouraged, for God's care will be extended to us in all conditions in which we may be placed.... In the afternoon services I addressed the Saints for about an hour. I spoke of the reformation which this people will affect in the world, and warned the Saints against the evils of Babylon, especially against the failure to have children, and said we should accept them as blessings from the Lord, and endeavor to teach them correct doctrines and habits. We should teach them to work as well as to study. After I finished Father spoke for 25 minutes against infant murder, and false doctrines, both of which evils are being introduced into our midst....

Thursday, October 19, 1893:

At 2 o'clock I went to my Quorum meeting in the temple, at which were present all of the Presidency, and Bros. L. Snow, F. D. Richards, B. Young, F. M. Lyman, J. H. Smith, George Teasdale and myself. George Gibbs acted as clerk. We dressed in our robes, and Bro. Young was mouth in prayer. Father prayed at the altar. After prayers it was proposed and accepted that the brethren of the Twelve who desire to do so may form prayer circles from those already formed, and have them meet in the temple. This will give the brethren opportunity to become familiar with this pleasant labor.

Father said he thought the brethren of the Twelve should be out in the world opening the gospel door to various nations. Pres. Woodruff said he felt that the gospel should go to Japan.[4] Pres. Snow said he believed one and all of the Twelve are ready to go whenever their services are needed....

Friday, October 20, 1893:

At 11:30 I went to a meeting of the Presidency and Twelve at the President's office. The first business considered was the statement that for purposes of spite and to prevent statehood Prosecuting Attorney Judd is determined to renew the raid against polygamists. He sent to Attorney General Olney the names of Father, Joseph F. Smith, H. J. Grant, myself and H. B. Clawson, with evidence concerning our violations of the law, and we are today informed that Olney has told him to prosecute these and all other cases of a similar

---

[4] Elder Heber J. Grant was eventually chosen to open the Japanese mission.

character. A friend of our people who has been working with Olney says he is determined to put a stop to all cohabitation cases, and our friend tells us that the prominent men are all watched. We voted for the Presidency to take such a course as they think best to stop these proceedings, and they hope it can be done by the intervention of a Chicago friend who knows Judd, and can probably bribe him to remain passive, by employing him as counsel in some case at law, and thus pay him a good retainer.

We next considered the Mexican Mission affairs. George Teasdale gave a report of the condition of the people, and the Church land purchases. It was decided to sell the lands to the settlers instead of continuing to hold it in bulk. It was decided that we will not extend the settlements too far into the interior of Mexico at present....

Saturday, October 21, 1893:

I spent some little time with Father in the forenoon talking over business. I told him of our financial situation, and he told me to continue to do the best I can, and to try every prospect to get money. He agreed to a reduction of the rent on our Main Street store, and on his Big House property....

The good news came from Washington today that the Senate had passed the bill which designs to return to the Church the personal property which was taken from it under the Edmunds-Tucker act.[5] This will place in the hands of the Trustee-in-Trust between four and five hundred thousand dollars with which to pay the debts of the Church, for the education of Mormon children, the repair of houses of worship and the support of the poor....

Wednesday, October 25, 1893:

Pres. Cleveland today signed the Church property bill, but the attorney general quibbles about his right to dismiss the case which is pending before the Supreme Court, notwithstanding the action of Congress which restores the property. It is hoped the officer will see his way clear to have the matter fixed as determined by the law-

---

[5] See AHC journals 10 January 1894 and note 2.

making power without much delay, as the Church is in great need of means.

Thursday, November 9, 1893:

At two o'clock I went to my Quorum meeting at which all of the Presidency were present, and of the Twelve L. Snow, F. D. Richards, J. H. Smith, H. J. Grant and myself; George F. Gibbs clerk. Bro. Snow was mouth in the opening of the meeting, and Pres. Woodruff at the altar…. After prayer there being no business, some of the brethren related their experiences in various ways. Pres. Woodruff told of himself and David Patten being in Tennessee on a mission. While there Bro. Patten had a journey of 40 miles to make one day, and when he went out to get the mule he had procured for this labor, he was on the ground nearly dead with the colic. Bro. Patten said: "See here, old fellow, this won't do! You have got to carry me 40 miles today," and with those words he stepped up to the animal, laid his hands on the animal, and blessed him. The mule immediately arose, and made the journey. Pres. Woodruff said that was the only time in his life when his faith had been tried, but he thought it strange for an Elder to administer to a mule, and thus do what seemed sacrilege in his mind at that time.

Bro. Joseph F. Smith told of his mother having one of her oxen become sick when she was coming to the valley with her family. The captain of the company said the animal would die, but she got out a bottle of consecrated oil, and got two of the brethren to administer to the ox, and it recovered. Father also had one of his cattle healed by the laying on of hands by himself. The animal accidentally got its leg badly hurt, and it looked as though it could no more travel, but Father slipped out after dark and administered to it, and it recovered and made the journey home.

Bro. Joseph F. Smith told about David Patten having seen and talked with Cain. Cain is described as being a very large man, his head being even with that of David Patten when the latter was seated on his animal. I always entertained the idea that Cain was dead, but my attention was called to the passage of scripture concerning the curse of God which should fall upon whoever should slay Cain. I supposed this meant whosever should kill his seed....[6]

Friday, November 10, 1893:

The *Tribune* this morning advises the Liberal party to divide on National Party lines, and test the sincerity of the Mormon people, saying that the party can be speedily reorganized if deception is practiced by the Church. This is a very good move, and one for which we can be thankful to the Lord. It is now to be hoped that all acrimonies of the past will be buried, and a reign of peace and prosperity be established in this Territory....

Thursday, November 16, 1893:

From this meeting I went to my Quorum meeting in the temple, but arrived too late to dress with the brethren. Bro. F. D. Richards was mouth in the circle. All of the Presidency were present as well as Bros. L. Snow, F. D. Richards, F. M. Lyman, H. J. Grant and myself; George F. Gibbs, clerk. After prayers Father referred to the unpleasant feeling which is growing up in Z. C. M. I. because of the tyranny of George Romney as the chairman for the Executive committee. Assistant Superintendent Rowe has resigned because of this, and several valuable employees have been discharged. It was decided to call a meeting of the Board next Monday and consider

---

[6] The following excerpt from a letter from Abraham O. Smoot to Joseph F. Smith reports his recollection of an experience told by Elder Patten: "As I was riding along the road on my mule I suddenly noticed a very strange personage walking beside me. He walked along beside me for about two miles. His head was about even with my shoulders as I sat in my saddle. He wore no clothing, but was covered with hair. His skin was very dark. I asked him where he dwelt and he replied that he had no home, that he was a wanderer in the earth and traveled to and fro. He said he was a very miserable creature, that he had earnestly sought death during his sojourn upon the earth, but that he could not die, and his mission was to destroy the souls of men. About the time he expressed himself thus, I rebuked him in the name of the Lord Jesus Christ and by virtue of the Holy Priesthood, and commanded him to go hence, and he immediately departed out of my sight. When he left me I found myself near your house" (Lycurgus A. Wilson, *Life of David W. Patten: The First Apostolic Martyr* (Salt Lake City: The Deseret News, 1900), 57-59).

these matters, and call a halt on the arbitrary way in which things are being run by Bro. Romney.

At 5 o'clock I met in the Temple with Bros. F. M. Lyman, George Reynolds and James E. Talmage to hear and revise the Lectures which Bro. Talmage is giving to the University Theological Class in this city, and which are to appear in the *Juvenile* as well as in book form. Bro. John Nicholson also belongs to this committee, but he was not present this evening. We listened to and corrected the first and second lectures....[7]

Wednesday, November 29, 1893:

I went to the President's office with Bro. James E. Talmage in the forenoon to get some doctrinal points answered by the Brethren concerning a change in the articles of faith, and about the subject of baptism an answer will be given after these matters have been submitted to the Quorum meeting this afternoon. About the Sons of Perdition it was said we can scarcely tell who will be consigned to this doom. That there will also be daughters of Perdition there is no doubt in the minds of the brethren.[8] It was explained that only such can become Sons of Perdition who receive a testimony of the Gospel—who receive the Holy Ghost, and the highest blessings of

---

[7] For further information on this committee of revision for *The Articles of Faith* by James E. Talmage, see James P. Harris, ed., *The Essential James E. Talmage*, (Salt Lake City: Signature Books, 1997), 52-55; and the biographical essay.

[8] Elder Rudger Clawson recorded in his diary the following about a similar discussion that took place amongst the First Presidency and Quorum of the Twelve Apostles some ten years later (26 March 1903): "There was some informal talk regarding the question as to whether there are, or would be, any women in hell. It was conceded that some women by their acts—namely, abortion, child murder after birth, and the poisoning of their husbands, and other criminal acts—merited a place in the lower regions. President Smith expressed the view that women who commit such crimes as those mentioned would receive punishment to the uttermost farthing, but that there would be no daughters of perdition. This, he said, was his view in regard to the matter, which also seemed to meet the minds of the brethren" (Stan Larson, ed., *A Ministry of Meetings: The Apostolic Diaries of Rudger Clawson* [Salt Lake City, Signature Books; 1993], 560). Neither of these doctrinal positions were formally presented to or sustained by the membership of the Church.

the Church, and then willfully deny the light they have obtained. Murderers who crucify Christ anew, or consent to His death, in that they shed innocent blood knowing at the time that they are thereby preventing the spread of the truth, will be subject to this penalty. The murderers of the Savior are not Sons of Perdition, for they did not know what they were doing, as Jesus said in His prayer while on the cross. Peter also preached repentance to them, and said they would be redeemed when the times of refreshing should come. If they were Sons of Perdition they should not have been prayed for, as we are commanded not to do so in the modern revelations.

In our Quorum meeting in the Temple at two o'clock all of the Presidency were present, and Bros. L. Snow, F. D. Richards, J. F. Smith, H. J. Grant and myself; George F Gibbs clerk. It was decided to change the fourth Article of Faith to read "We believe that the first principles and ordinances of the Gospel are," etc. This is to overcome the error which occurs where it says in the third article "we believe that mankind may be saved by obedience to the laws and ordinances of the Gospel", and fourth "We believe that these ordinances are," etc., when faith and repentance are not ordinances but principles.

It was also decided that only the form given for baptism in the Doctrine and Covenants shall be used in the administration of the ordinance, except in the performance of baptism for the dead in the temples, where for adults they use the words, "Being commissioned of Jesus Christ I baptize you _______ for and in behalf of _______ who is dead for the remission of your sins," etc. It was decided that this matter of temple work shall be considered later.

It was also decided that frequent baptisms will not be allowed, and that this sacred ordinance is becoming too common. . . .

Thursday, December 7, 1893:

At two o'clock I went to my Quorum meeting. Present: Pres. Woodruff and Smith; Bros. L. Snow, F. D. Richards, F. M. Lyman and myself; George F. Gibbs, clerk. Bro. Lyman was mouth in opening, and I in the circle. It was decided in answer to a question that people should wear only white garments whether they be cotton, woolen, or linen. Colored garments should not, however, be used.

In baptizing the person officiating should enter the water as well as the candidate. This is fully explained in the Doctrine and Covenants.

I read copies of some dispatches from a letter book of Pres. Brigham Young, which were written in the time of the Buchanan war. They are very strong in some places. Harry Timmons came to me today, and said an Outsider in this city had got possession of the book, and the Liberals desired to use it against Statehood this winter. He wanted to know if the Church would not buy it. The brethren desired me to see upon what terms it could be had....

Monday, December 11, 1893:

In the afternoon I was at the President's office, where Elder James E. Talmage read to the brethren his third lecture on the third article of faith. Some little discussion followed, but suitable corrections were made, and the final reading of the matter was approved....

Tuesday, December 12, 1893:

In the morning Bro. John R. Winder and myself met Harry Timmons in the *News* Office and bargained with him for the Letter book concerning which I gave the brethren a report last Thursday. We secured it by the payment of $200 cash, and a verbal promise of an additional $200 after we become a State, providing none of the content of this book are brought to the attention of the public in the meantime. This is to guard against the use of any copies which may have been taken....

Thursday, December 14, 1893:

The Utah Statehood bill passed the House of Representatives yesterday with not more than five opposing votes. There is a clause in the bill forever prohibiting polygamy in the proposed State, but otherwise its provisions are very liberal. We hope it will soon pass the Senate and receive the signature of the President, but fear action on it may be delayed some little. The Liberals in the city rejoice at its passage as much as the Mormons, and it now looks as if all the people of Utah will be able to meet as brethren and citizens of our common country without any of the animosities of the past. So may it be.

Sunday, December 17, 1893:

At one o'clock I came to town and met Mr. and Mrs. Wray, for whom I procured good seats in the tabernacle. John Henry Smith spoke on the good that religion has done the world, and felt that even false ideas concerning God are better than unbelief in his existence. After meeting I took my Gentile friends to my room where Mr. Wray read to me an article which he has prepared for his eastern papers. It was very good, and there were but few corrections to make in it....

Monday, December 18, 1893:

The Liberal Party held a meeting this evening in the Theater and decided to disband, nearly all of them being in favor of Statehood. Thus one by one the Lord is breaking down the barriers which oppose the onward march of His people. It is now a question which will be the stronger party—the Republican or the Democratic....

Saturday, December 30, 1893:

At 10 o'clock I met with Bros. John Nicholson and George Reynolds as a committee to listen to Prof. James E. Talmage read his lectures before the theological class, which he has already delivered. There were some few corrections, and we then passed them....

CHAPTER SEVEN

1894

Tuesday, January 2, 1894:

At 10 o'clock I went to the President's office and listened to the reading by Bro. James E. Talmage of three of his theological lectures to the Presidency and Committee of Revision. With very few alterations they were passed. In the course of the reading Pres. Woodruff related that his son Brigham Young Woodruff, who was drowned some years ago, related to his sister before his death the manner in which he would lose his life, it having been revealed to him. When the news of his death was telegraphed to Pres. Woodruff, who was then in Washington County attending a conference, he sorrowed at Brigham's death, and inquired of the Lord why this good boy had been taken. The Lord then revealed to Bro. Woodruff as follows: You are doing much work for your dead in the temple, and it is necessary that one of your seed should come to preach to those in the spirit world for whom you are doing this work. This satisfied Bro. Woodruff, and made him feel resigned to his loss....[1]

Thursday, January 4, 1894:

I read some proofs this forenoon and then went to the President's office and submitted to the brethren a letter I had written to Prof. Benjamin Cluff Jr., proposing that a stock company be formed to buy out the *Contributor, Intermountain Educator* and *Normal,* and issue in the place thereof a creditable educational journal, combining the features of all three journals. Father and Pres. Woodruff, who were present, approve of the plan.

Attended my Quorum meeting at two o'clock. All of the Presidency were present, and Bros. L. Snow, F. D. Richards, F. M.

---

[1] See the biographical essay for further information on this doctrine and experience.

Lyman, J. H. Smith, H. J. Grant and myself; George F. Gibbs, clerk. Joseph F. Smith was mouth in opening and Father at the altar. After dressing the matter of ordaining Seventies was considered. The First Seven Presidents desire the privilege of removing aged and infirm men, who do not desire to be ordained High Priests, into a quorum by themselves, as they cannot be used for active service. After some little talk about this matter it was voted that the aged brethren be not forced into positions which will not be congenial to them, and that no Seventies be ordained in the future, except in an emergency, unless the candidates have been or are going on missions. The matter was referred to the Twelve to so inform the Presiding Seventies. To our Quorum was also referred some communications from Elders in California asking that some able and prominent Elder or Elders be sent there to meet a Christian minister who is winning people from the gospel to his faith. Not to engage in debate, but to talk to the people about our principles. It was suggested that one of the Apostles and B. H. Roberts go....

Friday, January 5, 1894:

In the afternoon I went to the President's office where Dr. Talmage read his theological lecture, which he proposes to deliver to the class next Sunday, to the Presidency and Committee. The subject was the Holy Ghost, in which some changes were made to conform to the written word regarding this personage of the Godhead. The brethren felt that it would be better to say too little than too much, and when it comes to separating too closely between this personage of spirit and His powers, it cannot be done except by using the greatest care so as to obviate discussion in the future....

Wednesday, January 10, 1894:

The Supreme Court of the Territory today ordered the personal property of the Church returned to the First Presidency, in accordance with the act of Congress. Over four hundred thousand dollars are thus to be returned to the Church in cash. This will help to pay the debts which have accumulated.

C. S. Varian today introduced a memorial in the Legislature asking Congress to return to the Church all of its real estate just as has been done with the personal property.[2]

Friday, January 12, 1894:

...At 10:45 went to the Presidents office and heard the lecture of Dr. James E. Talmage on the Sacrament for the Theological Class next Sunday. There were very few corrections to make in it....

Tuesday, January 16, 1894:

At 2:30 o'clock I went to my Quorum meeting in the Temple. Present: Lorenzo Snow, F. D. Richards, Francis M. Lyman, John H. Smith, Heber J. Grant and myself. Also of the First Seven Presidents of the Seventies: S. B. Young, John Morgan, B. H. Roberts, George Reynolds and Rulon S. Wells. After singing John H. Smith offered prayer. President Snow then explained to the brethren present the wishes of the Presidency in regard to the ordination of Seventies, and told them not to crowd aged men from their positions, but allow them to remain as they are unless they desire to change. We were also told to only ordain to the office of Seventy such as are worthy, and have proved themselves so by either going on missions, or by preparing themselves to respond to any such call.[3] The matter of sending one of the Apostles to Southern California for a short time to preach the Gospel was then considered. After considerable talk it was voted to send Bro. F. M. Lyman, providing the Presidency have no objections....[4]

Tuesday, January 23, 1894:

At 11 o'clock I went to the President's office and met Mr. Jenkins of the *Denver Times*, who is out here for the purpose of writing an article for use in the Utah Statehood edition of his paper, which is

---

[2] Congress had confiscated a great deal of the Church's property as part of the anti-polygamy legislation and was now returning some of it. See biographical essay, note 38.
[3] See AHC journals 4 January 1894.
[4] Ibid.

owned and controlled by Senator Teller. Pres. Woodruff and Smith gave some information on the subject he has to treat. Mr. Jenkins evidently is possessed of considerable conceit. When he had gone Pres. Woodruff asked the brethren present (L. Snow, H. J. Grant, myself, besides Pres. J. F. Smith) what we thought of the proposition to let Dr. James E. Talmage become the president of the University of Utah, and thus release him from his position as one of the Faculty in the Church University. I felt that it would be a good thing to do, as it would give our people the supremacy in that institution. We are not able anyway to carry on the work designed in our Church institution, and when we are in a better financial condition Bro. Talmage can be recalled. In view of Pres. Woodruff's feelings I moved, and it was carried that Bro. Talmage be not released….

Thursday, January 25, 1894:

I was also at the President's office in the forenoon to hear the pleas of Joseph Kingsbury and William M. Stewart in favor of James E. Talmage accepting the Presidency of the University of Utah. Mr. Kingsbury, who has been considered an infidel, said his heart was with the Mormons, and he considered himself one of them. He thought this was an opportunity for our people which we should not neglect.

At two o'clock I met with my Quorum in the Temple. Present: Bros. Woodruff, J. F. Smith, L. Snow, F. D. Richards, F. M. Lyman, H. J. Grant and myself; George F. Gibbs, clerk. Pres. Woodruff told of John W. Young having obtained $6,000 from a widow of the Church in London with Kaibab bonds as security. John told her that he was in good standing in the Church, and the Lord had revealed to him that she was to loan him the money. She is likely to lose it all….[5]

The Presidency of the University of Utah was next considered. All present seemed to favor the appointment of James E. Talmage to the position, but after considerable talk it was decided to hold the matter

---

[5] John W. Young's business dealings were of such a dubious character that at his suggestion and with the concurrence of his Brethren, he had been dropped from his position as a Counselor to the Twelve Apostles.

in abeyance till we can hear from Father on the subject. A telegram was therefore prepared and sent to him on the subject.

Bros. F. D. Richards, F. S. Richards and myself were appointed a committee to revise the bills which are presented to the Legislature, and on which our people in that body may desire counsel, and report our findings and judgment to the Presidency. This is to prevent as far as possible the passage of improper legislation....

On my suggestion the selection of a suitable room in the Temple for the various prayer circles to meet was left to Pres. L. Snow and John R. Winder. On motion of Bro. Joseph F. Smith the Twelve were then told to go ahead and organize the Circles, and bring them into the temple for their regular meetings. I was instructed to take hold of Father's old circle; H. J. Grant will look after Pres. Woodruff's; F. M. Lyman to Joseph F. Smith's; John Henry Smith to his Father's; John W. Taylor to his father's; and so on till enough circles are organized.

Bro. Roskelly of the Logan temple is having a considerable number of persons who are dead sealed and adopted to him. This is right where people request it, but he should not try to induce them to take this course through their surviving relatives, or in their own cases, if alive. Pres. Woodruff will write him to not try to get people to be thus sealed to him, but where they ask it of their own free will it will be proper....

Monday, January 29, 1894:

At 11:30 I went to the President's office and reported with Bros. F. D. and F. S. Richards that we think the Mechanics' Lien law now pending in the Legislature is a very bad measure. Steps will therefore be taken to kill it. Pres. Woodruff favors the plan which I suggested to him of having the University of Utah and the Agricultural College of Utah united under one Board of managers, and with one President, but leave them in their present locations until some future time....

Pres. Woodruff says he has decided to let James E. Talmage become the President of the University of Utah....

Thursday, February 1, 1894:

At 2 o'clock I attended my Quorum meeting. Present: Pres. Woodruff and Smith; F. D. Richards, H. J. Grant and myself; George F. Gibbs, clerk. The opening prayer was offered by F. D. Richards, and at the altar by Pres. Woodruff....

Thereafter we listened to some few letters which were written about 30 years ago by Pres. Brigham Young to William H. Hooper, when the latter was in Congress. Some fellow in town desires to sell them to the Presidency, but it was decided that they contain nothing which would do us any injury if published, and they will therefore not be purchased unless offered at a very low figure....

We looked at a room in the east end of the temple to see if it will be suitable for circle meetings. It can probably be arranged to answer the purpose, but it is very small....

Saturday, February 3, 1894:

I had a talk with Ben Rich in the afternoon. He owes the *Juvenile* office some money for printing his book, but now offers to turn the entire edition over to us, if we will release him from his obligation, and give him a thousand copies, which I agreed to do. He wants to get the *News* sermons to print in his Idaho paper—*The Silver Hammer*, but I did not promise to let him have them....[6]

Thursday, February 22, 1894:

I then went to Father's farm, where I arrived at 10:45. He had 60 of his children and grand-children together for the purpose of talking to them. We sang and opened by prayer, after which Father spoke for about an hour on the subjects of frugality, obedience and tithing. He urged us all to be careful with the means which God has entrusted to our care, to be strict in the payment of our tithes and offerings, and to be obedient to the priesthood and to our parents. His remarks were very good and timely. In answer to questions Father said the tithing of the wives and children should be credited to the head of

---

[6] As the official organ of the Church, the *Deseret News* regularly published sermons given by General Authorities.

the household, if he was the person who originally provided the means, till the children become of age. The standing High Council, to which reference is made in the Doctrine and Covenants, refers to the men who were chosen when there was only one Stake of Zion, and is not applicable to the present time.[7] Abraham in speaking of his only son refers to Isaac as being the only son of promise, or in the sense of only meaning the choice son....

Sunday, February 25, 1894:

I read a short time at home, and then went to town. I attended Talmage's Theology class at noon, and heard him discourse very excellently on the subject of the gifts of the Gospel, and the Bible and Book of Mormon. I was at meeting at 2 o'clock. Three persons were called to come to the stand, but none responding, I spoke for 45 minutes on the way in which individuals and communities make themselves feared and respected. Heber J. Grant then occupied 15 minutes on the subject of prejudice, and told instances in which this feeling was exhibited. He said we are opposed to home-made goods merely because of the name, for he had placed the home-made article at times in imported wrappers, and people pronounced them good, while the eastern article in home-made wrappers was condemned. Then he reversed the process, and the appearance condemned the best goods. He told of a cat being drowned in his mother's well. Her boarders would not taste of the water without commenting on its nastiness, though the well had been thoroughly cleaned out. He therefore pretended to bring some water from a neighboring well, which was pronounced excellent, when in reality it was from the original well....

Wednesday, February 28, 1894:

About 6 o'clock I went to Emily Clawson's to a birthday party given in honor of her mother, Sister Emily Partridge Young, who is 70 years old today. There were a large number of relatives and friends in attendance, and a very enjoyable evening was spent together. Pres.

---

[7] See D&C 102.

Joseph F. Smith spoke for a few minutes in a very touching way, and referred to Sister Young as having been a wife of the Prophet Joseph, and he felt to bless her for her fidelity to the cause of God....

Thursday, March 1, 1894:

At 2 o'clock I went to my Quorum meeting. Heber J. Grant was mouth in the opening, and I prayed at the altar. It was decided that the case of women who marry Gentiles, and then desire to enter the Temples and do work, will be considered and decided on the individual merits of each case, and no general rule shall be adopted.

Some people try to escape the effects of their sins by saying the same were forgiven at the Temple dedication. Only such sins were then forgiven as were known and truly repented of, and not such transgressions as were concealed....

Saturday, March 3, 1894:

Judge Phillips of Missouri today decided the case in which the Josephites sued the Hedrickites for the possession of the Temple lot in Jackson County, Missouri, at Independence, in favor of the Josephites. His ruling is unjust, because the Hedrickites hold a tax title to the property, and have been in possession of it for many years without dispute. The Judge in his opinion took occasion to say that the Josephites form the real Mormon Church, and that the Utah Church is in the wrong. His decision does not affect us at all, but makes many persons in the neighborhood of the Temple lot feel insecure in their property, as many only hold their property under the same conditions which surround the Hedrickites.[8]

---

[8] The Josephites, or Reorganized Church of Jesus Christ of Latter-day Saints (now known as the Community of Christ) were litigating with the Hedrickites, or Church of Christ—Temple Lot, for ownership of land in Independence, Missouri, which Joseph Smith had marked as the center place of Zion where a temple was to be built. See Joseph Fielding Smith, *Essentials in Church History* (Salt Lake City: The Church of Jesus Christ of Latter-day Saints and Deseret Book, 1961), 134.

Tuesday, March 6, 1894:

At 10 o'clock I went to the President's office, where, after considerable preliminary talk, we considered the railroad matters. After some little discussion a motion was made that we go ahead with the proposed undertaking, but just as a vote was about to be called, it was decided to adjourn, subject to call, for the reason, as I subsequently learned, that Pres. Woodruff was not feeling well, and did not desire to be troubled with this matter at present....

Wednesday, March 7, 1894:

Was called to the President's office to a meeting at 10 o'clock....

We then considered the railroad proposition again. Some of the brethren favored going to Coalville only, Pres. Snow and Grant were dubious about starting at all, while Bros. Joseph F. Smith, F. D. Richards and myself were in favor of the whole proposition to build the whole line from Coalville to the Pacific Coast. The final decision was reached when Father said with great warmth and force, "I prophesy, in the name of the Lord, that if we will be united and go ahead with the work, we will succeed and be prospered." There was then a unanimous vote taken to prosecute the labor with all speed and vigor. Pres. Woodruff now said he felt that this was the right thing to do. We all seemed to feel easy at the result of the meeting, and I was particularly glad, for I have felt all along that it was the right thing to do. We will of course meet difficulties, but with faith and works they can be overcome....

Thursday, March 8, 1894:

At two o'clock I went to my Quorum meeting. Present: All of the Presidency, though Father came in after prayers; L. Snow, F. D. Richards, H. J. Grant and myself; George F. Gibbs clerk. Pres. Woodruff opened by prayer, and Pres. Snow was mouth at the altar. We sustained Elias Kimball as President of the Southern States Mission in place of his brother Jonathan Golden, and decided that he had better not take his family with him to that field.

It was decided that Pres. Snow write to John W. Taylor, and urge him to come home to Conference, and that he then attend to his ecclesiastical duties, and not neglect them as he has done the last six months.

Some talk was had about Spiritualism and secret orders, which some of our people are joining, and it was said that we should use all our endeavors to check these things....

Monday, March 12, 1894:

I am 35 years old, and my son Abraham, or Junior as we call him, is 8 years old today. I baptized and confirmed the latter in the Temple today, Pres. Lorenzo Snow having arranged for the heating of the water for my especial use.

I feel ashamed of the little progress I have made in the world during the time I have lived in it. I wish I could do more while I still remain....

Wednesday, March 14, 1894:

President Woodruff today decided that the Church will help to sustain the Utah University for the coming two years, inasmuch as the Legislature failed to appropriate a sufficient amount of means. It is expected, however, that Bro. James E. Talmage will become the President of that Institution.

Friday, March 30, 1894:

[8 _ lines were cut from this entry.]

REMARKABLE STATEMENTS: Oliver B. Huntington relates in an article in the *Young Woman's Journal* that Joseph Smith the Prophet's father, once gave his mother a patriarchal blessing in which he promised that her body should never see corruption. It was supposed this meant that she should live till the Savior came, and then she should be changed. To the surprise of the family, however, she died in July, 1839. Some years later, in removing her body from the place where it had been deposited to a new location, it was found that the body was in an incorruptible state, and had the appearance of wood. The features, form, etc., were as natural as life.

Bro. Huntington claims that he was promised the blessing of preaching the Gospel to the inhabitants of the moon, whose people the Prophet is claimed to have said, are generally about six feet tall and live to be about 1,000 years old. They dress quite uniformly in the style similar to the Quakers.[9]

Sunday, April 1, 1894:

I was engaged in reading at home till nearly noon, when I took the car for town. I attended Dr. Talmage's theological class in the Assembly Hall at 12:30, and after he had delivered his lecture on the Gathering, I adjourned the class *sine die*, by authority and direction of the First Presidency. He spoke first about the adjournment, and I then explained that it was because of his numerous duties in other directions, and because it was only designed originally to continue the class till April, that it was decided to close. I expressed my appreciation of Bro. Talmage's labors, and a hearty vote of thanks was tendered him.[10] I advised the people to attend their Sunday meetings, and thus learn theology. George Reynolds made a few supplementary remarks, and urged the S. S. teachers who had attended this class to carry into practice the methods and items they have gained. Apostle B. Young was present, but he would not speak.

I went direct to the Tabernacle services, where Bishop O. F. Whitney delivered a very excellent discourse. He spoke of the prejudices of some people which will not permit them to carefully and impartially study Mormonism. He then referred to our preexistent state, and produced scriptural evidences to prove that our condition here is to some extent the result of our condition before we came to the earth. He then spoke of Joseph's call to the Work, and treated briefly of the first principles of the Gospel, closing with a strong testimony to the truth of the religion we have espoused....

---

[9] This description from Oliver B. Huntington has been used by anti-Mormons to belittle Joseph Smith and the Church. For a discussion of this statement, see Gilbert W. Scharffs, *The Truth About the God-Makers* (Salt Lake City: Publishers Press, 1986), 119-20; see also *History of the Life of Oliver B. Huntington, written by Himself,* 1878-1900 (n.p., n.d.), 10; copy in author's possession.

[10] These lectures given by James E. Talmage were eventually compiled into a book and published by the Church with the title *The Articles of Faith,* now a classic in LDS doctrinal literature. For further information about this project, see AHC journals, 16 November 1893 and note; see also the biographical essay.

Monday, April 2, 1894:

In the afternoon I was at the President's office for a short time where the Presidency urged upon Pres. Snow and several of the Twelve who were there the necessity of investigating John W. Taylor's affairs, and seeing that he attends more faithfully to his ecclesiastical duties, and less to his personal affairs. He returned this morning from Canada, where he has been laboring for nearly six months almost entirely in his own interests....

Tuesday, April 3, 1894:

I then went to my Quorum meeting in our room. Present: Lorenzo Snow, Franklin D. Richards, Brigham Young, Francis M. Lyman, John H. Smith, George Teasdale, Heber J. Grant, John W. Taylor and myself. Bro. M. W. Merrill came in later. After singing and prayer by George Teasdale, Pres. Snow expressed his pleasure at the union and love which are characteristic of this Quorum at present. He did not believe anything would ever occur to divide us, and hoped such would not be the case. "I feel that we should get into a condition to know the mind of the Lord at all times. If our eye is single to the glory of God, our whole bodies will be filled with light. If we do everything for the purpose and with the view of forwarding the work of the Lord, we will never fail, but will be successful in everything.

F. D. Richards: "Sometimes our prayers are not answered in the way we desire, and we feel disappointed; but if we are faithful, and that which we desire is for our good, the Lord will accomplish that for which we ask as he thinks best, and we will afterwards see that the way in which it has been done is much better than we could have anticipated."

B. Young: "I find it a constant struggle to keep anywhere near the line of my duty, I have so many temptations to overcome. I cannot say that I do as near right as I know how, for this is not the case, but I am trying to improve."

F. M. Lyman reported the labors of himself and B. H. Roberts on their recent mission in southern California. They held many meetings, visited numerous people, and did all they could to spend their time in spreading the truth, but to all appearances their labors are unavailing. Two young Elders who have labored in that section 9 months have not made a single convert, nor have they been fed and lodged, hence the people will be left to their own sins, and misery. The only [way] to get the truth before the people at all is to rent halls, and advertise, and then the results are doubtful.

John H. Smith next spoke. He hoped the Presidency would give permission for all the Twelve to be together once each year to attend conference, and thought the best time would be at the April conference. The expense of their coming from the mission field would be slight, and he felt that the renewed faith of such brethren by association with the Quorum here at home would more than compensate for the time and money thus expended. He also reported the labors of himself, Pres. Young and George Teasdale in Old Mexico....

We now sang a hymn for relief, after doing which Pres. F. D. Richards presented in a very pleasing way to Pres. Snow, he being today 80 years old, a beautiful basket of flowers, a gold pencil, and a gold pen and pencil combined. Pres. Snow replied in a very nice way, expressing the hope that we would each live to be over a hundred years old, and then be translated and live eternally. "These gifts may fade and decay, but the feeling which prompted their bestowal I will never forget in time or eternity."

George Teasdale expressed his pleasure at this meeting, and then reported his recent visit to all the wards of Juab Stake, where he found the people feeling very well.

Heber J. Grant: "I feel sorry that Bro. Thatcher is not with us. I am sure he would feel better physically and spiritually were he to attend to his apostolic duties. He has sometimes opposed measures which have been adopted by the Presidency and Twelve, and this because he had not met in Council to have them explained. I sometimes feel that propositions made are unwise, but after I have met with the brethren and had the business explained, I have seen eye to eye with all the Quorum. So it could be with Bro. Thatcher. We cannot always understand the purposes of God. Richard W. Young wanted to resign his position in the army immediately after completing his course in school, and I thought it would be best for him to do so, but Pres. John Taylor said he should remain in the army until later. All could see the wisdom of this counsel subsequently: Richard was stationed on Governor's Island near New York City, and went daily to the city where he studied law and graduated with honor, thus gaining a profession which he would not have acquired had he resigned as he first intended. How marvelously God works is illustrated in the case of a man now living in Idaho, and a member of the Church. He formerly resided in England, and when Bro. F. M. Lyman was there many years ago this man was sitting in a room not far from where Bro. Lyman was preaching. He overheard the sermon, and the principles taught so riveted themselves on his mind that he could never get away from them, and he finally joined the Church and emigrated. He attributes his conversion to that sermon of Bro. Lyman."

John W. Taylor: "My personal business has engaged my time in Canada for some time past, but it was necessary for me to be thus engaged or let my creditors go to the dogs, which to me would be worse than death. I hope to get out of debt soon, my prospects being better than ever before. The lands I control are the best in America, and I am now negotiating with an English Colonization Co. to sell them the lands. If I succeed I will make a million dollars, which I will use in paying the debts of every member of this Quorum, and give the remainder to the Church. In a recent letter sent by Pres. Snow he spoke of the terrible financial condition of the people, but said the clouds would eventually pass, and prosperity would shine on the people. I believe this with all my heart...."

M. W. Merrill: "I feel that we should keep out of debt. I do not owe a dollar, though I have 55 people depending on me for support. They keep themselves as much as possible, and I do what I can for their aid. I oppose mortgaging, as there is only about one in ten who can redeem property thus encumbered. In early days I was given 100 acres of land in Bountiful, Davis Co., by Pres. Young. I only kept a third of it myself, and divided the remainder among my co-religionists. When Pres. Young heard what I had done he said, 'You shall never want bread, nor shall your children, if you will keep the commandments of the Lord.' Hard times came afterwards, but I always had [enough] to eat and to give to others. There is safety in following the counsel of the Priesthood. One man who felt bitter towards Pres. L. Snow for some counsel he had given him, went to Montana, where he soon afterwards died a miserable death, and all his children who were opposed to Pres. Snow also died. The wife, however, who was a good woman lived to return to Utah, and join the people."

I then spoke concerning the growing evil of card playing, and other things which are leading away our young people. I hoped to do some little towards the saving of the children of men. We now adjourned till tomorrow, and Bro. B. Young pronounced the benediction....

Wednesday, April 4, 1894:

I spent some little time in the offices till ten o'clock, when I went to my Quorum meeting in the temple. All were present except Bros. Moses Thatcher and A. H. Lund.... After some preliminary remarks by Pres. Snow, Bro. Lyman spoke of his having met Gideon Carter on his recent visit in San Bernardino. He is a son of Gideon Carter who was killed in the battle of Crooked River in the early days of the Church. This man followed Lyman Wight from Nauvoo to Texas and testifies that the party practiced plural marriage. They did so until the laws of the land strictly prohibited it, and they were unable longer to escape its penalties. Lyman Wight said that the principle was too pure to be practiced by this generation. Carter said he heard Lyman Wight speak of a Council of Fifty over which Father John Smith presided. Wight was a member, and so sacred was his obligation to that body that he expressed himself as ready to crawl on his hands and knees to meet with the same, if it should have been convened by John Smith. Wight considered that each of this council was authorized and empowered to build up a Church in any part of the earth. Bro. Lyman then spoke of John W. Taylor's affairs, and said he felt that each member of the Quorum should correspond with Pres. Snow when absent for any length of time from the meetings.

He also felt that Bro. Teasdale should be released from the Stake Presidency of Old Mexico, and be allowed to travel as an apostle.

There was some desultory talk, and Pres. Snow then brought up Bro. Taylor's case, and said he felt that each of the apostles should hold himself free from business, so as to be ready at any time to answer the calls made on them by the Presidency. On these grounds the operations of John W. Taylor in Canada have been unwise and improper.

John W. said he accepted the reproof, and was willing to do whatever the brethren said for him to do in regard to the disposition of the 700,000 acres of land which he controls in Canada. There was considerable talk among various brethren about this matter, but it was left undecided, and we adjourned at one o'clock with prayer by myself. We went in a body to the funeral of Jesse W. Fox, which was held in the Assembly Hall, which was well filled with people....

F. D. Richards said that when our inheritances are assigned us in the hereafter he knew no person whom he would sooner trust to run the chain or drive the stakes for his lot than the deceased.

Father said he first became acquainted with Bro. Fox in Nauvoo, when he acted as a school-teacher. He was a good man, and I have no doubts as to his future, for he kept both his first and his second estates, and has earned his reward. Efforts are now made to make people believe there is no resurrection, but we know there is, and that we will all be saved if we are faithful. Our suffering and trials in life are not a mere accident, but are ordered for a wise purpose.

Pres. Woodruff said he never could mourn at the death of a good person, and could not do so in this case. He felt very sorry when the Prophet and his brother were murdered, not because of their death, but because he realized what their death would cost the nation. These things are what we all have to meet.

This closed the services and Joseph Horne offered prayer....

Thursday, April 5, 1894:

Was in town by 6:30 o'clock, and posted some of the books, dictated some letters, and looked after general business till 10 o'clock, when I met with the Quorum and Presidency in the temple. We had singing and prayer by John Henry Smith. President Woodruff then spoke: "I have felt we are too strict in regard to some of our temple ordinances. This is especially the case in regard to husbands and parents who are dead. Heretofore we have not permitted wives to be sealed to their dead husbands unless such husbands were in the Church, nor have we permitted children to be sealed to dead unbaptized parents. This is wrong I feel. I was sealed to my father, and then had him sealed to the Prophet Joseph. Erastus Snow was sealed to his father though the latter was not baptized after having heard the Gospel. He was, however, kind to the Prophet, and was a Saint in everything except baptism. The Lord has told me that it is right for children to be sealed to their parents, and they to their parents just as far back as we can possibly obtain the records, and then have the last obtainable member sealed to the Prophet Joseph, who stands at the head of this dispensation.[11] It is also right for wives

---

[11] Elder Boyd K. Packer has explained this revelation thus: "The Saints knew they were to perform baptisms for the dead. They knew that there was to be a linking of the generations. They knew that families were to be united through sealings or 'adoptions.' They were baptized for the dead, but kept only sparse records of this ordinance work. They were in some cases sealed or adopted to prophets of this dispensation.

"During the several years that the saints were on the move to the West and preoccupied with the troubles of the period, these matters were not clarified. When the Saints were established and temples…were under construction, it was time to have these matters set in order. It was during the closing years of the ministry of President Wilford Woodruff that this instruction was given by revelation.

"President Woodruff was a prophet uniquely qualified to accomplish this setting in order. In 1894, near the end of his ministry, having received instruction through revelation, he laid the foundation for genealogical work in the Church" (Boyd K. Packer, *The Holy Temple* [Salt Lake City: Bookcraft, 1980], 194; see also 195-206).

President Woodruff's journal records the following for this date: "I met with the Presidency and Twelve Apostles upon the subject of endowments and adoption and the following is a revelation to Wilford Woodruff upon that subject." There follows a page of blank space where President Woodruff probably meant to, but did not, write the revelation. President Woodruff's sermon at general conference (8 April) and Elder Cannon's journal entry here are two of the best sources available for ascertaining the content of the revelation. The revelation was accepted by the

whose husbands never heard the Gospel to be sealed to those husbands, providing they are willing to run the risk of their receiving the Gospel in the Spirit World. There is yet very much for us to learn concerning the temple ordinances, and God will make it known as we prove ourselves ready to receive it. In searching out my genealogy I found about four hundred of my female kindred who were never married. I asked Pres. Young what I should do with them. He said for me to have them sealed to me unless there were more than 999 of them. The doctrine startled me, but I had it done. When in St. George I found I had more dead for whom I desired to do a work than I could possibly attend to. I had none of my family with me, and one day the Lord told me to get the young people of that city to give me a birthday present by coming into the temple and being endowed for my dead. Pres. Young approved of the plan, and in this way I got my work done, some of Pres. Young's family helping me to do it. At that time I also had several of my dead kindred sealed to each other."

Father said: "I am thankful for what has been revealed. This matter has weighed for a long time on my mind. There has been a disposition since the days of Nauvoo for men to seek to add to their future kingdoms by having dead persons sealed and adopted to them. Amasa Lyman once said, 'When it comes to the game of kingdoms, I can hold my own with any of them,' meaning that his following was as large. Now, however, the danger of clannishness and divisions is averted, and we can show respect to the parents which God gave us, and through whom we doubtless chose to come before we were born into this world. Adoptions to certain men naturally led men to seek counsel from those to whom they were thus united, and consequently the Presidency and general priesthood was set to one side. This new order will also prompt us to be careful to obtain the correct record of our fathers. The man who is at the head of the Church should always be consulted and decide in cases where children find that some one or more of their ancestors are unworthy of having their offspring

---

First Presidency and the Twelve. See also Elder John Henry Smith's journal entry for the same date in *Church, State, and Politics*, 307.

sealed to them. In the days of Nauvoo baptisms for the dead were performed in the Mississippi River, and without any record of the same being kept; this was because of the people being anxious to do the work after the revelation was given, but it all had to be done again. I was thus baptized for many. Men were also baptized for women, and women for men, which was improper, but it was because the Lord had not revealed all that was necessary concerning the doctrine. My mother's dying charge to me was to do the work for our dead. I hail this word of God today with delight."

Pres. Woodruff said he knew that where honorable men of the earth had no posterity in the Church, God will reveal it to some person, so that the work can be done for them. For two nights in succession in St. George the spirits of the signers of the Declaration of Independence had appeared to him, and asked him to do their work. He did so, Bro. McAllister having baptized him for all of them. While doing so the room seemed filled with the Spirit of God. Father said he had been baptized for Thomas L. Kane and some members of Congress whom he knew to be good men. He expected to do the work for others. Each of the apostles now spoke in turn and expressed himself as delighted with the new order of things. F. D. Richards said he had traced his paternal and maternal ancestry back to those who came over the ocean in the year 1620.

Pres. Snow said, and Pres. Woodruff coincided with the view, that very, very few of those who die without the Gospel will reject it on the other side of the veil. F. M. Lyman wanted to do the work for the redemption of his Father Amasa, as soon as the Presidency felt it would be right for him to do so. John W. Taylor said he had seen the Prophet Joseph and the Savior. Joseph was the biggest man of this generation. John W. had been baptized in the Manti temple for Pres. Juarez of Mexico. M. W. Merrill said these instructions were in accordance with some views expressed by Pres. Taylor at the opening of the Logan Temple. "My father heard the Gospel, but did not receive it, though my mother did. He died and I did the work in the Logan temple for him. I did not intend to seal my mother, who was now dead, to him, but one night they both appeared to me, and my father looked angry with me. The night after I was baptized for him he appeared to James A. Leishman, the temple recorder, and my mother was with him. Bro. Leishman described them both to me accurately, though he had never seen them in life.. My mother did the most of the talking to Bro. Leishman, which was her characteristic in life. They desired to be sealed to each other. I therefore did as they desired, and the next night after doing so my father met me in the temple, embraced and blessed me, saying, 'God bless you my son! You are my savior and redeemer.' Since then he has not visited me."

I expressed my pleasure at the revelation we have had this day.

Pres. Joseph F. Smith, who came in late said, "The Lord revealed to the Prophet Joseph, after showing him his brother Alvin who died before the Gospel was revealed, in the Celestial world, that those who would have received the Gospel had they lived will obtain every blessing to which those who receive it in the flesh are entitled. I endorse the word of Pres. Woodruff with all my heart."

Father said Heber C. Kimball once told him he was a direct descendant of the Savior of the world.

Pres. Woodruff expressed his pleasure at the unity of the brethren.

Father now spoke of the unfortunate condition of the people at present in regard to marriage. A man in Pima married the widow of a deceased brother. He did not realize till after the Manifesto was passed his true condition. Now he is raising up seed to his dead friend, while he himself is likely to be left without posterity. Then there are men whose wives are barren, and are likely to be without representatives in the earth. Young widows are left with the alternative of marrying Gentiles, or remaining single all their lives. It seems that something will have to be done sooner or later to remedy these conditions. My son David died without seed, and his brothers cannot do a work for him, in rearing children to bear his name because of the Manifesto. I believe in concubinage, or some plan whereby men and women can live together under sacred ordinances and vows until they can be married. Thus our surplus girls can be cared for, and the law of God to multiply and replenish the earth be fulfilled. There is the danger of wicked men taking license from such a condition, and of good people taking offense thereat, but such a condition would have to be kept secret, until the laws of our government change to permit the holy order of wedlock which God has revealed, which will undoubtedly occur at no distant day, in order to correct the social evil. I do not say that this plan is the right one, but I appeal to the Lord to reveal what will be right in the matter to avert threatened evils.

Pres. Snow: "I have no doubt but concubinage will yet be practiced in this Church, but I had not thought of it in this connection. When the nations are troubled good women will come here for safety and blessing, and men will accept them as concubines."

Pres. Woodruff: "If men enter into some practice of this character to raise a righteous posterity, they will be justified in it. The day is near when there will be a difficulty in the way of good men securing noble wives. There are terrible afflictions at the door of this nation which will take their minds away from this people."

Father now offered prayer. We then had the sacrament after it had been blessed by Pres. Snow. At the table Father made a motion which was carried, that hereafter the Twelve who may be abroad upon missions be allowed to return home to the annual conferences of the Church provided it can be conveniently arranged for them to do so. After the Sacrament Pres. Joseph F. Smith offered prayer and the Presidency withdrew, though not until a motion was carried to the effect that the Sacrament in the future be no more administered in the large Tabernacle, but in the Ward evening meetings.

Pres. Snow expressed his pleasure at the expressions of John W. Taylor, and said he and all the brethren of the Quorum should get free and keep in that condition so far as it is possible. He told of an experience of his youth, when one of his wives, 16 years old, was seduced by a man in this Church who was an editor, and this girl was afterwards sealed to her seducer without Bro. Snow's knowledge. This man afterwards wanted to go to the temple, but he was not allowed to do so until he had obtained the permission of Bro. Snow. This editor afterwards raised several children by the woman he seduced. We must be ready to endure all things, and take them uncomplainingly. Bro. Merrill did wrong in allowing his family to send a complaining letter to the Presidency concerning the requirement made of him by Brigham Young, a few weeks ago, to make an apology in meeting for having hurt the feelings of some of the brethren in Richmond.

Bro. Teasdale said George A. Smith was once accused of adultery, and was threatened with excommunication unless he confessed having done so. He preferred to say what was untrue, and suffer under the load than to lose his standing, but his innocence was subsequently proved.

Bro. Young said Bro. Merrill had the proper spirit when he made his confession, but he did not have it now.

Bro. Merrill in replying did not show the proper spirit. He said he had not felt well towards Bro. Young for years, because he had married one of his daughters to an unworthy man, without the consent of her parents. He had also hurt his feelings in the Richmond confession affair.

Bro. Young said he did not know about having married Bro. Merrill's daughter as accused.

Pres. Snow said he saw that Bro. Merrill did not have the proper spirit now, and he was willing to leave his matters for his further consideration.[12]

John W. Taylor said he had been riding with a Gentile who said he had made an effort to have a former member of our Church admitted into the Knights of Pythias order, but when he heard that this man had been cut off from our Church after a High Council trial, he and other Gentiles did not have much confidence in or respect for him. This shows how much our Church tribunals are respected by non-Mormons.

---

[12] Regarding this matter, the journal of Marriner W. Merrill records for 5 April: "Then the decision of Apostle B. Young, which he made some months ago in relation to myself and others, with which myself and family were not satisfied, was discussed by President Snow, B. Young, myself, F. M. Lyman, H. J. Grant, J. H. Smith, George Teasdale, and the trend of the discussion was that the said decision was right and my family was wrong in sending their protest to the First Presidency" (Melvin Clarence Merrill, ed., *Utah Pioneer and Apostle Marriner Wood Merrill and His Family* [n. p.: Marriner Wood Merrill Heritage Committee, 1980], 175).

Heber J. Grant said it was revealed to him as he was traveling among the Moquis that he was called to be an apostle because his father according to the flesh, Jedediah M. Grant, and the Prophet Joseph, to whom he rightfully belonged, had requested it. Seymour B. Young was made one of the First Seven Presidents of the Seventies because his father had requested it.

We adjourned to meet on Tuesday, July 10th, at 2 o'clock. We had a hymn and prayer by F. D. Richards....

Friday, April 6, 1894:

I attended to business at the offices till 10 a.m., when I went to the general conference in the tabernacle. All of the Presidency and Twelve were present except Bros. Thatcher and Lund. There was also a good attendance of the Priesthood and people from all parts of Zion. After prayer by Joseph F. Smith Pres. Woodruff expressed his pleasure at the nice weather and favorable circumstances under which we can meet. He was also pleased at the number present, and hoped we will exercise our faith so that nothing may be taught but what the Lord will approve.

I then spoke for 27 minutes on the subject of prayer, and its effects upon those who do pray.

Bro. Merrill followed for 27 minutes, and said we should give more attention to the training of the young so that they will not desire to waste their time in playing cards, and in other things which are injurious. He believes that young men should come up regularly through the various quorums of the Priesthood, so far as it is possible for this to be done.

John W. Taylor spoke 25 minutes on the first principles of the Gospel, taking for his text a part of the first chapter of Galatians....

In the afternoon meeting Heber J. Grant spoke upon the necessity of teaching our children in their youth the way of life and salvation, and not leave them untaught until they grow up, for then they cannot learn as readily. Those people are in error who think it right to let their children grow to man and womanhood before teaching them the Gospel under the plea that they should be allowed to choose for themselves. The Lord tells us to teach our children before they are eight years of age.

George Teasdale reported the condition of the Mexican mission, and said we should be contented to labor where the Lord places us. He then spoke on the first principles of the Gospel.

John Henry Smith spoke of the divisions which sometimes exist in Stakes and Wards because of the decisions which have been given by the Church courts. Thus the spirit of criticism grows, and extends sometimes to the general authorities of the Church. It is improper, and should be overcome by the Saints.

I took Bishop Pratt of Hinckley home with me to supper, and we returned to the Priesthood meeting at 7 o'clock in the Tabernacle. At this meeting Bro. Winder, counselor to Bishop Preston, was the first speaker. He said that about $100,000 had been expended for the benefit of the poor, during the past year, and only about 40% of it had been paid by the people, the remainder having been paid by the tithing office. The tithing has decreased about 25%, and some of the Stakes had used locally 75% of what has been paid.

Father said it is not right for Saints to be moving from one place to another without seeking counsel. They should settle down, and not run to this and that place because some flattering reports are received from some new and good part of the country. We should seek the counsel of the Priesthood where we live, and then follow the advice given. We are not as wise in politics as we should be. In a very short time we will be the most influential people between the two oceans, if we will only be wise, and use the opportunities which God has given us according to the dictates of His spirit. We should not be greedy for office. It is ruinous to communities and individuals. It is this which is a cause of intense party feeling. In the Church men who seek office are not those who are called. We must overcome the feeling of sectionalism. Men should be elected to office not because they come from a certain part of the country, but because they are fitted for the position. We should feel that men will look after the interests of one part of the country as well as they will for another. The mismanagement of affairs in one part of the country where Saints are located, reflects upon all. Do not elect men to office who will take any liberties with public funds. Pres. Young was led to use several forms of baptism during his administration, but it was for a special purpose. We should adhere to the form given in the revelations of the Lord, except as we are instructed otherwise by the man who stands at the head of the Church. In ordaining and blessing people, we should use simple language, and where instructions have been given on these matters we should strictly follow them. In praying we should not be tedious or long....

Pres. Woodruff said that when he was in the midst of a body of men like those present tonight, he feels as though he would like to rent the veil and give them a view of the other world. "I also feel that I would like to have the Presidency and apostles throw off all worldly care and go into the world and preach the Gospel for the last time." He warned us against the false Christs and other bad men who are wandering about trying to deceive the people....

Saturday, April 7, 1894:

I was at the offices till 10 o'clock, when I went to meeting. F. M. Lyman was the first speaker. He spoke of the succession in the Presidency of the Church, and testified to the power held by the present authorities.

Bro. Brigham Young, F. D. Richards and Lorenzo Snow each spoke for a short time on the principles of the Gospel, bearing their testimonies to the truth of this work.

At noon I dictated some letters. In the afternoon the authorities of the Church were sustained,...

Pres. Joseph F. Smith then spoke in favor of the Tabernacle Choir, who should be sustained by the people in their concert this evening, as they need means for the purchase of books, etc.... He said the Presidency deprecate [discourage] card playing and round-dancing, and they desire the Priesthood in the Stakes to set examples before the people which will lead them to abandon these evils. He spoke in opposition to secret societies. They rob men to some extent of their agency, and place yokes upon the necks of members which are grievous to bear. We have every principle in the Church necessary to the temporal or spiritual welfare of the Saints. He spoke against the false doctrines which are being circulated trying to convince people that God, Jesus Christ and the Holy Ghost are one in body. It is our privilege to know the Scriptures, and not be deceived by wicked men....

Sunday, April 8, 1894:

At 10 o'clock I was at meeting, where Pres. Woodruff announced the doctrine of the sealing of children to parents as far back as it is possible to trace the genealogy, and then seal the last member to the Prophet Joseph. He also spoke of wives being permitted to be sealed to their dead husbands who were not in the Church, providing they will run the risk of their receiving the Gospel hereafter.

Father spoke upon this same subject, and showed the excellence of the plan which God has established for the redemption and uniting of the whole human family.

At noon I went home and had dinner with Mina, and in the afternoon according to the request of F. D. Richards went to meeting in the Assembly Hall, which was filled in addition to the large Tabernacle being crowded. The speakers in the meeting were H. J. Grant, myself, Moses Thatcher, Seymour B. Young and F. D. Richards, and the subject of most of our remarks was the revelation concerning the sealing as announced by Pres. Woodruff this morning. In the Tabernacle Father and Pres. Woodruff were the speakers....

Monday, April 9, 1894:

I was in the offices till 10 a.m., when I went to a meeting in the Assembly Hall of the general Church authorities, the Presidents of Stakes, Bishops of Wards and their counselors. After the usual opening exercises Pres. Joseph F. Smith said that when brethren to whom communications have been sent concerning their ability and willingness to take missions bring their replies to Bishops for their endorsements, the Bishops should not merely sign their names, but should certify to the correctness of the statements the letters contain. We want men for missions who are in every way qualified for labor abroad. A certain Bishop came to the Presidency at one time, and wanted to be ordained a deacon, teacher, priest, and elder because he had not held these offices before being made a Bishop. He was told that the Melchizedek Priesthood which was conferred upon him when he was ordained a Bishop embraced all the lesser offices. He was finally satisfied with this explanation, though he had been very unsettled before. While it is advisable for men to be trained in the lesser offices, it is not necessary for them to receive these ordinations if they are called to labor in the more advanced positions.

George Q. Cannon: "In selecting men for missions we should be discriminating, and select those who are fitted for the work. While all are told to thrust in their sickles and reap, all are not fitted for special work, and it needs judgment to determine who are qualified for certain labors. We are anxious to have a normal training school at Provo which will prepare our young people to take positions as teachers in any school in the land. Benjamin Cluff, Jr., has been in the east to gain the information necessary to take charge of such an institution, and we think we have the necessary instructors in our midst to direct such a college as will be second to none in the country. Circulars are being sent out to school trustees asking them how many and what class of teachers they need. These circulars are issued by Gentiles. We should employ our own teachers so far as possible, and not discriminate against those of our faith in favor of non-Mormons. Chancellor Harkness of the University of Utah said he was in favor of our Utah raised teachers."

Brigham Young: " I know of some young men who were ordained deacons who allowed the Bishop to do all their work. They were not properly trained. Some young men who go on missions are totally unfit for the labor required of them. One young man who had been in the mission a month came to me and confessed he had sinned at home so as to be unworthy of the Priesthood. He said he only came on a mission because of public opinion at home being in favor of such a course. Another young man came to Liverpool and had Utah cow-dung on his boots, he not having had sense enough to clean his boots during the whole trip. We should train and instruct our young men at home before we send them abroad."

F. M. Lyman: "Because the Stake High Counselors are called upon to sustain the decision of the Stake President, some of them seem to think they are at liberty to criticize the decision rendered, and to call to account this presiding officer. Apostles are authorized by the Presidency to regulate all the Stakes of Zion, but High Councilors do not possess this authority. They are not even empowered to travel in the Stakes and regulate matters there, except as they are called to do so by the Stake Presidency. When the Presidency of a Stake formulate a decision it must be sustained by the High Council of a Stake, in which case it becomes a High Council decision, and a President has no right to change it in and of himself. Superior courts should always try to sustain the decisions of the lower courts unless there is something radically wrong with the decision already rendered. Presidents of Stakes should always consult with their counselors in making up their decisions. Where the majority of the High Councilors are opposed to the decision, a re-hearing must be had. Thereafter, if not decided, the case should be sent to the Presidency of the Church."

Question by Anthony Ivins: "Should High Councils try property rights?" Answer by Father: "Where legal rights are involved it should be determined by the courts of the land, but equitable rights may be considered by the Church tribunals." In answer to another question it was said that where the two counselors to a Bishop disagree with him, it does not become a decision. Uncle Angus Cannon referred to a ruling of Pres. Taylor to the effect that the decision of a Bishop was superior to the objection of both of his counselors. Father said that the question had not been submitted by Pres. Taylor to his counselors, or they would have opposed such a conclusion. Pres. Woodruff upheld the view first mentioned.

In blessing people only the one who is mouth should speak aloud, and the others should not mumble his words, but should repeat them mentally. P. P. Pratt says the first confirmations of the Church were performed mentally and not orally. It is improper and unnecessary for all Saints coming to Utah from abroad to be baptized. This ordinance should not be made too common. It should only be administered when the candidate is cut off from the Church or disfellowshipped. Men who go to the temples should be ordained Elders before they come there, or in the Wards to which they belong. Garments worn by those who have been through the temple should be made of white material. Union knit suits, such as some of the sisters wear, are not proper to be worn as temple garments, but if used at all, should be over the garments. It is not always necessary for those who go to the temple to be re-baptized. Sometimes where people have not known the date of their first baptism, they have been re-baptized so as to get the record complete. A Bishop and one counselor can make a decision, but not two counselors alone. People who leave off their garments are not in good standing in the Church. We should be wise in political matters, as the eyes of the nation are upon us. No man who joins the various secret societies and takes their oaths, is worthy of a recommend to go to the temple. They draw away from us, and are bound to sustain their own members against all others. Pres. Woodruff here said: "Such are not worthy to go to the temple or bear the Priesthood."

George Teasdale: "We do not want the people to come to our settlements in Mexico who smoke and drink, or do other wrong things. We want men who will obey counsel, and not play cards, round dance, etc., and who will live honorable and good lives."

Pres. Woodruff: "I traveled thousands of miles as a priest and baptized people I had not the authority to confirm. Boys should be called early to the Priesthood so that they become acquainted with its duties. Encourage fast-day donations and the payment of tithes in your Stakes. Some of us belonged to a Masonic Lodge in Nauvoo, but no good came of it. We found fellow-members were plotting against the Church leaders, and seeking their death. We should not join the Masons, Odd Fellows or other such organizations." We were dismissed about one o'clock by prayer by Pres. Lorenzo Snow....

Thursday, April 12, 1894:

At two o'clock I was at my quorum meeting. Present: All of the Presidency, L. Snow, F. D. Richards, Brigham Young, F. M. Lyman, J. H. Smith, George Teasdale and myself; G. Gibbs clerk. Bro. Lyman said a woman had come to him with the request that her mother, whose husband died in the Church, but was demented, be released from her father, and be sealed to Bro. Lyman. The latter did not want the President to consent for this to be done, and his desire was granted, and the woman is to be told to leave her father sealed to her mother as is now the case. It was decided that men who persist in calling themselves the Savior, King David, and other ancient worthies, and thus lead away some weak-minded people, should be handled for their fellowship, and that prominent cases of this kind be published as a warning to others.

The circular concerning baptism was read and considered, but as there was some difference of opinion concerning the wording of it, the subject was laid aside for future consideration. Pres. Snow said that in the days of Kirtland some of the apostates questioned the right of Joseph Smith to receive revelation on certain matters. Brigham Young arose, and placing the Bible, Book of Mormon and Doctrine and Covenants together said, "I do not care for what these books contain, when I have the revelations of God to me at the present time. I am guided by present revelation."...[13]

Father said...we ought to control the newspapers, the hotels and the livery stables for our own safety and good repute. God has sustained us so far, and I feel that he will continue to do so, and will bring us out of our difficulties with credit and honor. It is remarkable how we have got along. We look at what appears to be a mountain, but as we approach it in faith, the Lord removes it from our way....

Sunday, April 15, 1894:

I took the 8:05 a.m. train for Provo, and at ten o'clock was at the Quarterly Conference. After the presenting of the authorities John Henry Smith spoke for a short time, but his remarks were so disconnected and uninteresting that I could not follow him. He was followed for a short time by Edward Partridge who spoke of the United Order, and the good results which would follow its acceptance by the Saints. F. M. Lyman occupied the remainder of the

---

[13] This is a condensed version of a story told by President Woodruff as found in Conference Report, Oct. 1897, 22-23.

time in a very good discourse on debt, economy, and kindred subjects. He advised the people to pay what they are owing, and then to keep out of debt....

Monday, April 16, 1894:

Henry McEwan was thrown from his buggy yesterday, and died from the effects of the accident this morning. He was one of the pioneer printers, and a good man in his way....

Wednesday, April 18, 1894:

At two o'clock I attended the funeral of Henry McEwan in the Twelfth Ward Meeting House. There was a large attendance of Saints and strangers. George Teasdale spoke for a short time on the hopes which the Gospel gives us in the presence of death. I spoke for 15 minutes on the kind nature of the dead [deceased], and urged his sons to be true to their God. I also advised the friends to be kind to the widow and fatherless. James E. Talmage spoke of the change our bodies undergo by death, and said we are not lost by this ordeal, but enter into a new sphere of life. Charles W. Penrose occupied a few minutes in speaking of the resurrection....

Thursday, April 19, 1894:

At 2 o'clock I was at my Quorum meeting in the temple. Present: W. Woodruff, Joseph F. Smith, L. Snow, F. D. Richards, M. Thatcher, F. M. Lyman, J. H. Smith, George Teasdale and H. J. Grant, as well as myself; G. F. Gibbs clerk....

Pres. Woodruff said he felt to leave adoptions of the past remain as they are with few exceptions.

Pres. Woodruff said that in 1834 he was in a meeting to which the Prophet invited him, held in Kirtland. Joseph said, after several of the brethren had borne 5 minute testimonies, that they did not have any idea of the magnitude of the work in which they are engaged. It will go to the Rocky Mountains, and will eventually fill all of North and South America. When this prediction was made we were all in a little log cabin....

Thursday, April 26, 1894:

At 2 o'clock I went to my Quorum meeting. Present: Brothers W. Woodruff, J. F. Smith, L. Snow, F. D. Richards, B. Young, F. M. Lyman, J. H. Smith, H. J. Grant, J. W. Taylor and myself; George F. Gibbs, clerk.... Conference appointments were made. It was asked if John D. Lee, a son of the Mountain Meadows murderer, who is a good man, and is called on a mission, should go. It was decided that he should go to England, but assume his mother's maiden name.

A letter from Willard Snow of Ogden was read in which he asks advice about withdrawing from the secret society known as the Ancient Order of United Workmen. He says no oaths against our principles are administered, and he only went into the society because of the life insurance it affords him at a cheap rate. The brethren decided that it is best for all our brethren to disunite themselves from such organizations....

Thursday, May 3, 1894:

Attended my Quorum meeting at 2 o'clock. Present: Bros. W. Woodruff, J. F. Smith, L. Snow, F. D. Richards, F. M. Lyman, H. J. Grant, J. W. Taylor and myself; G. F. Gibbs, clerk.... After the conference appointments were made the appeal of the Hedrickites for financial aid was presented. They desire to carry the case of the Jackson County temple lot to the U. S. Supreme Court for adjudication, but they have not sufficient means with which to do it. The whole community is only worth $3,000. We decided that our Church is in no position at present to give them the aid they desire.

In response to a question of mine it was decided that there is no objections to our young men joining the Utah militia. Indeed the law may require them later to join, if they do not now become members of their own free will and choice....

Thursday, May 10, 1894:

At 2 o'clock I was at my Quorum meeting. Present: W. Woodruff, Joseph F. Smith, L. Snow, F. D. Richards, F. M. Lyman, H. J. Grant and myself; George F. Gibbs, clerk....

Past adoptions, it is decided by Pres. Woodruff, are to remain unchanged, but where desirable sealings may be cancelled.

It is not advisable for the Twelve, except in rare cases, to perform marriage ceremonies between those of our Church and Gentiles....

Sunday, May 20, 1894, [Salina, Sevier Co.]:

Speaking of Salina and the great number of non-Mormons living there, he [Bro. Jensen, a local leader] said that Pres. Brigham Young once said that it would require a very good Saint to live in Salina, and not lose the faith, as the spot on which the city is built has been the scene of many an ancient battle in times when the Nephites and Lamanites were at war with each other. The pass through the mountains is the lowest here of any place in the Wasatch range. The spirits of the ancient dead still hover around this place. Bro. Jensen says it seems as though all the apostates gravitate to this place....[14]

Monday, May 21, 1894 [Richfield, Sevier Co.]:

Heber [J. Grant] spoke 20 minutes on the powers and rights of the Priesthood, and I then spoke 45 minutes on love in families, conduct of young people, etc. Pres. Seegmiller then said a few words, expressing pleasure at our visit and the instructions which had been given. Conference then adjourned. The Elsinore choir furnished the singing, and during the services yesterday they sang a piece to the words "O my Father," which Bro. Durrans of Parowan received in a dream. He dreamed that he saw a Navajo blanket floating down a river, and as he watched it, he suddenly saw several Indians appear on it. They came to the shore where he stood, and one of them placed an instrument to his mouth something like a clarinet, on which he played the tune which was rendered, with the exception of one high note which he could not reach. Bro. Durrans arose and wrote out the piece. Sometime thereafter a birthday party was given at his house when one of the brethren spoke in tongues. In the course of his remarks he said that this tune was the one used by the ancient

---

[14] For further information on this subject, see Duane S. Crowther, *Life Everlasting* (Salt Lake City: Bookcraft, 1967), 164-66.

Nephites, just before the last remnant was slain at the Hill Cumorah about the year 421 A. D. It was a kind of lamentation....

Thursday, May 31, 1894:

At 2 o'clock I was at my Quorum meeting, at which all of the First Presidency were present, as well as L. Snow, F. D. Richards, F. M. Lyman, H. J. Grant and myself; George F. Gibbs, clerk....

...Pres. Snow reported that one of the basement rooms in the Temple had been converted into a vault for the safe-keeping of books. The report was accepted, and he was authorized to make whatever other changes he thought necessary for the good of the library....

Saturday, June 2, 1894:

I was in the offices a good part of the day, and had one of the most trying financial experiences of my life. A [*Deseret*] *News* office check was protested, we had no means with which to pay the *News* employees, and Dooley asked me to get Father's endorsement to a guarantee for our $15,000 overdraft. Father had me at the President's office, where he complained at my failure to give him a report of the *News* and *Juvenile* offices condition. His complaint is well-founded, and I intend to try and avoid giving him cause to find fault in the future. An attorney came to see me about the *History* account due Streicher, one of the canvassers, who threatens suit unless his account is paid in full. Skelton of Provo, who owes the balance of over $400 on an unpaid note, came to tell us he can do nothing at present, and apologize for his past failures to keep his word with us. Altogether I have had a most trying day, and one which I hope the Lord will enable me to avoid in my future experience....[15]

Sunday, June 10, 1894:

I then went to...the funeral of Francis A. Brown.... The building was completely filled, and the coffin was covered with flowers. Pres.

---

[15] For further information regarding Elder Cannon's financial circumstances, see the biographical essay.

Joseph F. Smith spoke for an hour concerning the dead, and said that Bro. Brown was one of the most perfect men he ever knew. F. D. Richards made a few remarks, and I then spoke about 15 minutes concerning my acquaintance with Bro. Brown, and his many excellent characteristics. I also told of the spirits of Apostle Merrill's parents having visited him after their death, and of I having seen my mother when I was dead during the typhoid fever, all of which proved to me that the spirits of the dead are not far removed from the earth....

Wednesday, June 13, 1894:

In the forenoon a man who had lost his horses, came to ask me where they could be found. He said he thought of going to a woman clairvoyant, but thought best to come to a prophet of the Lord to tell him where his animals could be found. I could give him no aid, and not knowing what counsel to impart, referred him to the Presidency....

Thursday, June 14, 1894:

I was in the offices most of the day, until 2 o'clock, when I went to my Quorum meeting. At this meeting there were present all of the Presidency, L. Snow, F. D. Richards, F. M. Lyman, J. H. Smith, H. J. Grant and myself; G. F Gibbs, clerk.... Thereafter we had some talk about L. D. Hickey, the present head of the Strangite organization, who has come out to Utah to see and talk to the Saints concerning the principles of the gospel, and give his testimony and views. He called to see me this morning, and had some conversation with me. He says the only difference between the Church to which he belongs and ours is that we believe the succession of the Presidency came through Brigham Young, and he believes it came through James J. Strang. It was decided that the Twelve should meet with him on Tuesday next, and hear what he has to say.[16]

---

[16] James J. Strang organized a splinter church after the succession crisis of 1844 and his excommunication. He claimed to have received a blessing from Joseph Smith designating him as his successor and to have translated some plates called the Book of the Law of the Lord. For further information, see James B. Allen and Glen M.

It was decided today that in cases where women had been sealed to men who were not their first husbands, and children who were not united to their natural fathers, these ordinances might now be performed for the dead husbands and fathers, in accordance with the instructions given at the last Conference, without referring each particular case to the President of the Church. In this case, however, no change will be made in the old records....

Tuesday, June 19, 1894:

At 10:30, as per appointment I went to the Historian's office to meet with the Strangite Apostle Lorenzo Dow Hickey, who wanted to see and talk with the apostles. Through the forgetfulness of Pres. Snow, he did not come at the time appointed, and F. D. Richards, F. M. Lyman, John H. Smith, H. J. Grant and myself waited for him over an hour, though we talked during this time with our visitor, who is 78 years old, and was baptized into the Church of Jesus Christ of Latter-day Saints 42 years ago, he professing still to be a believer in Mormonism, but feeling that James J. Strang was the proper leader instead of Brigham Young. He told of having heard Martin Harris preach in a Quaker meeting-house, when he was 16 years old, and a member of the Methodist Church, Martin at that time having been engaged with Joseph Smith in the work of translation. The Quakers gave Martin permission to preach to them in their house providing he would not use the manuscript of the Book of Mormon for reference, which was agreed to by the preacher. When Martin became engrossed in his testimony, he drew from his pocket a part of the Manuscript, at which all the audience arose, and quietly left the building.

Bro. Sirrine baptized this man Hickey into the Church, and Hickey being a good preacher, was immediately ordained an Elder, and sent out with Bro. Sirrine to preach. In their travels around they were followed and opposed by the father of Hickey, who was a rank Methodist. The abuse of this man became almost unendurable, and

---

Leonard, *The Story of the Latter-day Saints* (Salt Lake City: Deseret Book, 1992), 251.

one evening after he had been particularly abusive Bro. Sirrine said, "The Lord will curse that man, if He ever spoke by my mouth." The son said he responded "Amen." The persecutor did not believe any misfortune would follow this curse, and would frequently say, "The curse of the Mormon has not hurt me yet." The son now says, however, that after the curse was uttered, misfortune seemed to follow the old gentleman, and his cattle would die in the yard during the night, and other disasters followed, and when the man was old he swelled up, turned nearly black and died.

When Bro. Snow came he engaged in prayer at Hickey's request, and then Bro. Snow called on him to say what he desired. The old gentleman arose, and in a very solemn manner told of his conversion to the Church, and thereafter to Strangism. He says his testimony of the one is just as strong as of the other, and he knows that both Joseph Smith and James J. Strang were prophets of God. He showed us the book, which Strang claims to have translated from brass plates given him by an angel, and which he afterwards returned to the angel. It is called, *The Book of the Law of the Lord*, and purports to be a translation of some of the writings of Moses. Strang also received other plates which were found in the roots of a tree in Voree, in Wisconsin, and which plates were also translated, though these are not so voluminous as the other writings. These latter plates are still in existence, being now owned by a man living in Missouri. This man, who is an apostle of the Strangite Church, which organization is now broken up by the scattering of its 500 members, wants the Lord to move upon our hearts to print and scatter broadcast among the people this Book of the Law. He says Joseph Smith [III], the leader of the Re-organized Church is the real Patriarch of the Church, but he is not nor can he be the leader of the people.

While the old gentleman is perhaps unduly zealous, one cannot but admire his pluck in coming out here, and his fidelity to the cause with which he has been so long associated. He has been a polygamist, and believes it is right for good men to have more than one wife. We talked with him till 1:30,…

Thursday, June 21, 1894:

At two o'clock I was at my Quorum meeting, where all of the Presidency were present, as well as Bros. L. Snow, F. D. Richards, F. M. Lyman, J. H. Smith, H. J. Grant and myself, with George F. Gibbs as clerk. We…attended to considerable business. A report was given of our interview with Mr. Hickey of the Strangite Church, and of a meeting which Bros. Lyman and J. H. Smith had with him this morning in which they told him he was deluded and advised him to repent and be baptized. He laughed at their warning, however, and seems to be set in his religion.

It was decided that where people receive the Gospel in the world, they should not be encouraged to emigrate until they are firmly grounded in the religion by labor and experience, and especially where they are in good situations, with good wages shall they not be encouraged to emigrate to this place, where labor is so scarce.…

Thursday, June 28, 1894:

In the afternoon I was at my Quorum meeting. Present: All the Presidency, L. Snow, F. D. Richards, F. M. Lyman, H. J. Grant and myself; George F. Gibbs clerk. There was some talk about the Mexican Colonization Company, of which several of the apostles are members, and it was decided that others in Colorado and Mexico shall be chosen to fill their places. The Presidency of the San Luis Stake were recommended for positions on the Board.

We next had some talk about the Holy Ghost being a son of God as much as the Savior is, only that he does not possess a body of flesh and bones. This talk was called out by some remarks of Bro. Lyman in Sanpete to the effect that the Holy Ghost has a distinct entity, and is a son of God. While the general view is that this statement is correct yet it is not thought advisable to teach it, for we speak of conferring upon the members of the Church the Holy Ghost, which is impossible, if he is a person. The general view is that the power and force of the Holy Ghost is or may be likened to the sun in our firmament, which though a distinct body sheds abroad its light and warmth upon the earth and other planets. Joseph Smith says in one of the Lectures on Faith in the Doctrine and Covenants that two persons comprise the Godhead, and yet we believe in the Triunity. In another place he says the Holy Ghost is a personage of spirit, hence while the Holy Ghost is a spirit, and may be born of God, yet it is the mind of God and Jesus Christ, and is their agent, possessing power to fill the hearts of men, and to exist in inanimate things, giving them light and heat, as is the case with the sun, as explained in the revelations to Joseph Smith,…

Wednesday, July 11, 1894:

I was in the offices till ten o'clock, attending to business, and then went to the Temple to our regular Quarterly Quorum meeting. Present: Pres. Lorenzo Snow, F. D. Richards, H. J. Grant, M. W. Merrill and myself. Most of the other brethren were unavoidably absent, but Moses Thatcher should have been here. It was felt by the brethren that Bro. Snow should take up a labor with him because of his neglect of his meetings, even when he could just as well attend as not, he does not come. We spent the time till about 1:15 in reading that portion of the history which Bro. F. D. Richards had prepared. It was very interesting, as it was a narration of the events immediately preceding and following the martyrdom of Joseph and Hyrum. Bro. Grant and I alternated in reading. We adjourned our meeting till 2 o'clock on Tuesday, October 2nd of the present year.…

Thursday, July 12, 1894:

At two o'clock I went to my Quorum meeting in the temple at which were present President Wilford Woodruff, Father, L. Snow, F. D. Richards, H. J. Grant, M. W. Merrill and myself; George F. Gibbs, clerk.… We had some talk about the care of our poor. It is said that each emigrant from England, who is converted to the Gospel, costs in cash and time the sum of $2,000. It therefore seems too bad that they should be neglected after arriving here, and be allowed to become discouraged through lack of employment, and so often lose the faith. Father felt that the presiding Bishopric should take this matter in hand and see that our worthy poor are employed.

It was voted that the Logan temple hands be docked in their wages for one month's pay while the building is being cleansed, and they are at home....

Friday, July 13, 1894:

I was with Father at the President's office for a short time in the afternoon while he was explaining to Bros. George Romney, George H. Taylor and Francis Armstrong his ruined financial situation. He did so because their firm were dunning him for the payment of a note which Father endorsed for William, and which the latter is unable to pay. After he had told them how he was situated, all said they would not press him, but would like him to do something for them as soon as he possibly could. I felt very much humiliated to hear him talk to them as he felt compelled to do, and I very much wished William had been there to hear what was said....[17]

Saturday, July 14, 1894:

I was in the offices a good part of the day attending to my usual work. I found it necessary to reduce the working time of the employees of the *Juvenile* bindery one-third, and consequently reduced the weekly pay-roll an equal sum. They all felt well about it, and said they would prefer to work part of the time than to be laid off entirely....

Tuesday, July 17, 1894:

Pres. Cleveland today signed the Utah Statehood bill. This will enable us to become a State in the year 1896.... This constitution is then to be presented to Congress, and if approved will give our senators their seats on March 4, 1896....

In the evening I...went to my German Society.... Bro. Schoenfeld spoke of his having joined the Church, and said he was then in the German army, where he completed his six years' service.... He also told of the translation of the Book of Mormon in the French

---

[17] President George Q. Cannon often signed notes, something like co-signing a loan, for his children, and therefore obligated himself for their financial setbacks. For further information, see the biographical essay.

language by Lois Bertrand, under the direction of John Taylor and the presentation of a copy to Louis Napoleon III, who rejected it, and caused that Bro. Bertrand was exiled from his native land. It is a strange coincidence that Napoleon should himself be subsequently exiled, and die in this condition in a foreign land. Bro. Schoenfeld spoke of a prophecy made many years ago by Orson Pratt, which said that the sons of native born Germans would yet carry the Gospel to Germany, and open the door to that nation from which their fathers had been exiled, as in early years some of the native-born members of the Church had been banished from their homes because of their religion....

Thursday, July 26, 1894:

At two o'clock I was at my Quorum meeting in the Temple at which all of the Presidency were present, as well as L. Snow, F. D. Richards, B. Young, F. M. Lyman, J. H. Smith, H. J. Grant and myself; George F. Gibbs was clerk. ...We had some talk about statehood, and the brethren were advised to sustain the movement, but to encourage our people to avoid the lust for office, and to be a little modest in their desires for position....

Thursday, August 16, 1894:

At two o'clock I went to my quorum meeting. Present: Presidents Woodruff and Smith, Lorenzo Snow, Francis M. Lyman, Heber J. Grant and myself; George F Gibbs, clerk....

Concerning the proper position of the altar in a prayer circle—as to whether it should face the east or south—there is no rule, though the custom is to generally have them face the south. Pres. Snow says he always aims to face the chief temple in offering his prayers.

It was decided that the circles over which the Twelve preside be permitted to meet in the Elders' room, instead of in the basement where the ventilation is so bad, and the room so small....

Thursday, August 23, 1894:

At two o'clock I went to my Quorum meeting in the temple at which there were present: Pres. Woodruff, L. Snow, Moses Thatcher,

John H. smith and myself; George F. Gibbs clerk. Pres. Woodruff's counselors were in Ogden today on some business. We spent most of the time in talking over old experiences in the Church. The brethren told of the way in which Pres. Joseph Smith and Brigham Young sometimes scored brethren from the stand who had not done as they ought to have done. Those brethren who took these whippings meekly and kept the faith have been since blessed of the Lord. It is a remarkable fact that each man who has presided over the Church has been thus tried in his feelings by his superior officer....

Friday, August 24, 1894:

I had some talk with Frank in the forenoon about the demands of Col. Trumbo and Gen. J. S. Clarkson for pay for their services in securing statehood for Utah. They doubtless worked hard, and did much good, but the price they ask is very high, for Trumbo not only wants a senatorship, but he and Clarkson also ask a heavy interest in the proposed railway from this city to California. They have doubtless promised the friends who worked for Utah's admission many things that will not be in the power of Father, and others who are associated in the railway enterprise to fulfill. Father is worrying himself sick over the matter,...

Sunday, August 26, 1894:

I went to the Fifth Ward meeting in the evening...I then spoke for an hour on the prophecies which must yet be fulfilled before Christ comes, warning the people not to place any private interpretation on the scriptures, but in reading them to try and be filled with the spirit by which they were written.

Tuesday, August 28, 1894:

In the evening I rode down with Father, who told me of the relief he felt from placing the deals between the Presidency and Trumbo and Clarkson about railroad matters in the hands of Frank Cannon, Nephi Clayton and W. W. Cluff, who are to thus relieve the brethren of the annoyances which have heretofore worried them sick....

Thursday, August 30, 1894:

At two o'clock I went to my Quorum meeting. Before engaging in our council, we looked around the temple grounds a little, and decided about the erection of a fence so as to permit visitors to walk around the temple and view the grounds….

The Josephites claim that at the organization of the First Presidency after the death of the Prophet Joseph, he [Wilford Woodruff] opposed Brigham Young's appointment, and say he saw no remarkable manifestations such as are described by Orson Hyde, wherein the ground shook to such an extent that the people ran from their houses in order to see the cause of the commotion. It is President Woodruff to whom I am now referring as having taken this part against Pres. Young. Pres. Woodruff says this is not true, for in all things he was united with the Prophet Brigham. He says he does not remember any particular manifestations at the time of the organization of the Presidency….

Friday, September 7, 1894:

I was at my usual work most of the day. I met with Elmina S. Taylor and her two counselors, Marie Y. Dougal and Mattie S. Tingey, and Susa Y. Gates in the afternoon to talk over *Young Women's Journal* matters. I told them I thought the magazine was doing very well considering its youth and the dullness of business generally. They all promised to do all they could for its success in the future….

[3 lines were cut from the original journal entry for Thursday, September 20, 1894. Six words remain readable next to the left margin of the page.
today told…
to Walter W…
intention to…]

[September 22, to the first half of September 27, 1894 has been removed, including one page having been torn out of the original journal.]

Thursday, September 27, 1894:

At two o'clock I went to my Quorum meeting at which were present Father, Joseph F. Smith, L. Snow, F. D. Richards, B. Young, F. M. Lyman, J. H. Smith, H. J. Grant and myself; George F. Gibbs clerk....

We then had some talk as to whether or not it was advisable for the brethren of this Quorum, and the priesthood generally to register and vote. It was thought best for them to do so where they safely can, but most of the brethren present today felt that they cannot conscientiously take the prescribed oath. While in meeting a message came saying that Pres. Cleveland has granted a new amnesty to all who have been convicted of polygamy or cohabitation, restoring to them all their civil rights, providing they have lived according to the law since the amnesty proclamation of Benjamin Harrison. It is this latter clause which bears the sting, and works against so many of our people, myself included....

Friday, September 28, 1894:

The Utah Commission today modified the registration oath to agree with the President's Amnesty proclamation, so that a person only has to swear that he will observe the laws of the country, and especially the one relating to polygamy and cohabitation in order to be allowed to vote. I could very well take the oath in its present form, but think I had better not do so.

[The entries for September 29 and the first part of 30 have been snipped from the journal and amount to approximately 10 missing lines.]

Tuesday, October 2, 1894:

At two o'clock I met with my Quorum in the temple. All of the members were present excepting Bro. A. H. Lund, who is in England on a mission.... Pres. Snow addressed a few words to us and then gave the meeting into our hands....

I was first called to speak, and in my remarks referred to the great increase of sexual sins in the territory, and said I had heard of some of our people using preventatives to conception. I told of my faith in the promise given us sometime since by Pres. Snow that the Lord would assist us this once out of our financial difficulties. I hoped this help would be soon given. I referred to the public feeling with the people on account of the association of the Presidency with Col. Trumbo, who is a corrupt fellow.

Bro. Merrill spoke of the great work to be done in the temples for the salvation of the living and the dead, and felt that the Saints should be kept alive on the subject. He referred to the evils of debt, and hoped the Church and individuals would soon be relieved.

John W. Taylor made a very few remarks expressing the desire that the Lord will bless us in our meetings.

Heber J. Grant spoke at some length on the Word of Wisdom, and expressed a hope that something might be done to check the evil, which now seems to be rapidly growing....

Wednesday, October 3, 1894:

I was at my Quorum meeting at ten o'clock, which was opened by prayer by Brigham Young. George Teasdale spoke of the trials which he and the Saints have undergone in Mexico, because the government has imposed unlawful taxes on them, and other difficulties have arisen which have tried them. Nevertheless, they have been blessed by the Lord, and are happy.

John Henry Smith spoke briefly of the political situation, and said he feared a revival of the old "liberal" party, unless we use wisdom in our affairs.

Francis M. Lyman said that we must sustain the Presidency in all they do. It is not our privilege to set them right if they are wrong, but that belongs to God. They have a right to call us into question. He hoped the Lord will help us out of debt. About half of the Twelve are in this bondage, and unless the Lord does come to our rescue it looks as though we would fail. This load of debt injures our influence to some extent.

Some people feel that men who have children by their plural wives commit adultery. He has tried to correct this feeling wherever he has met it.

He felt that fasting and prayer should be more faithfully observed by the Saints than it generally is.

Moses Thatcher said he believed that Statehood would bring us so much relief that we can live with the wives we now have unmolested, and many other blessings will we enjoy.

At 12 o'clock we took our adjournment till 4 o'clock....

At 4 o'clock the Quorum met again. Brigham Young spoke first. He thinks the principal items now needing our attention, and those which are most neglected are the paying of tithing and the Word of Wisdom. There are many things going on with the authorities which he cannot understand, but he always feels that they are right. When the Bullion, Beck and Champion Mining Co. was organized he did not feel right about it, but he prayed to the Lord and thus received information that it was proper for the brethren to engage in that enterprise. My faith is that the Lord will see us safely through all our difficulties if we will not complain of Him or His servants. The Presidency have too much to do. They should leave the trifling things which occupy so much of their time to others who can just as well attend to them, and they should devote themselves to the weightier things of the Church.

John W. Taylor said he did not feel under obligations to sustain the Presidency in anything about which they did not consult him and the Twelve, and he rather complained of their organizing the Utah Company for profit, when they had rebuked him for his efforts to make money out of the sale of lands to the brethren and strangers. Bros. Thatcher and Richards both mildly rebuked Bro. Taylor for the spirit he manifested. Pres. Snow spoke of the great apostasy in Kirtland, and said we must not partake of such a spirit. Sidney Rigdon one day spoke boastfully of his riches, and said God had given him his wealth because of his faithfulness, but when the Kirtland bank broke all his supposed wealth was gone, and he and Joseph had to flee for their lives. The failure of this bank was necessary in order to reveal the hypocrites who were in that place.

At six o'clock we adjourned till tomorrow, I offering the benediction....

Thursday, October 4, 1894:

At this time I met with my Quorum, all the brethren being present excepting Bro. Thatcher, and he came about noon. Prayer was offered by John Henry Smith. Each of the brethren then occupied about 10 or 15 minutes in speaking . I inquired what was to be done in the case of men who persistently disregarded the Word of Wisdom, the law of Tithing, and who neglected their plural families. The only answer I received [was] that such [a] person should be considered weak in the faith.

Bro. Merrill once said that if all the people would pay an honest tithing he would agree to call on them for no other donation of any kind.

John W. Taylor had nothing to say.

Heber J. Grant said he believed we would be more blessed in sustaining the Presidency in things we do not understand than in those things about which we are consulted, still I wish that our leaders would consult us about matters of such importance as the Utah company, because sooner or later we will have something to do with it. He expressed a wish to do just as the Presidency desire.

Pres. Snow felt that we should keep in the utmost secrecy the proceedings and counsels of our meetings. "I do not care what the brethren say so long as they close with the desire to do as our leaders direct."

George Teasdale said he had heard Erastus Snow say that ordinances and temple labors done by such as do not pay their tithing, observe the Word of Wisdom or who neglect their families will be of no avail. The Aaronic priesthood embraces the law of tithing, and these lesser matters, but to the Melchizedek priesthood belongs the law of consecration.

John Henry Smith said that Gen. McCook said to him that he would despise any man who would desert his plural wives. "I was called out last night to visit a child sick nigh unto death with the typhoid fever, whose father scarcely ever visits it. I felt that the Lord would punish such a man."

Francis M. Lyman said that some of the apostles and leading men in breaking the Word of Wisdom do more harm than all the other brethren by their teaching can do good. I do not believe there is any proper excuse for any person in the Church to break the Word of Wisdom. It is dangerous ground for me to take to try and weaken the influence of the Presidency. It is the invariable rule that God blesses those who stand by the brethren. We should sustain them fully, for it is not our place to correct them, and the people should sustain us with equal diligence.

Brigham Young said Patriarch John Smith would have been asked to resign or keep the Word of Wisdom during the time of his father had it not been for the pleadings of Joseph F. Smith. Pres. Young and others desired to make Joseph F. Smith the patriarch of the Church. If this had been done we would have had a prophet and patriarch equal to those who were slain in Carthage Jail. He spoke of Trumbo's influence with the Presidency which he had deplored, and also felt some little disappointment when John Q. became the editor of the Church organ. Still he had defended as best he could these matters before the people.

Franklin D. Richards felt it to be the duty of the brethren to steady the ark, for this was the labor of the priesthood in days of old, and he only was slain who attempted to do it because he did not hold the priesthood.

After a few remarks by Pres. Snow of an encouraging character, our meeting adjourned till the second Tuesday in January at 2 o'clock p.m.

We now prepared the sacrament, which was blessed by Pres. Snow, and we ate of it in company with Father and Joseph F. Smith, who joined us. Pres. Woodruff was too sick with a severe cold to be present. This done Father and Joseph F. Smith addressed us in regard to our duties as the leaders of the people. The latter was very vehement in telling us that our duties required us to be out among the people, teaching them the ways of God, instead of spending our time at home with our business. He said in substance, to me, "Here is Bro. Abram H. Cannon with the work of two or three men on his shoulders. I say to him in the name of Israel's God that it is his duty to get relieved as soon as possible, and get out among the people." He also felt that the apostles should be relieved of work in the temples.

The counselors to the President should also travel and not be shut up to do the work which clerks can be hired to do. When he had finished his remarks Father and several of the brethren spoke in a more moderate way, but all felt desirous that more work should be done by the apostles among the people than is now the case....

Friday, October 5, 1894:

I was at the offices dictating letters till ten o'clock when I went to the conference, at which the attendance of the priesthood and people was very good. All of the Presidency and eleven of the Twelve were present. Father gave a synopsis of the work which is being done at home and abroad. He encouraged the Presidency of the various Stakes to call young men to labor in the ministry at home among the people. Advised all to seek for revelation, which it is their privilege to enjoy, that all their labors may be approved of God. Elders are now told not to encourage the too speedy gathering of new converts to the truth from foreign lands, but rather to leave those baptized for a time in their homes till their faith and experience in the Gospel gives them some stability.

Brigham Young was the next speaker. He felt that it was time for the people to observe the Word of Wisdom and the law of tithing, so that the land may be sanctified to the people. He heard from this stand twenty years ago that this revelation was now a command of the Lord, and we cannot therefore afford to disregard it.[18] He felt that we had already had talk enough about these principles, and we should now begin to carry them out.

Joseph F. Smith: "We are needing missionaries to labor in Norway, Sweden, Holland, Germany, the Holy Land and other places, but young men who fail to keep the Word of Wisdom, are not worthy to fill these positions. If the Saints would refrain from the use of those things which are forbidden there would remain in the territory enough money to pay all our debts.

---

[18] This account agrees with the official reason (as given in Church handbooks) for considering the Word of Wisdom a requirement instead of simply a wise suggestion—that Church leaders had earlier declared it a commandment to the Church.

At noon I was at the office attending to business.

Met at two o'clock, and listened to Apostle Snow speak. He said we will have difficulties to meet, but the Lord has placed incentives to do right before us. If we are faithful we will become as God is, and enjoy all the blessings and privileges of so exalted a being.

Francis M. Lyman: Those who sin after having once been forgiven will have all their former sins return to them. Bishops depend too little on the Fast-day donations for the care of the poor, and too much upon the tithes. The people should be encouraged to pay their donations, and strictly observe the monthly fast which the Lord has instituted. In our Fast Meetings we should pray for those who are in any kind of distress, as well as to occupy the time in bearing testimony.

John Henry Smith spoke on the subject of prayer, and urged the people to observe family devotions.

At the close of this meeting I went to the offices for a short time and attended to business, and then also in the German meeting for a few moments, but sat in the back part of the building so that I would not be called to speak....

At 7 o'clock I was at the Priesthood meeting....

Heber J. Grant spoke strongly in favor of helping the poor, and concerning the paying of tithes. He knew the Lord would bless those who are faithful in attending to these duties. Father also made some good remarks on the same subjects. He said God would take away the power of any person who seeks to weaken the influence of the Presidency and leading men. These men have been called to their positions by the Lord. He also spoke in favor of funds being raised to complete the statue of Pres. Brigham Young. Meeting then adjourned.

Saturday, October 6, 1894:

I was at the offices a short time in the morning, and then went to the temple, where the Twelve met to select a suitable person to fill the vacancy in the First Seven Presidents of Seventies, caused by the death of John Morgan. The following brethren were nominated: Richard W. Young and James E. Talmage by John W. Taylor;

William Spry by F. M. Lyman; John C. Cutler, Willard Young and James H. Anderson by Brigham Young; Joseph L. McMurrin by myself; William J. Kerr by Moses Thatcher and Edward Stevenson by John Henry Smith. The latter became our unanimous choice, with Joseph L. McMurrin as second and William J. Kerr as third selection. We then adjourned and went to the tabernacle services. Moses Thatcher was the first speaker. He advised the people to avoid all acrimony and hatred in political matters. One old lady met him and John Henry Smith walking arm in arm on the street. She expressed her pleasure at this sight, as she had believed them to be embittered against each other because of their political differences. We ought to be able to differ in these matters, and still be Saints. Morality is something which should be encouraged.

George Teasdale among other remarks of an excellent character made this promise: "I say unto you who are in financial difficulty that if you will pay your tithes and offerings in faithfulness before the Lord, you shall be delivered. It is a time to repent. This is the mind and will of the Lord."

Heber J. Grant spoke on the Word of Wisdom, and urged officers of the Church who cannot keep it to resign their positions. Last year we spent about six dollars in breaking this commandment of God for every dollar we paid in tithing. He spoke of the folly of sending our money out of the country for things which we can as well obtain at home.

At noon I was at the offices for a short time attending to business

In the afternoon meeting John W. Taylor spoke of the evil spirits which are abroad among the people which are seeking to deceive them. The spirit of healing is possessed by the Christian Scientists, but it is and has been with the Church of which we are members. We must trust the Lord, and He will bless us with every needful gift. He said he knew that the Utah Company organized by the Presidency would prosper.

Bro. Merrill spoke of temple work, and urged the people to do their duty in this respect. He also spoke against debt.

I next spoke for half an hour on revelation, and tried to encourage all the Saints to seek for this blessing. I also told the Saints not to bother the Presidency with their trifling matters, but to settle all minor affairs between themselves....

Sunday, October 7, 1894:

Both meetings of the conference were crowded today, and in the afternoon an overflow meeting was also filled. In the forenoon Father occupied the rest of the time in a powerful discourse on the deceptions of these days in a religious way, the immorality which exists, the care we should exercise in politics, etc. He said that those who destroy their offspring or consent to such an act, or who take measures to prevent the having of children God will curse, and their names will be lost from the earth. He warned all against the evil practices of the age.

Pres. Woodruff added a few words of testimony to what had been said, and called upon the people to observe the Word of Wisdom. He said that if he and John Smith the Patriarch could not keep this law of God they should resign their positions. This was direct counsel to John Smith, who is a notorious smoker, and also drinks sometimes.

At noon I went to my offices and read.

In the afternoon the general authorities were presented and sustained, Edward Stevenson being called to fill the vacancy in the First Seven Presidents of Seventies occasioned by the death of John Morgan. Several reports were also read. Franklin D. Richards then made a few remarks on the Godhead.

Joseph F. Smith then spoke on the subject of allowing our sons to obtain homes among the saints instead of us driving them away by our selfishness to seek homes in remote places away from the body of the Church. He also advised early marriages, and told the young people not to wait till they were rich before getting married, but to start in a humble way and God would bless them....

Thursday, October 11, 1894:

Was at my Quorum meeting at two o'clock. Present: All of the First Presidency, L. Snow, F. D. Richards, Brigham Young, F. M. Lyman, J. H. Smith, George Teasdale, H. J. Grant and myself; George F. Gibbs clerk....

The time of the meeting was then occupied in listening to and correcting two articles concerning remarkable manifestations in the St. George and Manti temples, as written by M. F. Farnsworth. These were so amended and changed that only enough for one article was obtained from both. The article is to appear in the *Contributor*.

Friday, October 12, 1894:

In the afternoon I was at the temple, and assisted in setting apart and instructing about twenty missionaries for various parts of the world. While here Jesse Cannon [a nephew] came with the folks and was administered to by J. F. Smith, H. J. Grant, George Reynolds, John Nicholson and myself, Heber anointing with oil, and John Henry blessing him.

Saturday, October 13, 1894:

In the forenoon I went with Uncle Angus and Jesse Cannon to the office of the eye doctor, Lyons, who yesterday desired to remove the injured eye, so as to save the other from loss by sympathy. I emphatically protested against the operation, and therefore merely a little film or covering was removed, and it was decided to await further developments. I believe God will heal the eye, if faith is exercised, and therefore told the folks they must not be crying about him, but show their faith by their cheerful countenances. In the afternoon I assisted in administering to Jesse in the temple, and was mouth in sealing the anointing. I felt led to promise him a full recovery if he would exercise faith….

Sunday, October 14, 1894:

On my way to the seven o'clock train for Ogden, I called and administered to Jesse, who seems to be improving….

Monday, October 15, 1894:

I called early in the morning and administered to Jesse, and then went to the office and attended to work for a short time….

I returned home with the folks at 6:10 , and spent the evening in reading. We called to see Jesse Cannon on the way to the farm. He was in the temple today and was administered to. While there a dream he had a few nights since was fulfilled: Pres. Snow came and anointed his eye, and told him he should recover the full use of it. All the time while he was receiving the administration he heard the most beautiful singing,…but none of those present heard it.

Tuesday, October 16, 1894:

In the evening I was at home reading proofs. I called in the forenoon and administered to Jesse Cannon, who is rapidly recovering.

Friday, October 19, 1894:

I also had a talk with Father about the *Juvenile* business, which made him feel somewhat discouraged because of our heavy indebtedness. I told him we were doing our best to keep up our expenses, and get a little ahead. We had a talk with the Presidency about the *History of Utah*, and they gave Bishop Whitney notice that they were through with him so far as writing on it is concerned, now that he has finished the third volume. I suggested that we hire a cheaper man, and a better worker to write the biographies for the fourth volume. It was thought that this will be the best thing to do.

Father also spoke to me about taking some good girl and raising up seed by her for my brother David. He mentioned the daughter of Theophilus Davis, who has said she will never marry at all unless I become her husband, but I told him I knew but little of her character. He told me to think the matter over, and speak to him later about it. Such a ceremony as this could be performed in Mexico, so Pres. Woodruff has said….[19]

Sunday, October 21, 1894:

I went to my room and spent part of the forenoon, and at noon called to see Jesse Cannon, but he had gone to the temple to be blessed. I took lunch at Aunt Sarah's, where Mina and the children

---

[19] See the biographical essay and Appendix One: Plural Marriage Issues in the Abraham H. Cannon Journals.

also ate. I was at the Tabernacle at two o'clock, and heard Eli H. Peirce speak for 50 minutes.[20] He spoke of the universality of salvation, and advanced false doctrine, that is, so far false that he made it appear that all men would be saved regardless of their sins here upon the earth. His sermon might have been considered a good Universalist discourse. Father corrected the impression he had made, and read from the Doctrine and Covenants and Book of Mormon to show that there will be a very severe punishment meted out to those who sin, and so great will be their torture that it will seem to be eternal. He also referred to the case of Nehor, who in the days of Nephi taught such doctrines, and thus did great injury to the Church. I felt very miserable all the time Bro. Pierce was speaking, and he was called at the earnest solicitation of Joseph E. Taylor who was presiding. Father wanted Bro. Brigham Young to speak….

Monday, October 22, 1894:

In the forenoon Prince Galatzin of the Russian Imperial Council of State, and Lieutenant General of the Russian army came into the *News* Office to purchase some books. I was asked in German, which language he speaks fluently, as well as French, where he could see Pres. Woodruff. He desired me to show him the office, which I did, and introduced him to the President and Father, with whom he had some conversation. He was accompanied by a local Catholic priest. To my astonishment he was given permission by Pres. Woodruff to visit the temple under my guidance, and both these gentleman passed through the holy place, Bishop Winder going with us.[21] They were

---

[20] Eli H. Peirce was a member and business manager of the Tabernacle Choir and also an insurance agent. Today he is little known except as the assembler of an impressive LDS book collection which was sold to Harvard University in 1914, shortly before he died. The collection was remarkably large and complete and became the foundation of Harvard Library's Mormon holdings. For further information, see Alan K. Parrish, "The Eli H. Peirce Collection of Mormon Americana at Harvard University," in David J. Whitaker, ed., *Mormon Americana: A Guide to Sources and Collections in the United States* (Provo, Utah: BYU Studies, 1995), 239-59.

[21] Evidently President Woodruff made more than one exception such as this, allowing a "Gentile" or non-member of the LDS Church to tour a dedicated

much struck with the elegance of the place. I also took them through the Tabernacle and Assembly Hall, with all of which they were much pleased. He leaves tonight for Russia, because of the severe illness of the Czar, who according to all reports cannot live very much longer; indeed his death is daily expected....

Henry A. Woolley died this morning from a complication of diseases resulting from kidney disorders. He was a very excellent man, and I have been associated with him in several businesses in which we were both directors. He is a young man who seemed likely to have a long lease on life. He died the victim of overwork and worry, and too many are following in his footsteps.

Wednesday, October 24, 1894:

[A small triangle shaped portion of text has been cut from the original of the right side of this entry. I have inserted what I guess to be the most likely missing words.]

I went to the funeral of Henry A. Woolley in the afternoon at two o'clock. The services were very peaceful and quieting, and the remarks were consoling.... His wife feels reconciled to his death, as he seemed to be going blind, he having lost the use of one eye entirely.

After meeting I went to the President's office and talked with Father about taking a wife for David. I told him David had taken Annie [Cannon his?] cousin, through the veil in life, and suggested she might be a good person [to have?] sealed to him for eternity. The suggestion pleased Father very much, and [as Uncle?] Angus was there, He spoke to him about it in the presence of the Presidency. [He does?] not object providing Annie is willing. The Presidents Woodruff and Smith both said they were willing for such a ceremony to occur, if done in Mexico, and Pres. Woodruff promised the Lord's

---

temple. Elder Marriner W. Merrill recorded the following in his journal under date of 13 November 1891: "On yesterday one Gentile by the name of Miller viewed the interior of Logan Temple by permission of President Woodruff, which is the first outsider that has ever seen the inside of this Temple" (Melvin Clarence Merrill, ed., *Utah Pioneer and Apostle Marriner Wood Merrill and His Family* [n.p.: Marriner Wood Merrill Heritage Committee, 1980], 148).

blessing to follow such an act. Father said Uncle Angus should sound Annie on the matter, and I was willing to leave it in that way.[22] The feelings of Uncle Angus are not very pleasant today, as Dr. Lyon tells him that Jesse's eye must come out, or he may lose his other eye, and perhaps his life. I have not been able to feel this way, but believe the Lord will heal him, if he and those about him will exercise faith. I am therefore opposed to the operation. Jesse came to my Circle at six o'clock, where I had opened with prayer, and Orson F. Whitney was mouth at the altar.... I also went to Uncle Angus' with Bro. Stevenson after the Circle and administered to him. Several promises have been made him of his complete recovery, if he will have faith, and I believe these promises will be fulfilled. The Presidency would give Uncle Angus no counsel as to what he should do in this case, but thought he ought to follow the feelings of his own heart, and these seem to be to have the eye removed. I protest against it in my feelings....

Thursday, October 25, 1894:

I was up at two o'clock, and after dressing went to see Jesse Cannon. I sat with him till 6:30, attending to the changing of the cloths on his eye, and praying for him. I then went to the office and attended to my usual work all day, except when at my council meeting in the temple in the afternoon. I called on Jesse in the evening, and administered to him. He seems somewhat improved today, and the doctor says he is some better.

At two o'clock I was at my Quorum meeting. Present: All of the Presidency; L. Snow, F. D. Richards, B. Young, F. M. Lyman, George Teasdale, H. J. Grant and myself; George F. Gibbs, clerk.... We had some talk about temple ordinances, and then branched off to politics, in the discussion of which considerable warmth was shown by some of the brethren. Brigham Young felt the temple was not the proper place for the discussion of such subjects, but nevertheless the matter was continued till the desire of the Presidency was expressed

---

[22] See the biographical essay and Appendix One: Plural Marriage Issues in the Abraham H. Cannon Journals.

that the Republican ticket should win in the Territory. This desire seemed to annoy Heber J. Grant, and in speaking to me on politics he manifested an anger or suppressed spirit which surprised me. The warmth he showed astonished me very much....

Saturday, October 27, 1894:

I had a talk with Uncle Angus about his daughter Ann, and he gave me full and free permission to ask her to become the wife of my brother David, and seemed to wish that she would look favorably on the proposition, though he did not want to influence her in the least against her own will. He said he would give her counsel if she desired it....

[The entry for Tuesday, October 30, 1894, has been entirely removed.]

Wednesday, October 31, 1894:

Jesse Cannon then came in and was anointed by Bro. Wright, and Edward Stevenson was mouth in administering to him. He is daily improving....

Thursday, November 1, 1894:

At two o'clock I went to my Quorum meeting, where all of the Presidency were present, as well as Lorenzo Snow, F. D. Richards, F. M. Lyman, H. J. Grant and myself; George F. Gibbs, clerk.... We then had read the articles of incorporation of the proposed Genealogical Society of Utah, and it was resolved that F. D. Richards proceed to complete the organization, and that he become its president....

Saturday, November 10, 1894:

At 10:30 o'clock I was at the President's office where a number of the Twelve and the Presidency met George Teasdale and A. F. Macdonald to consider Mexican land matters. The necessity of more colonists for that country was urged by Bro. Teasdale, and the Twelve were told to be on the lookout for suitable persons to go there and live. It was also decided to continue John Henry Smith for the present as president of the Colonization Company. Plural families can well live in that country without molestation, and even plural wives can be taken without any conflict with the laws of that country....

Sunday, November 11, 1894:

I was at my room most of the forenoon, though I called to see Brigham Young, who has been quite sick, but is now so much better as to be able to go out, which he was this morning, and Jesse Cannon, who is now rapidly recovering.....

Wednesday, November 14, 1894:

This morning I was busy in the office writing letters and attending to other business till 10:30 o'clock, when I went to the temple and met with all the members of my Quorum excepting A. H. Lund, who is in England, and Moses Thatcher, who is sick. The subject we considered was the letters concerning the education of our missionaries previous to sending them out to preach, as suggested in letters received from John W. Young, B. Cluff, Jr., and John T. Miller. All of the brethren excepting myself made some remarks, with the result that we felt it proper for our young men to study the language of the people among whom they expect to labor previous to their starting out. We also felt that the Professors of the B. Y. Academy are not competent to teach the youth their duties in the Priesthood, but need very much to get the spirit of the Gospel themselves, which some of the brethren say they do not now possess. Indeed Bro. Cluff is said to have opposed some advice on the Word of Wisdom, which had been given by Bros. Lyman and Grant. I have myself felt for some time that the B. Y. Academy was drifting away from the real spirit of the work of God, and the teachers pay too much attention to psychology, and too little to the truth as found in the scriptures. The feeling is to call Bro. Cluff and his assistants to an account on these matters. We do not see any way in which to pay money in large sums to rent a hall in London, as suggested by John W. Young, though we all felt it would be a good plan to have a missionary fund from which to obtain funds with which to buy for various tracts and other things which would help the work along. It is felt that all we now desire done can be accomplished with the organizations now formed in the Priesthood, and that to go ahead and form new ones would be a detriment to the cause. We decided to present our views to the Presidency tomorrow in five minute speeches by each of the brethren....[23]

At six o'clock I was at my circle meeting, where we were increased by the attendance of Eli H. Peirce, who expressed his union and good feeling for each member of the Circle, and his faith in the Gospel and the authorities of the Church.....

I also called to see Jesse Cannon, whose eye is rapidly recovering....

Thursday, November 15, 1894:

At two o'clock I was at my Quorum meeting, where all of the Presidency were present, as well as L. Snow, F. D. Richards, B. Young, J. H. Smith, George Teasdale, H. J. Grant and myself; George F. Gibbs, clerk. F. D. Richards opened with prayer, and George Teasdale was mouth at the altar. Thereafter each of the Twelve, beginning with myself, expressed his views concerning the letters which we considered in our Council meeting held yesterday. We were united in the feeling that we cannot establish schools in which to prepare Elders for missionary labor, nor can we recommend the establishment of priesthood classes in the Provo B. Y. Academy. We do advise those young men who are called to foreign missions to study the language for a time before leaving. We were requested to place our decision in writing, and I was appointed to assist Bro. F. D. Richards to prepare it....

Friday, November 16, 1894:

I was at the President's office for a short time in the afternoon. While there the Presidency were talking about the spirit which has

---

[23] For another account of this meeting, see Melvin Clarence Merrill, ed., *Utah Pioneer and Apostle Marriner Wood Merrill and His Family* (n. p.: Marriner Wood Merrill Heritage Committee, 1980), 182.

resulted from the political campaign. He [Pres. Woodruff] said that for a long time Moses Thatcher has not enjoyed the Spirit of God, and he has fears for him unless he repents. He told of the spirit which led away from the Church in early days six of the Twelve Apostles. He said that the Prophet Joseph frequently did peculiar things in order to try those who were about him. One Sunday two Methodist preachers came to visit him in his house. He talked with them for some time, and then took a coal from the ash pan and marked on the floor. He then jumped, and said to one of the brethren present that he could not jump as far. This very much offended his sanctimonious visitors, when he opened out on them and said he merely did it to try them, as he perceived they were visiting him merely to find some sin in him. When Pres. Woodruff first met him and his brother Hyrum they were coming in from target shooting with pistols, which they held in their hands. Bro. Joseph remarked that he was intending to go up to Missouri, and thought he would have to do some shooting, and wanted first to see if he could hit anything.....

Wednesday, November 21, 1894:
There was a sham battle today at Fort Douglas between the U. S. soldiers and the militia. It attracted a large number of spectators, though many were disappointed in the display.

In the evening I took Annie Cannon with me to hear the lecture of General Lew Wallace....

Thursday, November 22, 1894:
At one o'clock I went to the home of Heber J. Grant to dinner, as all of the Presidency and Twelve who are in town had been invited to attend, it being his birthday. He is 38 years old. As he is going to Wayne Stake this afternoon, we could not remain with him but a short time. He is a very remarkable man for one so young, and has done a vast amount of good in his time....

Sunday, December 2, 1894:
I went to...Kaysville...for the conference meeting at ten o'clock.... Bros. F. D. Richards and F. M. Lyman were also at this

conference. The forenoon was occupied by Bro. Lyman speaking 55 minutes on the trials the Saints have experienced in the Word of Wisdom, tithing, donations, etc., and I occupied 35 minutes in confirmation of what he said, and in warning the Saints against vice and immorality.

We had dinner at the home of John R. Barnes. In the afternoon Bro. Richards spoke for 45 minutes concerning our temporal duties as referred to by the brethren this morning. He spoke excusingly of aged people who use tea, coffee and other forbidden articles, but after he had gone to the train Bro. Lyman said in a few closing remarks that aged people were more blamable for using these things than are the young, and he told them in the name of the Lord that they should refrain....

Tuesday, December 11, 1894:

In the evening I took supper at Aunt Amanda's, and then went to the Lyceum, taking Mina and Annie with me, and saw the operetta of Cinderella, which was well rendered by a company of society people of this city, whose object was charity....

Thursday, December 13,1894:

At two o'clock I went to my Quorum meeting. Present: Wilford Woodruff, Joseph F. Smith, Lorenzo Snow, Moses Thatcher, Francis M. Lyman, John Henry Smith, Heber J. Grant and myself; George F. Gibbs, clerk....

Pres. Snow said that he gleaned from the remarks of the Presidency at the office a few days ago that where a man is faithful to all his covenants, he will not lose his wife in the world to come even though she obtain from him a divorce in this life. Where men are untrue to their families and their God they will be left without wife or child in the future existence....

Sunday, December 30, 1894:

Frank came to see me in the afternoon, and spent some little time in conversing about various matters of business....

He told me that Trumbo and Clawson had made a demand of the Church for 17% of the personal property which the government returned from that which was escheated some years since. These parties claim that it was through the efforts and influence of a California law firm that this property was returned. The Presidency at one time agreed to give a certain percent to any party which would obtain favorable action on the petition for the return of the fund, but the parties who now claim the rake-off have no more right to the sum demanded than I have. The Presidency tendered $35,000 but this it is claimed is not enough to satisfy the attorneys, though I believe Trumbo and Clawson are the ones who are not satisfied. To my mind this demand, which it is said will be collected by suit unless promptly and fully paid, is a case of blackmail, and I think the Presidency ought to have it exposed, so that they may know the traitors and wicked men with whom they are dealing. Frank desired my advice about joining the Masons, who are a powerful though secret organization in this country. He had been approached several times by influential men who desired him to join them, but he had done nothing in this direction, as he did not desire to do anything which would be wrong for a member of the Church. He feels that he would have more influence and power with leading men in the nation if he was a member of this body. After hearing all he had to say I could not feel that he would be doing any wrong in joining the Masonic fraternity so long as the vows he is required to take will not cause any retraction of the Gospel.... I had a delightful day reading and pondering on the principles of the Gospel.

Chapter Eight

1895

Wednesday, January 2, 1895:

At three o'clock I went to the meeting of the Deseret Sunday School Union officers, where our time was occupied in considering a proposed manual of instructions for the use of Sunday School teachers. I did not hear the whole article read, but what I did hear made no favorable impression on my mind. It seems to me to be crude in many parts, inappropriate in others. We are to consider it further before issuing it, if we do so at all....

Thursday, January 3, 1895:

I went to the President's office for a short time, where Pres. Snow, Brigham Young and myself were told of some unpleasantness which exists between Apostles Moses Thatcher and M. W. Merrill, because of some remarks which the former made in Paris, Idaho, reflecting on the latter. The matter has been referred to the Apostles for settlement, and in doing so Pres. Woodruff and Father hoped that the position of Bro. Thatcher would be examined thoroughly in order to have him change his attitude, which will otherwise lead him sooner or later from the Church. He has not been for a long time in full harmony with his Quorum or the Presidency. Father said he would lose the faith unless he repents....

At two o'clock I met with my Quorum. Present: Pres. Woodruff, Father, (Pres. Smith is at home sick), L. Snow, B. Young, F. M. Lyman, H. J. Grant and myself. George F. Gibbs, clerk. We had little business to do, and merely engaged in prayer without clothing in our robes. Father was mouth. The correspondence relating to the difficulty between Bros. Thatcher and Merrill was handed Pres. Snow, and I read it to the members of the Twelve present. Bro. Thatcher is charged with having publicly said that an apostle from

""

Cache Valley had been rebuked by the Presidency for teaching politics from the stand, and he had been forced to make a public acknowledgement. This has reference to Bro. Merrill, but is untrue, and Bro. Thatcher fails to deny that Bro. Merrill was the man intended when the latter wrote to him, but on the other hand dodges the question, and claims a misquotation of his remarks. Several prominent Church members who were in the meeting, however, corroborate the newspaper's report. (the *Post*) of the remarks....[1]

Sunday, January 6, 1895:

At two o'clock I went to the tabernacle, and was very unexpectedly called to speak. Bros. Brigham Young, John H. Smith, Heber J. Grant and J. W. Taylor were all there, and I supposed one or more of them would occupy the time. I spoke, however, for 70 minutes on the first principles of the Gospel, and temple work, urging the Saints to give more attention to the latter, and asking strangers to investigate the plan of salvation, with prayers to God, and assuring them of answers to their prayers. I felt quite free in my effort, and hope it did some good....
[The next 3 lines were cut from this entry at the bottom of the original journal page.]

Tuesday, January 8, 1895:

I was at my Quorum meeting in the temple at two o'clock. There were present Lorenzo Snow, F. D. Richards, B. Young, F. M. Lyman, John Henry Smith, Heber J. Grant, John W. Taylor, M. W. Merrill and myself.... John H. Smith excused himself for part of the afternoon, as his presence is required in Court where the election cases are being heard, in which John is one of the contestants from the 3rd precinct in this city. Pres. Snow was pleased to meet so many of the Quorum, and desired the time used as was thought best by the brethren. The case which we were to investigate between Bros.

---

[1] For further information on this episode between Marriner W. Merrill and Moses Thatcher, see Melvin Clarence Merrill, ed., *Utah Pioneer and Apostle Marriner Wood Merrill and His Family* (n. p.: Marriner Wood Merrill Heritage Committee, 1980), 184-85 (8, 9, 10, and 17 January).

Thatcher and Merrill could not be conducted because of the absence of the former through sickness. Bro. Snow said the brethren would see times in their lives when it would require all the faith and strength which they had gathered by former experience to withstand the temptations which would be placed in their paths, but if they proved faithful the Lord would make them mighty and powerful men in the earth. He loved all his brethren, and desired their continued prosperity and blessing.

Bro. Richards spoke of the necessity of careful and complete records being kept by the various organizations of the Church. There was great neglect in this particular in all the stakes, and he desired the brethren to use their influence to have a reformation in this respect among the people, so that correct and full history of the various parts of the Church might be made. He expressed his full fellowship for all the brethren of the Quorum.

John Henry Smith made a few remarks previous to those of Bro. Richards, because his absence may be necessary tomorrow. He had only the best of feelings for all the brethren, and hoped they entertained the same towards him.

Brigham Young said he had sometimes had dark hours in his life, but was very grateful that the Lord had not tried him at such times beyond his power to resist. He hoped to be able to live in such a way to constantly have the spirit of God to be with and direct him in all his labors.

Francis M. Lyman said he had at times found it almost impossible to talk to the people when he arose on his feet. He felt that this is occasionally due to his own misconduct, but he hoped to be able to so control himself as to be able to claim the blessing of the Lord. He desired during the present year to do more than he ever had done for the work of the Lord....

Wednesday, ,January 9, 1895:

At ten o'clock I went to my Quorum meeting at which all the brethren who were present yesterday were in attendance except F. M. Lyman and J. H. Smith, who went to Ogden to attend the funeral of

Sister Callister, the mother-in-law of the former, and John W. Taylor, who went to Ogden on some private business.

Just before meeting started Brigham Young said that when the Saints were in Nauvoo, Edwin D. Woolley nearly killed his animals in driving across the plains of Illinois, for fear he would not arrive at the home of the Saints before the Savior appeared—so near did he think His approach was.

After singing and the opening prayer by Brigham Young, Bro. Heber J. Grant gave voice to his feelings. He regretted the presence of so few of the brethren. He desires to be in a position to accept in the proper way whatever changes may come over the people. There has already been a wonderful transformation in the attitude of the Gentiles towards us since Pres. Woodruff said at the dedication of this temple that the time had now come for Zion to be favored. He regretted the position which Bro. Thatcher had taken, but believed it was because he had withdrawn himself from the association of the Quorum, and had persistently disregarded the wishes of the Presidency in regard to his position in politics. Until he repents of this spirit Bro. Grant does not believe his feelings will improve. The speaker [Bro. Grant] told me privately after the meeting that he believed the foundation of Bro. Thatcher's decline in faith and works was his withdrawal of his Bullion-Beck dedicated stock, from the pool in which Pres. Taylor placed it, and the using of the proceeds thereof for his own private purposes. The speaker expressed the belief that there is a spirit of reform among the people. M. W. Merrill was pleased to be with us. He felt he had not had the advantages in the Church that some of his brethren had enjoyed, as he was the only member of his family who had gathered with the church, and his brothers and sisters had opposed him. Still the Lord had been very merciful to him, and he desired to do that which will be pleasing to his Maker. He did not know for certain that Bro. Thatcher's remarks about which the trouble had occurred were meant for him, but he believed they were, but even if not for him, they should not go out uncorrected. He had not the least ill-feeling toward Bro. Thatcher for what he had said, but the speaker in writing to him for an explanation of his remarks, had been acting under the direction of the Presidency.

I made a few remarks expressing my desire to correct evils which I discover in myself, and to do all I can for the work of the Lord. I believe the course Bro. Thatcher is taking is causing a division of the people of Cache Valley into factions, and I therefore feel that the matter should be promptly and thoroughly corrected.

We now adjourned for noon,...

At two o'clock we met again at the temple, and spent two hours nearly in reading 50 pages of the History of the Twelve which had been compiled by Bro. Richards. The narration dealt with the time when the apostles went on missions just before the martyrdom of the Prophet, and their return to Nauvoo....

Since the new year there seems to be a more hopeful feeling in financial circles, though there is not much improvement in collections. I do hope things will ease up in the near future, for it is difficult for me to get along.

Thursday, January 10, 1895:

At ten o'clock I was at the temple at my Quorum meeting. After singing, and prayer by Francis M. Lyman, John Henry Smith spoke of his recent trip to the irrigation congress at Denver and to the Trans-Mississippi Congress at St. Louis, where the Gentiles with whom our people met seemed particularly anxious to court their favor and make their acquaintance. It was wonderful how kind every one was to the Mormon delegates from Utah, and Father was made the chairman of the latter convention for the ensuing year. The brethren had the opportunity, which they accepted, of allaying much prejudice against the Mormons, and of giving some correct information concerning our principles and practices.

Pres. Snow expressed his astonishment at the wonderful change which has taken place in the minds and hearts of outsiders concerning the Mormons, and he hoped we would be able to endure the flattery and favor of the world as well as we have endured their persecutions.

John W. Taylor told of the favor which we have found with many prominent Canadian officials. The present premier, McKenzie Bowell, has visited our settlement in Canada, and gained by his associations with Sister Card a very good impression of our people, and a good idea of our principles. He is our warm friend. There are at present about 700 of our people located in Canada. Bro. Taylor said his financial affairs seem to be improving, and he hopes soon to be out of debt, so that he can magnify his calling as an apostle. When he left Salt Lake City some time ago he was promised a blessing by Pres. Snow, and he felt he had received it at least in part. He related many instances of healing which he had witnessed in fulfillment of his promises made under the inspiration of the Lord, all of which made him greatly rejoice. One child troubled with St. Vitus' dance had been instantly healed. Hyrum Grant's son, who was in the insane asylum, was taken therefrom at John W. Taylor's advice, and after being administered to by his father, who removed him from the asylum, he was healed. In conclusion he said he knew the Lord will relieve these men of their financial burdens, because their hearts are right before Him.

While he was speaking Moses Thatcher entered. He looks and feels poorly, but desired to be with us today.

We took a recess from 12:15 till 1 o'clock. At the latter time Pres. Snow said we would hear now the differences between Bros. Thatcher and Merrill, when he felt sure they could be amicably settled. I then read the correspondence which passed between these two brethren, as also some written testimony obtained by Bro. Merrill concerning remarks made by Bro. Thatcher which he considered improper. Also the sermon delivered in Paris [Idaho] in October last about which the trouble arose. The following extract is that which is considered objectionable: (I do not quote the exact words.) "There was an apostle over in Cache Valley who arose among the people with the reins tight in his hands, and the bit firm in the mouths of the Saints, as he supposed, and told them that the Presidency wanted them to vote a certain way. Well, the matter soon came to the surface, and the consequence was he was tried for it. The case was referred to my court for hearing, and the eyes of all Israel were upon that case. The testimony of every person in the congregation where this was done was taken, and when the record was read over it was adjudged that the Apostle did wrong, and he had to go before the people and ask their forgiveness."

Some charges and countercharges passed between Bros. Thatcher and Merrill, and then the members of the Quorum were asked to express their views on the matter, as to how it can best be settled. Bro. Richards thought that the best and easiest way was for Bro. Thatcher to write a denial of the remarks credited to him, inasmuch as he says he did not make them, and to publish this denial in the *Paris Post*. In this view Brigham Young, Francis M. Lyman, John Henry Smith, and Heber J. Grant agreed, as well as Pres. Snow. John W. Taylor thought that nothing but discord would result from such publication, and did not therefore favor it. I was in harmony with this latter view, and felt that even if these remarks had been made they were of too little consequence to make so much trouble about them. I did not believe this investigation would have occurred had this statement been made by any other member of the Quorum, as I felt there was some prejudice against Bro. Thatcher, due, doubtless, to his continual absence from the meetings of the Quorum. Bro. Thatcher said he was willing to do whatever the brethren decided was best, but he could not help but feel it would be a mistake to publish the proposed denial. As it still seemed to be the wish of the majority, he asked for a little time in which to prepare his statement, and an adjournment was therefore taken till next Thursday at 11 o'clock....

Friday, January 11, 1895:

I also had a long conversation with Bro. Thatcher, who feels quite sore over the injustice which he feels has been done him by Bro. Merrill and the brethren who yesterday investigated the case. I said all I could to encourage him, though telling him of my desire to be united fully with my Quorum in its decisions....

Monday, January 14, 1895:

Pres. Woodruff and Smith sent for me today to learn what I had to say about the remarks which I made in my Quorum meeting on

Thursday last in favor of Bro. Thatcher, and concerning them. I repeated as near as I could what I had said, and they approved of it. The feelings which the Presidency had against Bro. Thatcher, were those, I felt, which his own neglect of his meetings, and the counsels of the Presidency had created, and I believed he could remove them by meeting more frequently with the brethren, and thus learn of their wishes and feel of their spirit. Pres. Woodruff said he did have feelings against Bro. Thatcher because of his fight against Father, and his continual opposition to the course which the Presidency desired to take. Pres. Smith believed that Bro. Thatcher has been dishonest in his actions politically, and had continually opposed his Quorum and the Presidency, for which reasons he was hurt in his feelings towards Bro. Thatcher. I told the Brethren I was in full accord with their views and policy, and would do whatever they desired of me so far as I possess the power and ability....

Thursday, January 17, 1895:

At 11 o'clock I was at the temple at my Quorum meeting at which there were present: Pres. Lorenzo Snow, Brigham Young, Moses Thatcher, F. M. Lyman, J. H. Smith, H. J. Grant, M. W. Merrill and myself. John W. Taylor came but excused himself because of some important matters which needed his attention. After singing and prayer by John H. Smith, Bro. Thatcher said he was glad to be here, and hoped to ever be ready to make amends for misconduct or mistakes. He then read a letter to the editor of the *Paris Post*, in which he fully denies the statement attributed to him as mentioned in our meeting last week, and makes full reparation, as far as it is possible to Bro. Merrill for the aspersion supposed to be cast upon him. After the statement had been read Bros. Young and Merrill both said they were fully satisfied with it. On motion of Bro. Lyman we voted to approve the statement made, and then Bro. Thatcher asked that it be submitted to the Presidency to see if they are pleased with it. Pres. Snow then made a few remarks in which he expressed the hope that hereafter when any difficulties arose between the brethren, they will endeavor to settle them without calling the attention of the Quorum thereto. He felt jealous of the unity of the

Twelve, and hoped we would allow nothing to arise to separate us from the love we should bear towards each other. We now took an adjournment till two o'clock, to meet with the Presidency....

Met with my Quorum at two o'clock. All the brethren who were present this morning except John Henry Smith were in attendance this afternoon, and in addition thereto Pres. Woodruff, Pres. Joseph F. Smith and F. D. Richards. It was announced that Bro. Thatcher had presented his letter to the Presidency, and it had been approved. It was decided that hereafter our weekly meeting is to be held at 11 o'clock in the forenoon so as to allow time for Bros. Moses Thatcher and Merrill to come from Logan and after meeting with us return the same day if they so desire. We had some talk about Mexican matters, and the President asked us to look out for families who desire to go to Mexico, as there is need of some colonists in that country in order to secure some privileges of land, etc., from the government. We also had some conversation about the Tabernacle Choir. Prof. Stephens has been talking of resigning because he felt his labors were unappreciated. The brethren of the Presidency told him to remain in his position, and they promised him all the aid in their power to continue the success of this musical organization....

Thursday, January 24, 1895:

At 11 o'clock I was at my Quorum meeting in the temple. Present: Wilford Woodruff, Joseph F. Smith, Lorenzo Snow, Franklin D. Richards, Brigham Young, Francis M. Lyman, John Henry Smith, M. W. Merrill and myself; George F. Gibbs, clerk....

Francis M. Lyman, myself and Bishop Preston were appointed as a committee to consult with the present Church attorneys, and then to decide whether it is better for the Church to engage them for whatever work has to be done or retain them in regular service as is now the case at the rate of $5,000 per year for Franklin S. Richards and $3,000 for LeGrand Young. We are then to present our report to the Presidency.

Pres. Woodruff said it has been told him that Moses Thatcher was in the habit of setting men selected as Bishops apart to that office after having ordained them High Priests instead of also ordaining them Bishops. He said this was wrong, for every call to an office must be accompanied by an ordination, while an appointment could be made by setting apart.

It was decided to increase the salary of Evan Stephens from one to two thousand dollars per year, and then engage all his time in the service of our tabernacle choir. It was also decided to give him all possible help in his efforts to bring the choir to a high state of perfection.....

Thursday, February 7, 1895:

In the evening I was at Father's with my family, as he had a family reunion, at which nearly all the children had some part to perform, either in giving sentiments, reciting, singing or otherwise....

I told of Father's failing to appear for trial, when I was sentenced to prison for cohabitation, when he would have most likely been killed, had he been present. Since then honors have been heaped upon him, showing how God blesses those who are honest and upright in their actions....[2]

Friday, February 8, 1895:

At 11 o'clock I was at a meeting of Cannon, Grant & Co., where we were trying to find some way in which to raise funds to pay notes of $45,000 due in the east, but could devise no means. We finally decided that Bro. Grant should write that we have the matter in hand and will report further as soon as possible. While meeting Father predicted that we would soon be relieved by obtaining enough money with which to pay all our debts, and to do all that we desire in righteousness. Pres. Young knew of the existence of gold mines in these mountains, but desired them to be concealed until the people had the wisdom to use the wealth which God would give them for the accomplishment of good. In one place a gold mine was located and a shaft was sunk on the vein, from which pay ore was taken. A tunnel was then driven, but the vein was never discovered again, and even in the shaft the vein was not again found, it having vanished, as

---

[2] For further information, see the biographical essay.

it had been said that treasures would vanish. Joseph Smith knew of the existence of treasure which the ancient inhabitants of this continent concealed, but he did not reveal the location so far as known to any living person. These riches will undoubtedly be discovered at some future time....

Wednesday, February 13, 1895:

Returned home...and went to the President's office to a meeting of the trustees of Young University. We spent two hours in discussing the best plans for disposing of the vacant lot in the 18th Ward which was donated by the heirs of Brigham Young for the erection of a school to bear his name. We finally decided to donate it to the Latter-day Saints' College of this Stake providing they can use it for this purpose, and that they will erect a building thereon to be called the Brigham Young Institute. Willard Young and Spencer Clawson were appointed a committee to devise ways and means for the purchase of several interests of heirs who refused to donate their shares for the purposes of education, as designed by their father....

Thursday, February 14, 1895:

At 11 o'clock I was at my Quorum meeting in the temple. Present: All of the Presidency, L. Snow, F. D. Richards, J. H. Smith, H. J. Grant, J. W. Taylor, M. W. Merrill and myself; George F. Gibbs, clerk. Pres. Woodruff opened with prayer, and John W. Taylor was mouth at the altar. Pres. Woodruff then asked the brethren to exercise their faith in behalf of the Church, that relief might come from the financial difficulties in which we are now placed. John W. Taylor said he thought we should borrow money from abroad at a low rate of interest, and get the brethren of the Church to endorse the paper. The experience of Cannon, Grant & Co., was related in this connection. Pres. Woodruff said we are sure to find relief under the blessing of the Lord, but how and when it is to come he could not say. Heber J. Grant related that when in New York trying to borrow money, at the time when the State and Zion's Savings Banks were about to close their doors, he found money being loaned at 20% per annum. He had vainly tried to borrow at this rate.

He prayed to the Lord for help, and said he was willing to lose $50,000 on a loan of $250,000 providing the Lord would help him to get the amount. Within ten minutes of the time he offered this prayer John Claflin of New York started out to find Heber, and when they did meet he offered Heber the money on the very terms which the prayer had said he would give for the amount. The money saved our banks. Pres. Snow remarked "You may be sure the Lord is a good business man."…

Sunday, February 17, 1895:

I was reading at home for a short time in the forenoon, and then went to my room, where I read and studied until meeting time, when I went to the Tabernacle services. Father occupied the time in speaking on predestination and forgiveness of sins. He said that no person is elected to be damned, but men are given their agency, thus having power to fix their own future condition. All who repent, except those who shed innocent blood or sin against the Holy Ghost can be forgiven and saved. He encouraged all to repent, and to live as near the Lord as possible.…

Thursday, February 21, 1895:

I was in the offices until 11 o'clock, when I went to my Circle [Quorum] meeting in the temple, at which there were present all of the Presidency, L. Snow, F. D. Richards, F. M. Lyman, J. H. Smith, H. J. Grant, J. W. Taylor, M. W. Merrill and myself; George F. Gibbs, clerk. Heber J. Grant opened with prayer and John Henry Smith was mouth at the altar. We then considered an application from B. H. Roberts to endorse his new book entitled *A New Witness for God*, which has been examined by a committee consisting of F. D. Richards, George Reynolds and John Jaques, and very highly approved by them. It was decided to allow him to use the report of the committee in any way he may desire, but it was not thought [proper] for the Presidency and Twelve to endorse the publication.

Father next read a letter he had received inquiring if the Apostles of old laid on hands and conferred the Holy Ghost as is now done in the Church. He desired to answer the letter through the *Juvenile*, but desired first to obtain the views of the brethren on the subject. Bro. Joseph F. Smith has some views which Father was desirous to hear, and he also expressed himself on the subject. He believed that the apostles of Jesus received the Holy Ghost as it is now bestowed—by the laying on of hands. He thought this was the order of the church with regard to all members. Bro. Smith holds, and so declared in a sermon delivered in Franklin within a few weeks, that the Apostles did not enjoy the gift of the Holy Ghost until after the Savior was slain, for he tells them that when He went away the Comforter should be sent to lead them into all truth. He believes the Saints of old enjoyed a measure of the Holy Spirit, but not the Gift of the Holy Ghost. Father took the ground, and he was supported by Pres. Woodruff, Lorenzo Snow, F. M. Lyman, H. J. Grant and John W. Taylor who spoke, in the position, that the Apostles had the Holy Ghost conferred upon them by the laying on of hands before the death of the Savior, but that they enjoyed it in greater measure after his death and resurrection. In support of this Father cited the scriptures where Peter enjoyed the Holy Ghost in testifying that Jesus was the Christ, the Son of the living God. Then John the Baptist is said to have been filled with the Holy Ghost from his mother's womb; also the facts that the Apostles healed the sick by the power of the Holy Ghost. Bro. Smith admits that these things are true and were done by the power of the Holy Ghost, but says this power and the gift of the Holy Ghost are two different things. It is a very fine distinction which he draws. He also feels uncertain as to whether Judas committed the unpardonable sin in betraying the Son of God, but all who spoke felt sure that Judas was guilty of this sin. In the before mentioned sermon Pres. Smith said Peter lied before God when he denied the Savior. Father thought this an improper statement, which Bro. Smith admitted was the case. The result of the discussion was that the views of all were nearly the same, but Pres. Smith said he was hurt that Father should bring this matter before this Quorum, where he had been humiliated and mistreated. Father asked his forgiveness, and said he only desired to obtain the views of the brethren upon the question propounded and not to humiliate any of the brethren in bringing the matter up. Had there been the least idea in his mind of a discussion or ill feeling in regard to the subject, he would not have presented the case, but would have spoken to Pres. Smith alone about it. Good feeling was restored before we separated....

[The last three lines of the journal entry for March 9, 1895 were cut out, leaving the following 3 words still readable on the left side by the margin:
I learned...
ed him...]

Thursday, March 21, 1895:

At 11 o'clock I met with my Quorum. Present: Bros. Woodruff, Joseph F. Smith, L. Snow, F. D. Richards, B. Young, F. M. Lyman, J. H. Smith, J. W. Taylor, M. W. Merrill and myself; George F. Gibbs, clerk. The opening prayer was offered by Brigham Young, and F. D. Richards was mouth at the altar. We decided to employ Franklin S. Richards as Church attorney for the coming year at $3,000 per year Church pay, he being the only legal help we think it necessary to employ at present. This conclusion was reached only after some little discussion, some being in favor of the dividing of this amount between F. S. Richards and LeGrand Young.

We voted $25 per month tithing pay to William C. Dunbar in Church pay to help him in supporting his family, he being constantly employed in the temple....

Tuesday, March 26, 1895:

I learned today through Franklin S. Richards, who had an interview with Judd on Sunday night, that Mormons were furnishing the prosecuting attorney with information about their brethren. He (Judd) says he is examining this testimony, and if he finds it correct he will prosecute the cases....

Patriarch William J. Smith came in the office today and said he would like to give me a blessing, which I was very glad to receive. It was reported by Frank Chamberlin and is as follows: Blessing: Given under the hands of Patriarch William J. Smith upon the head of

Abraham H. Cannon, son of George Q. Cannon and Elizabeth Hoagland, born March 12, 1859, at Salt Lake City, Salt Lake County, Utah.

Brother Abraham, greatly beloved of the Lord, I place my hands upon thy head in the name of Jesus Christ, the Son of the living God, and by virtue of the Holy Priesthood which I bear, being a Patriarch in the order of the Holy Priesthood, and in the name of Jesus Christ, I seal and confirm upon your head all your former blessings, baptisms, confirmations, washings and anointings, and the blessings of the Holy Priesthood that have been conferred upon you shall increase upon you. You shall be mighty in bearing testimony before the Saints of God, and the spirit and power of God shall be upon you and they shall know that you are a servant of the Most High God; and the spirit and power of your apostleship shall rest upon you to the full desire of your heart. You shall heal the sick, you shall cast out devils, and you shall perform all manner of miracles that are necessary for the salvation and redemption of Israel.

You are greatly blessed and beloved of the Lord; thou art one of His noble sons; He has a desire unto thee, and has appointed thee to come forth in this day and generation to perform a mighty work of the redemption of His people of the House of Jacob.

I bless you that you may live whilst you desire life and life is sweet unto you. And I say unto you that if you desire it with your heart you shall never taste of death; you shall rise triumphant in the earth, and meet your Redeemer at his coming, and ever be with your Lord. The Lord loves thee because of thy integrity, thy honesty, thy virtue, thy faithfulness in promoting His cause. Thou shalt cause the hearts of thousands to rejoice, and thousands shall call thee blessed of the Lord, and rejoice to hear the sound of thy voice.

I importune my Heavenly Father that he will give His guardian angel charge of you to protect you from harm and danger, from plagues and pestilence, and from the destructive elements that are coming upon the earth to destroy the wicked from the face thereof. And I say unto you that the spirit of Babylon, which is spiritual wickedness, shall not have power and dominion over you. The Lord watches over you, and you are as in the hollow of his hand; and you shall become mighty and great in the Church and kingdom of God. Your faith shall be like unto the faith of Moses and the brother of Jared, and if it necessary to command the sun or the elements, they shall obey you, and you shall have power to do and perform any miracle whatsoever for the salvation and deliverance of Israel.

I bless you with health, with life and with power that you may run and not tire, and walk and not faint; that you may be active in body, limb and joint. I pray the Lord my God to breathe the breath of life upon you, that you may be filled with life, with vigor, with energy and with power to go forth in your calling, to stand up as one of the great and noble of the earth, for it is what thou hast come and been reserved for to this day and this dispensation, to assist in the redemption of Zion and the gathering of Israel. Thou shalt live to see Israel gathered from the four corners of the earth and Zion established and the kingdom of God set up never more to be thrown down, and thou shalt stand as a Savior upon Mount Zion to be gathered back to the Center Stake, and minister in that holy Temple, and the temples of God for the salvation of your Father's house, your ancestors, and assist in the redemption of the house of Israel. I bless you as one of the One hundred and Forty-four Thousand saviors that shall stand upon Mount Zion. I bless you and seal you up against the powers of darkness and the destroyer, that death, hell, and the grave may have no dominion over you, and that you may be filled with that love which emanates from God, the Father, through Jesus Christ His Son; and that the glory of God, the glory of the Heavens may rest upon you, and when you stand up in public or in private to bear testimony of the Gospel of Jesus Christ, the glory of God shall be upon you, and the Holy Spirit shall give you utterance and eloquence, and you shall not be excelled upon the earth nor in the Church of God by man. I bless you to be good and to be great and to be faithful in all time to come, and seal you up to eternal life with the holy resurrection, to come forth in the morning of the first Resurrection with all thy Father's house, to inherit a kingdom of Glory that shall never fail thee, for thou art of the pure blood of Israel of the lineage of Ephraim, Even so, Amen.

Saturday, March 30, 1895:

Orson F. Whitney made a very good speech in the Constitutional Convention today in favor of Woman's suffrage, in which he opposes the ideas and arguments of B. H. Roberts as expressed yesterday and the day before. Both are said to have made excellent speeches....

My brother Frank wrote me a letter from New York which I today received in which he urges me to take better care of my health, and predicts great disaster to me unless I do so.[3] He has urged Father to get me relieved from the *News* Office. He says the latter is much pleased with my manipulation thus far of Bullion-Beck matters, which news made me feel very much pleased. I only hope I can continue to aid and satisfy Father in all business which he entrusts to my care.

Tuesday, April 2, 1895:

At two o'clock I was at the meeting of my Quorum in the temple. Present: Lorenzo Snow, F. D. Richards, Brigham Young, Francis M. Lyman, Heber J. Grant, George Teasdale, John W. Taylor and myself. After singing, prayer was offered by Heber J. Grant. The absence of the other brethren was due to the fact that Bros. Thatcher and Merrill are sick; John Henry Smith is in the Constitutional Convention, and Anthon H. Lund is in England.

Pres. Snow said we should try to be happy under all circumstances, for in the end everything will come out right. The thing for us to do is to put our trust in the Lord and his promises, when He will take care of us.

I was next called to speak. I felt that more work should be done by us in the missionary field at home and abroad. Many people are living and dying without the knowledge of the truth, and here at home the labors of our missionaries who return home could be used to advantage in talking to the strangers who come within our gates. I would like to be in a position to labor more than I now do for the work of God and the salvation of souls.

---

[3] Abraham's journals occasionally hint of health difficulties that he endured. This prediction from Frank proved true, as Elder Cannon lived little more than one more year. See the biographical essay.

John W. Taylor and Heber J. Grant, who just returned on this morning's train for the East were both too tired and sleepy to talk much.

George Teasdale told some of his experiences in Mexico. More good could be done if the people were more united, nevertheless the Saints are doing very well. They have planted out a large number of trees and are making other improvements. With scarcely an exception the people observe the Word of Wisdom, and in the ten years they have been there not a single case of forced marriage has occurred. One great cause of this purity is that the people have refrained from round dancing, and have not used spirituous liquors. The example the Saints set is also having an effect for good, as at least one man ceased using tobacco because he saw that our people refrained from it.

We now adjourned till tomorrow, with prayer by Brigham Young....

B. H. Roberts made what is said to have been a very brilliant speech against woman's suffrage in the Convention today. Some of his remarks grossly offended the ladies, but others it pleased. I hope he will not get a big head over his popularity.

Wednesday, April 3, 1895:

At ten o'clock I was at the temple, where all the brethren who were present yesterday met again, and also Bro. M. W. Merrill. We opened by prayer from George Teasdale and singing. Francis M. Lyman said there seems to be a greater exertion on the part of the people to keep the Word of Wisdom and other laws of the Church, than has ever been the case, and the improvement is gradual and not spasmodic, which is a good sign. Two brethren are said to have died from their efforts to keep the Word of Wisdom, but even if this is the case the lives of thousands will be prolonged by the observance of this law. These brethren are Christensen of Colorado, and Anderson of Manti. He felt that between now and the November election the Apostles should freely circulate among the people, so as to prevent the acrimonious feelings which accompany a campaign. We can do much more to prevent trouble than to overcome it when once done.

He finds the brethren generally willing to accept counsel, and follow it. He rejoiced to know that in all his travels with the brethren of this Quorum he had never had any quarrel with them, nor has he or any of the Quorum failed to accomplish any mission which has been assigned to them.

Brigham Young said Bro. Thatcher made a remark at the close of our last quarterly meeting of which he wanted an explanation. It was: "You know that your father was prejudiced against Orson Pratt." Bro. Young denied this knowledge, but he would wait for his explanation till a favorable opportunity to get an explanation.[4] The Saints need the visits of the apostles, for they are hungry for the Word of the Lord. Unless the Presidency call us to labor elsewhere, I feel it is our duty to be out traveling among the people. We are gaining the confidence of many who are not of our faith. Only yesterday an Arizona man who has large financial interests in the South proposed to turn over to us all his business if we would take it, as he said he felt sure no advantage would be taken of him or his family when the Saints had his property in charge. This spirit will continue to grow....

At two o'clock I was again in the Temple. Bro. Merrill told of the great changes which have occurred in this valley and territory since the Saints first settled here. He could see the hand of the Lord in it all. The Lord had been his friend all the time. Once when he attempted to wade Platte River, while on the way to the Valley, he got beyond his depth, and being unable to swim, sank twice, and was about to go down the third time as he felt what seemed to be a sandbar under his feet. On this he was able to stand till help reached him from the shore. The Saints should not call on the Church for help in every undertaking, as they are getting in the habit of doing. They should help themselves. He told of a Bro. Larson who was called from Cache Valley to a mission in Scandinavia. He tried, but

---

[4] Brigham Young and Orson Pratt had experienced some occasional disagreement about some of Elder Pratt's doctrinal teachings and this had resulted in official public rebuke of Elder Pratt's speculations. For further information, see James R. Clark, *Messages of the First Presidency*, 6 vols. (Salt Lake City: Bookcraft, 1965-75), 229-40.

in vain for some time to get the money, but he was not daunted. He said he would be ready to start on the day appointed, and would walk to New York, and would then work his way across the ocean. He afterwards, however, secured the money in some way. We should pay our tithing, and in so doing God will greatly bless us.

F. D. Richards next spoke. He congratulated Pres. Snow on this, his eighty-first birthday, and expressed hope that he might live to be a hundred years old. (Bro. Richards was himself 74 years old yesterday.) "The Lord many times excuses us for sins committed in our inexperience and youth in the Church, but when we get to be older, and have advanced in the Priesthood we must learn to do nearer what is right. We should be ready to respond to every call made upon us, and never make excuses. The early Elders went on missions when sick and only covered with rags, but they did not know of such a thing as to say 'I will go if I can.' We should not go into debt to our enemies. If we must borrow let it be of our brethren and friends." We then spoke of the newly-organized genealogical society, and invited the brethren to join and take a life membership, which costs only $12. The funds thus procured are to be used in procuring English books of reference.

Pres. Snow said he was so happy in hearing the testimonies of the brethren that he could shout hosanna, if it were proper to do so. He felt that the Lord would not permit one of this Quorum to be lost, but He would exercise a care over them for the remainder of their lives. He hoped Bro. Roberts could be made to see the danger of obstinacy and pride, and that he would not lose his desire to serve the Lord above all things.[5] It would be proper for the Saints to seek counsel, and not to sell their inheritances in Zion, but it would not do to teach such things in public.

---

[5] B. H. Roberts had, to some degree, walked the same path politically as Moses Thatcher and found himself at variance with the First Presidency. Eventually he saw his errors, repented, and returned to full fellowship with the presiding quorums, becoming a powerful advocate and defender of the Church and its doctrines. For further information about B. H. Roberts' experiences, see Truman G. Madsen, *Defender of the Faith: The B. H. Roberts Story* (Salt Lake City: Bookcraft, 1980).

We now adjourned till tomorrow, with prayer by John W. Taylor....

Thursday, April 4, 1895:

At 10 o'clock I was at the meeting of my Quorum in the Temple. After singing prayer was offered by Brigham Young. We then decided that when we adjourn today's meeting it shall be till 2 p.m. on Tuesday, July 9th of the present year.

John W. Taylor said that an apostle has no right to join any political party, or do anything else of a grave character, without first consulting the Presidency. The Gentiles in this city are glad at the conduct of Roberts, for he has betrayed the Church in what he has said and done. We must be united in politics so far as to seek and follow counsel, or we will be driven out of this country. No man has the right to act contrary to the counsel of the President. B. H. Roberts has broken his covenants, and should be called to an account. We will become free if we will listen to the advice of the Presidency. There is some talk of a raid being renewed in this territory, but I have no fear of it. I testify by the Spirit of God that the Presidency will soon be relieved of their financial difficulties, and means will be tendered to them to meet all their obligations, for men of means will have confidence in the Church and its authorities. Further, we will in a short time be free to live unmolested with our families in this city, if we will be united in our course. Moses Thatcher might today be a well man, if he would do as his covenants and his brethren require. He must however, accept and follow the counsel of the Presidency, or I fear he will die. Bro. Merrill will yet become thin and live to do much good. Every dog in the country seems to be barking at Pres. George Q. Cannon. He is a man of God, and the Spirit of the Lord is upon him, and I do not care if he is the power behind the throne, so long as he stands as he thus has done to protect the interests of the Church and people. He has always stood in the breach at home and abroad to defend Zion, and this is the cause of the attack upon him. My greatest wish at present is to get out of debt.

Heber J. Grant also felt that Bro. Thatcher might be made well, if he would follow the counsel of his brethren, for this was the promise given to him when we administered to him. We must sustain the Presidency, and God will then bless us. I cannot sustain Bro. Roberts in the course he has taken.

John Henry Smith, who just entered started to speak, but was interrupted by the entrance of all the Presidency, and George F. Gibbs. He then said that all the Gentiles in the Constitutional Convention were united in their opposition to the woman's suffrage provision of the Constitution. A great many of our people are in the same condition of opposition. George R. Emery went around his Ward—the sixteenth—and found that 100 out of 150 were opposed to this principle. Pres. Woodruff said he feared the Constitution would be defeated if woman's suffrage was not a part of it. A great many people believe that the opposition of O. F. Whitney and Roberts to each other in this proposition was because of Church counsel they have received, when the fact is he advised Roberts to not oppose this doctrine.

Pres. Joseph F. Smith felt it necessary for woman's suffrage to be a part of the Constitution. B. H. Roberts has done more to injure us in the last two weeks than any ten Liberals have done in the last fifteen years. I consider him the assassin of the liberties of this people.[6] Next to him I am told that John Henry Smith has done more than any other man to injure the cause of woman's suffrage, from his having spoken enthusiastically of the ability and courage of Roberts in doing as he had done.

Some little discussion now followed, all of which was favorable to the adoption of this article, until Father arose and said: "I have deplored the agitation of the Prohibition and woman's suffrage question. I believe we can better wait for a time to get suffrage for the

---

[6] B. H. Roberts believed that women lowered themselves when they participated in the political process and therefore opposed women voting. See Jean Bickmore White, "Woman's Place is in the Constitution: The Struggle for Equal Rights in Utah in 1895," *Utah Historical Quarterly* 42 (fall 1974): 344-69; and Carol Cornwall Madsen, ed., *Battle for the Ballot: Essays on Woman Suffrage in Utah, 1870-1896* (Logan, Utah: Utah State University Press, 1997).

women, than to force the matter now, and thus array against us the opposition of the Gentiles. It gives the opponents of Statehood the opportunity to work strongly against the Constitution. Things which are right in themselves it is not always wise to attempt. D. M. Stuart once tried to excommunicate a man from the Church in Scotland who was worthy of being cut off, but Bro. Stuart was not possessed of wisdom to do it, and the Presidency of the mission had to go to his help. The secret ballot in this territory was opposed by me at one time in this territory, but subsequently, when the proper time had arrived I advised it, for if we had not established it Congress would have done it for us. My views are very clear as to the course we should take in regard to this question in order to be safe, still if my brethren are united in their views I will vote with them, realizing, however, at the same time that I am thus voting to endanger Statehood.

Bro. Teasdale was strongly in favor of omitting from the Constitution, or at least submitting the question of woman's suffrage to the vote of the people, but other brethren desired the provision in the Constitution. The result was a lack of union on the subject, and hence the matter was left for the members to do as they desired.

The Presidency withdrew for a short time to fill an appointment, during which time we sang some hymns. About four o'clock we partook of the Sacrament, after it had been blessed by Father. Then our meeting adjourned with prayer by Pres. Lorenzo Snow.

After meeting I was at the office for a short time attending to business. In the evening I was at Father's talking with him about various business matters. He told me of his having deeded to Hiram B. Clawson his big house in the 17th ward for the use of Clarkson, Trumbo, and others. I told Father that I felt certain he will yet find that Clawson receives some pecuniary advantage from this deal. Indeed, I told Father that I knew of Clawson having had a rake-off on sums of money which the Church once paid U. S. Marshal Benton to keep him quiet during the raid. I opened my heart to Father in regard to Clawson, and told him of his double dealings....

Friday, April 5, 1895:

I was in the offices sending drafts to the east, answering letters, and doing other business till 10 o'clock, when I went to the Tabernacle services, where the attendance was somewhat small. After the opening exercises Pres. Woodruff expressed his pleasure at meeting with the Saints, and hoped the Spirit of the Lord would direct our services at this conference—the sixty fifth annual Conference of the Church. I was next called to speak, and occupied 25 minutes in urging the Bishops and other leading men to look after the idle men of their Wards and try to find something for them to do, so that discontent may not find place among the Saints, and that hard times may by industry and thrift be abolished.

M. W. Merrill next spoke: "I know this is the work of the Lord, for I have had many evidences of its divinity. We should seek the Lord in secret prayer for we can thus obtain the power with the Almighty which cannot be obtained by public prayer alone. I endorse the teachings given to keep the people employed. We should not be so ready to call on the Presidency for help, but should be anxious to make our own way in the world. I visited one Ward in Cache Stake, where the Bishop desired to build a meeting house but before he had hauled one load of rock, or done a day's work towards the building he had called on the Church for an appropriation. This being refused by the Trustee-in-Trust, he had decided to postpone the erection of the building until some help could be had. This spirit of dependence is wrong, and was not known in early days in these valleys."

John W. Taylor: "There is a spirit now abroad in the Church among those who have lost the faith, which would kill the servants of God if the opportunity was only given. We should overcome this spirit. We break our covenants when we speak against the anointed of the Lord. There are assassins lurking in the grass about the men of God, who would destroy the characters as well as the lives of the good and great. I am glad there is fault found with the servants of God among the wicked, for it is an evidence that the Lord is urging them on in the path of duty, and this is what makes the adversary angry. Wicked men would like the watchman to step down from the towers of Zion, so they might work their vengeance and destruction. In our

Councils all the brethren speak freely their minds, but when we come to the vote on any question, we are united." The morning services now closed, and I spent two hours at the offices attending to business.

At two o'clock was again in meeting. Heber J. Grant spoke first: "The success of the Church is assured so long as we do our duty by it and ourselves. Lazy people seem to die young, and it perhaps is a good thing, for we can very well spare them. The worker is generally blessed with health and long life, but of course immoderate work is injurious. One ward in this stake only paid 15% of its supplies for its poor, and the Church was required to make up the remaining 85%. A Bishop of one Ward in the Church boasted that he had been a success, for he had never called on the people of his Ward for a donation, but had procured all that his poor needed from the Church. He was later displaced from his position for incompetence. It is a blessing to those who give as well as to those who receive donations, and no Bishop has a right to deprive his people of their blessings in this respect."

George Teasdale: "All who are converted establish a character for themselves, and do not depend upon the bauble of reputation for their welfare among the people. I am reminded of the saying of Shakespeare, 'Though thou be chaste as the ice and pure as snow, thou shalt not escape calumny.' The brethren of the Church are proving the truth of this statement, for whatever their motives or actions they are misconstrued. The Savior did not care for his reputation, but sought to establish a character which could not be offensive to His Master. The world has no cause to fear us even if we do acquire political power, for we will only use it for the good of our fellowmen. We should have faith in the administrations of the Elders and not depend so much upon the skill of doctors. We should keep out of debt as much as possible, at least so far as our enemies are concerned."

Pres. Woodruff: "From boyhood I have made it the rule of my life to avoid debt. I scarcely ever gave a note and those which I did give were for others and not for myself. Since becoming the President of the Church, however, I have become deeply involved, principally because of the demands of the government upon us, for this was the beginning of Church indebtedness. The people should be urged to pay their tithing and Fast-day donations, and to cease calling on the Church for help. This done and it will not be long before we will be able to pay all our debts. Individuals should also seek to pay their obligations, and thus maintain a good credit. I believe the government will yet restore to us our real estate."

President George Q. Cannon: "I do not believe there is a tithe of the suffering in Utah that there is elsewhere in this country. If we are not as much blessed as we should be it is our own fault, for as a rule the suffering we endure is due to our neglect of the counsel which has been given us. The Church has done much for the people, and they naturally turn to it when in distress. This territory could not have been settled had it not been for the Church organization, for many settlements would have gone down but for the help which the Church has extended to them. Men should now seek to sustain the Church by their money and influence. Not that there is any desire to blend Church and State, but Church can be made very effective in maintaining order and peace in the community. Oregon was first settled by a Government grant of 500,000 acres of land to those who first went there, but Utah had nothing to aid it. On the other hand we were helpful to those who desired to come to this land, for we sent as high as 500 teams loaded with flour to the Missouri River each year to help the emigrating Saints. No people on this continent have a better credit than this people, and it should be so. Our bonds should be as good as government bonds. Some of our enemies have been trying to injure our credit, but the Lord will over-rule it for good. I personally hold everything I have for the welfare of Zion. Thousands of the Saints feel the same way. The time is not distant when men of wealth will place their money in the hands of the Saints for their use, because they will have confidence in their integrity and honor. In the School of the Prophets one of our covenants was that we would not go into debt without first knowing how such debts were to be paid. We have not fully lived up to this covenant. The Prophet said that when this people reached a condition where they would not care for money, then they would have it in abundance."…

At 7:45 I was at Priesthood meeting, where John Henry Smith was speaking when I entered. I was unable to get the thread of his remarks.

Father spoke on irrigation matters. "We are at present held up as examples of successful irrigators, but unless we are careful we will be outstripped by others around us. We should be careful with our water-rights, or we are likely to lose some of them. Our fruits are not now fit to export. We should improve them. The day of large farms is past, and we should now seek to adopt the methods of intense farming which prevail elsewhere, thus producing from the soil all that it can possibly yield. We should not sell our inheritances in Zion, but should rather encourage our boys to secure a piece of land, and then hold it sacred...."

Saturday, April 6, 1895:

I was at the offices attending to various business matters until ten o'clock, at which time I went to the Tabernacle. Among other things I wrote to Frank a long letter about Father's affairs. At the morning services Francis M. Lyman was the first speaker: "The Church organization is a perfect one when all the Quorums are full, and no person need be over-worked. The officers are all chosen of God, and not because they have sought appointments. The Lord will sustain His Priesthood, and vindicate the course He has taken with regard to the affairs of His Church."

Brigham Young: "I desire a State government, but I desire more than this the union of the Saints in the work of the Lord. Those who are without faith in the Priesthood, have but little faith in the Author of the work. Men may choose us in the work of God, but if we are united they will not be able to accomplish much. Statehood would free us from the tyranny of some petty officials. I do not want any office in the government. I want to be in a position to accept the advice of my brethren, so that I may be led of God by His word today instead of that which was revealed hundreds of years ago. We have served the Lord in adversity, can we do so in prosperity?"

Franklin D. Richards: "An important feature of the latter-day work is the keeping of records. Every family, ward and organization should provide themselves with suitable records, and keep them in good and full condition. The journal of Pres. Woodruff has furnished the Church with much valuable information, which would otherwise have been lost. Children should be encouraged to keep daily records of the events of their lives. Old men should make a history of their lives. All organizations in the Church should keep full and accurate records of everything of importance which occurs. These latter should be the property of the public, and not private. John Whitmer once kept some early Church records, but when the Church tried to obtain the same, and the Prophet Joseph asked for them, Whitmer refused to deliver them up. We have since got a full copy of the same. The Savior was able to prove his descent by the genealogical records which had been kept. Abraham found by the records of his day that he was entitled to receive the priesthood, for in olden times the people were careful in keeping records. Records should be made in the time when events occur, and there should be no procrastination."

Father urged the procuring of the best paper for the keeping of the records, as poor paper will decay, and records will thus be lost to future generations. Good ink should also be used.

At noon I was at the offices reading proofs, and was also at the President's Office for a short time talking with Father, who was transferring his 17th Ward property to Hiram B. Clawson.

In the afternoon meeting we had the Church authorities presented, and some reports were read of various organizations. The Sunday School report showed that there are 690 schools organized with a total membership of 91,976 officers, teachers and pupils, and of these 81,921 are children. The Church report shows a membership in the Church of 160,595 officers and members, though the report is not correct, some of the Wards having failed to report. Including children under eight years of age the report showed a membership of 220,773 souls, of which 7,045 are drawing support.

Lorenzo Snow now spoke of his association and acquaintance with the Prophet Joseph, and bore a strong testimony to the divinity of his mission. He then spoke of the work being done in the temples for the living and the dead, and urged the Saints to take advantage of the opportunities offered them to redeem those who have passed away.

Sealings of those who died without the knowledge of the truth are quite numerous, and there is a disposition to extend every opportunity for the work to be accomplished according to the unions formed while the parties lived in the flesh....

By request Dr. James E. Talmage made a few remarks upon the evils of using tobacco. "We should not avoid the use of tobacco to avoid the penalty which follows its application, but because it is forbidden by the law of God. It is most difficult for the body to recover from the effects of using tobacco, and the effects of it are transmitted to posterity. Those who are born with the taste for tobacco, have a burden entailed upon them which it will be difficult to unload. The intellectual powers are much injured by the use of this weed. During a cholera plague which visited one place in the western country, the report was sent out that every intemperate man had succumbed to the disease, while many who had avoided the use of tobacco and liquor had recovered. [Illegible] tobbaco student in the United States stands at the head of his class in college. Franklin said he thought tobacco bad, for he had never seen an honest man who advised any of his dearest friends to contract the habit. A great many boys use tobacco, and its use generally leads to other vices."

After meeting I met Simon Bamberger. I told him of my suspicions concerning Clawson's actions in getting possession of Father's property, and informed him of Clawson's conduct in getting possession of his present stock in the Bullion-Beck Company....

In the evening I went to the city with my folks to watch the search light which is being used from the top of the Templeton Hotel to advertise Old Dominion cigarettes. The lights, of which there are two, are very powerful.

Sunday, April 7, 1895:

I was engaged in reading at home until time for meeting, when I went to the tabernacle. Pres. Woodruff spoke first: "There has been a warfare between the powers of light and darkness ever since the fall of Lucifer. The Lord raises up holy men and prophets at various times to warn the wicked of their destruction unless they repent, and thus He never allows them to be destroyed without first giving them an opportunity to repent of their sins and be saved. Joseph Smith was one of these men. He did a mighty work for the good of mankind, but as is the case with other prophets, he has been misunderstood. He had enemies among his nearest friends, for at one time in Kirtland members of the Twelve, and even the witnesses to the Book of Mormon turned against him, and sought to take his life. They were smart men according to the ideas of men, and sought to direct the affairs of the Church, and this was the cause of the apostasy. Only two of the apostles who were then in Kirtland stood faithfully by the Prophet. I was a seventy, and was visited by the apostates, but I told them they would all go to hell if they did not repent. One apostle stood in the aisle of the Kirtland temple and cursed the Prophet. As the sacrament was passed to him, he seized a piece of bread and threw it into his mouth, like a mad dog. He thus ate and drank damnation to his soul. He afterwards drowned himself. No man will ever see a repetition of those scenes. We are too near the end. Those whom God has now chosen will be true to the end. We should watch and pray, however, that we fail not. I hope I may live to see the union of the priesthood and people. All that has been spoken will be fulfilled. When Joseph and Hyrum met with nine of the apostles for the last time, shortly before his death, he was transfigured before them, his face shone like amber, and he gave us all the keys of the kingdom. He told us we must warn the world or God would hold us accountable. I am the only one of that Quorum now left. These apostles and the Presidency are united. Whatever we do that is wrong we will have to atone for. I want you Elders to cease troubling about who God, and the other holy personages are. We know enough about them for our salvation, and when we get where they are we will know more."…

Pres. Joseph F. Smith said: "One of the most important acts of our Conference is to hold up our hands in covenant to sustain the authorities of the church. Some think nothing of this ceremony. Those who violate the Word of Wisdom do no greater evil than those who violate their covenants to sustain the Authorities. I am sorry we have to bother ourselves so much about financial matters. Jesus gave no concern to these things, yet He had the power to combine the elements to feed the hungry, to turn water into wine, and to obtain money with which to pay taxes. He was thus capable of teaching men the way of temporal as well as spiritual life. If men were wise they would not exhaust themselves in their mad rush for wealth. We even feel unsatisfied with the use of our natural strength in seeking wealth, and therefore take stimulants to enable us to do more and go further in our desires to become rich. We will be judged by the Lord for evil-speaking, and for every violation of the laws of God. Perhaps one cup of tea or coffee would do us no harm, but it is the violating of the law of God that does us the injury. You may depend upon it that such men as seek to avoid being counseled of the servants of God for fear they will advise him different to his inclinations, will be condemned of the Lord. They seek to be a law unto themselves, and hence abide in sin."

At noon I was at my room engaged in reading. At two o'clock I was at the Assembly Hall overflow meeting, with Brigham Young, George Teasdale and Edward Stevenson. Bro. Teasdale was the first speaker: "We are of little use in the work of the Lord till we are converted to the principles which the Lord reveals; then we become good workers. With some, conversion comes easily, and with others it is difficult. One man in London many years ago bore his testimony to the truth, and in his remarks said with an oath that he would never deny the Gospel. He was old at the time, but when I came to this county he was with the Morrisites, and was an apostate to the truth. It will not do for us to be boastful. We must be humble, and be diligent in our secret prayers, or we will be lost." He then gave a little account of the labors of the Saints in Mexico, and said the Lord was blessing the people there who serve Him.

Edward Stevenson: "I heard the Prophet Joseph say fifty-one years ago that he had given all the keys of the church into the hands of the Twelve Apostles. He said it mattered little then where he went, as the power and authority are now on the earth to build up and consummate the work of the Lord among all nations. I heard Joseph say that this Church should never be overcome and wherever the majority of the Saints and the records were found there would be the true organization. When Joseph delivered his last sermon an outsider was standing near me, and when Joseph finished I turned towards him, and saw tears trickling down his cheeks. He said, 'I will never again raise my voice in opposition to that man.' The words of the Prophet had a wonderful effect upon him."

I next spoke for half an hour on the evils of divorce, and the terrible social evils which are growing up in this nation. I warned the Saints against partaking of this spirit of the world which means destruction to all who possess it.

I went to my room for a short time, and then attended the German meeting, where I listened to some remarks by Karl G. Maeser,...

I went from this meeting to the Sunday School conference in the tabernacle, where we had a good attendance. After the usual opening exercises the authorities were sustained....

Karl G. Maeser: "The excellence of a structure depends upon the superiority of the foundation. Success in teaching depends upon the nature of the instructions and methods of imparting them. When a teacher ceases to learn he ceases to be of use in the day or Sunday school. The history of the church, and biographies of leading men furnish a sufficient number of interesting incidents to illustrate every principle, without there being any necessity of resorting to myths to illustrate the truth. If a child discovers that a teacher is telling an untruth, though it be only to illustrate a principle, the child is apt to lose faith in its teacher."

The choir rendered a song.

Heber J. Grant next spoke: "We need funds for paying the expenses of those who travel to visit the conferences, to procure printing, charts, books, and for other purposes, hence we instituted Nickel Day, which is now changed from September to the last Sunday in October. Every pupil and teacher in each school should donate a nickel each at that time. The Mexican Sunday schools did this last year, and only one other Stake in Zion has done so. Some schools have even kept all the money they did collect, instead of only 20% which each school is entitled to retain for its services in collecting."

Francis M. Lyman spoke on the subject of the Ten Commandments. "Every Sunday school teacher and pupil should know the Ten Commandments and repeat them each morning in addition to our own prayers and the Lord's prayer. We should make them a part of our daily practice, for it is the oldest moral code in existence. We should make our schools attractive and powerful for good."

I next occupied ten minutes in speaking upon the necessity of speaking loudly, clearly and distinctly in school, so that the children may be all the time interested in what is being done. Examples should also speak louder than words in all our teachings to the little ones.

Father next spoke: "A Sunday school superintendent should be appointed in each mission in the world, for in this way great good can be accomplished. The instructions for the schools should all come through the General Board, and should not be issued promiscuously by Church schools or academies except as they are approved by the officers. One of the catechism cards says that one of the blessings derived from partaking of the Sacrament is the forgiveness of sins. This answer, though in a measure correct, is misleading, and should be changed. Baptism is for the forgiveness of sins, though our sins will ever be forgiven us when we truly repent of them and in humility and faith ask the Lord to forgive us."…

Monday, April 8, 1895:

I was in the offices attending to the mail and doing other business until ten o'clock, when I went to a meeting of the Priesthood in the Assembly Hall. After the usual opening exercises permission was given the brethren to ask any proper questions. Canute Peterson of Sanpete Stake asked: "How long shall we bear with men who are well off, but who fail to pay one farthing in tithing or donation to help the Church?" As the subject of tithing was thus presented Father read a list of the amounts used of the tithes by the Stakes….

There is an average used by all the Stakes of 55%. The average used by all the Stakes is somewhat less this year than last. The average amount paid by each tithe payer is $19.05. An idea prevails that the tithes are not properly used by the officers of the Church, and this is used by some as an excuse for not paying tithing. No faithful Saint will use such an excuse for neglecting a duty. If the Church means are improperly used, those who are guilty will be held accountable. Some ask if they are expected to pay tithing on the increase of cattle which have once been tithed, and that have been fed on hay that has also been tithed. If we are so strict in our dealings with the Lord, we may expect him to be equally close with us. I have not felt it wise to excommunicate non-tithe-payers, but they should be labored with, and made to see, if possible, their duty, and then be encouraged to perform it. Some do not like to pay tithing because it is generally concentrated in Salt Lake Stake, and thus builds it up at the expense of the other Stakes. This is a lame excuse. The effort should be made by the Presidents of Stakes to consume as little tithing as possible in their Stakes, and should at least support their poor without using tithing with which to do it. Davis and Sanpete Stakes have determined to sustain their poor without Church help. The Church should not be called to aid so many enterprises, but the settlements as well as individuals should be self supporting. The determined man always succeeds in his labors, whether spiritual or temporal.

John B. Maibin asked to what extent those who join secret societies are entitled to the blessings of the House of the Lord.

Francis M. Lyman said: If we would give the value of one meal in a month to the poor, they would be placed beyond want. Father said we should fast twenty-four hours, instead of only for one meal. A monthly fast is worth more than a family physician. All we take with us to the other side of the veil, is the good deeds we perform. We should donate for the erection of the monument to Pres. Brigham Young. Nothing will dry a man up so quickly as to stop giving of his means for the good of the Church, and a man who fails to pay his tithing is not worthy to hold position in the Church.

Pres. Woodruff said that Father is the largest tithe-payer in the Church, but Father in explaining this matter later said that he had tried for many years to pay something as a consecration, and as there was no other fund in which to get credit than that of tithing, he had obtained credit for a larger tithing than he really should pay. He wanted by this means, however, to prepare himself and his family for the adoption of the law of consecration when it is again restored. He had sometimes borrowed money in order to pay into the Church for a consecration. Pres. Woodruff said that if the brethren could be with him for a few days, and thus see the demands which are made upon the Church for financial help they would then see the necessity for the Saints paying their tithing fully and promptly.

Pres. Hess of Davis Stake asked if all the shrinkage and loss of produce was charted to the Stakes and wards in which it occurs. Bishop Burton responded that nothing else could be done, but Father said the presiding officers should see that there is no waste or shrinkage. Where these is loss, however, from depreciation in prices, a column in the report should indicate this loss. The percentage of tithing used in Sanpete Stake is high because the temple is supported from this fund. Pres. Petersen in speaking of this subject also referred to the Pioneer Monument Fund, and said every Saint should feel it an honor to be able to contribute to such a fund.

Several of the brethren accounted for the large amount of tithing used in their stakes to the depreciation in values.

It was stated that the funds used for the poor in the year 1894 was $109,509.43 out of which the Church donated from the tithing $61,573.39. Father said that people who pay no tithing should not be recommended to the temples. Bro. Teasdale said this cannot be a land of Zion to us until we sanctify it by the payment of our tithes and offerings. This law pertains to the Aaronic Priesthood, but the Melchizedek Priesthood requires the offering of all we have to the extent of our lives, as well as our property and time.

Heber J. Grant said that only 31,410 members of the Church pay any tithing, which leaves nearly 10,000 families which pay no tithing at all. 10,115 people receive support from the Church. Neither the Church nor individuals would be involved [indebted] if all the people paid an honest tithing.

Pres. Hammond of San Juan Stake said that most of their donations were paid to Indians, of which there are a great number in his Stake. He inquired if the illegitimate child of a Mormon girl, who married a Gentile is worthy of a blessing at the hands of the Priesthood.

Pres. Joseph F. Smith said: "We should not withhold blessings from any innocent person, but bless them where the parents are willing. We must deal mercifully with those who do not pay a full tithing, and try to get them to do their duty. Where the Saints openly and glaringly neglect counsel, they should be dealt with, and not be permitted to receive the blessings of the House of God. We must, however, judge people according to their capacity. It is deplorable for our people to get united with secret societies, because they have a tendency to lead away from the Church. The members cannot attend their meetings, because they have to look after the rights of labor; others cannot pay tithing as they must meet their society dues; some cannot go on missions, as they will thus lose all the benefit of their payments into the society if they go away and fail to meet their monthly dues; and thus one thing after another arises in which those who belong to these secret organizations are prevented from doing their duties as members of the church. The presiding officer must use his judgment about conferring blessings on those who join these secret organizations.

Father said we should not make the ordinance of baptism too common among us. Even where Saints come from abroad it is not always necessary to baptize them before giving them a standing in the Stakes of Zion, for their recommends from the branches which they formerly belonged should entitle them to acceptance here.

Meeting adjourned....

At 2:30 o'clock I was at the annex, and assisted in setting apart 23 missionaries for various fields. Pres. Snow gave them some instructions, and told them not to seek to be eloquent, but to bear humble testimonies to the truth, and the seed thus sown would some time bring forth fruit....

Susa Y. Gates talked with me in the evening about her daughter Leah, and said she would like her to find a good husband. She would have been pleased for me to marry her, if it were possible.[7] She would

---

[7] Susa Young Gates' daughter Leah eventually married John A. Widstoe, a chemist who later became president of the University of Utah and a member of the Quorum of the Twelve Apostles.

also like her husband to get another wife, so as to fulfill the law of God....

Thursday, April 11, 1895:

At ten o'clock I went to the temple, but the meeting did not commence till eleven though the first-named hour was appointed. There were present at the opening, all of the Presidency, Lorenzo Snow, F. D. Richards, B. Young, F. M. Lyman, George Teasdale, H. J. Grant, J. W. Taylor, myself, James Jack, N. W. Clayton, W. W. Cluff and Pres. Collins Hakes of the Maricopa Stake; Also George F. Gibbs, who acted as clerk....

Bro. Hakes told of the expenditure of $1,200 annually for the benefit of the Indians in his Stake. It was voted to continue this appropriation. There are between eleven and twelve hundred baptized Indians now in the Maricopa Stake. Among these is one named Valenzuela who is a Seventy, and labors industriously among his brethren preaching the Gospel. The chiefship of the tribe belonged to him, but he resigned it in order to devote himself to the work of the Lord....

Friday, April 12, 1895:

Bamberger told me today that Keisel of Ogden had said he would use his money and time to defeat woman's suffrage if made a part of the Constitution. He believes, too, that such a step will call the old Liberal Party into existence. I told the Presidency of this matter, and Father and Pres. Woodruff think it would be wise to leave this provision out of the Constitution. Pres. Joseph F. Smith, however, says he would rather see Utah remain a territory than to see it become a State without woman's suffrage being a part of the Constitution....

[The last three lines have been cut from the entries for Saturday, April 13 and Thursday, April 18, 1895.]

Saturday, April 20, 1895:

At 7:45 I took the U. P. train for Provo to attend the Conference. The Presidency, Lorenzo Snow and F. M. Lyman were also in attendance at the meetings. I was taken by Sister Holbrook to the Roberts House, where I was very kindly entertained by herself and husband. At ten o'clock I was at the Tabernacle, where a very small attendance of the people greeted us. The Presidency of the Church took charge of the meeting. After the opening exercises David John reported briefly the condition of the Stake. The people of Provo are poor meeting-goers. The tithing and donations of the Saints have increased during the last year.

Edward Partridge supplemented this report. The officers are generally alive to their duties, but there is a general negligence among young people in regard to meetings. The home missionaries are doing good work. More time should be devoted to the training of the young people in the duties of their positions.

Pres. Woodruff: "I am very much astonished to see so few of the Saints present. When I heard of the Gospel in my youth I walked 130 miles in winter through deep snow to see the Elders and hear them preach. If we realized the importance of the times in which we live, we would be more attentive to our duties."

Francis M. Lyman: "The attendance today is much better than usual in this stake at the first meeting of the conference. I feel that the conferences of this stake should be held in the larger wards, and not be confined to Provo. Take the meetings to the people if they will not come to the meetings…. When Saturday is set apart for the holding of Conference every Saint should make that day sacred. We need young men for positions all the time, but we cannot find the right kind. There should be a number of young men in this Stake duly qualified to do duty in important positions in this Stake and Church. We do not find any, however, who are particularly prominent.

I spoke for 15 minutes on the necessity of the Saints seeking counsel on all matters pertaining to their temporal or spiritual welfare.

Father added a few words. He said we cannot neglect duty and still retain the full influence of the Spirit of God. Children should be taught that it is better to die in the Church than to live out of it. We should seek counsel of the authorities, and then have sufficient of the Spirit of God to testify…that the counsel we have received is right….

At one o'clock I was at Reed Smoot's house where the Presidency and we three of the Twelve held a council. We canvassed various brethren for the Presidency, but only when Pres. Joseph F. Smith suggested the following were we fully united: Edward Partridge for President; David John and Reed Smoot for counselors. Arthur Winter was present when we decided, but L. John Nuttall had withdrawn. It is rumored that the latter wanted the position, for he said at the funeral of Pres. A. O. Smoot that he dreamed of the latter's death, and thought he was called to fill his shoes.

At two o'clock the meeting was better attended. Pres. Snow took for his text the words of the Savior where He tells Peter to feed the sheep. The men who are called to preside over this Stake will need to feed the sheep, to be kind, liberal and to possess all the characteristics of Saints. We should do our temple work, and not leave it till it is too late to redeem our kindred. It is estimated that it will require the labors of 300 persons in each of 5,000 temples to labor night and day during the Millennium to redeem those who are dead, and who never heard the truth.

Pres. Joseph F. Smith read from the Doctrine and Covenants as to the manner in which officers in the priesthood should be chosen. "The Lord through the leaders is to make the nominations, and the people can then receive or reject them as they see fit. The Lord gave to the church the law of Enoch, as also the law of Celestial Marriage, but they were rejected, and were therefore withdrawn, thus relieving the Saints of the condemnation which would otherwise have followed their disobedience. We should all improve in our duties, and seek to more fully keep the commandments of the Lord. I think we should change the place of holding conferences in this Stake. I bless the people in the name of the Lord, who were in attendance at the meeting this morning. I felt humiliated at the meager attendance this morning, and felt it was a direct insult to Pres. Woodruff."

Pres. Woodruff told of his faith in the Prophet Joseph, which faith never wavered no matter what labor this man of God undertook.

Some were offended at Joseph's jolly manner, but I knew him to be a Prophet.

After Meeting I went to L. Holbrook's, and was conversing with the brethren for some time. Mame came down from the city this afternoon. We all had dinner together at the hotel.

A Priesthood meeting was held at 7:30, at which Pres. Woodruff felt unable to be present. Pres. L. Snow referred to the Kirtland apostasy, and contrasted the same with the union now existing among the brethren of the Presidency and Twelve. This same union should exist throughout the Church. A mighty work could then be done by the Saints. "Bishops are not expected to do all the preaching. They are to look after the people to see that all are provided for. Short prayers and sermons are generally the best for the people, and they make the speaker more popular. Paul once preached till a young man fell asleep in the window from which he fell and was killed. It might do for Paul to thus prolong his remarks for he had the power to restore the dead to life, but we had better not try to preach so long. Meetings should be made interesting as well as instructive."

Father next spoke: "A noted orator once said that the chief art of public speaking was to know when to stop. Some men have set forms for prayers and go through them regardless of the time or occasion. It is not always wise to speak till the spirit ceases to operate. Those who are listened to with the most eagerness are those who cease to speak when the audience is greatly interested, and anxious to hear more. Our wives and children should take part in the family prayer, and a good time to pray is just before supper, when the whole family is together. The Lord will remove obstacles from our way as soon as we need it. He only prepared the way before the Israelites as they enlarged, and needed more room. Our fast offerings should be made sufficient to meet the requirements of the poor. There are two among many things which we should specially seek now to encourage: First, respect for the Priesthood, which is now lacking because of the great influx of Gentiles, and because of the absence of the Priesthood from the people during the raid. Second: We should love each other, and establish union among us in all things."

Meeting now adjourned, and I went home with Jacob Gates, with whom Father also went. We talked some time before retiring, and Father told of some of his early struggles in California in establishing the printing office and conducting the work of the ministry, all of which was done through faith, and by determined work.[8]

Sunday, April 21, 1895:

I was reading for a short time in the morning, and at ten o'clock was at the tabernacle, which was well filled. Brigham Young and John Henry Smith were in attendance today. The former was the first speaker: "We represent all the people of the earth before the Lord, and we should feel the weight of this responsibility. We should shirk no labor which is necessary to clear ourselves of the blood of this generation. We should avoid too much frivolity, but concern ourselves with various matters."

John Henry Smith said that if we are honest in our hearts though we may go wrong the Lord will bring along something to change our course, and put us in the way of salvation.

Father next spoke: "The supreme desire with us should be to gain salvation and exaltation. Very many who started out with vigor in this work have been lost in the mists. We are predestined to be saved, but if we sin the Spirit of the Lord will be withdrawn from us. We should divest ourselves of everything that is contrary to the will of God. One of the greatest causes of apostasy is to speak against the Priesthood. We may feel justified in doing this, but such a course will grieve the Spirit of God. Another fruitful cause of apostasy is adultery. Some of us have had more wives than one, but so long as he confines himself to association with those whom God has given him, he can retain the faith, but as soon as a man has illicit intercourse with another woman, he loses the Spirit of God. By lustful desires and thoughts a man can also make his tabernacle unfit for the indwelling of the Holy Ghost. Then it is that we detect spiritual disease. When men disregard the counsels of the Priesthood, they

---

[8] For further information on this period of President Cannon's life, see Davis Bitton, *George Q. Cannon: A Biography* (Salt Lake City: Deseret Book, 1999), chapter 3.

must repent or lose the faith. We should pray often, and resolve to serve God and be pure in heart."

At noon I went with Prof. Benjamin Cluff Jr., to dinner.

Meeting convened at one o'clock. After the usual opening exercises Pres. Woodruff said that the Spirit of the Lord had indicated who should preside over this Stake. These persons were Edward Partridge for President, with David John as First and Reed Smoot as Second Counselors. All of them were sustained without a dissenting vote. The President is the son of the first Bishop of this Church, and the man who gave Pres. Woodruff his first mission.

Father said that six of the apostles had approved of these men, and it now remains for them to seek for the Spirit of the Lord, and be guided by it. We want these men to now work for the salvation of the people in this Stake.

Pres. Joseph F. Smith urged the people not to speak against these men in public, and thus weaken their influence. "If you have anything against them make it known to them privately, and thus settle your differences. It is a crime for me to embitter my neighbor against one who has offended me and I should keep my troubles to myself unless a third person is needed to establish peace for me. When one man avoids another there is something between them not right, and when brethren are afraid to counsel with the authorities, it is a sign to me that their business is not quite what it should be. You should confess your desires to the priesthood before you engage in enterprises, and get their counsel, and not wait until trouble comes upon you, and then seek counsel as to how you can escape. You cannot get counsel of the Lord if you neglect the authority which he has placed on the earth. My freedom prompts me to seek counsel, and it does not make me a slave to seek advice of men of wisdom and experience...."

Reed Smoot: "I did not know till five minutes before coming to this meeting that I was to be called to this position which has been assigned me. My past life has been in a business line, and I feel unfit for this position, but if it is the wish of the Presidency I will do my best to magnify my calling. I ask your prayers and faith, for I desire to do all I can to save myself and others."[9]

The brethren were now set apart on the stand, Pres. Woodruff being mouth in the case of Edward Partridge, Father in case of David John, and Pres. Joseph F. Smith in the case of Reed Smoot. The authorities were now presented, after which Pres. Woodruff made a few remarks in which he urged the Saints to be more attentive to their duties.

I went home with the brethren on the U. P. train, and spent the evening at home in reading.

Reed Smoot had a peculiar dream while on a mission in England. He dreamed that his wife who was then pregnant gave birth to twins, one of which died, and the other wasted away till it was a mere skeleton. The doctors held frequent consultations about it, and finally decided that it could not live. Still, he saw the child live and grow up. Events transpired just as he saw them in his dream, and after his return the living child was nigh unto death, but his faith because of his dream was strong that it would survive. Finally, when all the doctors gave it up, he said to his wife that he would give the child anything to eat that it craved. At first this treatment seemed to disagree with the little one, but it gradually grew in strength and size until now it is as healthy and strong as any of the children.

Thursday, April 25, 1895:

At 11 o'clock I was at my Quorum meeting in the temple. Present: All of the Presidency, L. Snow, F. D. Richards, B. Young, M. Thatcher, F. M. Lyman, G. Teasdale and myself. George F. Gibbs was clerk. The correspondence of G. C. Williams, commonly called Parson Williams, was read. He resides in Mexico, and claims to have been badly treated by brethren in authority in the Church, for which reason he desires to be dropped from the Church. The matter was referred to Pres. Teasdale and his counselors in the Presidency of

---

[9] Reed Smoot later became an Apostle and United States senator. When he was elected to the senate, the Church's enemies used the public forum provided by the senate to put the Church on trial in his name—the result being the famous Smoot hearings. See the biographical essay, note 29, for further information.

that Stake for them to see him, and learn his wishes, with the idea of making him feel right.

Pres. Woodruff gave a mild reproof to Moses Thatcher for his failure to seek counsel of the Presidency in regard to Constitutional Convention and other matters. All important matters should be brought to the attention of the Presidency before they are urged in the Convention. Father closed our meeting with prayer....

Thursday, May 2, 1895:

At 11 o'clock I was at the temple. Present: All of the Presidency, Lorenzo Snow, F. D. Richards, Brigham Young, Francis M. Lyman, J. H. Smith, George Teasdale, H. J. Grant and myself, George F. Gibbs clerk. We gave some consideration to the correspondence of G. C. Williams of the Mexican Mission, who feels that he has been badly treated by some of his brethren, and also feels to condemn the Church for allowing Isaac Haight, who is said to have been one of the leaders in the Mountain Meadows Massacre to remain in the Church after his participation in that terrible crime. In that massacre Williams is said to have lost fourteen relatives. He is himself considered a very good man, but because of the matters mentioned above he desires to be dropped from the Church. After some little talk on the subject, the case was referred to Pres. George Teasdale and his counselors from that Stake to consider and report thereon....

Wednesday, May 15, 1895:

I got the proof of my life-size photograph today. I had the picture taken yesterday for the annex of the temple, where Pres. Snow desires all the twelve to be placed. It was very good....

Friday, May 17, 1895 [On U. P. Train bound for St. Louis]:

I spent most of the day in reading, though I did some little writing on Heber J. Grant's typewriter....

Sunday, June 2, 1895:

At ten o'clock I was at the Conference in the Tabernacle, where the attendance was very poor. Remarks were made by Bishop

Preston. He urged the payment of tithes and the performance of daily duties in the Church to insure an exaltation. John Henry Smith spoke about prayer in the family and the asking of the blessing upon food. At noon I was at my room and at two o'clock again attended meeting, where the authorities of the Church were presented. Pres. Woodruff spoke a few moments and urged the Saints to teach their children to pray and to keep the other commandments of the Lord, that they may not be overcome by the judgments which are to come upon the world. Pres. Joseph F. Smith occupied the remainder of the time. He made reference to the great revivalist Moody's remarks in Liverpool, where he said that a ragged boy was one day told by an artist who desired to procure his picture, to call at his office on a certain street where he should receive a shilling. The boy ran home and told his mother of the gentleman's promise, and she, desiring him to present a good appearance, washed and cleaned him and dressed him in his best clothes. When he appeared at the door he was not recognized by the painter and was sent away without his reward. This illustration was presented by Moody to call to the minds of the people the fact that God did not care for men until they sinned, when He is very anxious to reclaim them. Consequently men should not be as that little boy and seek to clean themselves up and dress themselves in their best, but appear as they are before the throne of God and He will reward them notwithstanding their sins. A home missionary, it was claimed by Pres. Smith, has been preaching doctrine similar to this, and Brother Smith proclaimed loudly against it. The prodigal son was not received so warmly because of the sins but because of his repentance. And God does not desire to encourage sin in His children, but is pleased when the sinner repents, though the penalty for sin must be fully paid before redemption comes....

Monday, June 10, 1895 [Parowan, Iron Co., Utah]:

We left Parowan this morning about six o'clock and drove about eighteen miles to Cedar City,... Arriving at Cedar City brother Lund and myself were given breakfast by Pres. Uriah T. Jones,...

A brother of Pres. Jones yesterday left for the Provo Insane Asylum, he having lost his reason immediately after returning from a mission in Wales, where he suffered greatly from indigestion. The family were feeling very bad about this misfortune, for which, however, no one was particularly to blame, as his sickness was a result of illness of about eight years standing. He attempted a short time since to take his life. His recovery seems doubtful. He is so emaciated through long fasting that it seems scarcely probable that his body will endure what may be necessary to effect his recovery.

Just after finishing breakfast Mr. Thomas Taylor, ex-Bishop of the 14th Ward in Salt Lake City called to see me and gave vent to considerable abuse of the Authorities of the Church in general and Father in particular. He said that my visit to the city and to the South was calculated to defeat his plans for the construction of a road to San Diego, he having already secured the co-operation of influential and moneyed men to carry through his project. He says that the Authorities of the Church have persistently interfered with his arrangements, and they have followed him with a determination to ruin him, which he cannot understand. He threatens that a continuation of this persecution, as he calls it, could lead him to publish a statement giving what he said would be damaging testimony against Father and the other members of the Presidency. He will then appeal to the people to know if they will sustain such men in the positions they occupy. His whole conversation was that of a man partially insane. I invited him to publish any statement which he might have or could procure, and assured him that nothing he could tell would injure Father or the brethren, as their whole conduct through life was of a character that they need not be ashamed of it. I told him further that his talk this morning had deprived me of all respect and regard which I had entertained for him in the past, and suggested that no further conversation was necessary, as I did not care to listen to his abuse of men whom I respected and loved; nor could his feelings prevent me doing anything I could to encourage the building of a railroad through Southern Utah. The fact that he has said for twelve years past that he was just on a point of constructing a road, and had failed to do so up to the present time, is an evidence of his inability to accomplish what he has hoped would be done. The brethren living in Cedar tell me that he has no association with the people, and is considered by them as a man unworthy of their respect and confidence....

Tuesday, June 11, 1895 [Pinto, Washington Co., Utah]:

We partook of a good breakfast and started on our journey about six o'clock. I called on Bishop Knell as we were leaving the city, and paid my respects to him. We travelled some fourteen miles to the Mountain Meadows, where we viewed the spot in which the terrible massacre of one hundred and twenty-six people occurred, September 27th, 1857. The monument of rocks that was built some years ago by the soldiers to mark the spot, has fallen down through the effects of storms and the cutting away of the ground, there being now a deep gully where formerly was a grassy meadow. It was at this spot that John D. Lee was executed some years ago for his complicity in the murder, it being proven in the United States District Court that if he did not personally plan the massacre he was the leader in the attack, and his hands were dyed in the blood of the victims. One could not help but feel sad in visiting this lonely spot and in thinking of the terrible crime which occurred here, though after the surrender of the besieged emigrants, who were on their way to California, they were marched to the top of the hill in the Mountain Meadows about a mile and a half distant from the first attack, and were there massacred in cold blood—men, women and children being indiscriminately slaughtered, with the exception of seventeen infants who were unable, it was thought, to understand the terrible event which had occurred. This latter tragedy was the most terrible because the victims were without arms, they having surrendered them to the Militia and the Indians, under the solemn pledge of the officers that they should be protected. The Meadows are now occupied at the north end by a small settlement called Hamblin. In the hollow about a half a mile distant from the monument there is a ranch with cultivated land around it extending nearly to the monument, all of which is owned by Joseph Burgess, who accompanied us to the scene of the murder. As we went down to the monument we passed a rather prominent, round-topped hill, on the summit of which it is said Isaac Haight, who was the ecclesiastical leader of the people at the time of the massacre, and Col. William H. Dame, who was the Colonel in command of the militia, had a bitter quarrel after the occurrence of the tragedy, one charging the other with the responsibility of the crime....[10]

Thursday, June 13, 1895; St. George, Washington Co., Utah:

I had the pleasure of meeting Brother Samuel Knight with whom I conversed about the Mountain Meadows Massacre, he being able, of all living men, to give the best account of that horrible affair, as he was an eye-witness to part of it. He informed me that there was only one other man, and that Pres. Daniel H. Wells, to whom he had given the narration, but he seemed to have no hesitation in telling me of the event, though he expected me not to use it in any way: He had only recently been married when the news of the coming of this emigrant train reached his ears. He and his wife were living at the north end of the Mountain Meadows when the emigrants passed along, and they inquired of him where they could procure pasturage for their animals, and rest for themselves for a few days before starting out on the deserts to the west. He directed them to the south end of the valley where grass and water were abundant. Some of the emigrants were very boastful and seemed to be filled with a wicked spirit. The Territory was at that time under martial law, as the United States army was approaching from the East. These emigrants said that they would go to California and raise a company of soldiers, returning to attack the Mormon people on the west, and thus destroy the people and their homes. These boastings they had expressed through the settlements of the people in the north, and it had a tendency to aggravate the Saints who had already suffered so much at the hands of mobs. After the emigrants had been located at the south end of the valley a day or two, a message came from the authorities in Cedar City, but whether they were the military or ecclesiastical authorities who gave the command Brother Knight does not now remember. This message, which he accepted as an order that could not be disobeyed without imperiling his own life, commanded him to

---

[10] See also AHC Journals, 11 January 1891 and 13 June 1895.

go to the South, in the neighborhood of St. George and Santa Clara, and instruct the Indians to arm themselves and prepare to attack the emigrant train. This attack it was proposed to make at the junction of the Santa Clara and Magotsu, a point which we day before yesterday passed, as we came down a very steep incline, before we arrived at Gunlock. Brother Knight did not return with the Indians, but remained to do some necessary work on the ranch which he and another brother owned near where Santa Clara now stands, but after laboring there two days he and his companion, feeling anxious to know what had occurred at the Meadows, mounted their horses and started for the place. While passing through the willows only a short distance to the south of the place, they were accosted by John D. Lee. He informed them that an attack had been made upon the emigrants, who had formed a corral of their wagons and were defending themselves. The Indians had surrounded them as far as they could, without exposing themselves to danger, and some of the emigrants had been killed. As Brother Knight passed on the way to his ranch at the north end of the valley he saw the militia camped at a place where Joseph Burgess's house now stands, and on reaching his home he heard considerable shooting, which made his wife very nervous, she having but recently given birth to his first child. He did not go to the scene of the firing, however, but remained at his home until a message came requiring him to hitch his team to his wagon, there being only one other team in the valley, and proceed with it to the south end of the valley where the arms of the emigrants were to be loaded into his wagon, together with the children who were unable to walk, he being thus informed that the besieged had surrendered. He refused to go at first but was told that he would himself be punished if not slain, and his team and wagon would be taken anyway. Against the protests of himself and wife he was thus forced to answer the call made upon him, though his feelings, as he says, were most terrible. Arriving at the place of attack his wagon was loaded with the arms of the emigrants, on top of which was piled some bedding and thereon the wounded and some women and children were placed until his wagon was loaded to its utmost capacity. He then proceeded on his way, together with the other wagon, which was similarly loaded.

Those who were able to walk were then formed in line and they proceeded towards the north end of the valley where his ranch was located. As they reached the summit of a slight elevation, shots were fired from the oak brush on the side of the road, and then occurred the butchery of the unarmed and helpless men, women and children, the Indians and white men taking part alike in the slaughter. One man he particularly noticed as being blood-thirsty. His name was Stewart, now dead. He seemed to be filled with an insane desire to slaughter as many as possible, and he hewed them down without the least mercy. The scene was most terrible, and the bodies of the victims were left upon the hill until the following day when a slight hole was dug in the ground and the slain were thrown into it, though the wolves subsequently uncovered the remains and picked the bones. Not until some years later were the skeletons buried decently. That same night, Haight, Dame and others took supper at Brother Knight's house, and he learned from their conversation that none of the general authorities of the Church had sanctioned or encouraged in any way the dastardly deed of which these fanatics were guilty. Indeed the authorities knew nothing about it until after the terrible event had occurred. The then Bishop of Cedar City, Klingensmith, died alone and friendless on the desert, an outcast and hunted renegade. Some years after this occurrence Haight died in exile, despised and deserted, and all those who took part in this bloody deed, so far as they are known, lived miserable lives and died horrible deaths. It seems as if the hand of God was against them for their crimes, which no straining of their religion could excuse or justify.[11]

On our way home through the fields, Brother Lund and myself visited the somewhat famous stone, a little south of St. George, which is covered with hieroglyphics. Prof. Lockwood of the United States Geological survey, who died with the Greely expedition to the North Pole, said he thought them Egyptian. The face of the stone is covered with curious inscriptions which undoubtedly have some meaning. The ravages of time are fast removing them from the exposed rock, though some of them are still very distinct.

---

[11] See also AHC journals, 29 January 1891 and 11 June 1895.

Wednesday, June 19, 1895:

Father arrived this morning from the East…. Father's health has not been very good, though he is feeling better today than for sometime past. I had some talk with him during the day about business matters, and also spent a few moments with him and Pres. Smith in Mr. Meyer's company. Pres. Woodruff is absent from the office, as his health has been extremely poor of late through the failure to obtain sleep at night. The fact is he is worrying too much about business to be able to obtain the needed rest. Asthma is also troubling him considerably….

Thursday, June 27, 1895:

I spoke to John A. Evans this morning about accepting the Management of the *Deseret News* Publishing Co. It was with reluctance that he consented to do so, as he had some fears concerning the financial part of the undertaking. He might well be fearful in regard to this, as I have advanced since I came into the office over ten thousand dollars to pay the most pressing bills. I think, however, that the future will bring sufficient business to meet all expenses, as there has been quite a revival in our affairs within the last two months. John Q. does not much like the change, for the reason, I suppose, that he cannot as well annoy me with his petitions for financial help as he could were I associated in the office with him. In the afternoon a meeting of the *Deseret News* Pub. Co. was held in my room; present; John Q. and Angus J. Cannon, John A. Evans, Walter J. Lewis and myself. After I had called the meeting to order I tendered my resignation as the Manager of the Company, and on motion of John Q. seconded by Walter J. Lewis it was accepted, for the reason as John explained, that he had realized for a long time that my labors in the office were unjust to myself, because of the severe toil it required of me in connection with my other numerous duties….

Sunday, July 14, 1895:

I spent the forenoon at home and at my room engaged in reading, and in the afternoon I attended the Tabernacle services, where there was a very large attendance, the gallery being thrown open, and the whole building being comfortably filled. A large number of the audience was composed of teachers who are visiting Salt Lake City, they having come from Denver where their convention was held a few days since. Greatly to my surprise I was called to speak. I arose with such trembling as I never before experienced in arising to address a congregation. I occupied an hour and five minutes in speaking of our views of education—that the mental, moral, physical and spiritual part of man should be equally trained in order to attain perfection, and then referred in brief to the principles of the Gospel in which we believe. I found considerable freedom in speaking after I got started....[12]

Monday, July 15, 1895:

I met a number of visiting teachers today, all of whom expressed their pleasure at the sermon which I delivered yesterday, which gave them a better idea of Mormonism than they had heretofore had. I was told that the remarks would allay considerable prejudice among our visitors and among those with whom they associated in their homes. I trust that good will result from their visit to our city.

Friday, July 26, 1895:

There is considerable excitement at present in Idaho and Wyoming, in the neighborhood of the Yellowstone National Park because of the Indian uprising. Several weeks ago ten Indian bucks were arrested for killing elk in the Park, contrary to law. As they were being conducted to prison to await trial, they tried to escape, and several were killed. This act started them on the war-path, and some families of white people in Jackson's Hole are reported massacred.

---

[12] For Sunday, 14 July, the journal of Richard S. Horne, an early pioneer, school teacher, and acquaintance of Elder Cannon, states: "I attended the Tabernacle services and heard an excellent discourse from Apostle Abraham H. Cannon. About one thousand teachers from the Denver Convention were in attendance" (Richard S. Horne journal, Family and Church History Department of The Church of Jesus Christ of Latter-day Saints archives, 58; unpublished typescript copy in editor's possession).

Saturday, July 27, 1895:

At 9:30 a.m. I went to the train and met the Presidency and party who just returned from their Alaska trip, in good health and spirits. Pres. Woodruff finds some difficulty in breathing because of the altitude, but has been very well during his absence....

Tuesday, July 30, 1895:

At 11 o'clock I was at the President's Office to a meeting that was called to talk about politics. Present: All of the Presidency, Lorenzo Snow, F. D. Richards, Brigham Young, F. M. Lyman, H. J. Grant, The Presidency of this Stake, John T. Caine, F. S. Richards, S. R. Thurman, Judge William H. King, and George F. Gibbs, clerk. John T. Caine presented the matter we came to discuss. He said there was a fear among the Gentiles that the Church intended to use the women to accomplish the things they desired in a political way. The Democrats had chosen some prominent Church women to take part in their proceedings with the result that Uncle Angus as President of this Stake had asked them to resign their offices or cease mixing in politics. If such was to be the course of the Church Bro. Caine thought it would result in discord and bitterness on the part of Gentiles. The Democrats wanted the Presidency to say how far the people and officers of the Church are to be allowed to engage in politics without being considered in bad standing in the Church. F. S. Richards, Thurman and King each spoke in confirmation of Bro. Caine's statement, and expressed the fear that the withdrawal of the prominent women from the political field at this time would cause the Church and some individuals trouble. Bro. Thurman, who is the assistant prosecuting attorney for the U. S. at Provo, says that the policy of Judd is to pass unnoticed all cases under the Edmunds-Tucker law, unless the matter is so flagrant as to cause comment in public. The Gentiles, with the possible exception of a very few, are anxious to see the past buried, and do not want any revival of past difficulties. It was felt by the attorneys present that the women will be allowed to vote this fall, as the enabling act provides for all legal voters of the proposed state of Utah to be permitted to vote for the constitution and the State officers. Thurman said he made one of the conditions of his accepting office under Judge Judd, that he would not be called to prosecute those of his co-religionists who violated the Edmunds-Tucker law, and though Judd had a list of 350 persons who were guilty of these crimes, it was not believed he would use it. Considerable discussion ensued as to who should be allowed to take active part in politics from among the prominent men and women in the Church. Caine, Thurman, F. S. Richards, Joseph E. Taylor and Penrose were in favor of all the members of the Church being given perfect freedom to accept office, stump the country or do anything else they might desire in this regard. Judge King felt that the high ecclesiastical officers of the Church should and could be kept out of active work, and could thus act as balance wheels among the people. Uncle Angus explained in a 30 minute talk the position which he had taken. He gave counsel for all the Bishops and counselors, Presidents of quorums and associations, etc., to refrain from politics in every way further than to vote. This was non-partisan advice.

We took an adjournment for 25 minutes to get some lunch, and on re-convening Pres. Woodruff asked each of the Twelve and Presidency to express their views. Pres. Snow was not in favor of leading brethren and sisters engaging in politics, but they should devote themselves to the affairs of their callings.

F. D. Richards was in favor of turning all the brethren and sisters loose to do as they thought best in these matters.

B. Young said he was inclined to Democracy, but thought any Church official who neglected his calling for political office was making too great a sacrifice.

F. M. Lyman desired the prominent brethren and sisters to avoid politics, but thought it wise for them to attend primaries in order to see that good people were chosen for position.

H. J. Grant did not favor at first the movement of the sisters in politics, but now they were engaged in them, he thought it would be unwise for them to be recalled.

I was in favor of the prominent Church officials of the Church and Stakes keeping out of this business. I expressed my contempt for those who continue to make threats about starting the raid in order to force the Presidency to declare themselves in regard to politics. We have made sacrifices enough to satisfy the most exacting men who are honorable, and we have proved our integrity in what we have done. We do not want our straightforwardness now questioned.

Pres. Joseph F. Smith was in favor of giving the men and women of all classes perfect freedom in their political affairs.

Father felt that the sisters and all others should be constrained from declaring the politics of our dead leaders, and should teach the doctrines of their respective parties. Joseph Smith taught the most advanced Republican doctrines, and Brigham Young held office for four years under a Whig administration. He was also a devoted protectionist. Our salvation in a political sense will be assured by showing to both parties that they have a fighting chance in this territory. They will not want to offend us, but will seek our favor. It would be best for Zion to have the parties nearly equally divided, and leading men should avoid office. The day will come when office will be forced upon our leading brethren who are modest and seek to avoid prominence in political affairs. The lust for office is a curse to many young men, and should be overcome. The sisters must not use their religious meetings to promote their political cause.

Pres. Woodruff felt that the leading men and women should keep out of active politics. He regretted the course the sisters had taken, but now that they have gone so far, it will be better to let them finish this campaign on the lines which have been marked out for them.

It was therefore decided to give freedom to the men and women of the Church to finish this campaign as they think best, and yet the general counsel is that the leading men take no very active part in the political arena.[13]

We adjourned at 5 o'clock,...

Wednesday, July 31, 1895:

The Indian scare in Idaho and Wyoming is about past, as there was more talk than evil deeds done in this affair. The Indians were the injured parties in the scare.

Thursday, August 1, 1895:

At 11 o'clock I was at the temple at my Quorum meeting. Present: All of the Presidency, L. Snow, F. D. Richards, B. Young, J. F. Smith, and myself; George F. Gibbs, clerk. We approved of three Bishops which had been selected to fill vacancies in the Weber Stake. We decided to give no advice with our present limited knowledge, concerning the disincorporation of Grantsville City, but to leave it to the people themselves to act as they think best.

Brigham Young was appointed to act with the Presidency and High Council of the San Juan Stake in trying Soren Jensen for his continued opposition to the authorities of his Stake and Ward....

---

[13] Discussions such as this one are what eventually led to the issuance of the so-called Political Manifesto, a document issued by the First Presidency that required men holding high Church position to get permission from the First Presidency before running for political office. This was in accordance with the nature of their callings and the formal charge they received at the time of their ordination—that they would place their callings first in their lives. Some of the Brethren, including Moses Thatcher (who refused to sign the document) and B. H. Roberts (who reluctantly signed it), strongly opposed it, believing it was but a tool the First Presidency could use to approve those they desired for a position and stop those they did not. They felt this curtailed their freedom in the political process. While these reasons may have had some elements of truth, it is also true that these men had accepted a high calling, accompanied by a sacred charge, and in so doing had freely bound themselves to limiting consequences. For the text of the Political Manifesto, see James R. Clark, ed., *Messages of the First Presidency*, 6 vols. (Salt Lake City: Bookcraft, 1965-1975), 3:272-77.

Sunday, August 4, 1895:

I went with Mina to the Hot Springs in the forenoon and had a bath which weakened me very much, but did me good, I believe. I then went to my room and read for a short time. At two o'clock I was at the Tabernacle services for a short time—the services only lasting an hour and a half—and heard a very good discourse by Franklin D. Richards concerning the Book of Mormon....

Tuesday, August 6, 1895:

I met with the Presidency for a short time.... Pres. Woodruff said while I was there that Reed Smoot had just been to see if Father would run for the senatorship of the new State. I asked upon which ticket he would run. He said he did not want the position, and would only accept of it if the Lord desired it. I could see from Father's remarks that it would not require much urging to get him to accept of the nomination. I said that Frank ought to be informed if this was Father's feeling, as both Frank and Father could not hope for office.

At one o'clock I was at the Co-op Furniture Co. with Father, where he selected some furniture for his houses.

At two o'clock I was at my quarterly Quorum meeting in the temple. Present: L. Snow, F. D. Richards, B. Young, F. M. Lyman, J. H. Smith, H. J. Grant and myself. After singing and prayer by F. M. Lyman, Pres. Snow spoke for a short time. He felt that these meetings should be most sacred to us, and nothing should be allowed to interfere with our prompt attendance at them. Bro. Thatcher would be better in his health if he would attend the meetings of his Quorum. Bro. Merrill has no reasonable excuse for his absence. The early apostles of this dispensation on many occasions quarreled, and were not united; so was it also with the apostles in the time of Jesus; but God has given us a union which I hope will ever continue. We must not oppose the authorities over us, but do as David said was right—not raise our hands or voices against the Lord's anointed.

Brigham Young said Bro. Merrill has never attended meeting in Richmond or partaken of the sacrament there since the trouble was settled by himself and Bro. Lyman over a year ago, in which Bro. Merrill was required to make some acknowledgements to the people for his conduct in politics. Bro. Young felt personally injured by this conduct on the part of Bro. Merrill. Bro. Lyman was appointed to take up a teacher's labor with Bro. Merrill tomorrow on this matter. We occupied the remainder of the time in reading from the manuscript History of the Twelve, which F. D. Richards had prepared....

Wednesday, August 7, 1895:

At ten o'clock I was at the temple where all of those present yesterday were in attendance as also M. W. Merrill. Heber J. Grant opened with prayer, and we had some singing.

Pres. Snow advised us to avoid becoming discouraged though we may sometimes make mistakes. We must seek union and perfect love.

Brigham Young: "I feel well in my labors. The apostles are growing in power to overcome evil and to control their passions and feelings. I found some disunion in Cache Valley, and believe Moses Thatcher partakes of this spirit. I feel that he ought to be sent away from the country for a time till he has full chance to recover his health, and so that he can also get a better spirit than he now enjoys. Outside Stakes should be more often and regularly visited by the apostles. Our appointments should be made in a systematic manner. George Teasdale should be released from the Presidency of the Mexican Mission and be allowed to return home to work among the Stakes of Zion. There is no union in the Presidency of the Mexican Mission, Bro. Teasdale and his counselors, MacDonald and Eyring, continually working at cross purposes. I think the Saints in Mexico should become citizens of that country, which would aid them in obtaining many rights which are now denied them."

Some discussion now ensued as to the person who should be chosen to preside in Mexico, and Anthony W. Ivins was the unanimous choice of the brethren for the position, though he is now very much tied up in business in Southern Utah, as well as in his position as counselor in the Presidency of the St. George Stake.

We adjourned at 12:10 with prayer by Francis M. Lyman, and met again at 1:30 p.m. We further considered the Mexican Mission presidency and decided to recommend to the Presidency of the

Church as our first choice for that position Anthony W. Ivins; second, Richard W. Young; third, Richard R. Lyman. George A. Smith, George F. Richards, Joseph S. Wells and M. W. Merrill, Jr., were also prominently mentioned in connection with this position.

F. D. Richards referred to the work he had done on the history of the Twelve Apostles, and desired to receive any criticism or encouragement for his work which the brethren see fit to give at any time.

Francis M. Lyman felt that there is sufficient work at all times among the Saints to keep all the brethren of the Quorum busily engaged in the ministry. "Our labors have generally been approved by the Presidency. We should encourage early marriages among our young people to prevent them from committing sins against virtue."

Benediction by M. W. Merrill....

Thursday, August 8, 1895:

I was reading proofs and dictating letters until ten o'clock when I went to my meeting in the temple. Prayer by John Henry Smith, and we had the usual singing.

Pres. Snow asked the views of the brethren concerning Japan as a country now ready for the preaching of the Gospel. Pres. Richards said Japan is a country far advanced in civilization, and it seemed an opportune time now to try and gain a foothold there for the sending of our missionaries. I explained in some detail the negotiations which are now pending between the Presidency and Mr. Stanton, which will most likely result in the sending of myself or some other brother to Japan to complete the arrangements for the connection of the steamship line with our proposed railway. This explanation made further talk upon this subject unnecessary.

John Henry Smith said he had nothing more to say than that he was in full fellowship with his brethren.

Heber J. Grant read a good letter from Anthon H. Lund, in which some of his labors and travels were detailed. Bro. Grant then expressed himself as desirous of mingling more among the Saints then he had done, and suggested the apportionment among the Twelve by a committee the various conferences so that we may know for some time ahead what places we are expected to visit. This suggestion met with approval, and Brigham Young, F. M. Lyman and John Henry Smith were appointed such committee.

While Bro. Merrill was speaking the Presidency entered, and our talk ceased. Pres. Snow called attention to the condition of the Mexican Mission, and suggested the releasing of Bro. Teasdale from his present position. Brigham Young and John Henry Smith enlarged on the remarks of Pres. Snow. Pres. Woodruff then expressed himself as in favor of the plan recommended, and Father therefore moved, and it was unanimously carried, that George Teasdale be released from the Presidency of the Mexican Mission, and that Anthony W. Ivins be appointed to succeed him; and that the latter be allowed to act without counselors until he finds men whom he desires to have aid him in the Presidency....

A question from Cache Stake was asked, as there seems to be a difference of views even among the Twelve upon the point. Bro. Thatcher holds that Sec.102 of the Doctrine and Covenants makes it imperative that at least seven members of each High Council be present to transact business, and that no more than five alternates can act in any High Council. Father maintains, with several other brethren, that alternate High Councilors possess all the powers and authority which are given to regular members and they can consequently be called to fill any number of vacancies which may occur because of the absence of regular members. After some little talk Pres. Woodruff said there never would be a time or condition when the work necessary to be done would be delayed or stopped by the negligence of one or more men, consequently when enough regular High Councilors were not in attendance to do the business, alternates should be chosen to continue and do the work needful. In the absence of a Bishop a High Priest could be chosen temporarily to perform his duties....

Wednesday, August 14, 1895:

Pres. Woodruff asked me today what I thought of Father's candidacy for the senatorship from Utah. I told him I thought the sacrifice was a greater one than Father should make. If he ran on the

Republican ticket, which I believe would be the one he would choose, it would antagonize all the Democrats, and I felt that the place he had won for himself in the hearts of the Saints was too valuable to be sacrificed for a political office. Besides, he was too much needed in the Church at home for him to leave. Pres. Woodruff said he felt just as I do.

Thursday, August 15, 1895:

At 11 o'clock I was at my Quorum meeting at which all the Presidency, L. Snow, Brigham Young, F. M. Lyman, J. H. Smith, Heber J. Grant, George F. Gibbs and myself were present. It was reported that some trouble exists in the Panguitch Stake through some of the prominent brethren having accused Pres. Jesse W. Crosby, Jr., of embezzlement, and he having lodged a counter charge of defamation of character against them. Bro. Lyman and two other apostles are to go there in two weeks and settle this matter.

Brigham Young was appointed to settle some difficulties which exist in the San Juan Stake between Bro. Soren Jensen and some brethren in high ecclesiastical positions.

A list of outside conferences was read to which members of the Quorum seldom go, and these were apportioned out to the four foot-loose members of this Quorum who are to see that these places are visited at least twice a year. Brigham Young was appointed to the eastern stakes; Francis M. Lyman to the Southern Utah stakes; John Henry Smith to the northern stakes, and George Teasdale to the Arizona and Mexican stakes. This is the apportionment made by the committee selected in the meeting of the Twelve last week.

Some talk was had about Charles W. Stayner and his doctrines of reincarnation. The fear was expressed by some of the brethren that Bishop O. F. Whitney has become somewhat indoctrinated with these ideas.[14] The matter was called up by the reading of two

---

[14] The AHC journals occasionally refer to rumors that Bishop Orson F. Whitney had begun to believe in reincarnation. While it is difficult to determine whether or not this may have been true, to any extent, we do know that Bishop Whitney was called to the Apostleship by President Joseph F. Smith in 1906, where he served faithfully until his death in 1931.

resignations which were sent to Bishop Whitney by a wife and grand-daughter of the late Joseph Young, they having lost the faith through the acceptance of Christian Science. It was decided to take no action on the resignation of the wife who is now eighty years old, and scarcely responsible for her actions....

Friday, August 16, 1895:

Was at the President's office part of the forenoon where we considered the indebtedness of the B. Y. Academy at Provo, for most of which the estate of Abraham O. Smoot is now held. The amount is over $50,000. It was felt that the Church must assume this, receiving in return all the property of the institution. A committee, consisting of William B. Preston, John Clark and Charles S. Burton, was appointed to see what can be done in the way of funding the whole indebtedness, and thus securing a low rate of interest....

Saturday, August 31, 1895:

...The Republicans have held their convention and nominated Heber M. Wells for Governor, and Clarence E. Allen for Delegate to Congress. They did not name their senators. The Democrats have nominated Joseph L. Rawlins and Moses Thatcher for the Senate, B. H. Roberts for the House, and John T. Caine for the Governor.

Judge Merritt and Bartch have ruled that the women are not to be allowed to vote this Fall but must wait until we are admitted as a State, as it is only our State Constitution that enfranchises them.

Monday, September 2, 1895:

This morning Dr. R. B. Pratt cleaned out my left ear, which has been quite deaf since I left Coronado. She removed therefrom a large amount of wax and other foreign matter, which restored my hearing. The right ear is permanently deprived of part of its power, the cause being cold...in the head. It has been defective for a long time past.

Tuesday, September 3, 1895:

At two o'clock I was at the funeral of Elizabeth C. Taylor, in the 14th Ward Hall. The speakers were Joseph Horne, Joseph F. Smith and Father, all of whom gave comfort to the sorrowing relatives, and advice to all present. This woman was the second wife of Pres. John Taylor, and is Father's own aunt. She was 84 years old. She was well educated, yet in the early days of the valley was ready to do any kind of labor to help her husband provide for his family....

Thursday, September 5, 1895:

At 9:30 I met with the Presidency and read to them my report of travels and business done, which pleased them very much. At 11 o'clock I met with my Quorum in the temple. Present: All of the Presidency, Lorenzo Snow, F. D. Richards, John H. Smith, Heber J. Grant and myself; George F. Gibbs, clerk. We had some talk about the injurious effects of the use of cocaine, which is a drug similar to opium, and sometimes leads those who use it to commit suicide. Bro. Richards told of a certain woman who is in the Church, and who contemplated committing suicide. She decided one night to commit the deed the following morning, but while asleep she dreamed that she had done the deed, but when her spirit desired to leave the grave where her body was confined she was told to remain there until she died a natural death. Because of this restraint she suffered indescribable tortures, and when she found it only a dream she decided to suffer anything here on earth rather than to take her own life. Father said he believed some suicides would meet a second death. H. J. Grant was told to warn Bishop O. F. Whitney against carelessness in regard to attending meetings, as also to urge him not to become too intimate with Miss Babcock, or the Stayner brothers....

Sunday, September 8, 1895:

I took the nine o'clock train for Farmington where I attended the Quarterly Stake Conference, which was held in the bowery. Pres. Joseph F. Smith and Heber J. Grant were also present....

I expressed pleasure that the women would not be allowed to vote this Fall because of the fear that their doing so may injure the chances of statehood; it is also better for them to have time to study the principles of the two parties before aligning themselves with either.

Besides, this is to be a very hot campaign, and it will be better for the women to be free from the turmoil and bitterness which will ensue. I referred to the great need of missionary work in the world, and spoke of the opening which seems to be presented by Japan....

Meeting reconvened at one o'clock,... Pres. Joseph F. Smith then spoke for 55 minutes. He scored me for remarks which He thought were intended to oppose woman's suffrage, but in his understanding of which he misjudged me, for he reaffirmed my statements in his sermon. Bro. Grant tried to correct him while he was speaking, but it only made Bro. Smith the more firm. He said I had no right to boast of my independence in politics, which reproof was good for me. He gave a very good political talk....

Thursday, September 19, 1895:

At the hour named [11 o'clock] I went to my Quorum meeting in the temple. Present: W. Woodruff, Joseph F. Smith, Lorenzo Snow, H. J. Grant and myself; George F. Gibbs, clerk. It was decided in answer to a question which was asked that where persons are guilty of sexual sin, they are to be made to confess before as few as are absolutely necessary in order to make the plaster as large as the sore.

Pres. Woodruff dismissed us with prayer....

Thursday, September 26, 1895:

I was in the offices engaged as usual until 11 o'clock, when I went to my Quorum meeting in the Temple. Present: Pres. Woodruff, Joseph F. Smith, L. Snow, F. D. Richards, George Teasdale, H. J. Grant and myself; George F. Gibbs, clerk. Edward Partridge, president of the Utah Stake asks if all the elders engaged in administering the Sacrament should kneel while the blessing is being asked, or only the one who is mouth. On motion of Joseph F. Smith he was answered that only him who is mouth should kneel, though Bro. Smith thinks there is no doubt it was intended in the revelation that the congregation should kneel, but the size of the Church now prevents this being carried out.

It was sometime since decided by Pres. John Taylor that a baptism is not legal unless the person officiating enter into the water with the candidate.

Bro. Partridge desired the Church to furnish means with which to pay the janitor of the Provo Stake Tabernacle, there being now about $700 due him. The answer was sent that other stakes pay their Stake House expenses, and Utah must do the same. The amount should be collected from the various wards which are benefited by the building.

Pres. Woodruff expressed his disapproval of the conduct of Moses Thatcher and John W. Taylor in absenting themselves from our Quorum meetings on their private business, without first securing the consent of the Presidency. It is a neglect of their duties as apostles. Moses Thatcher has been sick, but when he is in this city attending to business matters, he does not visit our meetings, which shows how little interest he has in them. Several of the brethren expressed disapproval of Bro. Thatcher's conduct, but John W. Taylor did ask permission to go to Europe, as he hoped there to sell his Canada land, and thus get out of debt.

Dismissed with prayers by George Teasdale....

Sunday, September 29, 1895:

Richard Horne told me yesterday of the remarkable healing of his almost blind and very feeble daughter, who has been ill since birth, by the faith and prayers of her young brother, who is a deacon, and blessed her one day that she might recover. The family are delighted, and praise the Lord for this blessing, which came in so unexpected a way.[15]

---

[15] For 28 September 1895, the journal of Richard S. Horne states: "I read Artie's [Arthur, son of Richard] Vision to Apostle A. H. Cannon. He was well pleased with it and expressed his opinion that it should be published and suggested that I write full particulars to the First Presidency. I did so." For 28 November 1895, the Horne journal records, "The last two numbers of the *Juvenile Instructor* contain Artie's Vision and Lizzie's [daughter of Richard] experience with the adversary" (Richard S. Horne journal, Family and Church History Department of The Church of Jesus Christ of Latter-day Saints archives, 58; unpublished typescript copy in editor's possession), 63, 67; See also Richard S. Horne, "A Remarkable

Tuesday, October 1, 1895:

Word comes from Missouri that the State Supreme Court has decided that the Temple lot in Independence, Missouri, belongs to the Hedrickites, instead of to the Josephites as the district court had decreed. We are glad of the decision, as the Hedrickites are favorable to us, and want our Church to own the plot of ground.

At ten o'clock I was at the Temple at my regular quarterly Quorum meeting. All of the Twelve were present excepting John W. Taylor, and Anthon H. Lund. After the singing, which I led, prayer was offered by George Teasdale. Pres. Snow then expressed his pleasure at meeting so many of the brethren. He hoped our union would increase. He referred to the part of the Word of Wisdom, in which the use of meat to excess is forbidden. He said we have no right to slay animals or fowls except from necessity, for they have spirits which may some day rise up and accuse or condemn us. Beasts are the servants of the people here, and will be so in eternity. Whenever we partake of animal food, we eat that which has cost an immortal life. Unless famine or extreme cold is upon us we should refrain from the use of meat.[16]

Franklin D. Richards: "The Prophet Joseph said he expected to own his horse and dog in eternity. The apostles should engage in no labor that will occupy their time or attention other than their calling as messengers of the Lord, unless they first obtain the permission of the First Presidency. This principle has prevailed in the Church from the beginning. Pres. Young once said that if every person who had heard his testimony of the truth had been as faithful in spreading the truth as he had been, the knowledge of the Gospel would have spread all over the earth."

Brigham Young: "If I do wrong I want my brethren to give me a chance to make the matter right. I was filled with terror a few days ago to hear a conductor on a train which brought me to this city from San Juan tell of the organization which exists among the various labor organizations in this country by which they can spread disaster

---

Healing," *The Juvenile Instructor* 30, no. 21 (1 Nov. 1895), 660-63; and 30, no. 22 (15 Nov. 1895), 689-92.

[16] See D&C 89:12-13; see also D&C 49:18-19.

and destruction all over this country in a very short time. This man said that at the time of the Pullman strike there were plans laid, and the word had gone forth that every city of size in this country would be fired at a certain time on a certain day. This plan would have been carried out but for the interference of the government in the trouble, which action frightened the would-be destroyers."

We adjourned at 12 o'clock for two hours.... At two o'clock we met again and after singing, Moses Thatcher spoke. He referred to the intelligence of animals, and said we can impart of our spirit to them. We should treat them kindly, and not kill them unnecessarily. "We ought to teach our people to have respect for age and for the Priesthood, for much carelessness exists in this respect." He asked the forgiveness of the brethren for anything he has done to offend them, and said he had none but the best of feelings for the Presidency and Twelve.

Francis M. Lyman: "I approve of the teachings concerning the eating of meat and killing of animals. I met in Bunkerville on my recent trip, Orange L. Wight, the eldest son of Lyman Wight. He has been out of the Church since the days of Nauvoo, until very recently, when he was baptized. He once had three wives, one of whom is now in the California insane asylum at Highlands. He now lives with his daughter at the above named place, and is 78 years old. He was personally acquainted with the wives of the Prophet Joseph, and when Young Joseph [Smith III] tried to get him to join in the organization of the Josephite Church, which organization proposed to deny plural marriage, Orange told him he might as well deny all the other principles, as plural marriage was just as true as any of them. Orange followed his father into Texas, where an organization was effected and for some time maintained which claimed to be divine, the mistake of Lyman Wight being that he felt every apostle had the right to establish and maintain a Church wherever and whenever he saw proper."[17] Bro. Lyman related of the joining to the

---

[17] Lyman Wight, an Apostle and close friend of the Prophet Joseph Smith, left the body of the Church after the martyrdom of Joseph and Hyrum Smith and traveled with some followers to Texas, where he set up a short-lived church, under his own authority. He was excommunicated in 1848 and died in Texas in 1858.

church of several old-time Mormons, and said he could not help feeling sorry for these men who have lost so much time and so many blessings by their apostasy.

Some desultory talk was now had in which the following truths were told: Joseph Smith tried the faith of the Saints many times by his peculiarities. At one time he had preached a powerful sermon on the Word of Wisdom, and immediately thereafter he rode through the streets of Nauvoo smoking a cigar. Some of the brethren were tried as was Abraham of old. The Prophet said that the Scripture concerning the putting of new wine into old bottles referred to the teaching of the Gospel to old traditionated people, many of whom were unable to stand the new truths. Even baptism for the dead was once unacceptable to the Saints.

John Henry Smith spoke of his inclination to eat meat, which he believed, however, he could overcome. He also told of his trip to the irrigation congress, and the kind attentions he and the brethren received.

I dismissed the meeting till tomorrow with prayer....

Wednesday, October 2, 1895:

I spent the whole forenoon at the offices working on the accounts of the *Young Woman's Journal,* so as to prepare a financial statement for them.

At two o'clock I was at my Quorum meeting in the temple, where the same brethren were in attendance who were present yesterday. After singing Bro. Merrill opened with prayer.

George Teasdale was willing to be directed by the Presidency, but hoped he might be allowed to live in Mexico, and visit from there the Arizona stakes of Zion. Many people desire to move away from our Mexican settlements as they think they can better their financial condition, but those who obey counsel and remain are the best, and will be blessed of the Lord.

Heber J. Grant expressed his willingness to abstain from the use of meat, if it is desired. He would like to take a foreign mission if his circumstances would allow it, but he is at present very heavily involved.

M. W. Merrill told of a dream or vision his son, Alonzo, had while presiding in the Friendly Islands Mission, from which he only recently returned. He was troubled with the disease which is common in those islands, and gradually grew so feeble that he felt he must die. He sent for the six Elders who were laboring there to come in that he might give them instructions about their further labors. Before they arrived, however, he felt it was not right for him to thus give up, and he consequently asked them to administer to him, which was done and he felt some relief. The same evening as he lay on his couch he saw one of his brothers from home enter the door. His name was Hazen. Alonzo inquired where another brother was, for it was the other whose administration he desired to receive. Hazen responded that he was at home, but that he had come all the way to himself administer to Alonzo. He then came forward, lifted the netting which covered the sick one, and anointed his whole body with oil, using while doing so almost the same words which are used in the temple ordinance. He then administered to Alonzo, and promised him a complete recovery, if he would only exercise faith. The next morning the Elder arose in good health but weak, to the astonishment of his companions and the Saints, and he completed his mission, returning home in safety.

Bro. Merrill told of his experience in Mill Creek Canyon, by which the slipping of a log, which he was trying to load on his wagon pinned him to the earth, where he would have frozen to death, but for the interposition of divine power, which, while he was unconscious, relieved him from his position, and placed him on his wagon, which was also loaded for him, and when he regained his senses he found himself on his way home. His experience, however, compelled him to lie in bed for six weeks thereafter.[18] Bro. Whittle had a similar experience. He was in the canyon where a falling log fastened him to a tree stump. As he lost consciousness he saw two men walking along the side of a mountain. When he recovered he

---

[18] For further information on this account, see Bryant S. Hinckley, *The Faith of Our Pioneer Fathers* (Salt Lake City: Deseret Book, 1956), 180-82.

was astride one of his horses, with the other animal tied to this horse's tail.

Bro. Merrill testified to the truth of plural marriage, the divinity of which was revealed to him when he was a boy. Those who honor that principle God will bless.

He next told of a vision he had some time ago, in which he visited the other world, and was told by his heavenly guide that some of the houses he saw were occupied by the Prophet Joseph, Hyrum and other men of this Church. A group of children among whom was his own dead girl was pointed out to him.. He met a young lady neighbor in that realm, and when he expressed surprise at seeing her, she said she was only there temporarily, but would soon return to remain. When he awoke he told his wife that this young lady would soon die. Not long thereafter she was taken sick, and went for Bro. Merrill to administer to her. She then drew his head to her mouth and feebly whispered that she was now going to the place where he had met her a short time previously. In five minutes she was dead.[19]

Bro. Richards told of Bro. Stowell having died, and seeing on the other side Joseph, Brigham and other brethren, all of whom seemed very busy in the work of redeeming the dead. A dead child of an acquaintance of his called to see its parents, but they did not recognize it because of its growth.

Heber J. Grant told of the dream of John Rowberry in which he thought he fell from a ship and was drowned. He went to a most beautiful country, where he met Orson Pratt, who said he was in heaven. He also met others. Bro. Rowberry told this dream to Orson Pratt, who was then alive, and was told that when he died he would meet in heaven the very persons he had seen, as they would precede him. When Orson Pratt died, Bro. Rowberry remarked that it would be his turn next, and it was indeed so.

Pres. Snow had a letter read from Almira Miller Pond, in which she tells of the visit of her dead husband and his instructions to her concerning temple work. Her husband also told that a young lady of

---

[19] For further information concerning this account, see J. Berkeley Larsen, "The Reality of Life After Death" (address to the Brigham Young University Student body, 6 October 1953), 4.

the family would soon die, which event occurred three weeks thereafter....

Thursday, October 3, 1895:

At 10 o'clock I was at my Quorum meeting in the Temple, where we had the addition of John W. Taylor to our number, he having returned last night from Europe, where he has been on private business for the past two months. Singing was had, and F. D. Richards was mouth in prayer. Just before the meeting Brigham Young said that Moses Thatcher has a hard heart, for he told the Presidency in an interview he had with them yesterday or the day before that none of the Twelve have any backbone, for they are trying to deprive him of the very thing which Christ died to establish, which was the free agency of man.

After Bro. Snow had made a few introductory remarks I spoke of my experience when my spirit left the body during my illness with the typhoid fever. I also told of how strong I was when I did not use meat at all, and expressed the belief that our people would be better and stronger by refraining from the use of animal food entirely....

John W. Taylor said he had not accomplished the work which called him to England, and did not know when he could. He said several people of means are talking of locating in Utah, because they desire to escape the wickedness and dangers which abound in the world. He met John W. Young in England. He is laboring very hard to get means with which to pay his debts, so that he can preach the Gospel. It is also John W. Taylor's wish that he may be able to do this with his own affairs.

Some talk was had about the Japanese Mission, and the feeling was very strong that an apostle should open it up at no distant day....

The Presidency now entered and we spread the tables for the Sacrament. Pres. Snow offered prayer, and Father blessed the emblems. Before we partook, Pres. Woodruff expressed his pleasure at being with the brethren, and hoped the Holy Ghost would guide us in all we do now and in the future....

Friday, October 4, 1895:

I was in the offices attending to business till 10 o'clock, when I went to the general conference, which was well attended by officers and members of the Church. When singing and prayer had been offered Pres. Woodruff made a few opening remarks in which he expressed pleasure at meeting with the Saints and expressed the hope that the Spirit of God will be with us.

Lorenzo Snow read from the Doctrine and Covenants, and said confusion now reigns in the world, and troubles increase, but we should seek for the Holy Spirit to guide us, so that we may now and ever be undisturbed in the performance of the duties which are required of us. We will all of us at some time or other need supernatural aid, and if we have faithfully kept the commandments of God, we will receive it just when we need this help. He encouraged the Saints to do their temple work. There are now about 170 missionaries working in the temples.

Heber J. Grant said the presiding authorities should encourage the Saints to pay a full tithing and also their donations, and should then see that the tithing gets into the hands of the Presidency to meet the heavy bills which are continually presented to the Church for various matters. All commands of God are given for our blessing, and by observing them we overcome all selfish feelings. The man who feels that he is unappreciated in the Church is the one who fails to mingle with the Saints, and to be guided by the Spirit of God. We should honor our Priesthood, and those who preside over us.

John W. Taylor: He told of his being in London 13 days ago, and of the misery and poverty which he there witnessed. He also saw the necessity for the preaching of the Gospel for those who worship at all bow down for the most part to images. Our prosperity comes because of our having received and obeyed the Gospel, but if we exalt ourselves we can be abased. My mother left several brothers and sisters in England when she came to Zion. They are now all dead, but of those who came to Utah, there is a large flock.

Between the meetings I was at the offices attending to business. Was at meeting in the afternoon.

George Teasdale spoke on the remarkable fulfillment of prophecy in connection with the latter-day work. Said we must lay aside all our weaknesses when we accept of the Gospel. He bore a strong testimony to the truth.

John Henry Smith spoke of the necessity of spreading the Gospel among the nations of the earth.

M. W. Merrill urged the people to be more attentive to their temple work He read extracts from the writings and sermons of Joseph Smith to show that the work in the temples for the dead is the most important of any which devolves upon the Saints. Only about three quarters of a million baptisms for the dead have occurred in all the temples combined since they were opened until the end of 1894.

Pres. Woodruff added a few words of confirmation to the remarks of Bro. Merrill. God will hold us accountable for this labor, and if we neglect it we will be condemned....

Saturday, October 5, 1895:

I was in the offices from seven till ten o'clock attending to business. I then went to meeting. Francis M. Lyman said that men in this Church never lose the fellowship of the people so long as they do their duty. There is no power given to Satan to compel us to do wrong, but when we work evil it is because we yield to our own wicked desires. We should perform all our temporal labors with a view to building up Zion on the earth, and for the purpose of laying up treasures in heaven. This Church could not be run one hour with books alone, for it requires the living oracles to guide the affairs of the work of God. Men of God always talk without fear or equivocation, for that which they say will invariably be fulfilled.

Brigham Young: "There is a union and intensity of purpose among the Saints that is not to be found elsewhere. We cannot be one with the world and retain the Spirit of God. They may repent and become one with us. The Spirit of God is not with the man who thinks that drinking, gambling, prostitution and kindred evils are necessary to a community, and such things should be banished from among us." He then read of various revelations to show what terrible events are to occur in the last days as a punishment against the wicked.

Franklin D. Richards delivered a very interesting sermon on the Book of Mormon—the manner of its delivery to Joseph, its contents and divinity.

At noon I was at the offices....

Was at meeting at two o'clock, and was the first speaker. I felt very free during the 25 minutes I occupied, and had for my subject obedience. This principle should begin with the children , and should continue in the organizations of the church. Pres. Joseph F. Smith congratulated me on my sermon after meeting, and said he could agree with every word of it.

Moses Thatcher said that obedience was founded on intelligence. It is said we can readily forgive those who injure us, but those who we injure, never. We should only exercise the authority of the Priesthood in kindness. Love begets love. A man who will deceive others politically would not hesitate to deceive them in any other way. We should not allow the matters of little weight to break the friendships of years.

Father next spoke: "When the Latter-day Saints live as they should they know the voice of the true Shepherd. For a time after the death of the Prophet Joseph it looked as though Sidney Rigdon would be chosen to succeed him, but I remarked one day in the printing office where I was working that I did not believe God would choose a traitor or a coward to lead his people. For a time it looked as though I would be kicked out of the office.[20] Pres. Young was chosen as the leader, however, with unmistakable clearness, and with equal certainty was John Taylor selected, and subsequently Wilford Woodruff, to stand at the head of this work. Disobedience results in the loss of faith and the Holy Ghost. We possess independence and all those characteristics which make a great people, and God will work through us greater miracles than have ever yet been done, if we

---

[20] Young George Q. Cannon had learned the printing trade under Elder John Taylor while working in the Church printing office in Nauvoo. See Lawrence R. Flake, *George Q. Cannon: His Missionary Years* (Salt Lake City: Bookcraft, 1998), 24-25.

will but keep his commandments. We are left with no ground to stand on, when we resist the counsels of the Priesthood." He then referred to the purity and excellence of the stock of those who laid the foundations of this commonwealth, about nine-tenths of them being from new England. He also told of the unparalleled march of the Pioneers to this land, and the hardships they endured in the early years.

Just before the meeting closed Father protested against the people leaving the building before the benediction was pronounced....
Sunday, October 6, 1895:

At ten o'clock I was at the Tabernacle, which was crowded. Pres. Woodruff spoke of the spirit of revelation, and the necessity of our being in possession of the same. He referred to his boyhood days, and his great desire to hear the Gospel, and enjoy its gifts, but this was denied him for some time, and such men as Dr. Porter and Rev. Baws told him the gifts enjoyed by the ancient Saints are no longer necessary. Zera Pulsipher baptized myself and brother. When in England I was one time moved to tell the people to whom I was speaking that I would not meet them again for some time. Why I did so I could not tell, but being led of the Spirit I traveled 80 miles south, and in eight months had baptized about 2,000 people, including 45 preachers, and had numerous chapels at my disposal. These people had been praying to the Lord for some one to come and teach them the true Gospel. John Benbow, who was among this number was very wealthy, and wanted to lay all his property at my feet for me to use, but I would not touch a dollar of it. Satan lives today, and tries to tempt the servants of God, but I feel safe in saying that he will not be able to lead any of these apostles astray, nor will they give this people any wrong counsel."[21]

Pres. Joseph F. Smith: "I do not know where I could go if I left this Church. I think one cause of the friendly feeling of the world towards us at present is because of our temporal prosperity." He then gave a very powerful discourse on the subject of home industry, and

---

[21] Further information regarding President Woodruff's missionary experiences is found in Preston Nibley, comp., *Three Mormon Classics: Leaves from My Journal, My First Mission, and Jacob Hamblin* (Salt Lake City: Bookcraft, 1988), 5-111.

the encouragement they should receive from the people. He referred particularly to the Sugar Factory, and said that should be sustained against every other institution of its kind in the country.

At noon I spent my time in reading at my room.

At two o'clock I was at the overflow meeting in the Assembly Hall, where Brigham Young presided. C. D. Fjelsted was the first speaker. He said we are far more blessed than people in the world. We are compelled, however, to work out our own salvation. Gentiles hire ministers to take care of their souls, doctors to take care of their bodies, and lawyers to take care of their property.

Heber J. Grant said it was necessary for us to practically apply the principles of the Gospel. We should give home industries our continued and most loyal support.

Anthony W. Ivins spoke on the greatness of the latter-day work, after having read a little from the words of Jeremiah the prophet. His remarks were very encouraging.

I then spoke briefly on the curse, which followed the disobedience of the Jews, and warned the Saints against following their example....

Seymore B. Young spoke for a short time on missionary work, and encouraged the brethren to prepare themselves for such labor at home and abroad.

Brigham Young made a few closing remarks about our duty in relation to accepting the word of the Lord as it comes to us through the proper authority....

Monday, October 7, 1895:

I was busy in the offices until ten o'clock, when I went to the Assembly Hall to the Priesthood meeting. After the opening exercises Lorenzo Snow spoke a short time on Temple work, and urged the presiding authorities to keep this subject before the people. He said those who labored in the temple would carry a good influence to their wards. He hoped we would never have to close the temples because of persecution or because of the neglect of the Saints.

Bro. Merrill told the people to keep private records of the work they do, so as to avoid calling on the temples to furnish them abstracts of what they have done.

Uncle David said that some of those to whom the St. George temple had furnished abstracts had made mistakes in copying the same. For this reason he would hereafter require those who desired abstracts to furnish the books in which they desire them copied, so that errors may be avoided.

Pres. Woodruff said every elder should keep a complete and careful genealogical record.

Franklin D. Richards spoke of temple work, and also invited the brethren to take life memberships in the genealogical society which has recently been started.

Pres. Joseph F. Smith said the same patriotism which we have shown in our religious affairs should be manifested in regard to the sustaining of home industries, and if trusts are formed to break down our struggling businesses we should work against them. The time may come when we will be cut off from the outside world for our supplies. If this does happen we will be in a bad condition if we are not self-sustaining. Though outside concerns may reduce the price on some goods which we here manufacture it will be only for the purpose of closing down our factories, and they will then raise the price when there is no competition. We have the living oracles in the Church, and their counsel must be sought. The moment a man in authority decides to do as he pleases, he steps on dangerous ground. One of the Twelve and one of the Seven Presidents of Seventies have done wrong in accepting obligations without first consulting and obtaining the consent of those who preside over them. No man surrenders his manhood by seeking the advice of his superiors."

Heber J. Grant bore a very strong testimony to that which Pres. Smith had said. He would rather have the confidence of the Presidency and Twelve than that of the whole people otherwise. He expressed the hope that politics would not be allowed to cause us to lose interest in the work of God. He spoke strongly in favor of home industries, and said the stores would carry home-made goods, if the people demanded them.

Pres. Woodruff said we must sustain ourselves in temporal matters or we will place a weapon in the hands of our enemies with which to injure us.

Father next spoke: "Stake superintendents of the Y. M. M. I. Associations should be consulted by bishops and other presiding authorities when selections of local officers is made. Statistical reports should be furnished promptly and correctly. The brethren should connect themselves with the State Irrigation Society, which will distribute reading matter which will be valuable to every farmer. The waters of the country should be secured, and be held in reservoirs for the use of the settlers, and not for speculative purposes. The influence of every man should be exercised to secure a large and favorable vote in favor of the Constitution. We should all be in favor of Statehood with the remembrance of the wrongs which we have so long suffered. Those who pay tithing receive more in return than they give. To pay to the Lord is a good investment. I would not have said what Pres. Smith has, but I am glad he did so, for it is the truth, and where men have done wrong they should correct their mistakes, and try to do better."

L. John Nuttall urged the brethren to keep their titles clear and their organizations perfect, so that no question may ever arise in regard to their ecclesiastical property.

Pres. Woodruff bore testimony to the truth of what Father and Pres. Smith had said. He had been in the Apostleship for sixty years, and had never known an Apostle to take upon himself any obligation that was to occupy his time or attention outside of his calling without first obtaining the permission of those who presided over him. If he did do so he lost the faith.[22] A man does not lose his manhood by doing what is right.

Heber J. Grant spoke a few words in favor of the Brigham Young monument.

After some desultory conversation the meeting adjourned....

---

[22] This statement was directed at Moses Thatcher, B. H. Roberts, and a few others holding high Church office, who were resisting their leaders' counsel to get permission from them before seeking political office, a course that would distract them from their ecclesiastical callings.

Wednesday, October 9, 1895:

I had a long talk with Dan Seegmiller, of the Presidency of Kanab Stake, whom I was led to suspect of having stolen at least one of my mares that I sent south to be herded some years ago. There were three mares neither of which was ever returned to me, and I was told by several reliable parties that he had sold one of them. He satisfied me that he was innocent, as the animal he sold was very much like mine, but was not her. I begged his pardon, for my wrong accusation, and we parted the best of friends.

Bro. Seegmiller told me of a conversation which he had with George W. Thatcher[23] on the evening after the Priesthood meeting when the latter exclaimed that he never felt "so G___ D___ mean in all my life." He said that Father was encouraging the attack against Moses Thatcher and Roberts so that he could secure for himself the nomination for Senator, but George Thatcher acknowledged that it was for the purpose of preventing this that they had nominated Thatcher and Roberts....

Thursday, October 10, 1895:

I went to the seven o'clock train, and bade Father goodbye, as he is going east for a few days. I then went to the offices and worked till 11 a.m., when I went to my quorum meeting in the temple. Present: Wilford Woodruff, Joseph F. Smith, Lorenzo Snow, F. D. Richards, Brigham Young, Francis M. Lyman, George Teasdale, Heber J. Grant, John W. Taylor and myself; George F. Gibbs, clerk. Some talk was had about Church divorces. Joseph F. Smith holds that where the President gives a divorce it disunites the couple for time and eternity, for the same power which unites them together dissolves the bond. No man is justified in putting away his wife, however, save for fornication, and this, as explained in the pamphlet issued in the days of Joseph the Prophet, is alienation.

We now had some talk about politics. B. H. Roberts has written a letter to the Presidency justifying the course he has taken, but it does not make the matter right, so said Pres. Woodruff. It was decided

---

[23] George W. Thatcher was the son of Moses Thatcher.

that Heber J. Grant should visit Powers and try to pacify him, which was subsequently done, when Powers said the Church had a perfect right to discipline its members, but his only objection to the remarks of Joseph F. Smith was the application which was being made of them by the Republicans, who said this was an evidence that the Presidency of the Church desired the defeat of the Democratic party. We were dismissed with prayer by Brigham Young....

Saturday, October 12, 1895:

Both the *Herald* and *Argus* today condemn in unmeasured terms Joseph F. Smith's remarks at Monday's Priesthood meeting, and they cry "Hands Off," or threaten the disbandment of the Democratic Party, and vigorous opposition to statehood.[24]

Monday, October 14, 1895:

Pres. Woodruff issued a card in this morning's *Tribune*, which was confirmed by Joseph F. Smith in the *News*, in which the statement is made that no Church influence is used or sought to be used by the authorities in political matters....

Wednesday, October 16, 1895:

I went home to supper, and at 8:30 Mame and I went to the home of Hyrum B. and Emily Clawson to the wedding reception of their daughter Lulu, who was today married to Seymour B. Young, Jr. The house was crowded, but it seemed to me the guests were invited more for the presents they would bring than for the sociability. I spent a dreary two hours in standing around, and then went home without getting any refreshments.

Sarah and I have been married seventeen years today.

Thursday, October 17, 1895:

At 11 a.m. was at my Quorum meeting in the Temple. Present: Wilford Woodruff, Joseph F. Smith, Lorenzo Snow, Brigham Young, Francis M. Lyman, Heber J. Grant, John W. Taylor and myself;

---

[24] See AHC Journals 7 October 1895.

George F. Gibbs, clerk. Pres. Woodruff said LeGrand Young had suggested that the Twelve issue a document containing the statement that the Saints are politically free, but it was felt that we had already done enough of this kind of thing, and the fear was expressed that even were we to do as suggested, Moses Thatcher might refuse to sign with us. Pres. Woodruff said that Moses Thatcher's discontent began at the death of Pres. Taylor, when he sought to rule the Twelve, at which time he also attacked Father in a vicious manner, and charged him with great wrongs, which he had never done. Heber J. Grant said he had seconded Moses' efforts to down Father at that time, but he had since seen the error of his ways, and repented of them, which Moses had never done.

Joseph F. Smith told of a quarrel which George W. Thatcher and Lyman H. Martineau had in Logan, in which each called the other a liar, and they would have come to blows had not friends interfered. It was over some political matters. Bishop Preston also charges George W. Thatcher with his defeat for the Democratic nomination for Governor, George feeling that Preston's nomination would injure Moses' chance for the Senate.

John W. Taylor was mouth in dismissing....

Sunday, October 20, 1895:

I arose quite early and went to Ogden on the 7 a.m. U. P. train to attend the Stake Conference. Pres. Joseph F. Smith, John W. Taylor and Edward Stevenson were also there....

John W. Taylor advised the people to possess their souls in peace. We must not allow ourselves to become excited, for it is always unsafe to tie to an excitable person. Politics must be made subordinate to the Gospel. The day will come when the Priesthood will govern in all things. Our troubles come from the desire to have our own will instead of doing the will of the Father. The devil is the foundation of all strife....

In the afternoon I spoke for 40 minutes. I told the people to be careful not to misquote the brethren as well as not to misjudge them. We are liable to be deceived in our hearing, seeing, as well as by our other senses. If we slander or malign our fellow-men, we will have to pay the penalty of this sin. We should study politics and use them wisely, but in all things we must be sure to avoid any betrayal of the brethren.

Much to my chagrin and astonishment Edward Stevenson occupied the remainder of the time, this preventing Joseph F. Smith from speaking. He referred to ancient prophecies concerning the great latter-day work, and showed how the Lord had fulfilled the same....

Monday, October 21, 1895:

I went to the office very early, and attended to some work, and then took the nine o'clock train for Ogden. I went direct to the meeting....

Pres. Joseph F. Smith then delivered a very powerful testimony of the Gospel, and gave instructions to parents concerning the proper care and rearing of their children. He told of the terrible consequences which will follow those who neglect their duties to their offspring. Better for such never to have had children than by their conduct to have inspired infidelity and disobedience in the hearts of the children. He told of one man who had apostatized, and reared his children out of the Church; in his old age he had reunited himself with the Church, but all his family were without faith, because of his apostasy. "All evil-doers are sons of perdition until they have atoned for their sins, but those on whom the second death will have a part are the unredeemable sons of perdition, to whom reference is made in the Doctrine and Covenants." He said he did not favor the union of Church and State, but he did not want the state to interfere with the discipline which the Church sees fit to give its members. Politics reminded him of the Sandwich Islander who told his wife to put some water on some ink powder he had purchased. She did so, but made it too thin. The result was a quarrel in which he accused her of using too much water, while she protested that there was not enough ink powder. The result was a separation, and it required nearly all the elders in the mission to get them reconciled again....

In the afternoon the authorities were sustained and I then spoke for half an hour on the duty we owe to vote for statehood, and presented some reasons for our taking this course. It will bring freedom, and give us greater influence at home and abroad. I also encouraged idlers to move into the country and secure land for cultivation, and to make themselves homes.

Pres. Joseph F. Smith spoke for 15 minutes in favor of statehood. He thinks we will find it cheaper than our present form of government. We are to receive 8,000,000 acres of land with statehood, in addition to two sections in each township, and the sale of this land will no doubt more than off-set our increased expenses.

John W. Taylor spoke interestingly for half an hour on the same subject....

Tuesday, October 22, 1895:

The reconvened Democratic Convention met today in the theater. It was a very noisy gathering, according to all reports, and resulted in the issuance of an address denouncing Church interference, and referring to Bro. Lyman having used an influence in politics which was entirely improper. He is charged with having urged the election of Frank J. Cannon in Garfield County, when he was not in that county at the time charged nor after Frank's nomination for Congress. Pres. Lorenzo Snow says he never saw such a terrible spirit among members of the Church since the days of Kirtland as that which he witnessed today in the theater among the brethren.

Thursday, October 24, 1895:

Until 11 a.m. I was busy in the offices. At this time I went to my Quorum meeting in the Temple. Present: All of the Presidency, Lorenzo Snow, Brigham Young, F. M. Lyman, H. J. Grant, M. W. Merrill and myself; George F. Gibbs, clerk. We had some talk about the political situation. Father said that Moses Thatcher [and B. H. Roberts] were wrong in feeling and saying that the Presidency of the Church have no right to dictate them in their political actions. Had they entertained such feelings when they were made general authorities of the Church they would never have received his vote. It was felt that these brethren must be labored with so that such doctrines be not accepted by the Church as correct.

We had some talk about re-incarnation, which doctrine it is feared is entertained by Orson F. Whitney, George C. Parkinson and others. It was felt that these and any other persons who believe in this false idea, should be corrected. Father dismissed with prayer....

Sunday, October 27, 1895 [Oxford, Idaho]:

We had a short visit with Counselors Sol. Hale and M. F. Cowley before conference began. Pres. George C. Parkinson is now in Utah campaigning for the Republican party.

At ten o'clock we met in Conference with a reasonably good attendance of people....

I then occupied an hour in speaking on family government, and the evils of back-biting.

At noon we had a talk with Sol. Hale and M. F. Cowley about the re-incarnation ideas of George C. Parkinson. The former had never been approached by his president on the subject, but Bro. Cowley said he had learned from Bro. Parkinson's own lips that he entertained some belief in this false doctrine, for he had brought supposed proof from Scripture to sustain his position. At the time the Stake Academy building was dedicated during the present year Pres. Parkinson had his house dedicated, and though Apostle Merrill was there, he was not asked to offer the prayer, but Orson F. Whitney was. Orson thereafter blessed Bro. Parkinson and his family, and was in turn blessed by Bro. Parkinson. George C. Parkinson has told his counselors that he will yet be one of the Twelve Apostles, and Orson F. Whitney said that the only reason he was not made an Apostle when I was chosen was because he violated the Word of Wisdom, for he had been selected, but when it was learned that he was guilty in this respect, he was voted down. This was not the case; his name was mentioned, but he was never chosen for the place....

Thursday, October 31, 1895:

I dictated a number of letters in the morning, and then went to my Quorum meeting at 11 o'clock. Present: All of the Presidency;

Lorenzo Snow, Brigham Young, F. M. Lyman, J. H. Smith, H. J. Grant, J. W. Taylor and myself; George F. Gibbs, clerk....

There was some talk about Father's remarks in Brigham City on Monday last, wherein he charged some man (evidently meaning Powers) stole the election of Salt Lake City, when the Liberals were installed, and he was now at the head of another organization. Father denied in the *Tribune* having said any such thing as this, but when he came to question those who were with him at the conference, he became convinced that he had used such language, and his denial of it was due to a lapse of memory. He therefore feels very much chagrined and humiliated. He sent a verbal apology to Powers of the affair.

Bro. Lyman said he had been told by a prominent Democrat that the party intended to sit down on Father, Joseph F. Smith, F. M. Lyman, J. H. Smith, M. W. Merrill and A. H. Lund for their interference in politics, and some of the people have refused to vote for them as authorities of the Church.

A question was asked as to where adulterers should be required to confess their sins, as mentioned in the Book of Covenants. Pres. Woodruff said the acknowledgement should be as public as the offense, but no more exposure should be required than is necessary to correct the evil. After some discussion it was decided that where a public confession of this sin is necessary it should be made before a Fast meeting, or in presence of the Priesthood, but in no case before a public and mixed congregation.

Women married to Gentiles should not be allowed to receive their endowments, because of the secrecy enjoined upon them, which may arouse the jealous suspicions of their husbands. The President is, of course, allowed to make exceptions to this rule. Wives of apostates, if they retain the faith, are allowed to do work in the temples.

Meeting was dismissed with prayer by Francis M. Lyman....

Friday, November 1, 1895:
Father issued in tonight's *News* a card of apology for his remarks in Brigham City concerning Powers. It was received by Powers very gracefully, and he spoke publicly of the more exalted position which

Father had taken in his feelings by the manly and full acknowledgement of his error....

Saturday, November 2, 1895:

This morning's *Herald* attacks Francis M. Lyman for his alleged Church interference in politics. They make out a very poor case against him, for he can disprove their most serious charges....

...I took the U. P. train for Logan, on which were Heber J. Grant and John W. Taylor. We were met in Logan by Counselor Isaac Smith with buggies, and were taken to the Conference in the Tabernacle....

John W. Taylor spoke 35 minutes on the inaccuracy of our outward senses, which causes us sometimes to commit very grave errors, and misrepresent our brethren and sisters in what they say and do. He bore a strong testimony to the divine calling of the First Presidency, of which Quorum George Q. Cannon and Joseph F. Smith are just as good as Pres. Woodruff. We must sustain these brethren or lose the Spirit of God.

John W. Taylor and I took dinner with Isaac Smith. At the table John W. reproved Bro. Smith for his criticism of Moses Thatcher, who may have done wrong, yet he is not amenable to Isaac Smith. Bro. Smith took the reproof in a good spirit. Before going to meeting I called at Bro. Thatcher's house to see him, but he sent me word he was engaged. Joseph L. Rawlins and other political leaders were there, and I felt rather hurt that he would see them and not me.

In the afternoon meeting Jonathan G. Kimball spoke for 15 minutes, and urged the people to sustain the Priesthood. He related a dream which one of the apostles had in which he saw a small but very filthy stream winding its way through Cache Valley. It gradually increased in size, and as it grew the people timidly approached it and placed first their fingers, then their hands and finally their whole bodies in the polluted liquid. Those who would not bathe in this stream fled to the mountains for safety. He allowed the congregation to make their own application of this dream, which he evidently felt meant politics.

M. W. Merrill urged the Priesthood to attend to the details of their callings, and to be obedient in all requirements made of them.

After a beautiful hymn had been sung by the choir, Heber J. Grant spoke of the injury which will result from the spirit of fault-finding and back-biting which exists. People who indulge in such a spirit will lose the faith unless they repent.

After meeting H. J. Grant, J. W. Taylor and myself called on Bro. Thatcher. He seemed to be some better than when we last saw him. We remained with him for some time, and chatted pleasantly....

Sunday, November 3, 1895 [Logan, Cache Co.]:

At six o'clock I arose and accompanied Heber J. Grant and Orson Smith to administer to Theodore Petersen, who returned a short time ago from a mission because of ill health. It was said he was possessed of an evil spirit, which was the cause of our being called so early in the morning, but I saw no evidence of this being the case. He is undoubtedly troubled with consumption. We administered to him.

In the forenoon meeting I spoke for nearly an hour on the heroism which our elders manifest in going upon missions, and the devotion of their wives to the cause of truth. I urged the exaltation of politics to a high plane and not allow them to drag us down. I also encouraged the Saints to vote for statehood.

Moses Thatcher followed me for over 40 minutes. He also asked the people to vote for statehood, and said by so doing we would not become a part of the great image which Daniel saw, and which was to crush all the man-made kingdoms of the latter days. He told the brethren not to use their priesthood to afflict those who are under them, for God does not approve of such conduct....

Thursday, November 7, 1895:

At 11 o'clock I was at my Quorum meeting in the temple. Present, all of the Presidency, Lorenzo Snow, F. D. Richards, B. Young, F. M. Lyman, H. J. Grant, J. W. Taylor and myself; George F. Gibbs, clerk. Bro. Lyman read letters which he received from John R. Murdock and C. D. White of Beaver, in which they deny any Church interference in politics on the part of Bro. Lyman in 1891, to which J. F. Tolton makes affidavit. I was present at that meeting, and verbally testified that Bro. Lyman said nothing which I could not approve, and it could not be construed in any reasonable way as Church interference in politics. We indulged in some political talk, considering in connection therewith Moses Thatcher's Logan speeches, in one of which he said there was sufficient room in Utah for both the Church and the State, but if the Church interfered with the State, there would soon be no Church. He also used other unwise language. John W. Taylor said he felt that the leading Church authorities should be selected for prominent positions, and the idea should not be allowed to grow that because a man occupies a high ecclesiastical position, he should be shut out of political offices. Bro. Lyman inquired what the wishes of the Presidency were in regard to senators. He had till this morning been opposed to Father being chosen for this position, but now he felt it would be right for him to go as one of the first senators from Utah. Heber J. Grant also spoke strongly in favor of Father for the position. Pres. Woodruff expressed his desire that Father should go. At Pres. Woodruff's request I expressed my views in opposition to this selection, for I felt that Father would thereby lose the respect and confidence of a good part of the people, and besides, he had not worked for the Republican party, and was in no way entitled to the nomination by them. I felt, too, that his services were more needed at home than in Washington. We were advised to keep our conversation quiet until statehood is achieved....

Friday, November 8, 1895:

Father spoke to me privately today about his going to the Senate. He says he does not care to go, but I think it would afford him gratification to be sent. He hopes Frank will not feel disappointed should Father be chosen in his place.

Saturday, November 9, 1895:

While talking at Pres. [William W.] Cluff's after meeting he said that the exact center of the United States has been located at Col. Ogden's grave, about ten miles west of Independence, Missouri, the place designated by the Prophet Joseph Smith for the building of the Center Stake of Zion.[25] The most fertile spot in the country is also said to be within a radius of fifty miles of Kansas City, which would include the place where Joseph Smith said the Garden of Eden was located.

We spent the evening in pleasant conversation.

Sunday, November 10, 1895; Coalville, Summit Co.:

At two o'clock the attendance at meeting was very good. I spoke an hour and ten minutes telling of duties which must not be neglected at present if we would retain the faith of the Gospel. Women should try to exercise an influence for good over their husbands, and should encourage them in doing their duty.

Bro. Stevenson spoke for ten minutes. He said David Whitmer apostatized over a mere trifle: he thought the revelations of the Lord to Joseph Smith were published too soon, and also felt that the Church should be called merely The Church of Christ. Thomas B. Marsh lost his standing in the Church because of a quarrel about a pint of stripplings. He afterwards came to Utah and joined the Church, and one day called the people to witness what he had lost by his apostasy....

Monday, November 11, 1895:

I spent part of the forenoon and afternoon with Senator Fred T. Dubois of Idaho, who is on his way to Washington. He is much interested in the progress of Utah, though he was once a violent persecutor of Mormons in Idaho. He was U. S. Marshal for the State before it entered the Union, and no man could be more active than he in hunting down polygamists, but of late he has been a very good friend, and helped very much to make Utah a State. He told me privately that he thought it would be a grave mistake for Father to accept a senatorial nomination now, as he has done no political work, and to select him for the position now that the work is done would immediately raise the cry here and in the East that the Church and

---

[25] See D&C 59—Introduction; see also D&C 84:2-4.

State were united. He thinks the Senators should be Frank J. Cannon and C. C. Goodwin. I accompanied him to see the Presidency in the afternoon, and he expressed to them his views about who should be the senators. Father there said that he was in favor of Goodwin being selected as the Gentile candidate. Pres. Woodruff agreed with this view....

Tuesday, November 12, 1895:

In the afternoon I was at the President's Office.... I also had a talk with Father, who told me privately that he hoped Frank would go to the Senate instead of himself, and he said Frank should work for his own nomination. He told me to telephone to Frank that the Lord would overrule it all for the good of all concerned....

Thursday, November 14, 1895:

At 11 a. m. I was in the Temple. Present: All of the Presidency, Lorenzo Snow, F. D. Richards, B. Young, F. M. Lyman, J. H. Smith, J. W. Taylor and myself; G. F. Gibbs, clerk. On motion of Joseph F. Smith, seconded by F. M. Lyman, George Teasdale is to be called to locate his family in Utah as soon as Anthony W. Ivins is installed as President of the Mexican Stake, which Bro. Lyman will start south tomorrow to do.

John Ashman asks: To whom shall an illegitimate child be sealed? To the Father who died without marrying the mother, or to the woman who is alive and now married? Answer: To the woman. Question: A Mormon girl married a Gentile, and a girl was born who is now being raised by the father, the mother being dead. Can she be sealed to her grand-parents who are in the Church? She must wait till she is of age, and then choose for herself, unless the father consents for her to be sealed to her relatives.

Father felt that some investigation should be had of the conduct of Thatcher and Roberts before they receive any ecclesiastical appointments in the Church. Pres. Snow said he could not fellowship them until they made things right, nor could any of the Quorum do so. It was decided to leave any investigation of their affairs until after

Statehood, as trouble might otherwise ensue because of the exercise of Church discipline.

John Henry Smith said it was told him that the Democrats are preparing affidavits and a brief in opposition to statehood, and that Powers was at the head of the plan. The latter part was subsequently proved to be untrue....

I today learned from Ex-marshal I. A. Benton that out of the $5,800 which H. B. Clawson received during the raid as "hush money" to keep Benton from making arrests, only four payments of $500 each and one payment of $200 ever reached Benton. The remainder, $3,600 H. B. Clawson must therefore have retained for himself. I reported my findings to Father, who was pained and astonished.

Friday, November 15, 1895:

At 11 o'clock I was at the President's Office and accompanied Pres. Woodruff and Father to the Telephone Company's building, where we were shown through the most excellent and complete structure by Pres. George Y. Wallace and Supt. D. S. Murray. The building is entirely fireproof, and is prepared with every convenience for the accommodation of customers and employees. Mr. Wallace made a proposition to the Presidency that if the Church will take 15 telephones they will supply them for $52.50 per month. The reduction in the price is for the purpose of securing other customers among the Mormon people, of whom only three now have them in their homes....

Saturday, November 16, 1895;

I spent most of the day in the office at my usual work. In the afternoon I had a long talk with B. H. Roberts, who feels somewhat humble since his political defeat. He says he must engage in some remunerative employment in order to sustain his family. He justifies himself for the course he has taken in politics by reason of advice which he says was given him by Pres. Joseph F. Smith, which was in substance that all the brethren were at liberty to engage in politics, with the full approval of the Presidency. He presents a very plausible side of the story, but in some things he is not right in my opinion, especially in his views as to the rights of the Priesthood. I advised him to see the Presidency, and set himself right with them, but he did not feel that he could yet do so....

Monday, November 18, 1895:

I was engaged nearly all day in the offices and my room attending to business and writing on my journal....

Thursday, November 21, 1895:

At 11 a.m. I was at my Quorum meeting in the Temple. Present: All of the Presidency, F. D. Richards, H. J. Grant, J. W. Taylor and myself; George F. Gibbs, clerk. A letter was read for the Presidents of Stakes and presiding authorities generally, concerning the organization of Teachers Quorums, as also about the confessions of adulterers, the idea being to embody the desires of the brethren on these subjects as expressed in a recent meeting of our Quorum; but the letter was not sufficiently clear, and it was therefore laid over for more careful preparation. Some talk was had about a successor for Bro. Lund in the Presidency of the European mission. Bro. Grant said he had desired to succeed in this position, but his heavy financial load seemed to make this desire a thing which cannot be fulfilled for a long time to come. It was left for the Presidency to select a successor. Pres. Joseph F. Smith offered prayer. Thereafter some talk was had about the senatorial question. Pres. Woodruff expressed his wish that Father should go to the Senate, and said all our private talk in the future should be in this line.

Father said he hoped Trumbo would not go for two principal reasons: He is not a person whose manner and characteristics we would desire to represent us, for he is very ignorant, and then he would be, no doubt, a boogler, accepting bribes for services which he would have the power to render.

It was decided that George C. Parkinson be recalled from laboring in Trumbo's interest, and John W. Taylor was appointed to see and recall him. Later in the day, however, it was decided that Heber J. Grant should be sent to see Parkinson, and tell him some reasons why the Presidency do not want Trumbo to go to the Senate from Utah.

In the afternoon I was with Father at his office for some time. He there requested George M. Cannon to try and prevent the legislators from pledging themselves to any senatorial candidate before coming to the legislature....

Sunday, November 24, 1895:

At two o'clock I was at the Tabernacle, where the funeral of the last of Pres. Brigham Young's brothers occurred. Lorenzo D. Young was 88 years old, and has been a sufferer for a long time, so that death will be a relief to him. The speakers were F. D. Richards, Heber J. Grant, Myself, John W. Taylor, Joseph F. Smith and Pres. W. Woodruff. Testimonies to the good character and life of the deceased were borne, and some remarks were made upon the resurrection. All that was said and done was of a consolatory character....

Saturday, November 30, 1895:

In the evening I was at home engaged in reading proofs, and writing on the type-writer.

Monday, December 2, 1895:

In the afternoon at two o'clock was at the President's Office at a meeting. Present: All of the Presidency, Lorenzo Snow, F. D. Richards, John Henry Smith, Heber J. Grant and myself: John R. Winder and George Gibbs. The President stated that the Pioneer Power Co. of Ogden had expended over $50,000 on its property, which amount had been raised on the individual credit of the directors. The control of the Company is in the hands of the Presidency of the Church, and they desired to carry the work through to completion, because they believed it would be a benefit to Zion in whose interest they were working in this enterprise. The Company had unsuccessfully tried to sell its bonds, till now they have an offer from Mr. Bannigan, who purchased the Sugar Bonds, to buy $1,200,000 of the bonds providing he have a bond of $500,000 in bonds, and $300,000 of the preferred stock of the company,… In other words, he is to buy the $1,500,000 of bonds at 80 cents on the dollar, and the interest and principal of the same is to be guaranteed by the Church. His demand is a very heavy one, but there is no likelihood of our being able to do better. Pres. Woodruff desired to know if the brethren would approve of the endorsement of the Church on these bonds. The matter was considered at some length, resulting in all of the brethren voting for the motion which was made by Pres. Lorenzo Snow, and seconded by F. D. Richards, that we do give the Presidency our full support and faith in signing these bonds, and that we stand behind them in the doing of the same. John Henry Smith said he voted for the motion, though his conscience and judgment did not approve of the course which it was decided to take. He feared the credit of the Church might be injured by this action. Both he and F. D. Richards urged that we defer action till the majority of the Quorum are together, and thus get them committed to the policy, but the necessity for immediate action on this matter was urged, hence it was decided to take the vote of those present, and see others of the Quorum thereafter, and try to secure their sanction. Pres. Snow remarked that the Presidency would have the support of the Quorum of the Twelve in whatever they decided to do, even though the course they took resulted in financial failure. Father said he saw light in taking this course, and felt easy; this was also the feeling of Pres. Woodruff, which was the reason for his change of heart on the matter, for when the matter of endorsing the paper was first mentioned he repelled it instantly. Bishop Winder said he was at first very much opposed to the Presidency giving their endorsement as asked, but at the last meeting of the board, his feelings had suddenly and unaccountably changed, and he felt convinced it was the best and only thing to do. Pres. Woodruff evidently felt that this was the thing that ought to be done, and was very much relieved in his feelings when the vote of the brethren was in favor of the proposition.

After meeting Father was speaking to some of the brethren, when he said with the feelings which Pres. Woodruff entertained towards Moses Thatcher, it would not be wise for any of us to mention this matter to him. Father said Moses Thatcher's drawing away from his brethren commenced as far as his knowledge concerning it went, at a time when the Council of Fifty met in the old City Hall, and Moses opposed the proposition to anoint John Taylor as Prophet, Priest and King, and Moses' opposition prevailed at that time. Moses has constantly opposed the increase of power in the hands of the President of the Church....

Tuesday, December 3, 1895:

At noon I went to the President's office and checked off Father's bank book and then listened to a conversation which the Presidency had with violinist W. C. Clive, in the presence of George H. Thomas, who is a coronetist, and John Henry Smith and Heber J. Grant. Bro. Clive has refused steadily to join the Union of musicians in this city. He has been playing with the Salt Lake Theater orchestra until a few days ago, when a change was made in the leader, Willard Weihe taking the place of George Careless, the latter being a non-union man, and the former belonging to the union. The result is that Bro. Clive cannot play with Weihe unless he joins the union. He also lost a position as leader of the Opera House orchestra because he is not a Union man. The change in the leader of the Theater orchestra was made without it being known to Bro. Grant, who is the President of the Company, of the condition of affairs. Bro. Clive, who has refused to his own financial injury to join the Union from principle, and because he thought the Church did not approve of these organizations, now desires to know the mind of the brethren thereon. The Presidency could only re-affirm their opposition to the Union, and expressed their admiration for the manly stand Bro. Clive had taken. Pres. Woodruff said sorrow would come to this people if they join these unions. He felt they are opposed to the Gospel, and no Saint should find place among them. After hearing the talk of Bros. Clive and Thomas, the matter was referred to Bros. Grant and Smith, who are on the Theater board of Directors, to see what they could do for the relief of Bro. Clive. These brethren think a fight will result, but believe it will be best to tell Weihe that he must employ Clive, who has been at the theater so many years....

I went with Heber J. Grant and John Henry Smith to the house of the former in the afternoon, and assisted in administering to his son Heber S., who has been troubled for some time with hip disease. His suffering at times has been very bad, but since the fast in which the family engaged two weeks ago, he has been better. Patriarch John Smith also told him a few days ago in blessing him, that he should recover, and do much good for Zion....

Thursday, December 5, 1895:

At 11 a.m. I was at the temple at my Quorum meeting, where the following brethren were present: All of the Presidency, L. Snow, F. D. Richards, Moses Thatcher, John H. Smith, Heber J. Grant, John W. Taylor and myself; George F. Gibbs clerk. A letter was read from Brigham Young complaining of the improper conduct of Pres. F. A. Hammond of the San Juan Stake. He smokes and drinks thus setting such an evil example as to lead many of the young men to follow him in these bad habits. It was felt that an effort should be made to have him resign, and the Presidency will take the matter in hand to try and effect this without hurting his feelings.

Pres. Snow asked if it is allowable for people to wear any garment next to their skin except the garment provided in the giving of endowments. The decision was that the garments of the temple should be worn in all cases next to the skin.

We were dismissed with prayer by Pres. Woodruff....

Friday, December 6, 1895:

Was at the President's Office for a short time, where I desired to secure from the brethren some unqualified opinion and decision in regard to the senatorship for Father. Ben Rich had written me asking this question, and I desired to answer him. I told Pres. Woodruff that I considered it dangerous for Father and Frank to juggle longer with this question, as the result might be that both would lose it. I had already talked freely with Father, and he had expressed himself as unfavorable to his selection, but he desired me to see Presidents Woodruff and Smith. Pres. Smith said in answer to a request for his views that he would like Father to decide the question, but as far as his views are concerned he thought it would be better for Father to refrain from becoming a candidate at the present time. Pres. Woodruff then talked privately with Father, after which Pres. Smith, Heber J. Grant and I were told by the President that in his view Father should go to the Senate, but not this time. He felt it would be unwise to urge Father forward at the present time, and he was therefore in favor of sending Frank. All of us felt to raise both hands to sustain this decision, even H. J. Grant, who has been so desirous in the past that Father should go, says now that he fears it would be a great mistake for Father to be sent because of the feeling among the Saints in regard to this matter. I am greatly pleased at this outcome of a serious question....

Saturday, December 7, 1895:

...I took the R. G. Western train for the purpose of going to the Conference at Kaysville.... I went direct to the meeting house where Father was speaking on apostasy and some of the causes leading thereto. He said adultery was one of the most fruitful, for the spirit of God will not remain with an impure man or woman. He referred to the case of Amasa M. Lyman, who had been pure and upright, so far as he had been able to observe during a long and intimate acquaintance with him, during which time they had been on missions together. The only thing which he questioned in the conduct of Lyman was his fondness for Spiritualism, and to attend seances. He therefore asked Pres. B. Young after the apostasy of Lyman, what the cause was. Pres. Young said Amasa M. Lyman had once lifted his heel against the Priesthood of God in that he would not follow the counsel which Pres. Young gave him in regard to the forming of a company to go to California.

I bore testimony for ten minutes to the remarks which I had heard....

Sunday, December 8, 1895:

I went to Kaysville on the U. P. 8 a.m. train, where I attended Conference. Franklin D. Richards, Heber J. Grant, John W. Taylor and George Reynolds of the General Authorities being also present.

After the opening exercises Bro. Reynolds made some remarks in relation to the great work of preaching the Gospel, and the small extent of country we have as yet covered. He was followed for half an hour by Heber J. Grant, who spoke on the observance of the Word of Wisdom, tithing and kindred subjects. John W. Taylor occupied the remainder of the time in a discourse calculated to magnify the Presidency of the Church, and the general authorities, and to encourage the Saints to sustain them. He made some remarks which were scarcely proper concerning the mental and physical condition of Pres. Woodruff, who was unable, he said, to do the work of the Church without the help of his counselors. "As well might a baby be placed at the head of the Church as Pres. Woodruff without the aid of Presidents Cannon and Smith." The spirit of his remarks was just right, but his language was scarcely as well chosen as it might have been. He said those who voted against the Presidency or any one of them, voted against all of them.

His remarks were very timely, as he had been approached by two different members of the Church who felt to vote against Father, Pres. Smith and perhaps other brethren who had taken active part in politics. I was also told by Bro. Barnes, a young man, before coming to meeting, that some of the brethren desired to vote against Father, Joseph F. Smith and F. M. Lyman. I advised him to use his influence against any such thing, and told him those who could not sustain the brethren had better refrain from voting altogether....

Meeting reconvened at two o'clock, when Heber J. Grant presented the authorities, all of whom were unanimously sustained. John W. Taylor then explained that his remark concerning Pres. Woodruff made this morning, referred only to his ability to attend to the detail work of the Church, and had no reference to him as President and Prophet, for he is indeed the Prophet of God, and gives the Word of God to the people.

I then spoke about 40 minutes in relation to politics, and urged the study of the same, and care in the use of the same that they do not lead us away from the Church. Warned the people against corruption in politics as well as every other kind of evil.

F. D. Richards occupied the remainder of the time telling the people some of the results which will come to us as a people if we will remain humble and do as the Lord directs....

Monday, December 9, 1895:

I today hired Frank Chamberlin to do my type-writing,...

I called on Delegate–elect C. E. Allen today, who desired to talk with me about the rumor that Father is to be the Church candidate for the Senate. I assured him that such will not be the case, which information pleased him very much. He said such an event would result in the immediate belief that Church and State were united in Utah, inasmuch as Father has done no political work which entitles him to the place mentioned....

Tuesday, December 10, 1895:

I then went to the President's Office and read to Father and Pres. Woodruff a letter which I just received from Senator Fred T. Dubois, in which he urges the election of Frank and C. C. Goodwin to the Senate, because of the effect their election will have on the county in settling this old cry of the union of Church and State in Utah. Father does not think it wise for him to now issue a card refusing the senatorship, because this would show his hand to Trumbo, and allow him to form new combinations to secure his election, but under no circumstances will Father accept of the nomination for the senate, so he told me, and afterwards said the same to Ben E. Rich. I feared that Father's delay in making this public announcement might result in the defeat of Frank, because of so many members being at sea as between Father and Frank....

Thursday, December 12, 1895:

I was at the offices until 11 o'clock sending away statements, and writing letters. At the time named I went to my Quorum meeting in the Temple. Present: All of the Presidency, Lorenzo Snow, F. D. Richards, J. H. Smith, H. J. Grant and John W. Taylor besides myself; George F. Gibbs, clerk. A sample of knit garments was presented which were considered too tight. Pres. Woodruff said he could not feel to use any but those similar to the ones which were given him in the endowments.

Pres. Woodruff said there must be some investigation of the conduct of Moses Thatcher and B. H. Roberts before they can be allowed to actively engage in the work of the ministry. Roberts has accepted the editorship of the *Herald* without consulting the brethren, which is a bad sign, as it is bound to occupy his time and attention to the neglect of his ecclesiastical duties. His appointment displaces Charles W. Penrose, for whom it was thought some place might be found in the Historians Office in the writing of Church History, which is very much needed. Pres. Snow feels that we will not be justified in presenting Moses Thatcher and B. H. Roberts for the votes of the Saints at our next April Conference unless they repent and seek forgiveness of their brethren. John Henry Smith dismissed with prayer....

Thursday, December 19, 1895:

I then went to the Temple to my Quorum meeting, where all of the Presidency, F. D. Richards, Heber J. Grant, John W. Taylor and George F. Gibbs were present. We had no particular business to consider, but talked some of principle and politics. Father told of a vision which George C. Parkinson claims to have had in which he was visited in Liverpool while on a mission by a personage who told him that Brigham Young and Peter the ancient apostle, were one and the same person. When Bro. Parkinson propounded the question as to where Brigham was when Peter appeared to Joseph Smith and conferred upon him the Melchizedek Priesthood, the answer was that Brigham Young was asleep. He was first told by this visitor, however, that by pursuing a certain plan he would be able to arouse interest in the Gospel in the Liverpool Conference over which he was then presiding, and in which the Elders were in the habit of moving around in a certain groove. By following these instructions good results followed, which no doubt aided him in the belief that the remainder of the interview was genuine. Prayer for dismissal was offered by Heber J. Grant.

In the afternoon I was at the President's Office and did some business for Father. Matthias Cowley called while I was there and asked the President if there would be any objections to his running for Secretary of State in Idaho on the Republican ticket next Fall, if the party wanted him. The brethren approved of his accepting the office providing it came to him without his seeking....

Thursday, December 26, 1895:

At 11 o'clock I was at my Quorum meeting, where all of the Presidency were present, as well as F. D. Richards, Heber J. Grant, John W. Taylor, myself and George F. Gibbs. We had very little routine business to consider, but Pres. Woodruff stated that it is the will of the Lord that Father should go to the Senate the first session after Utah becomes a State, and said we should all use our influence to accomplish this object. He said this had been his mind all the way through but he had allowed the fear of misrepresentation and abuse to change his mind for the time being on the matter, but now he is convinced that the Lord desires this thing to occur as indicated. Father said in answer to the inquiry of Pres. Woodruff, that if he were not George Q. Cannon, but was judging merely as one of the Presidency, he would say that George Q. Cannon ought to go to the Senate, but personally he had no ambitions in this direction. Pres. Smith said he had felt opposed in his feelings to Father going, because of the effect it would have on the people and in the whole country, but if this was the will of the Lord, he would conform to it with all his heart. F. D. Richards and John W. Taylor were both unqualifiedly in favor of Father going, while Heber J. Grant and myself had felt that the decision of Pres. Woodruff about two weeks ago that Father should not go, was the proper thing, yet we were willing to do as the Lord directed and His servants counseled. Some talk was had as to who the other senator should be, and we felt that we would prefer O. J. Salisbury. None of us want Trumbo, Goodwin, Bennett or Brown. The vote to sustain this counsel of

Pres. Woodruff was unanimous, and we all agreed to work quietly for it.[26]

Dismissed with prayer by Father.

In the afternoon I wrote the decision of today's council to Frank, in accordance with Father's request....

Sunday, December 29, 1895:

I went to Provo on the 8:05 ...train, and went direct to the home of Jacob Gates, where I met his family, Patriarch Charles D. Evans of Springville, Lilian Hamlin and Leah Dunford of Salt Lake City. At my request Bro. Evans gave me a patriarchal blessing, which was as follows: "Brother Abraham, in the name of the Lord Jesus Christ, and by authority of the holy Priesthood, I lay my hands upon thy head and confer and seal upon thee a blessing as the Lord shall direct. Thou art a chosen vessel, sent into the world, for a holy purpose in the latter days, and hast been reserved in thy heavenly abode for thy work in the last dispensation. Thy lineage is through the royal seed of Ephraim—heaven-ordained and anointed, and has been preserved to this day, that the heirs of the Priesthood may receive flesh therein. Thou art a choice vessel because of thy lowliness of heart and of thy righteousness. The angel of the Lord has watched over thee from thy birth, and no son has revered his father and mother and been more obedient than thou hast. The glory of the Lord will be upon thee, and thy face shall shine therewith; and thy mind be a source of light and truth, and thy words be fitly spoken, and in every hour of need the inspiration of the Lord will be with thee, and hidden truths, the truths of the written word and those which will proceed from the Holy Spirit which are unwritten, shall flow to thee. And thy mind shall be a living fountain, from which thou wilt draw to feed the flock of Christ. Thy mind will be led out into new fields of thought—yea, into the deep things of the Lord, and profound wisdom and great depths of knowledge will open before thee; and thou shalt be astonished at the wisdom which the Lord will bestow

---

[26] This decision was short-lived, for on 14 January 1896, President George Q. Cannon "published a card in which he says that he is not a candidate for U.S. senator" (*Church, State, and Politics*, 340).

upon thee, for thy light will be as the light of the shining sun and thy wisdom exalt many. Thou wilt be great in the holy Apostleship, and thy power will increase with thy years; and thou wilt rebuke evil, which thou wilt hate, and evil doers will tremble before thee, and at thy rebuke devils will flee, and at thy touch the sick shall be healed, and God will honor thee. The elements will not have power over thee, nor the destroyer take thy life, for the work will continue and thy days be many on the earth. Thou wilt be as a rock of defense in favor of truth and righteousness, and thy pen and thy voice shall be set against evil, and no argument of the enemy will ever confound thy wisdom; for thy reasoning under the influence of the Holy Spirit, will be unanswerable, and the letter of revelation will spring into life before thee as a new creation. No weapon formed against thee shall prosper, and thy house shall be established forever; and every link in the chain of thy genealogy will be connected and perfected, yea, even to the time when Michael shall set one foot on land and the other on the sea, and declare time no longer. The heavens will be opened unto thee, and because of thy humility thy faith will triumph over every passion of thy flesh, which shall become obedient to the spirit of the Lord within thee; for the elements will obey thee and the angel of the Lord draw the sword in thy defense, and thy God will deliver thee. The arm of the wicked will fall powerless before thee, and thou wilt rebuke spiritual wickedness in high places. Rulers shall fear thee and feel rebuked by thy wisdom. The Lord will honor thee and thy children will revere and bless thy memory, and thou wilt never lack an heir to minister for thee and for thy house forever. Thou art born in a day of calamity and desolation. Thine eyes will behold great changes, for while thou livest nations will fall, and the plagues of the Lord devour many; but thou will stand and witness the redemption of Zion and behold her glory enter her center temple and gaze upon the faces of holy angels and hear their voices and wilt behold the face of thy Redeemer, and receive a crown of glory which will be imperishable, and thine inheritance will be sealed to thee both on the earth and in the temple of heaven. Thy feet will not stumble in the path of thy progress, nor thy guardian angel ever forsake thee. And thou wilt occupy the mansion prepared for thee from before the foundation of the world, and sit upon the throne of thy glory and exaltation forever and ever. And I seal thee up unto eternal life in the name of Jesus, amen."…

Tuesday, December 31, 1895:

I called at the President's Office twice on business, and in the evening took Father home with me, where he remained, as he [is] trying to avoid being interviewed by the newspaper reporters, who desire to learn whether or not he is or will be a candidate for the position of Senator. The rumor that he will be is widely circulated, and is causing considerable stir among some of the former Liberals, for they purport to see in this movement the hand of the Church. Father remained at Mame's.

I am thankful at the close of another year for the blessings which I have received, and though I have had many trials, I have been greatly blessed of the Lord.

Appendix One

✺

Plural Marriage Issues in the Abraham H. Cannon Journals

The practice of plural marriage, often referred to as polygamy, is a common theme running through the Abraham H. Cannon journals. Today, when most of the population of the world cares little about marriage and immorality has become an unnoticed, even expected, commonality, many wonder that polygamy could be an issue. The old charge of plural marriage to gratify lust has lost its sting. Today, people might wonder why the Mormons took the trouble to actually marry the other women, when it is so much simpler to live with them, forgetting commitment when it is convenient. Same-sex lifestyles are now considered politically correct and normal, and other types of perversion and immorality are increasing.

The doctrine and practice of plural marriage was revealed to Joseph Smith, probably in the early 1830s, although the revelation was not recorded until 1843. It is now found in the Doctrine and Covenants, section 132. It is perhaps the most misunderstood and ridiculed facet in all Mormonism. Carefully administered and controlled by the Lord through the presidents of the Church, only those approved and worthy could participate. The practice was partially halted in 1890 by revelation to President Wilford Woodruff in a document that came to be known as the Manifesto, and fully stopped by President Joseph F. Smith's proclamation in 1904, today known as the Second Manifesto. Since that time those who marry additional wives have been excommunicated from the Church.

Examination of the historical facts reveals that many of those clamoring the loudest against the Mormons' practice of plural marriage were hypocrites, living in adulterous relationships themselves, and it was this kind of hypocrisy that disgusted men like Abraham Cannon, who married their other wives by prophetic sanction, proper priesthood authority, and sacred covenant, and were then faithful to them.[1] They had deep conviction that what they were doing was right and approved of God by revelation to prophets (see

D&C 132). Elder Cannon himself taught "that none but those who had the divinity of this principle revealed to them should enter into its practice."

There are two plural marriage issues encountered in the journals that seem appropriate to review here. The first is the 1886 John Taylor revelation as it relates to the 1890 Woodruff Manifesto. "Fundamentalist" polygamists (non-members of the Church) desire to interpret a revelation given to President John Taylor regarding plural marriage as meaning that the practice would never cease in the Church. The second issue relates to post-Manifesto plural marriages and the Second Manifesto.

In 1902, Elder John W. Taylor, a son of President John Taylor, mentioned during a meeting of the Quorum of the Twelve that he had found a revelation among his father's personal papers. Elder Cannon recorded Elder Taylor's words of 1 April 1892: "John W. Taylor spoke in relation to the Manifesto: 'I do not know that that thing was right, though I voted to sustain it, and will assist to maintain it; but among my father's papers I found a revelation given him of the Lord, and which is now in my possession, in which the Lord told him that the principle of plural marriage would never be overcome. Pres. Taylor desired to have it suspended, but the Lord would not permit it to be done.'" The pertinent section of this revelation reads: "Thus saith the Lord, All commandments that I give must be obeyed by those calling themselves by my name unless they are revoked by me or by my authority and how can I revoke an everlasting covenant. For I the Lord am everlasting and my everlasting covenants cannot be abrogated or done away with; but they stand forever. Have I not given my word in great plainness on this subject?... I have not revoked this law nor will I for it is everlasting and those who will enter into my glory must obey the conditions thereof."[2]

Elder Taylor used this document as an excuse to disregard the 1890 Manifesto and other directives from the First Presidency mandating the discontinuance of the promotion and practice of plural marriage.

In 1905 Elder Taylor and Elder Matthias F. Cowley, a close associate, resigned their Apostleship over their inability to harmonize themselves with their quorum. In 1911, Elder Cowley was disfellowshipped and Elder Taylor was excommunicated. At his trial John W. Taylor again asserted that he had found the revelation among his father's papers. Joseph Fielding Smith made a copy of the document on 3 August 1909. The document was rejected by the Quorum of the Twelve Apostles at the trial.

A First Presidency statement of 17 June 1933 is often twisted by historians and others. It states that the copy of the "revelation" was not in the archives of the Church; it does not say the Brethren did not know of it or that some of them personally might have had a copy. Two important points are made in the statement: "It is alleged that on September 26-27, 1886, President John Taylor received a revelation from the Lord, the purported text of which is given in publications circulated apparently by or at the instance of [fundamentalists].... Furthermore, so far as the authorities of the Church are concerned and so far as the members of the Church are concerned, since this pretended revelation, if ever given, was never presented to and adopted by the Church or by any council of the Church, and since to the contrary, an inspired rule of action, the Manifesto, was (subsequently to the pretended revelation) presented to and adopted by the Church, which inspired rule in its terms, purpose, and effect was directly opposite to the interpretation given to the pretended revelation, the said pretended revelation could have no validity and no binding effect and force upon Church members, and action under it would be unauthorized, illegal, and void."[3]

The 1886 revelation never became the claim to authority by the polygamists until 1929. They did not publish it until 1938, although they had circulated copies. The document says nothing about authority but is only an affirmation of the principle of plural marriage. The 1890 Manifesto does not revoke the principle, but it does discontinue the practice.[4]

The doctrinal reasoning behind this issue was explained by Elder Bruce R. McConkie (then of the First Council of Seventy) in the following transcript, taken from a Church Educational System lecture he gave at Brigham Young University in 1967:

We've been considering plural marriage and approaching it from the standpoint that the Lord's law of marriage has always been one wife for one husband. This has been the case since the days of Adam to the present moment. It will so continue except for those periods of time when by revelation the Lord commands that plural marriage should be practiced. Sister A__ J__ asked me a question growing out of that concept which should probably be answered for everyone. She referred to a purported revelation that is attributed to John Taylor, indicating that plural marriage is going to be practiced everlastingly and always, that there's not time when it won't be. Consequently there will always be people who practice plural marriage even though it is not practiced by the body of the Church.

In that connection, we ought to have a few simple principles clear in our mind. The Prophet always taught that a man should have only one wife unless the Lord commanded to the contrary, and the prophet authorized it. The way these things work is this: There is priesthood on the one hand (which is God's power and authority), and then there are keys on the other hand. Keys are the right of presidency which authorize the use of the priesthood for a particular purpose. Peter, James, and John brought the priesthood, which is power and authority, and then somebody else came and gave the keys which authorized the priesthood today to baptize, to perform eternal marriages, and to preach the gospel in all the world—a whole host of uses. On the other hand, we can't use the priesthood today to resurrect somebody, because the keys have not been given and we are not authorized to use God's power for that purpose. The way the keys operate is that they center in one man at a time and that man is the President of the Church. They are conferred upon all the Twelve, but they lie dormant in them unless they become the senior apostle, because keys are the right of presidency and only one man presides over all others. So you can never perform an act by the authority of the priesthood, alone. You must have the authority of the priesthood and in addition you must have the authorization to use the priesthood for a purpose, which is keys.

I hold the Melchizidek priesthood but I cannot go out and resurrect someone because no one on earth or in heaven has authorized me to use my priesthood for the purpose of resurrecting somebody. When they do confer that key, I'll be able to do that. But somebody has authorized me to use the priesthood for the purpose of sealing couples in eternal marriage in the temple. So I go to the temple and seal people together. I didn't always have that right—until the one who has the keys gave me the right to use my priesthood for that purpose. Since he has I've been able to do it.

It takes priesthood and it takes keys and unless both of them are present an ordinance cannot be performed that is binding in heaven. The Lord gives the keys to the President of the Church in their totality. Hypothetically, the President of the Church could say, "we will not preach the gospel to the world," and all the missionaries would have to come home. Or the President of the Church could say, "we will not perform baptism" and nobody could ever perform another valid baptism. Or he could say "we will not perform any more plural marriages," and no one could perform a valid plural marriage. He could say celestial marriage itself will stop and it would stop because he holds the keys and gives the voice of God to the world. Nothing is valid and binding unless there is both priesthood and keys. If somebody comes along and says, "I can perform a plural marriage" you know automatically that's dishonest and it's not true. He can't do it unless the prophet of God authorizes it. This is the doctrine that completely removes all of the claims of all the cultists who think they can do something that is contrary to the present established discipline and order of the Church.[5]

Also of importance is the fact that President John Taylor, the receiver of the revelation, never attempted to put it forward as the will of the Lord to His people. It had to be found, reviewed, and decided upon years later, when the Lord had revoked His previous commandment and directed His Church in another course.

Post-Manifesto plural marriage is a highly complex and little understood segment of Mormon history. Those authors who have attempted to research and examine the scant evidence and sketchy data from this period have come away with as many questions as answers. In his biography of George Q. Cannon, historian Davis Bitton wrote: "A simple explanation would be Mormon perfidy—the Church leaders had never intended to abolish polygamy and would do what was necessary to perpetuate it. A gentler, more understanding explanation is that a transition period was inevitable.... The new plural marriages, not numerous compared to all the marriages being performed or to those of past decades, became a trickle. Finally, they were stopped."[6] As noted, this total cessation was a result of the issuance of the Second Manifesto in 1904.

An important consideration that must be understood is that those involved in post-Manifesto plural marriages left the boundaries of the United States to perform the sealings. This was to comply with President Woodruff's interpretation of the Manifesto, that it applied only to the laws of the land—the laws of the United States.[7] Great trouble and means were expended to meet this condition. Then, no matter what the protests and strategies of the Church's enemies, the agreements with the government were technically kept. Also, it seems reasonable to expect that as in any complex situation, occasional exceptions may be made, for the Lord's ways are not man's ways.

1 While not a specific plural marriage case, the following AHC journal entry makes the point: "In a fornication case tried yesterday before Judge Henderson in Ogden where the parties involved were not 'Mormons' the prosecuting attorney said it had come to be thought and remarked that the law against this and kindred crimes in this Territory was to be applied in a different way when 'Mormons' were defendants than when the accused were Gentiles, and the judge showed that this was his understanding.... How can we be expected to respect the law when such partiality is shown, and such manifest injustice is practiced? We at least must despise the law administrators " (7 January 1890).

2 Cited in Fred C. Collier, *Unpublished Revelations*, vol. 1 (Salt Lake City: Colliers Publishing Co., 1981), 145-46. It must be realized that this revelation is capable of more than one interpretation. Polygamous "Fundamentalists" *need* it to mean that plural marriage will never cease in the Church, else they lose justification for their immoral actions and become nothing but misled adulterers.

3 James R. Clark, comp., *Messages of the First Presidency* (Salt Lake City: Bookcraft, 1965-75), 5:315-30.

4 For further information on this revelation and "fundamentalist" claims, see J. Max Anderson, *The Polygamy Story: Fiction and Fact* (Salt Lake City: Publishers Press, 1979), 63-76; and Paul E. Reimann, *Plural Marriage, Limited* (Salt Lake City: Utah Printing Company, 1974), 185-224.

5 Bruce R. McConkie "Celestial and Plural Marriage," unpublished Church Educational System class lecture (BYU Lecture Series, summer 1967) 18-20..

6 Davis Bitton, *George Q. Cannon, A Biography*, 409.

7 Some writers have attempted to invalidate this point by insisting that marriages performed in Mexico, Canada, or on the ocean were still technically subject to the laws of the United States, especially after the newlyweds returned to their homes. Yet what must be ascertained is President Woodruff's perspective—how he would have viewed the matter—not how antagonistic legislation was phrased.

Appendix Two

Biographical Register

This register includes brief biographical information about the major characters whose names appear in the Abraham H. Cannon journals. This information has been taken from the following sources: *Deseret News 2001-2002 Church Almanac* (Salt Lake City: The Church of Jesus Christ of Latter-day Saints and the Deseret News, 2000); Andrew Jenson, *Latter-day Saint Biographical Encyclopedia*, vol. 1 (Salt Lake City: The Andrew Jenson History Company and the Deseret News, 1901); *Biographical Record of Salt Lake City and Vicinity* (Chicago: National Historical Record Co., 1902); Ralph B. Simmons, comp., *Utah's Distinguished Personalities*, Commonwealth Edition, vol. 1, (Salt Lake City: Personality Publishing Company, 1933); Gene A. Sessions, ed., *Mormon Democrat: The Religious and Political Memoirs of James Henry Moyle* (Salt Lake City: Signature Books, 1998), biographical appendix; and the Abraham H. Cannon journals. See also B. H. Roberts, *A Comprehensive History of the Church of Jesus Christ of Latter-day Saints*, vol. 6 (Salt Lake City: The Church of Jesus Christ of Latter-day Saints, 1930).

For information about the following—U.S. Attorney William H. Dickson, Colonel Isaac Trumbo, Judge M. M. Estee, C. C. Goodwin, J. S. Clarkson, and others mentioned in the A. H. Cannon journals as part of the polygamy raids, statehood political battles, and other anti-Mormon efforts—see Gustive O. Larson, *The "Americanization" of Utah for Statehood* (San Marino: The Huntington Library, 1971); and Edward Leo Lyman, *Political Deliverance: The Mormon Quest for Utah Statehood* (Urbana and Chicago: University of Illinois Press, 1986).

Caine, John T.

Born in the Isle of Man in 1829 and joined the Church in New York. Became Utah Territorial delegate to congress for five terms, where he helped the Mormon causes. Died in 1911.

Cannon, Angus M.

Born in England in 1834. Brother of George Q. Cannon. Father of Mina, Abraham's second wife. Became president of the huge Salt Lake City Stake from 1876 to 1904. Prominent in church leadership circles, he nearly had the visibility and influence of an Apostle; also prominent in Utah politics and business. Died in 1915.

Cannon, Frank J.

See the introductory and biographical essays.

Cannon, George Q.

See biographical essay.

Cannon, John Q.

See biographical essay.

Clawson, Rudger

Born 12 March 1857 in Salt Lake City. One of first to serve time in penitentiary for polygamy offenses. Called to apostleship by Lorenzo Snow; served as President of Twelve for 22 years. Sustained as a member of First Presidency, but never set apart to office. Kept journal similar to Abraham H. Cannon's. Son of Hiram Clawson, prominent businessman and secretary to Brigham Young. Died in 1943.

Cowdery, Oliver

Born 3 October 1806 in Vermont. Became acquainted with Joseph Smith and acted as his scribe in dictating the Book of Mormon. Became one of the three witnesses who saw the gold plates in heavenly manifestation. Tried but failed to translate from plates himself. Ordained to Aaronic Priesthood by John the Baptist. Became second elder of Church, and saw the Lord in vision in the Kirtland Temple (see D&C 110). Became disaffected and was excommunicated from Church. Rebaptized in 1848 and died in 1850 in Missouri.

Gibbs, George F.

Born in Wales in 1846, emigrated to Utah in 1868. Worked as a secretary to the First Presidency and the Twelve for sixty years, taking most of the minutes of the meetings of the Council of the Twelve during Elder Cannon's tenure as an Apostle. Died in 1924.

Grant, Heber J.

Born 22 November 1856 in Salt Lake City. Father was Jedediah M. Grant, a counselor to Brigham Young. Called to Apostleship at early age of 25, about which he received manifestation. Became prominent businessman. Served mission to Japan. Overcame large financial debts for himself and A. H. Cannon (after the latter's death). Became Church President in 1918. Considered friend by many important non-Mormon businessmen and national leaders. Died in 1945.

Harris, Martin

Born in 1783. Became associated with Joseph Smith in the publication of the Book of Mormon. Infamous for losing the first 116 pages of translation. Became one of the three witnesses who saw the gold plates and heard the voice testifying of their truth. Helped select first twelve Apostles. Left the Church but returned and was rebaptized later in life. Was said to have powerful testimony of the Book of Mormon. Died in 1875.

Hyde, Orson

Born 8 January 1805 in Connecticut. Ordained by the three witnesses as one of original twelve Apostles. Briefly fell out of favor and lost his Apostleship in May of 1839. Repented and was restored a few weeks later. First modern Apostle to visit Palestine. Died in 1878.

Ivins, Anthony W.

Born in New Jersey in 1852. Was active in Church and politics (Democrat); also served two missions. Ordained an Apostle in 1907 and later became member of the Heber J. Grant First Presidency. Died in 1934.

Jenson, Andrew

Born in Denmark in 1850, converted to LDS Church and became an assistant Church historian. Served several missions and authored a number of biographical and encyclopedic works chronicling the history and leaders of the Church. Died in 1941.

Kimball, J. Golden

Born 9 June 1853. Son of Heber C. Kimball. Called to First Seven Presidents of Seventy (First Council of Seventy) in 1892. Earned reputation as entertaining speaker; became folk-legend for occasional use of mild profanity and humor in speeches to conservative Mormon audiences. Died in 1938.

Lund, Anthon H.

Born 15 May 1844 in Denmark. Ordained Apostle (same time as A. H. Cannon) in 1889 by George Q. Cannon. Later became counselor in First Presidency. Died in 1921.

Lyman, Amasa M.

Born in New Hampshire in 1813. Became an Apostle and close friend of Joseph Smith in the 1840s. Father of Francis M. Lyman of the Twelve. Excommunicated in 1870 for preaching false doctrine (denying the need for the atoning sacrifice of Jesus Christ); died in 1877.

Lyman, Francis M.:

Born 12 January 1840 in Illinois. Son of Amasa M. Lyman. Became Apostle at age 40. Was a senior member of Twelve during A. H. Cannon's tenure as junior member. Father, Amasa, and son, Richard R., also became Apostles but were excommunicated. Died in 1916.

Maeser, Karl G.

Born in Germany in 1828. Joined the Church and emigrated to Utah, where he became a prominent educator (becoming the personal tutor of Brigham Young's children) and in 1876 started an academy in Provo that eventually became Brigham Young University. Died in Salt Lake City in 1901.

Merrill, Marriner W.

Born 25 September 1835. Ordained Apostle (along with A. H. Cannon) in 1889. Served for many years as president of Logan Temple. Is noted for receiving spiritual manifestations. Died in 1906.

Morgan, John

Born 8 August 1842 in Indiana. Called to First Seven Presidents of the Seventy (First Council of the Seventy) in 1884. Known as great missionary. Died in 1894.

Moyle, James Henry

Born in Salt Lake City in 1858. Became early Utah attorney, having been set apart to become such by President John Taylor. Became successful lawyer, businessman, and politician; also became assistant Secretary of the United States Treasury. Well acquainted with many church and political leaders. Father of Henry D. Moyle. Died in 1946.

Nibley, Charles W.

Born 5 February 1849. Became prominent and wealthy businessman. Called as Presiding Bishop of the Church in 1907. Lost most of fortune in later life. Called as counselor to Heber J. Grant in First Presidency in 1925. Died in 1931.

Nuttall, L. John

Born in England in 1834. Joined the Church and emigrated to Utah in 1852. Became bishop and stake president in Kanab, Utah. Became private secretary to President John Taylor in 1879 and was with President Taylor when he died in exile, at which time he began working with President Woodruff. Died in 1905 at age 71.

Patten, David W.

Born in New York in 1799. Ordained an Apostle in 1835 by the three witnesses, second in seniority only to Thomas B. Marsh. Considered loyal friend of Joseph Smith and the Church. Was said by some to have seen and conversed with Cain, the murderous son of Adam and Eve. Died as a martyr in the Battle of Crooked River in 1838.

Penrose, Charles W.

Born 4 February 1832 in London. Worked as newspaperman, politician, and defender of the faith until called by Joseph F. Smith to be an Apostle and counselor in First Presidency. Died in 1925.

Pratt, Orson

Born 19 September 1811 in New York. Brother of Parley P. Pratt. One of original twelve Apostles ordained by the three witnesses in 1835. In 1842-43 briefly rebelled and was excommunicated, but was rebaptized and re-ordained to Apostleship. Became possibly most prominent and educated scientist of early Mormonism. Because of speculation in written works was rebuked by Brigham Young, but reputation as doctrinal thinker has grown. Considered able defender of the doctrine of plural marriage. Died in 1881.

Pratt, Parley P.

Born 12 April 1807 in New York. Brother of Orson Pratt. Ordained one of original twelve Apostles by the three witnesses in 1835. Friend and supporter of Joseph Smith. Became early missionary, author, and defender of the faith. Shot by assassin near Van Buren, Arkansas, at age 50.

Preston, William B.

Born 24 November 24, 1830 in Virginia. Sustained as Presiding Bishop of the Church in 1884. Called John Q. Cannon (brother of

Abraham) as his second counselor in 1884. Deeply involved in Church financial affairs and politics. Died in 1908.

Reynolds, George

Born 1 January 1842 in London. Served as secretary to the First Presidency. Became test case for anti-polygamy legislation before U.S. Supreme Court. Called to First Seven Presidents of the Seventy (First Council of the Seventy) in 1890. Died in 1909.

Richards, Franklin D.

Born 22 April 1821 in Massachusetts. Ordained Apostle in 1849. Father of Franklin S. Richards, Church legal counsel. Died in 1899.

Richards, Franklin S.

Born in Salt Lake City in 1849. Son of Franklin D. Richards of the Twelve. Studied law privately; passed Utah bar and became LDS Church legal counsel and attorney for many Utah business enterprises, citizens, and Church leaders (including the Cannons's), especially during polygamy raid. Died in 1934.

Rigdon, Sydney

Born 19 February 1793 in Pennsylvania. Became friend and associate of Joseph Smith and participated in events of early Church. Served as counselor in First Presidency. With Joseph Smith experienced persecution (such as being tarred and feathered) and spiritual experiences (such as the vision of the three degrees of glory [see D&C 76]), but eventually left the Church and was excommunicated for his part in the succession crisis of 1844. Died in 1876.

Roberts, Brigham H.

Born 13 March 1857 in Warrington, England. Became prominent author, theologian, politician, speaker, historian, and defender of the faith. Resisted political Manifesto, but eventually signed. Had occasional disagreements with First Presidency; lost U.S. congressional seat because of polygamy. Called to First Seven

Presidents of Seventy (First Council of Seventy) in 1888. Died in 1933.

Smith, Hyrum

Born 9 February 1800 in Vermont. Older brother of Joseph Smith. Became loyal support to Joseph in his mission. Received Oliver Cowdery's position and became assistant president of the Church and Church Patriarch in 1841. Martyred with Joseph Smith in Carthage, Illinois, in 1844.

Smith, John Henry

Born 18 September 1848 in Iowa. Son of George A. Smith, prominent Church leader. Called as an Apostle at age 32; became prominent politician and community leader. Served as counselor to Joseph F. Smith. Died in 1911.

Smith, Joseph Jr.

Born 23 December 1805 in Sharon, Vermont. When 14 years old received vision of God the Father and Jesus Christ. Called of God to restore New Testament Church teachings and authority. Translated ancient record from metal plates known as the Book of Mormon. Became first president of The Church of Jesus Christ of Latter-day Saints. Practiced plural marriage in accordance with revelatory command (see D&C 132). Founded Nauvoo, Illinois. Experienced severe religious persecution throughout life, until martyred by mob at Carthage, Illinois, in 1844.

Smith, Joseph F.

Born 13 November 1838 in Missouri. Son of Hyrum Smith. As child drove wagon across plains to Utah. Served mission to Hawaii at age 14, ordained Apostle by Brigham Young in 1866. Served as counselor to John Taylor, Wilford Woodruff, and Lorenzo Snow, before becoming president of the Church in 1901. Issued Second Manifesto in 1904, terminating all future plural marriages. Considered doctrinal authority. Received vision of redemption of the dead (see D&C 138). Died in 1918.

Smoot, Abraham O.

Born in Kentucky in 1815. Father of Reed Smoot. An acquaintance of Joseph Smith, he became a mayor of Salt Lake City and Provo and was the Provo stake president for many years. Successful in business, politics, and Church service, he became one of the most influential men in Utah county. Died in Provo in 1895.

Smoot, Reed

Born in Salt Lake City in 1862. Son of Abraham O. Smoot. From a well-to-do family; managed the Provo Woolen mills and invested in other businesses. Was ordained an apostle in 1900. Elected to the United States senate, served for nearly 30 years, from 1903 to 1932. Senate seat was contested in what became known as the Smoot hearings. At these hearings Abraham Cannon's plural marriage to Lillian Hamlin became a national issue. Political career caused some to question his religious commitment, but always had support of the president of the Church; influential senatorial position allowed him to help the Church in many ways, including improving its reputation nationally. Died in Florida in 1941.

Snow, Lorenzo

Born 3 April 1814 in Ohio. Joined Church and received revelation that man could become like God. Became Apostle in 1849 and president of the Twelve in 1889. As president of Twelve, was A. H. Cannon's file leader. Showed unquestioned loyalty to First Presidency. Received personal visit from Jesus Christ at time of call as president of Church in 1898; also received revelation giving official reemphasis to tithing; died in 1901.

Stevenson, Edward

Born in Spain in 1820. Became well acquainted with Joseph Smith and many early Church leaders and events; many of which he wrote and spoke about throughout his life. Became member of the First Seven Presidents of the Seventy (First Council of the Seventy) in 1894. Died in 1897.

Talmage, James E.

Born 21 September 1862 in Hungerford, England. Became prominent educator, author, scientist, theologian, lecturer, university president, and then Apostle in 1911. Elder Cannon served on a Church reading committee which revised and approved the doctrinal content of Talmage's *Articles of Faith* lectures and book. Died in 1933.

Taylor, John

Born 1 November 1808 in England. Joined Church and became Apostle. Published Church organ in Nauvoo; taught George Q. Cannon printing trade. Was shot with Joseph Smith by mob in Carthage Jail in 1844 but lived. Became Church president in 1880. Father of John W. Taylor. Allegedly received plural marriage revelations. Died in exile on underground in Kaysville, Utah in 1887.

Taylor, John W.

Born 15 May 1858 in Provo, Utah. Son of John Taylor. Ordained Apostle by father in 1884. Strained relations with other Church leaders because of land speculation and refusal to accept Manifesto. Eventually resigned apostleship (1905) and later excommunicated (1911) for post Second-Manifesto polygamy. Died in 1916.

Teasdale, George

Born 8 December 1831 in London. Called to apostleship by written revelation to John Taylor (with Heber J. Grant) in 1882. Served for lengthy period in Mormon Mexican colonies. Died in 1907.

Thatcher, Moses

Born 2 February 1842 at Illinois. Ordained Apostle by John Taylor. Political aspirations and beliefs, along with bad health, morphine addiction, and stock ownership in B.B.&C. mine put him at odds with other Church leaders. Became inactive in Apostleship until dropped from quorum in 1896. Died in 1909.

Tullidge, Edward W.

Born in England in 1829. Joined the church and came to Utah, becoming a prolific writer. Founded periodicals in Utah and Idaho, wrote biographies of Joseph Smith and Brigham Young, and several local histories, some of which were published by George Q. Cannon & Sons. Fell into disfavor with Church leaders when he joined the Reorganized Church and used their names to sell his books. Died in 1894.

Wells, Daniel H.

Born 27 October 1814 in New Jersey. Became second counselor to Brigham Young in 1857. In 1877 became counselor to the Quorum of Twelve Apostles. Died in 1891.

Wells, Rulon S.

Born in Salt Lake City in 1857, Son of Daniel H. Wells, Apostle. Became a member of the First Seven Presidents of the Seventy (First Council of the Seventy) in 1893. Died in 1941.

Whitney, Orson F.

Born 1 July 1855 in Salt Lake City. Served lengthy term as bishop, which title became attached to his name. Became prominent local author, poet, historian, politician, and speaker; his *History of Utah* (four volume project) being produced in association with Abraham H. Cannon. Was ordained an Apostle in 1906. Died in 1931.

Woodruff, Wilford

Born 1 March 1807 in Connecticut. Joined Church and became immensely successful missionary. Became president of Church in 1889. Dedicated Salt Lake Temple. Journal considered highly valuable historical document for Church; received many visions and revelations, including one about death of A. H. Cannon. Issued Manifesto in 1890 that began eventual cessation of plural marriage. Struggled under burden of Church debt brought on by government persecution. Died in 1898.

Young, Brigham

Born 1 June 1801 in Vermont. Joined Church and became loyal friend of Joseph Smith. Succeeded Joseph Smith as president of the Church in 1847 after three years as president of the Twelve. Helped complete Nauvoo Temple, then led Mormon pioneers west to Utah in 1847. Founded Salt Lake City and began construction of Salt Lake Temple. Ordained several sons to be Apostles. Considered great leader and colonist in America. Died in 1877.

Young, Brigham Jr.

Born 18 December 1836 in Kirtland, Ohio. Son of Brigham Young; ordained Apostle at age 27 and became counselor to his father. Served in Quorum of the Twelve Apostles from 1877 to 1903, the last two years as its president. Journal records details of A. H. Cannon's death. Died in 1903.

Young, John W.:

Born 1 October 1844 in Nauvoo, Illinois. Son of Brigham Young. Ordained Apostle by father at age 19. Served in First Presidency until death of father, at which time became counselor to Twelve. Became businessman and railroad contractor. Business interests and money problems distracted him from ministry, until dropped from Church position by First Presidency and Twelve. Died in 1924 in New York.

Young, Seymour B.

Born 3 October 1837. Nephew of President Brigham Young. Became physician and acted as Abraham Cannon's doctor during his typhoid fever illness. Sustained to First Seven Presidents of the Seventy (First Council of the Seventy) in 1882. Died in 1924.

Zane, Charles S.

Born in 1831. Came to Utah in 1884 as Chief Justice of the Utah Territorial Supreme Court; also served on Utah State Supreme Court. A harsh anti-Mormon judge; sent many Mormon polygamists to prison. Died in 1915.

BIBLIOGRAPHICAL ESSAY

This bibliographic essay is not meant to be exhaustive, but its purpose is to comment on some of the more important studies involving Abraham H. Cannon and the significant contribution to Mormon history made by his remarkable journal.

Over the years Elder Cannon's life has received little attention from biographers and historians. The meager information available about him has made researching his life difficult. This problem is compounded by the loss of his 1896 journal. After the journals themselves and this "best of" abridgement, probably the next most informative work regarding Elder Cannon is Davis Bitton's *George Q. Cannon: A Biography* (Salt Lake City: Deseret Book, 1999). This scholarly and thorough treatment relies heavily upon Abraham's journals in portraying certain segments of the father's life and work, at the same time providing a few highlights about the son. At present, it easily becomes the foremost published work about President Cannon, although some Cannon family descendants have also accomplished much in this area. Another fine contribution concentrating more on George Q. Cannon's missionary activities and religious experiences is Lawrence R. Flake, *George Q. Cannon: His Missionary Years* (Salt Lake City: Bookcraft, 1998).

An interesting volume which has been of some use is Beatrice Cannon Evans and Janath Russell Cannon, eds., *Cannon Family Historical Treasury* (n.p.: Published by the George Cannon Family Association, 1967). Now something of a collectors item, this work (written from a family perspective and a blind eye to controversy) contains almost nothing about Abraham, but was informative regarding his ancestry and parentage.

Former Assistant Church Historian (and acquaintance of Elder Cannon) Andrew Jenson's brief article in *Latter-day Saint Biographical Encyclopedia*, vol. 1 (Salt Lake City: The Andrew Jenson History Company and the Deseret News, 1901), 167-68, provided some information, as did (another friend) Matthias F. Cowley in his *Prophets and Patriarchs of the Church of Jesus Christ of Latter-day*

Saints (Chatanooga, Tenn.: Ben E. Rich, 1902), 287-91. Both too brief to be very useful, these articles were so much alike that it was obvious one author had borrowed wholesale from the other. Other later authors, such as Richard S. VanWagoner and Steven C. Walker, *A Book of Mormons*, (Salt Lake City: Signature Books, 1982), and Lawrence R. Flake, *Apostles and Prophets of the Last Dispensation* (Provo, Utah: BYU Religious Studies Center, 2001), also used these earlier works for most of their short summaries.

After these volumes that contain mostly meager biographical material on Abraham, come a second category of scholarly works that, while not specifically about Elder Cannon, used his journals as a primary source for researching other historically important subjects such as Utah and LDS business, finance, politics and statehood, and plural marriage or polygamy. The two foremost of these are Gustive O. Larson, *The "Americanization" of Utah for Statehood* (San Marino, Calif.: The Huntington Library, 1971), and Edward Leo Lyman, *Political Deliverance: The Mormon Quest for Utah Statehood* (Urbana and Chicago: University of Illinois Press, 1986). These works constitute something of a commentary for the political entries in Elder Cannon's journal which have not received much attention in the present volume. They provide the context and explanations desired by those studying the history of Utah politics. Interestingly, both authors admitted that Elder Cannon's journals were the most important source for their respective books. Edward Leo Lyman wrote: "This young Mormon general authority, impressively candid and thorough in his daily journal entries, offered initial research leads to many developments occurring in this crucial period. In a real sense Cannon first suggested the course for further investigation of many of the subjects treated in the present work. Certainly the Cannon journal has been the most valuable single source utilized in this study" (304). And Gustive O. Larson wrote: "The writer is indebted to the journal for much helpful information relative to the political adjustments in Utah in the early 1890s" (285). And Lyman wrote this about Larson's work: "In 1970 Gustive O. Larson's *The "Americanization" of Utah for Statehood* was published. In what was the most extensive treatment yet of the Mormon struggle for statehood, the author relied heavily on the A. H. Cannon journal" (304).

Following these two authors lead, later historians would make similar use of the Abraham Cannon journals. Davis Bitton, in his biography of President George Q. Cannon referred to above, wrote: "For the next several years [the early 1890s], Abraham H. Cannon's magnificent diary, almost equal in importance to his father's for the years it covers, becomes one of our most valuable sources" (262). Then, in 1991 Thomas G. Alexander's *Things in Heaven and Earth: The Life and Times of Wilford Woodruff, a Mormon Prophet* (Salt Lake City: Signature Books, 1993), appeared, making thorough use of Elder Cannon's diaries, especially from chapter 11 on.

A study which concentrates on plural marriage issues is B. Carmon Hardy, *Solemn Covenant: The Mormon Polygamous Passage* (Urbana and Chicago: University of Illinois Press, 1992). Also mentionable is D. Michael Quinn's examination of post-manifesto plural marriage "LDS Church Authority and New Plural Marriages, 1890-1904" *Dialogue: A Journal of Mormon Thought*, 18, no. 1, (spring 1985), 9-105. This study, which evidences some of the stretching and manipulation of sources which so seriously compromise Quinn's later works, relied on the A. H. Cannon journal for several important conclusions.

Each of the above works would be seriously weakened without access to the excellent contents of Elder Cannon's journals. Though some of them evidence the liberal bias often present in academic works written by historians who view The Church of Jesus Christ of Latter-day Saints and its doctrines from a purely secular standpoint, the use of Abraham's journal has helped improve factual accuracy, context, and scholarship, in those studies.

Some important journals which have been specially helpful are Jean Bickmore White, ed., *Church, State, and Politics: The Diaries of John Henry Smith* (Salt Lake City: Signature Books, 1990), the journal of Wilford Woodruff (transcribed copy in editor's possession), and Melvin Clarence Merrill, ed., *Utah Pioneer and Apostle Marriner Wood Merrill and His Family* (n. p.: Marriner Wood Merrill Heritage Committee, 1980). These journals contained portions which were contemporary with Abraham Cannon's short life and shorter apostolic tenure. Within the select parameters of detail, length and depth of entry, and literary skill, Elder Cannon's journal is superior to these, yet they were still useful for further explanation and perspective.

For a standard historical reference for the time period covered by Elder Cannon's journals, see B. H. Roberts, *A Comprehensive History of the Church of Jesus Christ of Latter-day Saints*, vol. 6 (Salt Lake City: The Church of Jesus Christ of Latter-day Saints, 1965).

Complete publication information is given for each book or article used in the reference notes, including author, title, place of publication, publisher, date of publication, and the page number of the reference; therefore, no list of works cited is included here.

INDEX

unity among quorum, 149

Richards, Franklin S., 477
    employed as Church attorney, 372

Rigdon, Sydney, 477
    vision of heavens, 152-153

Roberts, Brigham H., 477-478
    against woman's suffrage. 376
    call to mission in east, 116
    guilty of cohabitation, 95
    on government discourse, 72
    thoughts on swearing and finding fault, 115

S

Sacrament, kneel when administering, 422
    to be administered in ward meetings, 315

Saints, discussion on political preferences, 142-143, 143n11

Salina, 327

Salt Lake Real Estate, selling of, 143

Salt Lake Temple, capstone to be set, 233
    capstone laying ceremony, 246-247, 246n6
    construction errors on, 78
    dedication services of, 6, 267-268
    desire of brethren for completion, 210
    preparation for dedicating, 255
    preparation for laying capstone, 243, 244
    use energies and means to finish, 258, 260

Sandwich Island choir, sang for President. Woodruff and George Q. Cannon, 92

Scientific and Literary Association, on the proposition to sell "Council House," 103

Sealing, revelation on, 3

Sealings and adoptions, discussion of, 170

Séance, power of, 167, 167-168n34

Second Manifesto, by Joseph F. Smith, 43

Selling of surplus property to Liberals, preparation for, 135-136

Smith, Eliza R. Snow, on thoughts of Prophet Joseph concerning ten tribes, 63

Smith, George Albert, on speaking with the spirit of George Q. Cannon, 51-52

Smith, Hyrum, 478

Smith, John Henry, 478
    Apostles' visits among Stakes, 150-151
    best to decline presidency of *Standard*, 179-180,181n10
    elected President of *Standard* Publishing Co., 178
    Gentiles opposed to woman's suffrage provision, 380
    on AHC's last days, 46

Smith, John M., desire for Twelve to gather annually for conference, 307

Smith, Joseph F., 478
    advice on marriage, 346
    be wise in financial matters, 388-389
    becoming efficient minister of Christ, 211
    counsel to Saints, 319-320
    counsel with leaders, 435
    divorce, 437
    duties of top Church leaders, 342
    favor of statehood, 441, 445
    feelings about Moses Thatcher's political actions, 256
    harm of secret organizations, 394
    households to be industrious, 283
    keep all commandments, 242
    Manifesto and families, 209
    manner of how officers in priesthood chosen, 397